HATE SPEECH AND POLITICAL VIOLENCE

BRIGITTE L. NACOS, YAELI BLOCH-ELKON, AND ROBERT Y. SHAPIRO

HATE SPEECH AND POLITICAL VIOLENCE

Far-Right Rhetoric from the Tea Party

to the Insurrection

Columbia University Press / New York

Columbia University Press
Publishers Since 1893
New York   Chichester, West Sussex
cup.columbia.edu

Library of Congress Cataloging-in-Publication Data
Names: Nacos, Brigitte Lebens, author. | Bloch-Elkon, Yaeli, author. |
Shapiro, Robert Y., 1953– author.
Title: Hate speech and political violence : far-right rhetoric from the
Tea Party to the insurrection / Brigitte L Nacos, Yaeli Bloch-Elkon, and
Robert Y. Shapiro.
Description: New York : Columbia University Press, 2024. | Includes
bibliographical references and index.
Identifiers: LCCN 2023028305 | ISBN 9780231214346 (hardback) |
ISBN 9780231214353 (trade paperback) | ISBN 9780231560290 (ebook)
Subjects: LCSH: Communication in politics—United States. | Political
oratory—United States. | Hate speech—United States. | Tea Party
movement. | Political violence—United States. | Conspiracy
theories—United States. | Obama, Barack. | Trump, Donald,
1946—Language. | Mass media—Political aspects—United States. |
Social media—Political aspects—United States. | United
States—Politics and government—2009–2017. | United States—Politics
and government—2017–2021.
Classification: LCC JA85.2.U6 N34 2024 | DDC 320.97301/4—dc23/
eng/20230824
LC record available at https://lccn.loc.gov/2023028305

Cover design: Noah Arlow

CONTENTS

PREFACE

This project began with the goal of examining partisan conflict and the role of the new online as well as traditional offline media in the rise of the Tea Party. We then expanded the research as events unfolded in the rise of Donald Trump and his Make American Great Again (MAGA) movement. Trump had won a great deal of respect and support among Tea Partiers when he made himself the voice of the anti-Obama conspiracy theories. Eventually, in Trump's own words, the Tea Party movement became Make America Great Again. Further, we recognized early on that the angry and often violent rhetoric of Tea Partiers was similar to Trump's and the hate speech of his supporters. We thought the results of the 2016 presidential election would put a damper on that rhetoric. We were wrong. Therefore, the book extends the story and our analysis through Trump's presidency and the 2020 election and its aftermath.

The main argument and general theorizing of the book concerns how communication became weaponized when the Tea Party, a reactionary social movement, quickly appeared and strengthened with the assistance of media insiders, GOP leaders, and conservative advocacy groups just months after Barack Obama, the first Black president of the United States, entered the White House. We argue that what we call the "interconnectivity of political communication" facilitated and even promoted the Tea Party during its first years along with anti-Obama conspiracy theories that were embraced by its supporters. The rumor that Obama was not born in the United States and therefore an illegitimate president became part of a toxic communication spiral when the reality TV star and entrepreneur Donald Trump made himself the public spokesperson of the "birther" lies. We examine how such weaponized communication—and the partisan conflict of which it was a part—played out in the tumultuous years that followed and ultimately led to the violence of the January 6, 2021, assault on the U.S. Capitol as a move toward overturning Trump's defeat in the 2020 election. The book provides a chronicle of the increasing level of partisan conflict and weaponized communication from the Tea Party to Trump and the political violence that ensued. As a result, what transpired has put American democracy at risk. As we discuss in the first chapter, other works have examined different aspects of these issues, but we offer a distinctive account that emphasizes the links between the Tea Party and the Trumpian MAGA movement.

This book has taken a while to complete. We owe great thanks to many individuals and institutions. We—especially Shapiro and Nacos—have been supported in many ways by Columbia University's School of Arts and Sciences, the Graduate School of Arts and Sciences, the Institute for Social and Economic Research and Policy (ISERP), the Department of Political Science, and the School of International and Public Affairs (SIPA). Bloch-Elkon is also grateful to the Bar Ilan University's Dean's Office of Social Sciences and the School of Communication.

For comments and very constructive criticism of earlier versions of the manuscript, we thank Lance Bennett, Larry Jacobs, Ben Page, and the anonymous reviewers who helped us improve the book immensely. At Columbia University Press, Stephen Wesley provided terrific support and especially assisted in moving quickly to publication once we completed our revisions. We owe special thanks to Ben Kolstad as our superb project manager and to Lois Smith for excellent copy-editing. We also thank Christian Winting, Marielle Poss, and ARC Indexing.

Many individuals provided direct assistance as well as organizational and logistical support. First, we thank the following former students for their able and important research assistance at various stages of our research and writing: Isaac Horwitz-Hirsch, Min Guo, Sidney Wiswell, Julia Cosgrove, Esterah Brown, Julia Schreder, Sayali Nagwekar, Helena Felsen-Parsons, David Anderson, Yu-Tung Tsai, Kristen Gonzalez, William Parish, Sunpreet Singh, Wilfred Chan, Daran Dooley, Adam Hyams, Tyler Trumbach, Ella Cheng, Emma Cheng, Vivian Tsai, Amber Tong Gao, Dan Louis, Sarah Kuranga, Rekha Kennedy, and Sam Frederick. At the manuscript's final stage, Eun Ji Sally Son provided capable assistance.

We are also grateful to Kay Achar, Emily Prince, Michael Scott, Holly Martis, Elizabeth Howe, and Eric Vlach at the Department of Political Science; Harpreet Mahajan at SIPA; at ISERP, its directors, Peter Bearman, Thomas DiPrete, Matthew Connelly, Alessandra Casella, and Jo-Ann Rivera; and Loran Morales Kando, Marylena Mantas, and Marianna Palumbo, Shapiro's collaborators on related work at the Academy of Political Science.

We could not have written this book without the mass media and public opinion data and other evidence available to us and to which we refer in the chapters, figures, and tables. We want to draw special attention to the many public opinion survey sponsors and polling organizations responsible for the extensive data that we have available today. We acknowledge the Roper Center for Public Opinion Research and its iPOLL database, which has been our go-to source for much national public opinion survey data. In particular, we have reported on our analyses of public opinion data from the NORC General Social Survey, the Pew Research Center, the Chicago Council on Global Affairs, and Gallup. We have benefited from communications about these data from colleagues at these respective organizations: Tom Smith, Rene Bautiste, Claudia Deane, Dina Smeltz, and Frank Newport.

Our greatest and warmest thanks go to our families, with whom we endured living and working during the COVID-19 pandemic.

Brigitte is most thankful for the support, feedback, and encouragement of her late husband, Jimmy, during the early years of our project. Today, he would share our concerns about the increase in partisan hostility, hate speech, and domestic political violence that threaten America's democracy he hoped our children and grandchildren would inherit.

Bob thanks his wife, Nancy Rubenstein, whom he once again gives credit for contributing to our debate about the title of the book (she came up with the title of our first book). She also, with good cheer and for too many months, left him alone at the computer and with his stacks of books and papers.

Yaeli is most grateful to her daughters, Liya and Neta Elkon, who were continuously supportive and understanding of their mother's involvement in this project, as they left their childhood behind and have been growing into beautiful young adults. Most important, along the way, they have learned a lot about precious democratic values and threats to democracy.

We owe our families big time. They helped make the book all the better for us, along with the others whom we have been so pleased to acknowledge. As always, full responsibility for all the deficiencies and shortcomings of our work, which now includes this book, is ours alone.

HATE SPEECH AND POLITICAL VIOLENCE

1

INTRODUCTION

From the Tea Party and Donald Trump's
MAGA Extremism to January 2021

Meteorologists predicted nothing unusual for Wednesday, January 6, 2021, in the Washington, DC, area. But apart from normal winter temperatures, there was nothing normal about that day. The "Save America" rally at the Ellipse near the White House, organized by activists in the Make America Great Again (MAGA) movement created by Republican president Donald Trump, turned into a breach of the U.S. Capitol and a violent attempt to prevent the certification of Joe Biden's election victory by members of Congress and Vice President Mike Pence. Republican senator Mitt Romney characterized the event as "an insurrection incited by the President of the United States."[1] Indeed, in the weeks before the attack, President Trump claimed falsely that he had won reelection in a landslide. He used his Twitter account, @realDonaldTrump, and public appearances multiple times to urge supporters to "Stop the Steal" of the election by the Democrats. For example, on December 19 he tweeted, "Statistically impossible to have lost the 2020 Election. Big protest in D.C. on January 6th. Be there, will be wild." On January 1, he used his Twitter account to mobilize his followers: "The BIG Protest Rally in Washington, D.C., will take place at 11:00 A.M. on January 6th. Locational details to follow. StopTheSteal!"

During a January 4 rally in Georgia ahead of two special elections for the U.S. Senate, Trump grandstanded: "If the liberal Democrats take the Senate and the White House—and they're not taking this White House—we're going to fight like hell, I'll tell you right now . . . We're going to take it back."[2]

At the January 6 rally, Trump began his seventy-three-minute speech with an attack on the mainstream media and Big Tech (the largest and dominant technology companies and their involvement in mass and targeted communication)—although both reported on or carried his propaganda day in and day out before and after he became president. He shouted, "We have hundreds of thousands of people here and I just want them to be recognized by the fake news media. Turn your cameras please and show what's really happening out here because these people are not going to take it any longer. It would be really great if we could be covered fairly by the media. The media is the biggest problem we have as far as I'm concerned, single biggest problem. The fake news and the Big Tech." A few minutes later, Trump piled on, "We don't have a free and fair press. Our media is not free, it's not fair. It suppresses thought, it suppresses speech and it's become the enemy of the people. It's become the enemy of the people."[3]

Trump repeated his tale of a huge election victory twice during this speech. "We won in a landslide. This was a landslide," he claimed. Getting to the very reason for this rally, he urged the crowd to act: "Now, it is up to Congress to confront this egregious assault on our democracy. And after this, we're going to walk down, and I'll be there with you, we're going to walk down, we're going to walk down. . . . Because you'll never take back our country with weakness. You have to show strength and you have to be strong. We have come to demand that Congress do the right thing and only count the electors who have been lawfully slated, lawfully slated."[4]

During his candidacy and presidency, Trump's relentless salvos of weaponized communication became the dominant feature of his political rhetoric.[5] The term "weaponized rhetoric, speech, or communication" is used here in reference to the content of spoken and written messages conveyed at public events or through various media with the goal of demonizing political opponents and societal "out-groups." Trump's populist vernacular of hate and division grew even sharper after he lost the November 2020 presidential election. On January 6, his language whipped the already combative crowd into a fury. Obviously perceiving their leader's attack speech as a call to arms, his supporters—among them well-organized and well-trained white supremacist, neo-Nazi, and antigovernment groups— invaded congressional buildings hunting for the "enemies" of the president and his supporters. Contrary to his promise, Trump did not join the crowd that moved furiously toward the Capitol. Instead, he watched the live TV coverage of the attack from the White House without making any effort to stop the rampage. He enjoyed watching his devoted supporters in MAGA hats who carried Trump banners and Confederate flags, used the poles of U.S. flags as weapons against Capitol police officers, and shouted "Hang Mike Pence."[6] Later, when Capitol and Metropolitan police, with the assistance of National Guard units, had secured congressional buildings, President Trump tweeted, "These are the things and events that happen when a sacred landslide election victory is so unceremoniously & viciously stripped away from great patriots who have been badly & unfairly treated for so long. Go home with love & in peace. Remember this day forever!"

Like supporters of the Tea Party movement a decade earlier, Trump and his most fervent followers launched their weaponized speech against anyone who was not loyal to the MAGA movement's leader. They did this regularly and in plain view. Nonfactual statements and foolish conspiracy theories were no longer spread merely among fringe groups but became part of mainstream politics. Trump's tweets about "rigged" election results and his declaration of love for "great patriots" who had maimed police officers and threatened the lives of vice President Pence, Speaker of the House Nancy Pelosi, and others were shocking displays of the most horrific consequence of his and his supporters' dangerous propaganda. As Timothy Snyder warned, "To abandon facts is to abandon freedom."[7]

How did the United States of America, the oldest continuous democracy, arrive at such a dangerous junction? Years of rising partisan conflict, the mass media's amplification of the Tea Party movement, and their embrace of anti-Obama conspiracy theories were crucial building blocks in the rise of Donald Trump. In 2019, President Trump told an interviewer, "The Tea Party was a very important event in the history of our country.

And those people are still there. They haven't changed their views. The Tea Party still exists—except now it is called Make America Great Again."[8] Trump was well aware that Tea Partiers along with Protestant evangelicals, many of whom were sympathizers of the Tea Party movement, composed the core of his political base from the moment he became the most prominent public advocate of the racism-driven anti-Obama birther conspiracy theory. The importance of the Tea Party in Trump's political scheme was crystal clear when he announced his run for the presidency with a laundry list of grievances and promises that mirrored the Tea Party's racist and nativist agenda.[9] Most important, as Trump became the leader of what was, in effect, a merging of the Tea Party and Make America Great Again (MAGA) movements, his aggressive rhetoric and outright hate speech helped to increase the existing political divisions to the level of hyperpolarization.

PERSPECTIVES ON THE TEA PARTY, ANTI-OBAMA CONSPIRACY THEORIES, AND THE RISE OF TRUMP

A multitude of books and articles have been published about one or another aspect of the Tea Party movement, the rise of Donald Trump, partisan conflict, and the role of the mass media and social media. The first scholarly books devoted to the Tea Party were authored by the historian Jill Lepore, the law professor Elizabeth Price Foley, and the political scientists Theda Skocpol and Vanessa Williamson. All three volumes contribute to our understanding of the formative period of the Tea Party. In a fascinating account, Lepore compares the modern Tea Party and its obsession with the American Revolution, the Constitution, and originalism to the 1770s and 1780s, concluding that the Tea Party's "originalism has slipped into fundamentalism."[10] Conversely, Foley praises the Tea Party's principles of limited government, U.S. sovereignty, and constitutional originalism.[11] Skocpol and Williamson offer a balanced and comprehensive analysis of the early

Tea Party's organizations, ideologies, and rank-and-file members; its early effects on the Republican Party; and its ability to get significant amounts of news coverage. Notably, these two authors recognize that in the earliest stage of the Tea Party the movement's activists were "right-wingers in the GOP orbit," including antigovernment extremists, among them militia groups such as the Oath Keepers, who would years later play a central role in the storming of the U.S. Capitol.[12] Parker and Barreto interpreted the Tea Party movement's early embrace and spreading of anti-Obama conspiracy theories as signs of their white members' fears about changes in their country that they perceived to be harmful to them.[13]

There is a rich literature describing one or another aspect of Tea Party propaganda, online sites, and communities; the role of cable networks; the mainstream media's news coverage; and the danger of weaponized communication at the disposal of strongmen leaders.[14]

There is also important, scholarly research that has considered social movements and contentious politics in the context of changes that have come with twenty-first-century information and communication technology. Before the breakthrough of social media as major communication vehicles, Yochai Benkler in his pioneering book, *The Wealth of Networks*, recognized, analyzed, and applied the transformation from an "industrial information economy" to a "networked information economy" that has allowed "cooperative and coordinated action carried out through a radically distributed, non-market mechanism that does not depend on proprietary strategies."[15] With the breakthrough of social media, however, Benkler, Robert Faris, and Hal Roberts show, in a further pioneering way, that these media did not dominate political communication. Rather, a strong one-sided ("asymmetric") communication sphere—"network propaganda"—on the political right emerged that substantially included existing media along with social media.[16] Social media—and its pathologies—was hardly the only influence on political discourse and was not the dominant force in the early 2020s.[17] Lance Bennett and Steven Livingston emphasize aptly that this new oppositional partisan sphere disrupted basic principles and institutions of American democracy.[18] A number of scholars researched and developed theoretical frameworks for the different ways in which contentious collective politics and social movements, including the Tea Party, used the new information and communication landscape.[19]

Other works deal exclusively or partially with Tea Partiers' and Donald Trump's obsession with anti-Obama conspiracy theories, the Tea Party's capturing of the Republican Party in the House of Representatives, Tea Partiers' (and evangelicals') crucial role in Trump's 2016 election victory, and Trump's political language.[20] While focusing on the 2020 presidential election, John Sides, Chris Tausanovitch, and Lynn Vavreck, for example, present and interpret valuable public opinion survey data on the increased political polarization that started well before Trump's entry into the electoral arena.[21] The partisan conflict at the level of political leaders that penetrated into the level of the mass public has been well documented—and it has continued and is important to emphasize further and more fully (see chapter 5).

A THEORY OF THE MASS-MEDIATED RISE OF THE TEA PARTY AND ANTI-OBAMA CONSPIRACY THEORIES

The main argument of *Hate Speech and Political Violence* is that political communication began to go into a toxic downward spiral when the Tea Party, a reactionary social movement, was hastily founded with the assistance of media insiders and conservative advocacy groups merely a month after Barack Obama, the first Black president of the United States, was inaugurated. We argue and support with our research what we call the *interconnectivity of political communication* that facilitated and even promoted the Tea Party during its formative first years and the anti-Obama conspiracy theories that were embraced by its supporters. The rumor that Obama was not born in the United States and therefore an illegitimate president became part of the toxic communication spiral when the reality TV star and entrepreneur Donald Trump made himself the public spokesperson of the "birther" lies.

As figure 1.1 shows, the traditional mass media and the new social media platforms and websites along with the perennial personal communications are vehicles for the transmission of political messages to and from

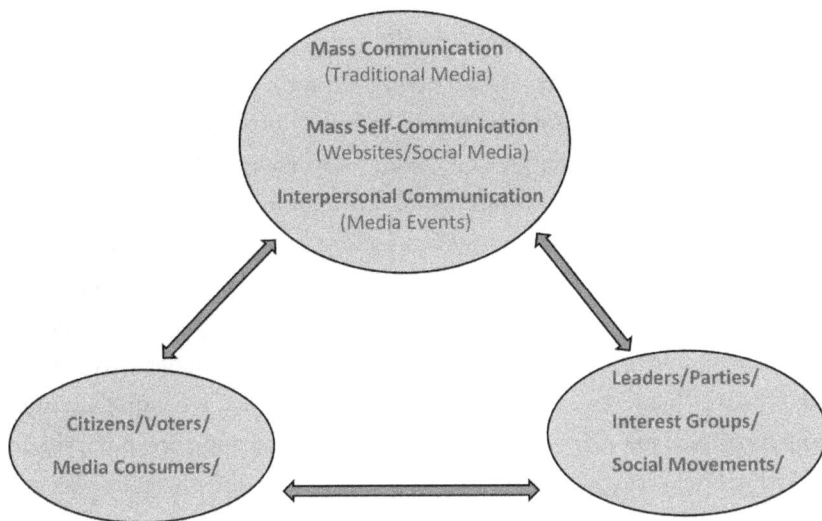

FIGURE 1.1 The interconnectivity of political communication and the rise of the Tea Party and anti-Obama conspiracy theories.

organized political entities and leaders (right corner) and citizens and voters (left corner).

The communicators in all three communication modes are participants in the political communication loop. What Manuel Castells calls *mass communication* and *mass self-communication media* were crucial contributors to and disseminators of uncivil and even weaponized rhetoric during the rise of the Tea Party.[22] But a great many of these toxic messages originated in interpersonal communication on websites and in the form of media events that remain part and parcel of modern-day politics and that tend to be staged in search of news and social media attention. Originally analyzed by Daniel Dayan and Elihu Katz, extraordinary media events, such as the public funerals of political leaders or the Olympic Games, required close organizational cooperation between governments and media organizations.[23] In the early stage of the Tea Party, the movement's activists organized mass protest rallies, often with the assistance and participation of Fox News's political talk show hosts, who highlighted the anti-Obama and anti-Washington outrage of its rank-and-file members and supporters. In this case, then, all three corners of the communication triangle were involved: mass media insiders and movement activists organized media events that attracted part of the general public—especially voters. These mass-mediated protests and the whole Tea Party movement were, according to Parker and Barreto, mostly organized against cultural, demographic, and political changes that Tea Partiers could not believe in.[24] Noting that contemporary "politics is primarily media politics," Castells characterizes the media environment as "the space of power making."[25] Similarly, as Khadijah Costley White put it, the news media are "not just a conduit through which political messages are conveyed to an awaiting audience, but a site in which political struggles, identities, activism, and rhetoric actually play out between media actors."[26]

In other words, the three communication modes shown at the top of figure 1.1 and separately in figure 1.2 are the pivotal parts of the interconnected political communication loop that we have described. The three communication types are not completely isolated entities; they are involved in symbiotic relationships in that they report, highlight, ignore, applaud, or condemn one another's messages. Our research shows how Tea Partiers and anti-Obama conspiracy theorists exploited the offline and online mass media and paved the way for Donald Trump's unorthodox candidacy and

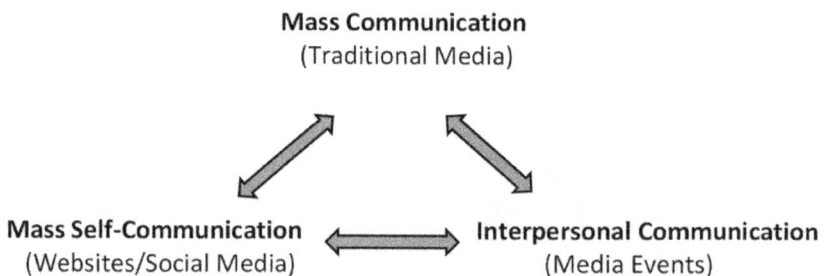

Mass Communication
(Traditional Media)

Mass Self-Communication   ⟷   **Interpersonal Communication**
(Websites/Social Media)   (Media Events)

FIGURE 1.2 The three modes of political communication.

presidency. Moreover, different partisan and ideological group members got their news then (and afterward) from an array of different online and offline information sources. The result was an insurmountable information and opinion gap between reactionaries to the right and progressives to the left of the ideological spectrum. For example, in December 2010, a few weeks after four dozen Tea Party–supported, first-time GOP congressional candidates won in the midterm elections, 52 percent of self-identified Republicans but only 9 percent of Democrats identified Fox News as their major information source. Conversely, whereas 22 percent of self-described Democrats named CNN as their primary news source, only 7 percent of Republicans did.[27] A decade later, the partisan gap had clearly endured: in mid-2020, 32 percent of Republican respondents named Fox News as their major information source, but only 2 percent of Democrats did. At the same time, 12 percent of Democrats preferred CNN as their primary news source, but only 2 percent of Republicans did.[28]

Our second argument is that the uncivil language of Tea Party radicals and anti-Obama conspiracy theorists was taken to an even greater extreme when Donald Trump entered the political arena. Bryan T. Gervais and Irwin L. Morris found similarities in the often incendiary rhetoric of congressional Tea Party members and Donald Trump. Incivility characterized much of the online speech of Tea Party supporters and anti-Obama conspiracy theorists.[29] Jennifer Mercieca characterized Trumpian rhetoric as an illustration of weaponized communication used by dangerous demagogues and pointed out that Trump "frequently explained his aggressive rhetoric by calling himself a 'counterpuncher,' but it often seemed he was the first to land a rhetorical punch."[30] This was certainly the case in the weeks before, on the day of, and in the weeks after January 6, 2021. Speaking of his own experience on that infamous day, then vice president Mike Pence, the major target of the angry crowd, told the ABC News anchor David Muir that Trump's words and especially a tweet from the president as the attack on congressional buildings unfolded were "reckless" and "endangered me and my family and everyone at the Capitol."[31] Obviously, Pence saw a causal relationship between Trump's rhetoric and the violent actions of his supporters.

We examine the rhetorical style and content of Donald Trump's tweets, speeches, and public statements and explore the groups and individuals who were most often targeted by his weaponized words. We also discuss the documented rise of lethal far-right violent extremism, including threats against members of Congress and other public officials during Trump's presidency (and thereafter), which suggest a relationship between violent speech and actual violence.

Last but not least, we use public opinion data to demonstrate how the reactionary agenda, inflammatory rhetoric, and political violence of the Tea Party/Trump era expanded the earlier partisan and demographic divisions in the United States into a hyperpolarized conflict and a threat to democracy. Forwarding past the conflict over the 2020 presidential election, while the major Trump-endorsed Republican candidates for the U.S. Senate (as well as other offices) lost their races in the 2022 midterm elections, the reactionary MAGA wing in the House's Republican majority caucus became more numerous and more influential in the party's thin majority. Moreover, Trump's early entry into the 2024 presidential race was a signal that he was in no mood to retire from politics.

WHEN POLITICAL OPPONENTS ARE SEEN AS ENEMIES

On the evening of January 6, a congressional majority and Vice President Pence certified Joseph Biden's presidential election victory—without the votes of six Republicans in the Senate and 121 in the House of Representatives. After the House impeached President Trump for his role in the failed insurrection, Republicans in the Senate prevented a guilty verdict in the impeachment trial. Republicans also opposed the formation of the House Select Committee to Investigate the January 6th Attack on the United States Capitol along the lines of the body that investigated the terrorist attacks of September 11, 2001. With the exception of two Republicans who had voted for Trump's impeachment, all the other members of the House Select Committee on January 6th were Democrats. The political and ideological polarization that had gradually widened for decades had now arrived at a trying crossroads during Trump's presidency.[32] Democrats and liberals on the one side and Republicans and far-right conservatives on the other side differed not simply on the pros and cons of particular policies but also on what was reality, truth, and fact. This division became even sharper after the January 6 nightmare. Democrats considered the efforts by President Trump and his supporters to keep him in office a serious assault on the very essence of democracy: the peaceful transfer of power after free and fair elections. Republicans downplayed the gravity of the incident or characterized the violent intruders falsely as tourists or members of the far-left Antifa movement. There was also a new twist in far-right conspiracy theories about the alleged enemy within that was working against MAGA patriots and their savior, Donald Trump: the hugely popular QAnon conspiracy theory claimed that "deep state" actors, among them FBI officials and other treacherous figures within the executive branch of government, had staged the attack of January 6 in order to smear the sitting president. In reality, the QAnon crowd was directly involved in the events of January 6. As the terrorism scholars Sophia Moskalenko and Clark McCauley found, "QAnon internet forums encourage followers to 'do the research' and 'connect the dots'—in other words, to function as collective myth-making platforms. It is on these platforms that QAnon discussed and planned 'the Storm' of January 6, designed to regain the 'stolen' presidency for Donald Trump."[33]

Calling nonsensical beliefs within the Trump movement "conspiracy theories without theory" and labeling them "conspiracism," Nancy Rosenblum and Russell Muirhead warned well before the insurrection attempt that "the conspiracists' assault on common sense produces disorientation. It creates a deep polarization about what it means to know something—a divide more unbridgeable than partisan polarization, for it becomes impossible to persuade, compromise, and even to disagree."[34] Early in the third decade of the twenty-first century, the political, social, and cultural rifts in the United States transcended the usual disagreements about policy preferences. Instead, millions of Trump Republicans considered Democrats as an existential threat to their image of America's democratic republic, and many were ready to fight for its survival. Similarly, millions of moderate and progressive Democrats and Independents considered many of Trump's fellow Republican leaders and followers as reactionaries and existential threats to liberal democracy.

However, neither the Tea Party nor the Trump movement or related conspiracy theories appeared out of the blue on the political stage. Both had deep roots in the steady rise of the so-called New Right within the predominantly white Republican Party that was in large part driven by fear and resentment of the Civil Rights and Voting Rights Acts in the 1960s and the emergence of militant Black groups during the same decade. Goldwater's New Right was determined to defend white supremacy. After all, "the hierarchy of caste . . . is about power—which groups have it and which do not. It is about resources—which caste is seen as worthy of them and which are not. It is about respect, authority, and assumptions of competence—who is accorded these and who is not."[35] Nathan Glazer and Daniel Patrick Moynihan wrote in the early 1960s that "religion and race define the next stage in the evolution of the American people."[36] Their prediction proved prophetic, especially at the beginning of the 2020s.

While there had been moderate and conservative factions in the GOP, the 1964 presidential campaign of Senator Barry Goldwater was a watershed in that "he and his supporters set the tone for the conservative movement ever after by mobilizing a base of right-wing populists, refusing to compromise with moderates, and pursuing a southern strategy (which Richard Nixon later took up further) aiming at attracting civil rights opponents to the GOP."[37] That strategy enabled him to win five southern states in defeat and opened that regional door further for Republicans going forward. From that time on, there were several major threads in the New Right's radicalism, most of all (1) the resentment and militant opposition toward actual or imagined changes in the traditional order of white Christian dominance; (2) the dissemination of conspiracy theories to pinpoint the enemies of the people at home and abroad; and (3) the attacks on the press that were seen as part of the evil cabal against patriotic Americans united in the New Right.

TAKING BACK OUR COUNTRY

Goldwater Republicans believed that "America has been largely taken away from them and their kind" and were "determined to try to repossess it and to prevent the final destructive act of subversion."[38] Goldwater lost to President Lyndon Johnson, but the New Right became energized by the defeat and began to fight relentlessly against progressive changes. Ronald Reagan's support from the New Right in 1980 had its roots in his strong backing of Goldwater in the 1964 campaign. Reagan used dog whistles such as "welfare queens," "forced busing," and "law and order" to appease both the New Right's ideologists and the moderates within the GOP. Notably, James Baker III, White House chief of staff in President Reagan's first term, recognized a close link between Reagan and the Tea Party. He told an interviewer, "People ask me what I think Ronald Reagan would think of the Tea Party. And I think he would be very, very comfortable with the Tea Party. I said, in fact, that I think he might be leading it. He was very, you know, he was seen to be somewhat revolutionary in his day."[39] President George H. W. Bush did not follow his predecessor's example of placating both factions within his party but showed his distaste for the New Right. In the 1992 primaries, he was challenged by Patrick Buchanan, who was not successful but had a strong showing in New Hampshire, which ensured the New Right's great influence at the GOP's national convention in Houston. There, in his so-called culture war speech, Buchanan laid out the New Right's clarion call for post–Cold War America: "My friends, this election is about more than who gets what. It is about who we are. It is about what we believe, and what we stand for as Americans. There is a religious war going on in this country. It is a cultural war, as critical to the kind of nation we shall be as was the Cold War itself, for this war is for the soul of America. . . . My friends, we must take back our cities, and take back our culture, and take back our country."[40]

Later, a Republican congressman from Georgia, Newt Gingrich, was ready for what he called the fight for "renewing American civilization" and to "put the GOP into a total war footing" against Democrats.[41] He was the engineer of his party's landslide victory in the 1994 midterm elections, when a new, antiestablishment class of "deep-dyed conservatives," mostly from the South, became members of both congressional chambers.[42] Gingrich taught them about the importance of attack language with use of words such as *traitors* and *radicals*.[43] He "pioneered a style of partisan combat . . . that poisoned America's political culture and plunged Washington into permanent dysfunction."[44] Halfway through Trump's presidency, Gingrich talked about "four great political 'waves' in the past half century . . . : Goldwater, Reagan, Gingrich, then Trump,"[45] without mentioning the equally influential New Right culture warrior, Patrick Buchanan. This perennial New Right battle cry of "taking our country back" from enemies within and outside was fueled by massive doses of oxygen during the rise of the Tea Party, its takeover of the congressional caucus in the U.S. House of Representatives, and, even more so, during the candidacy and presidency of Donald Trump.

CONSPIRACY THEORIES ABOUT EVIL ENEMIES

From his time as the self-appointed spokesman for the anti-Obama "birther" theory to his retweets of deranged QAnon messages from the White House, Donald Trump was the conspiracist in chief. Trump's longtime ally, the former New Jersey governor Chris Christie, wrote in his 2021 book, "Donald Trump was by far the most effective proponent of the birther conspiracy. He truly showed everyone how a lie like that can be exploited."[46] But just as House members and senators and politicians across the country became birther conspiracy theorists, many highly placed GOP elected and appointed officials signed on to the bizarre QAnon web of political lies.

During the Cold War, communists at home and abroad were the villains in Republican conservatives' conspiracy theories. As Senator Joseph McCarthy claimed in his opening salvo against traitors in 1950, "Today we are engaged in a final, all-out battle between communistic atheism and

Christianity. The modern champions of communism have selected this as the time, and ladies and gentlemen, the chips are down—they are truly down. . . . The reason why we find ourselves in a position of impotency is not because our only powerful potential enemy has sent men to invade our shores . . . but rather because of the traitorous actions of those who have been treated so well by this Nation."[47] Like McCarthy a decade earlier, Goldwater and his supporters believed in the same conspiracy theory; namely, that "the top government officialdom" was "infiltrated by Communists" engaged in harming the country's national interest."[48]

Adapting John Winthrop's mystical image of America as "a city on a hill," Ronald Reagan used it in the 1960s as a rallying cry "against rebellious students at home and Communist aggression abroad."[49] In the 1980s, the "shining city" as beacon of freedom became the core of President Ronald Reagan's conspiracy theory about an existential communist threat against America and the free world, "run from the heart of an 'evil empire.'"[50] This conviction influenced his foreign policy, including the "Contra" part of the secret Iran-Contra dealings that eventually was exposed as a major scandal. In the Iran-Contra affair, the Reagan administration engaged in the illegal funding of the right-wing Contras again the communist-backed Nicaraguan government via funds it raised by the secret sale through Israel of arms to Iran.

During Barack Obama's initial term in office, Patrick Buchanan was precise in pinpointing those from whom he thought white Christian Americans must take the country back when he wrote: "Our intellectual, cultural, and political elites are today engaged in one of the most audacious experiments in history. They are trying to transform a Western Christian republic into an egalitarian democracy made up of all the tribes, races, creeds, and cultures of planet Earth. They have dethroned our God, purged our cradle faith from public life, and repudiated the Judeo-Christian moral code by which previous generations sought to live."[51]

These complaints resembled the grievances expressed later in the "Great Replacement" conspiracy theory within alt-right and white supremacist/neo-Nazi groups that led to political violence: for example, to a death and multiple injuries at the "Unite the Right" rally in Charlottesville,

Virginia, in the summer of 2017; the mass shooting in a supermarket in El Paso, Texas, in 2019; and the attack outside and inside the U.S. Capitol on January 6, 2021. In no case did President Trump criticize the violent extremist elements responsible for this political violence. The Great Replacement threat was once more the direct and admitted motivation for the killing of ten Black people in the May 2022 mass shooting at a grocery store in Buffalo, New York.

THE PRESS AS VILLAIN

When President Trump chastised the media as "the enemy of the people" during the January 6 rally, it was the refrain of many such past attacks on news organizations and individual journalists during his public appearances and in his tweets. Earlier Republican presidents, too, were convinced that the most influential news media organizations were supportive of Democrats and liberals—no other president more so than Richard Nixon. While publicly not as combative in his attacks on the press as Donald Trump, Nixon was the only U.S. president besides Trump who considered the media to be an "enemy." Nixon entered the White House considering himself a victim of press bias in the past. He blamed news organizations for his loss in 1960 to John F. Kennedy, whom he claimed was their favorite candidate. After losing the 1962 gubernatorial race in California against the incumbent Democrat, Pat Brown, he told the press, "I leave you gentlemen now, and you will write it. You will interpret. That's your right. But as I leave you, I want you to know—just think how much you're going to be missing. You won't have Nixon to kick around anymore, because gentlemen, this is my last press conference."[52]

That was not his last press conference. Six years later, he ran again for president and defeated Lyndon Johnson's vice president, Hubert Humphrey. After Nixon won the presidency in 1968, the "battle lines had been drawn as they had not been in any previous administration."[53] Nixon's battle with the press was marked by a permanent offensive in the belief that attacking the media would increase his public approval in the midst of the faltering Vietnam War and the antiwar protests at home. His number one attacker was his vice president, Spiro Agnew, who drew on White House bullet points in his regular attacks against the media—an enemy elite—which he allegedly fought in the name of "the silent majority" of good Americans. The following points were used by Agnew and other White House officials as ammunition against enemies in the press:

- "A small little group of men who . . . enjoy a right of instant rebuttal to every presidential [speech]"
- A tiny small and unelected elite
- Subversive people who lived and worked in the suspect areas of New York and Washington and "read the same newspapers" and draw their political and social views from the same source
- A fraternity whose views do not represent the views of America
- Sinister people whom the average, honest, God-fearing American knew "practically nothing" about[54]

The press-president battle reached its most bitter apex at the height of the Watergate scandal, which had been brought to light by the reporting of two young *Washington Post* reporters, Bob Woodward and Carl Bernstein. Nixon and his supporters wanted to retaliate against the *Washington Post*. As Katharine Graham, the newspaper's publisher, recalled in her memoirs:

Of all the threats to the company during Watergate—the attempts to undermine our credibility, the petty slights, and the favoring of the competition—the most effective were the challenges to the licenses of our two Florida television stations. There were three separate challenges in Jacksonville and one in Miami. . . . Out of more than 30 stations in the state of Florida up for renewal, our stations were the only ones challenged.

Among the worst effects was the sharp decline in our stock price that naturally ensued, from $38 a share down to $28 in the first two weeks after the challenges, and continuing on down to $16 or $17, decreasing the value of the company by more than half. As for the direct effect on our finances, the legal costs of defending the licenses added up to well over a million dollars in the 2 1/2 years the entire process took—a far larger sum then than now for a small company like ours.[55]

The threats against the *Washington Post* showed how Nixon tried to act on what he told his inner circle: "The press is your enemy. Enemies. Understand that? . . . They're trying to stick the knife right in our groin."[56] Much later, for the same reason, President Ronald Reagan and his staff made great efforts to circumvent the national news media by creating "what amounted to a White House news service, feeding print stories directly to local news outlets."[57] But unlike Nixon and Reagan, Trump unleashed these constant attacks publicly, often in his face-to-face encounters with the press, at his MAGA rallies, and in his tweets. Except for his own propaganda arms among the cable networks, he called everyone in the media "liar," "enemy," "fake," and the like. This was an old and successful propaganda scheme of twentieth-century fascist leaders. In the words of one expert on tyranny: "As president, he used the word lies to mean facts not to his liking, and called journalists enemies of the people (as Hitler and the Nazis had done). Where the Nazis said 'Luegenpresse,' he said 'Fake news.' That president was on friendlier terms with the internet, his source for erroneous information that he passed on to millions of people."[58]

This created a climate in which Trump supporters threatened and, in several cases, attacked members of the media during his campaign and presidential mass rallies (see chapter 4). Trump also claimed that the liberal media was part of a dangerous global cabal that was an existential threat to American democracy. At the end of his 2016 campaign, he warned: "This election will determine whether we are a free nation or whether we have only the illusion of democracy, but are in fact controlled by a small handful of global special interests rigging the system . . . The establishment and their media enablers will control over this nation through means that are very well known."[59]

All in all, then, when the American democracy was at the brink on January 6, 2021, and thereafter, the roots of right-wing populism paired with conspiracy theories reached back into the 1960s, when GOP extremists laid the cornerstone in the New Right's foundation. More than half a century later, the Tea Party, a more extreme and activist reincarnation of Goldwater's New Right, and a crazy amalgamation of racist conspiracy theories formed a perfect storm for the coming of Donald Trump. When Trump made himself the celestial leader of the up-to-then leaderless national Tea Party movement, he was embraced most enthusiastically and thoroughly by social conservatives among Tea Partiers, who won the internal war over their libertarian brethren.[60] But, eventually, the libertarian wing, too, lined up behind the strong and especially competitive leader they wanted—Trump.

In *The Anatomy of Fascism*, Robert O. Paxton enumerated "mobilizing passions" as signposts for movements trending toward fascism. These included

- the need for authority by natural chiefs (always male), culminating in a national chieftain who alone is capable of incarnating the group's historical destiny;
- the superiority of the leader's instincts over abstract and universal reason; and
- the beauty of violence and the efficacy of will when they are devoted to the group's success.[61]

It seems that these were important markers on the Tea Party's and MAGA movement's road to the violent effort to overturn the 2020 presidential election results in several states.

THE TWENTY-FIRST-CENTURY MEDIA LANDSCAPE

The media landscape in the first decades of the twenty-first century was very different from that of 1964, when Barry Goldwater was the GOP's (and the New Right's) presidential candidate. Then and through the next decades, the three TV networks, ABC, CBS, and NBC, along with newspapers were the dominant news sources for Americans. There were no significant differences in the content of network evening news programs at the time,[62] and so the more than 55 million Americans who watched one of the three TV evening news programs by and large saw and heard the same public affairs information. To be sure, there were many other local and national news sources with different ideological and partisan views, but their consumption was limited to members or sympathizers of particular and small groups.

In the latter part of the twentieth century and even more so in the first decades of the twenty-first century, the media and information environment began to change from a low-choice to a high-choice system that weakened the reliability of public affairs information and fact-based political discourse.[63] As communication technology advanced, there were ever more opportunities for media expansion. Cable television in particular became increasingly a rival for the established TV networks after the establishment of CNN in 1980 as the first all-news outlet, followed in 1996 by the start of Fox News as a conservative network and in 2005 by the arrival of MSNBC as liberal counterpart to Fox. While cable and internet sites offered information alternatives in the latter part of the twentieth century, the coming and rapid expansion of social media platforms greatly increased communication and information sources in the first and second decades of the twenty-first century. Unlike in the low-choice media era, when newsroom gatekeepers could and often did nix unreliable information and sources, the high-choice system did not have quality controls informed by journalistic ethics for social media platforms, internet blogs, or podcasts. The American Society of News Editors, for example, demanded in its "Statement of Principles" that "every effort must be made to assure that the news content is accurate, free from bias and in context, and that all sides are presented fairly. Editorials, analytical articles and commentary should be held to the same standards of accuracy with respect to facts as news reports."[64] But when everyone can be an online publisher of written and spoken words, mostly political commentary, without regard to fact and truth, the lines between fact and falsity, truth and lies, become blurred.

This is particularly true when a country's highest official peddles lies day in and day out and those who serve him defend them as "alternative facts." The consequences are clear: "If nothing is true, then no one can criticize power, because there is no basis to do so. If nothing is true, then all is spectacle. . . . Post-truth is pre-fascism."[65]

From the day he announced his presidential candidacy in June 2015 through the 2016 primaries, Trump received more, and more positive, mainstream media coverage than both his GOP rivals and the Democratic front-runner, Hillary Clinton.[66] As a trio of political scientists concluded, "From the moment he entered the race. Trump garnered extraordinary media coverage, which helped to propel him to the top of the polls and helped to ensure that he stayed there."[67] In spite of giving candidate Trump such a crucial news advantage, the mainstream media ranked high as targets of all his tweet attacks from May 2009 through January 8, 2021, when Twitter closed his account. As figure 1.3 shows, of the tweets we identified

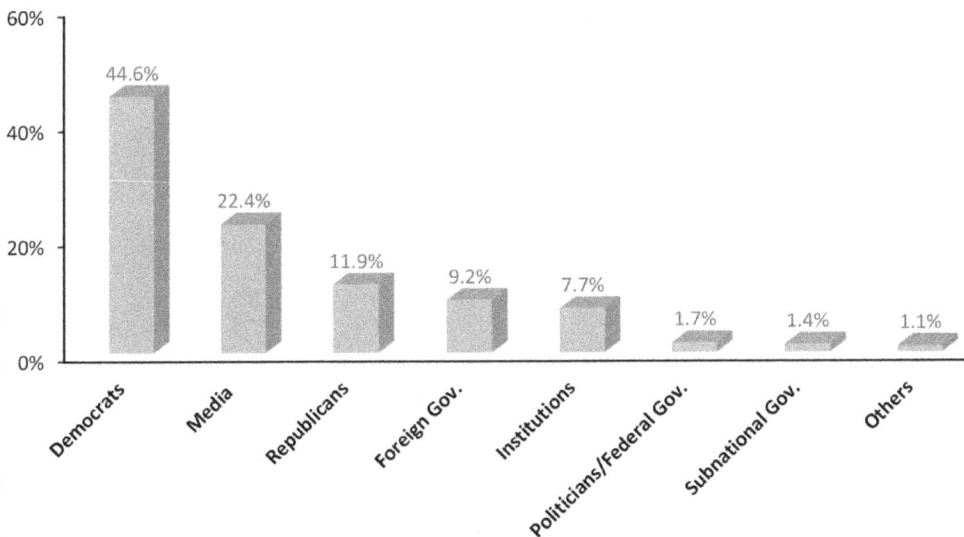

FIGURE 1.3 The targets of Trump's attack-tweet production.

Source: Compiled by the authors.

as rhetorical attacks, 22.4 percent targeted the media in general, particular news organizations, or individual reporters and opinion writers.[68]

This put the media in second place behind Democrats as targets of Trump's massive array of attacks. Because Trump lumped liberals and the media together in his "deep state" tale, one could argue that these "enemies" taken together were by far the preferred targets of his Twitter attacks. This constant vilification of news organizations and individual reporters and moderators took its toll with respect to the public's trust in the media. Not surprisingly, from 2015, when Donald Trump declared his candidacy for the presidency, to 2021, when he left office in the wake of the violent events of January 6, Republicans' trust in the media dropped precipitously—and to an unprecedented low of 11 percent, compared with the Democrats' 68 percent. This is shown in figure 1.4 (the question wordings for the survey trend data in all our figures can be found in the appendix).

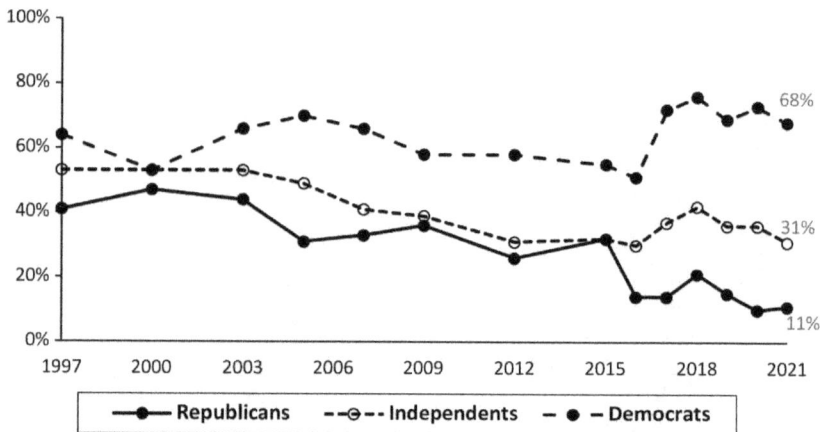

FIGURE 1.4 Trust in the media and partisanship.

Note: percentage great deal/fair amount.

Source: Gallup.

Trump understood the bifurcation of modern-day media into mass communication through traditional media and mass self-communication through social media platforms. Well before taking an active role in politics, he was preoccupied with the media as he sought to promote his business interests, his private life, and his love interests. It is telling that Trump's very first tweet (May 4, 2009) promoted his upcoming appearance on CBS's *Late Show with David Letterman*. He was obviously happy to make a guest appearance on the popular show, although Letterman had been critical of him. But once he began his transition from businessman and entertainment star to celebrity politician, Trump became extremely thin-skinned to any criticism reported in the news or expressed in media commentary. This was a strange reaction by a public figure who received generous media access before and after he became involved in politics and who was overly aggressive as a businessman and politician.

THE DOMINANCE OF RIGHT-WING
POLITICAL TALK RADIO

Although we did not systematically analyze the content of political radio talk shows, we believe that the dominance of corporate conservative and especially Christian radio networks contributed to the growth of far-right conservatism, the Tea Party, and the MAGA movement.

First, television in the second half of the twentieth century and then the internet in the twenty-first century overshadowed radio, their older cousin, as media of public affairs information. Many of the terrestrial radio stations aired music programs for faithful audiences with different musical tastes. However, as Jeffrey Berry and Sarah Sobieraj noted, "MP3 players, smart phones, Pandora, Sirius, and Internet radio have all badly injured the AM-FM radio business. Pandora, for example, allows individuals to go to a website, enter a song or symphony that represents their personal taste, and then have Pandora's algorithms create what is essentially the individual's own private radio station."[69] With dwindling audiences, advertising revenue shrank. Just as important, changes in public policy altered the AM and FM radio market,

(continued on next page)

(*continued from previous page*)

in that stations became attractive acquisition targets for large communication companies. First, the FCC's Fairness Doctrine, which required broadcasters to balance their programs with respect to political views, was repealed in 1987 during the Reagan administration; second, the 1996 Telecommunications Act, adopted during the Clinton administration, loosened the strict ownership limits of the past.[70]

Without the restrictions of the Fairness Doctrine and the limits on how many local stations one company could own, there was "a tidal wave of corporatization" as a majority of these predominantly small, mostly family-run local stations were bought by national companies.[71] Soon, a small number of national companies controlled the bulk of radio stations across the United States: iHeart Media, Inc. (formerly Clear Channel) owned 858 stations; Cumulus Media, 429 stations; Townsgate Media, 321 stations; Entercom, 235 stations; Saga Communications, 113 stations; and Salem Media, 109 stations.[72] Nationally syndicated political radio talk shows with "shock jocks" airing their extreme views and attracting like-minded audiences were a lucrative alternative to music or news programs. The most successful radio talk show hosts in terms of audience size were conservatives led by Rush Limbaugh, Sean Hannity, Dave Ramsey, Mark Levin, and Glenn Beck. For years, there was not one liberal host among the hosts with the top ten largest audiences in this radio genre. Moreover, all these hosts weighed in uniformly on the side of the Tea Party, related conspiracy theories, and Donald Trump's candidacy and presidency.

Salem Media, was by the time of Trump's presidency the largest of several media companies owned by members of the Council for National Policies (CNP), a conservative, Christian fundamentalist group established to remake the Republican Party in the image of the New Right. As Anne Nelson writes in her book *Shadow Networks*, CNP members managed to fill "the news hole in the heart of America," the vast area between the liberal East and West Coasts, with their radio programs. The "Lords of the Air," as Nelson calls them, "had a social agenda as well as a profit motive . . . Salem radio was designed to counter 'secular humanism' by building a platform for the best communicators to communicate biblical truth." Besides carrying religious programs, Salem also "rode the wave of conservative talk radio."[73] The CNP-linked radio companies—Salem, Bott, and American Family Radio—grew into an archconservative radio empire that "extended to at least forty-six states."[74] Taken together, the CNP media influence among Evangelicals was not lost on Donald Trump, who courted the group by pushing their conservative policy preferences and rewarding them with political appointments, thereby supporting their cause once he was in the White House.

POPULIST MOVEMENTS AND THE CENTRALITY OF COMMUNICATION

Public performances were always indispensable parts of contentious politics and social movements, "but only in the twentieth century—when public opinion, the media, and national states began to mediate between claim makers and their targets—did contention become a true performance for the benefit of third parties."[75] Contrary to its name, the Tea Party never strove to become a third political party. It began as a protest movement that became what Rachel M. Blum characterizes as an "intraparty insurgent faction," with an agenda of what Parker and Barreto called "reactionary conservatism" and with the intent to remake the GOP into the New Right party that Republicans from Goldwater on had imagined but not realized.[76] The Tea Party was from the outset a populist force in that it "represented the apex of a long distrust of elites and political insiders,"[77] and it became in less than a decade after its creation the perfect vehicle for a populist outsider to ride to power and to the complete dominance of the Republican Party. There has been an American tradition of powerful images conveyed through the media of clashes between the elite or the establishment and ordinary men. According to Michael Kazin, "Whether orated, written, drawn, broadcast, or televised, this language is used by those who claim to speak for the vast majority of Americans who work hard and love their country. That is the most basic and telling definition of populism: a language whose speakers conceive of ordinary people as a noble assemblage not bounded narrowly by class, view their elite opponents as self-serving and undemocratic, and seek to mobilize the former against the latter."[78]

To put it differently, social movements and populist movements depend on communication, whether person-to-person or through the mass media, to disseminate messages intended to persuade the receivers of populist rhetoric. Pointing out that political communication involves political actors and parties, the media, and citizens, leading scholars have concluded that the communicative tools used for spreading populist ideas are just as central as the populist ideas.[79] One might argue that communication is the oxygen of populism. Both Tea Party activists and Donald Trump and his MAGA movement are unthinkable without their heavy reliance on propaganda promoted through the media. And social media was the new communication vehicle that both the Tea Party and MAGA movements had at their disposal.

Notably, new types of media have been instrumental in publicizing the anger and hope and the grievances and reform demands of populist movements throughout American history. Tyler Branson considers new media forms the binding elements of populist movements. He singles out "the Populist Party in the 1890s circulating alternative newspapers, Father Charles Coughlin in the 1930s broadcasting sermons on the radio, [and] Ross Perot taking advantage of cable TV channels to campaign for the presidency." In each case, Branson writes, "populist rhetorical frameworks inform the relationship between social groups and technology."[80] Going further back to American Revolutionary times, the new media form was the political pamphlet, which was a major factor in stirring the revolutionary fervor in the American colonies.

But no earlier new communication technology was as consequential for the availability of alternative communication modes as the various social media platforms. They altered the information flows within the political communication paradigm.

While mass communication remains under the control of traditional media corporations and their gatekeepers, the more recent advances in communication technology, most of all the features of the internet, added a multitude of opportunities for mass self-communication whereby messages sent by individuals and groups circumvent the traditional mass media and their gatekeepers and can be received by mass audiences. Just as the conventional press pays a great deal of attention to and reports on competitors' scoops, the conventional and new media feed off one another's content, if only for competitive purposes.

Thus, modern-day social movements and especially those with strong populist leaders enjoy unprecedented opportunities to spread their messages through traditional media (print, television, and radio) and also to self-communicate their appeals and imagery on internet websites and on social media platforms. Most important, mass communication and mass self-communication along with interpersonal communication "coexist, interact, and complement each other rather than substituting for one another."[81]

The Tea Party, the related anti-Obama conspiracy theory craze, and the Trump-led MAGA movement used all three forms of communication and managed to conquer big chunks of what Castells describes as the power-making space.

FROM TEA PARTY EXTREMISM TO THE VIOLENT BREACH OF THE CAPITOL

In chapter 2, we examine mass self-communications and mass communication from the birth of the Tea Party in February 2009, just one month after the inauguration of President Barack Obama, to its remarkable influence in the 2010 midterm elections and its role during the 2012 presidential campaign. Our goal is to explore whether this movement, besides its birth on live cable TV, constituted yet another case in which a powerful new communication vehicle—the internet and its social media platforms—was instrumental in the emergence and growth of a populist movement or whether the mainstream media's own "newsroom populism" was equally as or even more important in heightening the public awareness of the Tea Party and its agenda.[82] We examine Tea Party websites and sample the content of posts and responses to them. We should note that since our research began in 2009, many of the links to websites and/or particular posts we cite are no longer available today. This is particularly the case for many links in chapters 2 and 3.

Assuming that mainstream media news coverage, too, was important in informing the public about the movement, we analyze the content of Tea Party coverage in major news, print, television, and radio outlets during two crucial periods: first, the summer of 2009, when, at the height of a severe recession, libertarian Tea Partiers were furious as they disrupted congressional town hall meetings in protest against taxes, government bailouts of banks, and President Obama's planned reform and expansion of health care; and, second, the period before and after the 2010 midterm elections, in which the Republican Party picked up sixty-three seats in the U.S. House of Representatives and six in the U.S. Senate, with most of the GOP newcomers endorsed and supported by Tea Party groups during the primaries and the general election campaign.

Chapter 3 is based on research on the intersections between anti-Obama conspiracy theories and mass communication and self-communication. We analyze the content of the conspiracy theory hub WorldNetNews.com and several nodes (most with Tea Party connections) that formed an expansive internet-based anti-Obama conspiracy network that spread two sets of interrelated rumors: first, that the forty-fourth U.S. president was born outside the United States and therefore not eligible for the highest office in the land and, second, that President Obama was a Muslim, not a Christian as he claimed. We describe the volume of reporting on the two anti-Obama conspiracy theories by broadcast, cable, and print media and conducted a systematic content analysis of four prominent, traditional news organizations (CBS News, CNN, National Public Radio, and the *New York Times*) in order to identify the sources and messages presented in the pertinent news reports. Finally, we explore and show how the mainstream media opened the information gates they controlled when Donald Trump made himself the birther spokesperson in chief—which was his first step in winning support of Tea Partiers for his future political plans.

Chapter 4 examines Donald Trump's hateful and divisive political discourse during both his campaign and his presidency and the targets of his verbal attacks—most of all racial, ethnic, and religious minorities; the news media collectively and individual journalists; as well as well-known politicians, mostly Democrats. Assuming that aggressive rhetoric by influential political leaders can also affect their supporters' words and deeds, we analyze Trump's online and offline hate speech, the rhetorical reactions of his followers, and the possibly violent consequences suffered by their declared enemies. We found that contrary to an old children's rhyme ("Sticks and stones may break my bones, but words will never hurt me"),

Trump's aggressive, divisive, and dehumanizing language was seconded by his followers, and they inflicted direct and indirect psychological and physical harm on those whom they excluded from their MAGA community.

Drawing on substantial public opinion survey and other data, chapter 5 puts into further historical and political context our argument that the Tea Party's propaganda and hardball politics as well as the impact of related conspiracy theories provided the opening for Trump's populist rhetoric, which evoked further powerful emotions—resentment and anger—toward the established political parties, their leaders, and their followers. This partisan conflict was strongly connected to increasing disagreements over nearly all major policy issues and to the increasing competitiveness of national elections. The emotional level of politics, as reflected in and amplified through the mass media and later social media, was closely connected to the substance of policies and politics and the consequences of elections for government policy making. The conflict had in fact begun long before the Tea Party and Trump and continued into the Biden presidency. It extended strikingly to the highly politicized reaction to the COVID-19 pandemic—producing a lack of unity and policy consensus during the most serious national health crisis in a century. This was followed by partisan battle lines being drawn on how elections are conducted and how votes are accurately counted.

Chapter 6 pulls together the most important findings of our research and connects them to the serious threats against American democracy before, on, and after January 6, 2021. We examine the background and motives of organized terrorists and unorganized insurgents who tried to prevent the congressional certification of Joe Biden's victory over Donald Trump and the ways in which social media platforms were used by MAGA activists and QAnon conspiracy theorists to spread the Big Lie and organize the Stop the Steal rally that preceded the storming of the Capitol. Although Trump and his violent supporters failed to prevent Vice President Mike Pence from certifying Joe Biden's victory, the intraparty insurgency started by Tea Party hardliners and intensified during Trump's reign remade the Republican Party in the image of the New Right's reactionary conservatism. Thus, the coup attempt by the sitting president and a clique of outside lawyers had significant support among GOP members in the U.S. House of Representatives and the U.S. Senate.

All along, first Tea Party activists and then President Trump and his GOP sycophants were far more interested in exploiting what some communication scholars call the "mediatization" of politics—the expansive influence of the media on politics, in addition to other aspects of society—by "mobilizing all available resources in the daily battles to influence and shape the news, mainly by accommodating the wants, needs, and standards of news worthiness."[83] The most shocking and outrageous rhetorical bombs thrown on Twitter or Facebook or on right-extreme networks such as Fox News, Newsmax, and One America News reverberated throughout the new media system and were more often than not magnified and amplified in the traditional media. Weaponized communication trumped (no pun intended) normal politics and governance. The result was extreme affective—highly emotional—political polarization that endangered the very foundation of American democracy, as the violent invasion of the U.S. Capitol on January 6 demonstrated.

Early in the twenty-first century, Robert Paxton warned that "fascism exists at the level of Stage One within all democratic countries—not excluding the United States."[84] Taken together, the following chapters closely examine the role of mass communication in the birth and growth of the Tea Party and anti-Obama conspiracy theories, both of which paved the way for the rise of Donald Trump and his inflammatory political rhetoric. This has had serious repercussions for American democracy to this day.

2

THE TEA PARTY MOVEMENT, THE MASS MEDIA, AND CONTENTIOUS POLITICS

On February 19, 2009, a month after President Barack Obama's inauguration, the on-air rant by a reporter for the financial cable network CNBC induced the birth of the modern-day Tea Party. Reporting from the floor of the Chicago Board of Trade, the world's largest futures and options exchange, Rick Santelli attacked the new administration's Homeowners Affordability and Stability Plan, which was designed to help certain homeowners prevent the foreclosure of their properties during the recession of 2008–2009. "The government is promoting bad behavior," Santelli screamed. "This is America! How many of you people want to pay for your neighbor's mortgage that has an extra bathroom and can't pay their bills? Raise their hand. President Obama, are you listening?" After characterizing homeowners with distressed mortgages as "losers," he trumpeted his remedy: "We're thinking of having a Chicago Tea Party in July. All you capitalists that want to show up at Lake Michigan, I'm going to start organizing."[1]

Santelli's rhetorical salvo may not have been the shot heard around the world, but it was heard around the United States. Financial types watched the original outburst on the cable TV channel CNBC; many more saw and heard replays of it on traditional and social media. The same day, an enthusiastic Rush Limbaugh aired the audio of Santelli's outburst and threw in one of his own rants when he said,

> This is Rick Santelli, reporter at CNBC, not a commentator. He is a reporter at CNBC on the board at the Chicago Board of Trade. And, as you can tell, there is tremendous upset over the mortgage bailout that was announced yesterday, subsidizing the losers, Obama picking the losers. . . .
>
> The idea that this would erupt in a market like this, where the traders were cheering, where the traders were whistling, where the traders were booing, this, ladies and gentlemen, is the reaction of people who have skin in the game. So, the point of all this, aside from what you heard, is that you are not alone. When the pulse of revolution starts, it just takes an action like this to inspire confidence in others who want to show up.[2]

On his radio talk show, Glenn Beck of Fox News was particularly taken with the anger he recognized in Santelli's voice. He interrupted his conversation with a female caller to his program to replay Santelli's audio repeatedly. "Pause it again. Do you hear his outrage again?" he said at one point. "Hear the anger?" Obviously recognizing an opportunity to get involved in Santelli's call to action, Beck told his listeners, "I believe this is the opening fire across the bow. When he said, 'President Obama, are you hearing this,' he couldn't have spoken truer words. This is the beginning that somebody in our government needs to finally pay attention. It is what I've been talking about that was coming for a very long time and that is disenfranchisement which will turn into anger and then turn into God knows what."[3]

The performances by Santelli, Limbaugh, and Beck turned the emergence of the Tea Party movement into a mass media spectacle comparable to attention-catching trailers for Hollywood blockbusters.

The idea of using the iconic Boston Tea Party to communicate contemporary antigovernment messages did not originate with Santelli but had been an effective weapon of both the political right and left in the past. For Geoffrey Kabaservice, the twenty-first-century Tea Party movement "was a throwback to the 'T-Parties' of the early '60s, part of the right-wing, anti-tax crusade of that era."[4] At that time, the "T" stood for tax, but its pronunciation ensured an association with the original Tea Party. In 1973, anti-Vietnam protesters chose the two-hundredth anniversary of the Boston Tea Party to stage an "Impeach Nixon" demonstration at Faneuil Hall. Their subsequent march "concluded with the reenactment of the Tea Party near the former site of Griffin's Wharf."[5] And two months before Santelli's rant, on the two hundred thirty-fourth anniversary of the original Tea Party in Boston Harbor, supporters of the presidential hopeful Congressman Ron Paul (R-TX) marched in snow-covered Boston from the State House to Faneuil Hall and "re-enacted the dumping of tea into Boston Harbor by tossing banners that read 'tyranny' and 'no taxation without representation' into boxes that were placed in front of an image of the harbor."[6] For the Libertarian/Republican Ron Paul and his supporters, this event "launched the modern Tea Party movement."[7] But while Paul and his camp got only some local press coverage, Santelli's passionate anti-government performance received the immediate attention of the national mainstream media. For the journalism professor Khadijah Costley White, "the Santelli moment illustrates the way that members in the news media actively constructed, framed, propelled, and instigated the Tea Party's ascent to public consciousness in a brand culture."[8]

On Tax Day (April 15) in 2009, Tea Partiers staged their first mass demonstrations throughout the country. In the prior ten days, Fox News promoted the events, relentlessly airing "more than 100 commercial promotions for the protests"[9] An estimated 300,000 people protested in 346 cities and towns. They expressed anger against the high level of taxation, the bailout of banks, high unemployment rates, growing budget deficits, and irresponsible government spending. The talk show host Sean Hannity of Fox News cheered Tea Party protesters in Atlanta, and former speaker of the House Newt Gingrich did the same in downtown Manhattan. The following is an exchange between Hannity and

Gingrich as they reported on Hannity's show, which was fully devoted to the Tax Day protests:

> *Hannity*: Mr. Speaker, I want to ask you one serious question. Because I am arguing and what's amazing about what has happened today all across the country, is that the American is—they're not thinking about themselves. They're thinking about their kids and they're thinking about their grandkids.
>
> And they're thinking about the future of this country. And that's why everybody here and everybody in New York and around the country inspires me here. But if we're talking about this kind of debt and this kind of deficit, is this really a battle between not limited government, and you know, less government Obama in which . . .
>
> (LAUGHTER)
>
> Is this now a battle between capitalism and socialism?
>
> *Gingrich*: This is a battle between families who care about their children and their grandchildren and who want them to have a decent life and politicians who are so greedy for power that they would burden our children and our grandchildren for a lifetime so they could get through the next election. This is a battle between responsibility and absolute power grabs by irresponsible politicians.[10]

The same day, Gingrich was more specific in attributing responsibility for all the government ills that protesters focused on. He called in to former U.S. senator Fred Thompson's (R-TN) radio talk show and told the host, "People have a growing awareness that the combination of the Obama administration and left-wing Democrats who dominate the Congress means a genuine threat to everything about their life."[11]

Some early Tea Party admirers, critics, and middle-of-the-road observers highlighted the crucial roles of influential Washington advocacy groups, such as FreedomWorks, then chaired by former congressman Richard (Dick) Armey, and Americans for Prosperity (AFP), founded and funded by David H. Koch of Koch Industries, an oil and gas conglomerate.[12] Well before the emergence of the Tea Party, these groups promoted libertarian values and advocated small government, fewer regulations, and lower taxes—especially for businesses and the wealthy. FreedomWorks' website (https://www.freedomworks.org/) claimed that the organization "recruits, educates, trains and mobilizes millions of volunteer activists to fight for less government, lower taxes, and more freedom." Similarly, the AFP website described that body as "an organization of grassroots leaders who engage citizens in the name of limited government and free markets on the local, state, and federal levels." Both organizations had plenty of resources and expertise in assisting Tea Party novices in winning, organizing, and mobilizing supporters.

Some observers claimed that Rick Santelli's rant on the floor of the Chicago Mercantile Exchange was an unprompted televised outburst that stirred immediate grassroots activism and organization through the new means of mass self-communication.[13] For others, Santelli was the strategically placed spark plug intended to ignite fireworks of publicity for the best-laid plans of political entrepreneurs who had social networks in place.[14] But whether or not it was a solo act or "the launch event of a carefully organized and sophisticated PR campaign in which Santelli served as a front-man, using the CNBC airwaves for publicity,"[15] the mass-mediated chant awakened the antigovernment emotions of ordinary people, and many of them joined the quickly emerging Tea Party movement.

As the April 15 demonstrations showed, less than two months after Santelli's "live" TV rant, the Tea Party had gained significant traction within the triangular political communication loop that we described in the introduction. That happened because from the outset, organized mass protest events against federal policies and politicians and smaller events received robust and ongoing mainstream media attention. Before we turn to the communication media, we examine in the next sections to what extent well-trained and well-financed political activists were instrumental in promoting and assisting the Tea Party and whether the Tea Party was a populist social movement from below or a creature of part of the mass public at large—or both.

WELL-TRAINED AND WELL-FINANCED ACTIVISTS AS TEA PARTY ORGANIZERS

At the outset, the key roles in the organization of the Tea Party movement were played by skilled community organizers at FreedomWorks, a libertarian antitax, antiregulation lobbying organization led by the former House majority leader Dick Armey. Only hours after the Santelli outburst, staffers set up the website IAmWithRick.com (no longer available), which linked visitors automatically to the blog "FreedomWorks Foundation's Taxpayer's 2009 Revolt." Two days later, Brendan Steinhauser of FreedomWorks posted, under the headline "How to Organize Your Own 'Tea Party' Protest," ten tips for building a local group. Among these tips was "Build an rsvp email list so that you can provide quick updates if something changes. You should also create a Facebook group so that the group can communicate with one another."[16]

While Santelli called for a Chicago Tea Party at Lake Michigan in July, FreedomWorks along with other conservative organizations and activists immediately used existing blogs, Facebook accounts, and—most of all—Twitter accounts to mobilize Tea Party protesters across the country to set up rallies on February 27, 2009—just eight days after Santelli's rant. Three days before the planned demonstrations, Steinhauser posted this guidance on FreedomWorks' website:

> FreedomWorks will be joining forces with Americans for Tax Reform, Smart Girl Politics, The American Spectator, Americans for Prosperity, Top Conservatives on Twitter, College Republicans, Heartland Institute, The National Tax Payers Union, The Young Conservatives Coalition, and local conservative political leaders.
>
> As we head into this protest, I would like to provide you with some guidance. The fundamental objective is to send a message to the public, government officials, and the media that is loud and clear, and the theme should be focused and consistent. . . . As such, we need to generate some key slogans that should printed [*sic*] clearly with LARGE

PRINT on posters. Below are some examples, but I would like to solicit more from all of you. The final 4–5 key slogans will be sent to everyone in a few days.

NO MORE PORK
NOBODY READ THE BILL
WASTE = STIMULUS
STOP WASTING OUR MONEY
PRIVATE SECTOR CREATES VALUE
NO TRANSPARENCY = NO CHANGE.[17]

The targets of this FreedomWorks propaganda guidance were conservatives who were deeply upset about Obama's victory in the November 2008 presidential election. Some of them were determined to duplicate or surpass the Obama campaign's use of social networking to win over voters—especially among the younger generation. Initially, Twitter perhaps became the most important communication vehicle and the emerging Tea Party a "case study of how Twitter can be used to mobilize political activists."[18] More importantly, as one observer noted, there were interconnections between and among the various social networks. "Much of the sharing is now facilitated by the fast-growing messaging site Twitter, where today the keyword 'teaparty' was one of the most frequently used terms," another observer pointed out. "Users sent out a flurry of updates about attendance, links to photos on Flickr and Photobucket, and videos on YouTube and other sites."[19]

Following the Tea Party protests of February 27, Steinhauser of FreedomWorks left no doubt about his organization's leadership role. "The taxpayer tea parties were wildly successful! Thank you to everyone who planned or participated in a tea party," he wrote. "But the movement is just beginning, and we need your help. We were able to organize dozens of tea parties around the country in less than a week, but now we must begin to plan bigger events in more cities, leading up to Tax Day on April 15th!"[20]

One of the quickly established national Tea Party organizations, Tea Party Express (TPE), claimed on its website that it "came into existence as the tea party movement was awakened by the famous Rick Santelli rant that swept across the country in February of 2009. This power and influence could not be ignored by the political establishment as the grassroots movement exploded onto the scene." In reality, TPE was founded by a California-based Republican political action committee, Our Country Deserves Better, which was closely linked to a long-time Republican operative and partner in a political consulting firm.

For critics, the Tea Party was "not a social movement, but rather a loose conglomeration of partisan interest groups set on returning the Republican Party to power."[21] Nancy Pelosi, then speaker of the U.S. House of Representatives, rejected the notion of a populist Tea Party movement. "This [tea party] initiative is funded by the high end—we call it astroturf, it's not really a grassroots movement," she said. "It's astroturf by some of the wealthiest people in America to keep the focus on tax cuts for the rich instead of for the great middle class."[22] Francis Fukuyama argued that the perceptions of Tea Partiers as a grassroots movement missed the mark. "Although the Tea Party is anti-elitist in its rhetoric, its members vote for conservative politicians who serve the interest of precisely those financiers and corporate elites they claim to despise," he wrote.[23] Theda Skocpol and Vanessa Williamson noted the irony of Dick Armey, a lobbyist on behalf of big business interests, emerging "along with his billionaire-backed organization as a national Tea Party spokesperson and advisor to GOP officials—operating in the name of a grassroots populist movement."[24]

THE TEA PARTY AS POPULIST SOCIAL MOVEMENT

For Tea Partiers there was no inconsistency here: they opposed and fought dangerous liberal, un-American elitists, not conservative soulmates, even if the latter happened to be among the most influential elites. And, indeed, the fact that professional activists paid by influential and wealthy political actors were instrumental in organizing and propagating the Tea Party from day one did not mean that the new kid in the political power space was not a social movement from below. Scholars consider what they call "contentious politics" as first steps on the way to potential social movements. According to Sidney Tarrow, an expert on social movements, "contentious politics occurs when ordinary people—often *in alliance with more influential citizens* and with changes in public mood—join forces in confrontation with elites, authorities, and opponents."[25] That was precisely what happened in the early days, weeks, and months of the Tea Party. Instant and early Tea Partiers, along with wealthy individuals and advocacy groups, joined forces so they could engage in contentious politics and confront political opponents in Washington, most of all President Obama and Democrats, whom they considered an elite out of touch with ordinary people.

Charles Tilly and Leslie Wood recognized three characteristics common in Western social movements:

(1) campaigns of collective claims on target authorities;

(2) an array of claim-making performances including special-purpose associations, public meetings, media statements, and demonstrations; and

(3) public representations of the cause's worthiness, unity, numbers, and commitment.[26]

In short, for contentious politics to succeed, social movements need to perform like actors on stage engage with and win the support of their targeted audiences. Following their original splash on television and radio, Tea Partiers—with the help of trained activists—displayed all the performative elements highlighted by Tilly and Wood as they built virtual and actual networks with many nodes and clusters. They found inventive ways to confront and interact with adversaries, and they rallied like-minded citizens around powerful cultural symbols related to liberty, patriotism, and the U.S. Constitution. Whereas the first two movement characteristics were marked by messages of anger, the third one—rank-and-file citizens making common cause against the powers that be in defense of their interests—was the positive antidote to anger in the combination of rage and hope that Manuel Castells identified as the crucial emotions in the formation of social movements.[27]

Tea Party activists and supporters considered themselves part of a populist grassroots movement and, according to the Tea Party Patriots' website (teapartypatriots.org), "a community committed to standing together, shoulder to shoulder, to protect our country and the Constitution upon which we were founded!" They claimed and seemed to believe that they were a movement of ordinary people rising up against an unconstitutional federal government and elites that curbed individual liberties and state rights, thereby violating the Constitution's esteemed values and principles. Asked what the Tea Party was, Armey characterized it as an "outside-the-body, bottom-up group" and a movement with people who "believe that the country is in serious danger by a government that's so excessive in its spending that it threatens the insolvency of the nation and their personal liberties."[28] Applauding the Tea Party's "unifying constitutional principles," Elizabeth Price Foley wrote, "It's fair to say there's no Tea Party, but there is a Tea Party movement."[29]

Commonly, such movements are neither the constructions of spontaneous grassroots actions nor mass public-elite alliances but the creations of individual charismatic leaders who utilize populist rhetoric and demagoguery to appeal to the fears and frustrations of ordinary people. Modern-day populist or so-called neopopulist parties and movements in particular "characteristically organize themselves around charismatic and strongly personalized leaderships and are immediately and exclusively identified with highly visible and controversial leaders."[30] But contrary to the typical case of neopopulism with one strong founder and leader at the top (e.g., Joerg Haider in Austria; Jean-Marie Le Pen followed by his daughter Marine Le Pen in France; and Geert Wilders in Holland), the Tea Party movement did not have one charismatic leader. Instead, even the founders and activists of the several nationally organized groups, such as the Tea Party Patriots (TPP) and Tea Party Nation (TPN), insisted that they were part of a leaderless grassroots movement with many activists in a few national and especially many local groups.

Nothing changed in this organizational arrangement in the years that followed. Yet, even without one singular movement leader, there were the early Tea Party heroine, Sarah Palin; other nationally known politicians, such as U.S. Senator Jim DeMint (R-SC), U.S. Rep. Ron Paul (R-TX), and U.S. Rep. Michele Bachmann (R-MN); along with TV and radio talk show stars (most of all, Glenn Beck and Rush Limbaugh) who had close links to the movement. Palin, the running mate of 2008 GOP presidential candidate John McCain and a much-admired celebrity among conservatives even after their electoral defeat, gave the Tea Party its most attractive public face and loudest voice during the movement's earliest stage.

In early 2010, a leading scholar of populism in America compared Tea Partiers to traditional populist movements, in that they "see themselves as virtuous common people against the immoral elites."[31] Students of populism disagree about whether populism is a form of communication or an ideology. For some, populism is "much more a style of political persuasion than a set doctrine."[32] Michael Kazin noted that the most revealing definition of populism is that of "a language whose speakers conceive of ordinary people as a noble assemblage not bounded narrowly by class, view their elite opponents as self-serving and undemocratic, and seek to mobilize the former against the latter."[33] Michael J. Lee recognized common rhetorical traits in populist movements regardless of their ideological bends: (1) the portrayal of "people" as the "heroic defenders of 'traditional' values; (2) the definition and labeling of "the enemy"; (3) the contradiction between the once fair "system" and the system as corrupted by the enemy; and (4) the "apocalyptic confrontation" as "vehicle to revolutionary change."[34] If "it is very difficult to translate the concepts of populism into a coherent ideological tradition," as Ben Stanley concluded, past populists of all stripes nevertheless managed to stitch together a collage of persuasive ideas about the people-versus-elite contradiction and the threat of alleged "enemies of the people."[35]

And so did the Tea Party.

Summing up the fears of the ultra-right movement of the 1950s and 1960s, Richard Hofstadter wrote that for the Cold Warriors of that time, "the old competitive capitalism" had "been gradually undermined by socialist and communist schemers."[36] Very similar sentiments were expressed and perpetuated by Tea Partiers, their sympathizers, and politicians closest to the movement. This was evident during the GOP primaries for the party's

2012 presidential nomination with several Tea Party favorites in the competition. Rick Perry, the Republican governor of Texas, aired an ad in which he charged that "Obama's socialist policies are bankrupting America. We must stop him now."[37] "He [Obama] is an Alinsky radical," Newt Gingrich said, accusing President Obama of being a disciple of the late left-wing Chicago activist Saul Alinsky. "He believes in fundamentally undermining the America we inherited," he added. "I believe in fundamentally rebuilding the America we inherited."[38] Michele Bachmann told voters on the day of the Iowa caucuses, "Iowans are rejoicing tonight because of that opportunity to reclaim our republic. We will do that. . . . We are unwilling to allow Barack Obama to implement socialism in the United States of America."[39] In short, the Tea Party grew quickly into a reactionary movement. According to Parker and Barreto, "People are driven to support the Tea Party from the anxiety they feel as they perceive the America they know, the country they love, slipping away, threatened by the rapidly changing face of what they believe is the 'real' America. . . . They hope to return to a point in American life before Barack Obama held the highest office in the land, before a Latina was elevated to the Supreme Court, and when powerful members of Congress were all heterosexual (at least publicly)."[40]

Tea Partiers also expressed distrust and hostility toward intellectuals—at least those with whom they disagreed. During the 2012 Republican primaries, presidential hopeful Rick Santorum, who considered himself part of the "Tea Party crowd," voiced his disdain for liberal intellectuals when he told supporters, "President Obama once said he wants everybody in America to go to college. What a snob. There are good, decent men and women who go out and work hard every day and put their skills to test who aren't taught by some liberal college professor that tried to indoctrinate them. . . . I understand why [Obama] wants you to go to college. He wants to remake you in his image."[41]

The disdain for intellectuals was a trademark of authoritarian populists and fascists in the twentieth century. According to Aldemaro Romero, Jr., "From Stalinism to Mao's 'Cultural Revolution' and Cambodia's Pol Pot on the left, to fascist regimes like Mussolini's, Hitler's or Franco's on the right, this movement has extended itself into violent connotations to the point that writers, artists, college professors, or just people wearing glasses . . .have been murdered by the thousands by those from oppressive regimes."[42] In his notorious book manifesto *Mein Kampf*, Adolf Hitler left no doubt about his disregard for the intelligentsia. In a chapter devoted to describing effective propaganda, Hitler wrote, "The art of propaganda lies in understanding the emotional ideas of the great masses and find-ing, through a psychologically correct form, the way to the attention and thence to the heart of the broad masses. The fact that our bright boys do not understand this merely shows how mentally lazy and conceited they are. . . . The purpose of propaganda is not to provide interesting distrac-tion for blasé young gentlemen, but to convince, and what I mean is to convince the masses."[43] In 1928, before the Nazis came to power, Hitler's propagandist-in-chief, Joseph Goebbels, said, "It is certainly true that the modern German cultural establishment produces every manner of nonsense. I know that this nonsense is poisoning the German national soul."[44]

Interestingly, after listening to Donald Trump and his supporters—many of them Tea Partiers—during campaign rallies in 2015 and 2016, one observer concluded that there was "resentment against the U.S. intel-ligentsia: the left-wing academia in its ivory towers, policy wonks moving seamlessly between prestigious universities and the government, journalists always happy to quote the so-called experts."[45] These attitudes may have been early signposts for the eventual declaration of war by President Trump and his movement against the "fake" media and against the Washington establishment, the so-called deep state within the federal government.

CHRISTIAN AND SECULAR TEA PARTIERS

It is ironic that within the Tea Party movement, "us-against-them" cleav-ages separated Christian conservatives concerned with mostly social causes from secular libertarians who demanded fiscal and other restraints on government. In one case, the leader of a local group "faced so many ten-sions in her flock that she split the group in two," meeting separately with "the Christian Tea Party" and "the regular Tea Party."[46] But whatever the local Tea Party leader perceived as the "regular" wing of the movement,

Tea Partiers were "on average, more religiously observant than the typical American" and "distinctively comfortable blending religion and politics."[47]

Then U.S. senator Jim DeMint (R-SC), like Sarah Palin, a darling of rank-and-file Tea Party supporters and the founder of the Tea Party Caucus in the U.S. Senate, praised the movement as the Great American Awakening. He said about Tea Partiers at a mass rally in Washington, D.C., "Their concern for our country's future seemed to have awakened their faith and stirred a sense of patriotism, civic responsibility, and a call to action. They knew their rights and freedoms came from God, not government, and they believed an expansive, debt-ridden government would destroy freedom in America."[48]

That DeMint described Tea Partiers' faith and their political agenda as going hand in hand was not unusual among politicians; in fact, it had been common since Ronald Reagan's presidency. Noting that previous presidents, such as John F. Kennedy and Jimmy Carter, had to assure Americans that their religion would not enter into their decision-making, Drew Westen identified the Reagan era as a turning point:

> By 1984, Reagan had redefined faith and morality. He openly embraced the religious right and its political agenda. . . . Reagan made his faith, and the interpretation of Scripture of a narrow and narrow-minded minority, the moral *foundation* of his presidency, on issues ranging from abortion to prayer in schools to fetal tissue transplant research. What Reagan so skillfully accomplished was a blurring of the distinction between the generic God of the founding fathers and the intrusion of *specific* sectarian belief into public policy—precisely the intrusion the founders had inveighed against.[49]

While the Tea Party did not have one charismatic leader, Ronald Reagan was its patron saint in the developmental phase of the movement. Sarah Palin drove this point home during her keynote address at the so-called inaugural Tea Party convention in 2010. She invoked Reagan's name five times. "We have a vision for the future of our country," Palin said. "It is a vision anchored in time tested truths: That the government that governs least, governs best. And that the Constitution—the Constitution provides the best road map towards a more perfect union. And that only a limited government can expand prosperity and opportunity for all. And that freedom as a God-given right and it is worth fighting for."[50] Paying tribute to Reagan toward the end of her speech, she said, "No longer with us, his spirit lives on and his American dream endures. He knew the best of our country is not all gathered in Washington, D.C. It is here in our communities where families live, and children learn, and children with special needs are welcomed in this world and embraced."[51] Eventually, the religious, culture-war wing, not the secular libertarian faction, gained the upper hand in the Tea Party movement; evangelical and libertarian values coexisted.

THE TEA PARTY'S PIVOTAL MEDIA LINKAGES

Regardless of how observers evaluated the influence of experienced partisan activists and ordinary citizens, many agreed that the media played an equal or greater role. Jane Mayer concluded, "FreedomWorks had not only the community organizers, the internet expertise, the propagandists at their disposal, they also bought conservative media celebrities to spread their narratives. The organization paid Fox News star Glenn Beck more than $1 million a year for using FreedomWorks' talking points regularly in his program." And the Republican pollster Frank Luntz claimed, "Glenn Beck's show is what created the Tea Party movement."[52] For Luntz there was only one person responsible for the birth of the Tea Party: "Glenn Beck's show is what created the Tea Party movement," he said.[53] Skocpol and Williamson identified three political forces as crucial in the creation to the new movement: "grassroot activists, roving billionaires, and right-wing media purveyors."[54]

We agree with those observations but argue further that not merely the right-wing variety but all the online and offline media contributed to the rise of the Tea Party. To put it into the context of our theoretical assumption, it was the connectivity of political communication among political activists, ordinary people, and the multiple types of media that grew the Tea Party into an influential political force. Therefore, we explore in the following sections how the early Tea Partiers used online media as meeting places and propaganda platforms and how all types of the mainstream communication media promoted the movement's messages and interests.

TEA PARTY ACTIVISM: FORESHADOWING THE EMBRACE OF TRUMP'S MAGA MOVEMENT

The website of the Tea Party Express (TPE), the well-funded group that engaged in on-the-ground activism and campaign financing, was a top-down space designed to indoctrinate and mobilize supporters without efforts to form a strong and interactive virtual community. TPE's opinion posts and columns were hard-hitting pieces of divisive demagoguery. As the 2012 election drew closer, the TPE's anti-Obama/anti-Progressive attacks joined the most extreme and hysterical right-wing propaganda against GOP America's public enemy number one, President Obama. Thus, in June, 2012, one TPE blogger spoke for many like-minded Tea Partiers when he posted this:

> Patriots, our president's bold aggressive attack on who we are as a nation is unprecedented. Obama has drawn a line in the sand proclaiming, THIS IS WAR! His anti-achievers vs. achievers; black vs. white; those who harbor disdain for America vs. those who love her.
>
> I am not talking about a foreign dictator pounding on the podium with his shoe at the UN, screaming, "We will bury you!" The person seeking to dethrone America as the world's super power is the current president of the United States, Barack Hussein Obama.[55]

Two months later, Lloyd Marcus, a regular TPE-blogger, wrote, "A majority of Americans realize that Obama is a far left, radical, socialist/

progressive, anti-American, lawless dictator. His reign of terror will end come November."[56]

In the Tea Party movement's contribution to what some scholars perceived as the remaking of the GOP in the face of Republican conservatism,[57] the TPE was more of an appendage to the GOP with an emphasis on campaign support for Republican candidates than a vehicle for reforming the party. For this reason, we selected three of the major national and originally unaffiliated Tea Party groups—Tea Party Patriots, Tea Party Nation, and Oath Keepers, the movement's military wing—from a multitude of national, regional, and local groups for our qualitative analysis of their online views and appeals, especially as they foreshadowed eventual support for Trump and the MAGA movement.

TEA PARTY PATRIOTS

In 2009, Amy Kremer and Jenny Beth Martin founded the Tea Party Patriots. Both of these "founding mothers of the Tea Party movement" were present at Donald Trump's infamous speech on January 6 before his supporters stormed the Capitol.[58] Kremer's pro-Trump group, Women for America First, was the permit holder for the rally at the Ellipse, where she told the cheering crowd, "I'm asked all the time, 'What happened to the Tea Party movement?' Well, here we are. We are just bigger than ever before! I truly believe in my heart that we would not have President Donald J. Trump were it not for the work that we've done over the past 10 years."[59]

Martin, the long-time leader of the Tea Party Patriots, was overshadowed on this day by Kremer. The two women had parted ways a few months after establishing the TPP back in 2009, and not in amicable terms. Both made lucrative careers as Tea Party activists: Kremer by first joining the rival Tea Party Express and jumping on Trump's bandwagon in the earliest stage of the 2016 presidential campaign with several Trump-related initiatives; Martin, by remaining the TPP's leader, eventually launching several separate TPP entities, all nonprofits seeking donations and supporting Trump after first backing Ted Cruz.

Back in the early months and years of the Tea Party movement, the TPP and two other major national Tea Party organizations, Tea Party Nation and the Oath Keepers, used their websites and social media pages to encourage fellow Tea Partiers to participate in online discussions. Activists posted opinion pieces and invited readers to leave their own comments. This created virtual communities of like-minded people bound by extreme political, social, and religious views that often reflected their fears and hopes, anger and prejudice, and sharp divisions between their "in-group" of patriots and the "out-groups" threatening the cultural and religious fabric of America.

The TPP introduced and maintained on its website a public affairs discussion board where posts by the so-called National News Group became springboards for a three-pronged narrative. First, there were constant attacks on Obama, members of his administration, Democrats, liberals, their wealthy supporters, and a political mainstream, including the media, alleged to be in cahoots with villains who were regularly described as socialists, communists, criminals, terrorists, and the like. Second, there were the glorifications of libertarian values—most of all limited government, free markets, and fiscal restraint—and of noble patriots fighting for these values; and calls to select candidates for political offices who were guided by Tea Party doctrine. Third, there was explicit resentment and suspicion of elites who served in government and other powerful institutions.

The following exchange was a case in point. Obviously worried about the future of Social Security and Medicare, a commenter named Lazaro asked in a mid-June 2012 post, "Can seniors still get their checks in the mail in 2013?"[60] Among the comments was one that showcased the Tea Partiers' distinction between good guys—in this case represented by GOP presidential nominee Mitt Romney—and the bad guys, personified by President Barack Obama. Lazaro wrote,

> If enough seniors vote for the man that will cause our economy to boom
> by freeing up the free market, there will be more than enough revenue
> to keep those checks coming. If too many seniors vote for the socialists,

they will finish killing this economy and seniors will be lucky to get anything at all. The only problems we've ever had were caused by big government, business-killing high taxes and overregulation interfering with the free market and spirit of average Americans trying to succeed and make a profit. Just look at any place else in the world and you will see what you'll get under the false hope and outright lies of socialism.

Another commenter predicted, "When Mitt Romney takes charge of the U.S. economy next January, the wealth creation will be the rising tide that lifts all boats. Unfortunately for most liberals this will be of scant comfort because they are all driving submarines."

Before the 2010 midterm elections, the TPP leadership claimed to be associated with twenty-three hundred local groups, but an investigative report "was unable to identify anywhere near that many, despite help from the organization [TPP] and independent research."[61] While the number of local groups and total membership was inflated, there was no doubt that the TPP was the most grassroots-oriented of the national Tea Party umbrella organizations, with the largest number of local groups, members, and state coordinators across the country.[62] These links between and among national activists, local groups, and individuals were crucial in organizing demonstrations in various parts of the country. June 13, 2012, was a case in point; "Minutemen calling all Minutemen Patriots" was the prominent appeal on the TPP website's opening page (www.teapartypatriots.org), with the following message:

We are calling on all Tea Party Patriots living within two hours of Washington, DC, to be Tea Party "Minute Men." When the U.S. Supreme Court issues its ruling on Obamacare we need you to join us.

The Supreme Court could rule at any moment between now and the end of June. Tea Party Patriots is organizing a rally and press conference in front of the Supreme Court. Many of you were there with us during the oral arguments and we are going to need your support again!

If you provide us with your phone number, we will call you when it's time to mobilize.

This was followed by a list of things to do in preparation for the event; for example, make signs, get bull horns, ask family members and friends to join the event. On the TPP Twitter page, there were a multitude of tweets with the same appeal in short form. The organization's Facebook page (856,000 "Likes" in mid-20012), too, called for volunteers for the mass rally in front of the Supreme Court. Within the next twelve hours, 525 people indicated that they liked the post and 37 left comments—all of them supportive of the planned protest. Some said they would sign up, others expressed regrets for living too far from D.C., still others said they would come if the Court decided in favor of Obamacare.

Eventually, the TPP's leadership focused mostly on the dissemination of propaganda and fundraising to support GOP candidates. The organization's website and its social media accounts asked site visitors to join the "over 3 million patriots who are already making a difference." Whatever the real number of those "patriots" was, eventually the TPP publicized mostly top-down propaganda but lacked the sizable virtual community of its formative years to receive these messages.

Although Ted Cruz was the TPP's national leadership's first choice among the GOP's presidential hopefuls in 2016, once Trump won the nomination, he was fully supported by TPP activists, most of all by Jenny Beth Martin. By that time, Martin had a strong foothold in Washington's GOP circles and was widely considered an asset in Republican campaigns. According to one account, the TPP's Citizens Fund "spent nearly $1 million on robocalls, telemarketing, and direct mail supporting Trump in the 2016 election."[63] Following Trump's victory in November 2016, Martin wrote in an opinion piece with the headline, "The Tea Party Movement Is Alive and Well—And We Saw Trump Coming." "Our organizations, our local tea party groups and the entire movement stand ready to serve as the ground troops in support of the implementation of the pledges President Elect Trump made during his campaign. His platform largely mirrors our movement's founding principles and causes: repeal of Obamacare, protect our borders, stop illegal immigration, restore fiscal sanity and get the government off our backs and out of our lives."[64]

She kept her word. The Citizens Fund, a PAC, contributed $1.2 million to Trump's 2020 campaign und later supported him during the first impeachment proceedings against him by organizing "End the Witch Hunt" protests. According to one report, "Tea Party Patriots Action spent $100,000 on TV ads attacking Deputy Attorney General Rod Rosenstein for his oversight of special counsel Robert Mueller's probe of Russian interference in the 2016 presidential election."[65]

TEA PARTY NATION

While the early Tea Party Patriots espoused libertarian principles, the competing Tea Party Nation group tried from the outset to appeal to both factions within the Tea Party, secular libertarians and conservative Christians, mostly Protestant evangelicals.[66] The organization described itself on its website (https://teapartynation.com/) as the home for conservatives and a "user-driven group of like-minded people who desire our God-given individual freedoms written out by the Founding Fathers. We believe in Limited Government, Free Speech, the 2nd Amendment, our Military, Secure Borders and our Country." By mid-2012, the TPN listed 516 groups, among them 31 Issue Groups (for example, Restore the Constitution; Veterans Against Obama; Christians United; Christian Soldiers-The Army of God), state affiliates across the United States, and eight fan groups, the largest of them including 795 Sarah Palin fans.

The frequent posts on the TPN's national forum and blog, often by the organization's founder, Judson Phillips, addressed TPN positions on important issues, asked provocative questions, unleashed attacks on Democrats and liberals, and warned the Republican Party establishment to implement the Tea Party movement's agenda or lose its support. More than the leaders of other nationwide Tea Party organizations, Phillips demanded that the GOP completely surrender to Tea Party orthodoxy. To that end, he worked on a "Tea Party Agenda" for the Congress along the lines of Newt Gingrich's "Contract with America," which Gingrich and others credited (whether true or not)[67] with winning the Republican majority in the House of Representatives in 1994.

Phillips's forum post of early May 2012 described his plan and asked for input from members. Within a month, more than twenty-five hundred visitors had viewed the post, and there were more than one hundred responses with issue proposals. A month later, another Phillips post asked the provocative question, "Should the Republican Party Survive?" In answering his own question, Phillips wrote,

> By 2008, the GOP was on the political endangered species list. Then along came the Tea Party. The Republicans claim they support the values of the Tea Party when they are at Tea Party rallies or when they are at home asking the voters to send them to Washington. But an amazing thing happens in Washington. They do not vote like conservatives. . . .
>
> Now, in what should have been the year of the Tea Party, the GOP has nominated the most liberal Republican ever selected to be the Presidential nominee of the Party. We must defeat Barack Obama. That is not open to debate. Obama must be removed from office. That means this time we must vote for Romney and we must vote for Republicans to replace Democrats.
>
> Should the Republican Party survive 2012? Should Mitt Romney be the last nominee this Party has and we see a new conservative party?
>
> That decision is in the hands of the Republican Party. If the GOP does not govern conservatively as soon as it gets to Washington, it will find conservatives finally bolting. If the Republicans continue to play the political games in Washington instead of cutting government and solving problems, the GOP will become the modern version of the Whig Party.[68]

Within one day, the post was viewed by 1,142 visitors, many of whom left comments that mostly agreed with Phillips's take that Obama must be defeated first before remaking the GOP in the image of the TPN.

Tea Party Nation members seemed to consider themselves as the pure Tea Partiers and to see other Tea Party organizations as coopted by the Republican establishment. Responding to several commenters' calls to consider the establishment of a third party, one man wrote, the "Problem is that no one [did] copy-write the name Tea Party, and pro Romney pro-establishment Tea Parties are out there and vocal. The tea party can be the catalyst, but anyone who wants to hang on to the MeToo idea should be kept out. If they have no core values or positions, let them stay with the GOP."[69] Mostly, though, the postings in TPN's forum, blog, and issue groups attacked, criticized, and vilified the evil enemies, most of all President Obama. Calling him a dictator, traitor, and socialist blogger, Marcia Wood wrote,

Obama is on the fast track now in his agenda to destroy America— Americans are gasping for breath and trying to stay afloat, but we're being manipulated and devoured by a desperate man, a would-be dictator who no longer hides behind closed doors.

He boldly improvises, rewrites and changes the laws of our land (Constitution) daring us to confront him. Even his own Administration is starting to realize that we have a mad man on the loose.

Democrats realize they're powerless and out of control because they put all their eggs in one basket betting on the "devil" who promised Americans jobs, smaller Government, transparency, lower unemployment, secure borders, a balanced budget and most of all unity.[70]

The next day, there were close to thirteen hundred views and dozens of responses, none of them less biting than the original blog post. One woman even suggested that there should be efforts to remove Obama from office before the end of his term. "I truly believe we can't wait until November," she wrote. "Who knows this may encourage others and maybe Obama may step down or get charges for impeachment before November. God works mysteriously. God gives us the tools to work with." A regular TPN poster proposed a more drastic way forward when he referred to militant anti-government groups as the last line of defense against the evil American government. In other words, for this Tea Party member, the last line of defense was violence.

At the end of August 2015, Karen Schoen posted a lengthy article on the TPN website under the headline "TRUMP; YOU'RE HIRED!" She told fellow Tea Partiers, "He [Trump] believes that if U.S. Borders were closed, and entitlements to illegals were stopped most would LEAVE! (remember, self deport). If illegal criminals were deported, trade agreements were restructured, Common Core was gone, and business-killing regulations were eliminated in the economy . . . America will become GREAT again." Commenters seconded her endorsement enthusiastically. One responder seemed to express their predominant sentiments when he wrote, "The next election is NOT about getting your party elected. It is about electing the right leader. If we get stuck with the old status quo, we are screwed as a nation. We only have one more election to get it right! GO TRUMP!"[71]

OATH KEEPERS

Founded by the Yale-educated constitutional lawyer Stewart Rhodes in 2009, shortly after the birth of the modern-day Tea Party movement, the Oath Keepers have been described, correctly, as "the Tea Party's military wing."[72] The group's mission statement, provided on its website (http://oathkeepers.org/oath/), revealed a radical antigovernment stand and an aggressive approach to politics. The first paragraphs stated,

> Oath Keepers is a non-partisan association of currently serving military, veterans, peace officers, and firefighters who <u>will</u> fulfill the oath we swore to support and defend the Constitution against all enemies, foreign and domestic, so help us God.
>
> Our oath is to the Constitution, not to the politicians, and we will not obey unconstitutional (and thus illegal) and immoral orders, such as orders to disarm the American people or to place them under martial law and deprive them of their ancient right to jury trial.
>
> We Oath Keepers have drawn a line in the sand. We will not "just follow orders."
>
> Our motto is "Not on our watch!"
>
> If you, the American people, are forced to once again fight for your liberty in another American Revolution, you will not be alone. We will stand with you.

Those active in or retired from the military branches, law enforcement, or other uniformed services were invited to enlist in the organization. Members or those planning to join pledged allegiance to the group's mission. In "testimonials" that were publicized on the organization's website, members and applicants for membership spelled out their grievances and what they considered effective remedies. Many posts were signed with full names, others with initials, still others were anonymous, and in some cases identifying information was deleted by the site administrator o protect a poster. The vast majority of testimonials and the comments they elicited followed the same script: the poster described his or her past or present service, lamented domestic enemies' violations of Americans' constitutional rights and values, and pledged to join the fight for America's freedom. The following testimonial from early 2012 exemplified this format.

When I took "The Oath" as a young Army officer in the 1960's to protect the USA against "all enemies both foreign and domestic" I never thought that the real danger would be the "domestic" one. I fought in Vietnam as a proud member of the 5th Special Forces Group, serving in an "A" team in the Central Highlands and also as a company commander of the Pleiku Mike Force. Now, over 40 years later, our biggest threat is our own government.

Our Federal and State governments are eliminating our freedoms granted to us by the Constitution for the sake of "security" after 9/11. The TSA, the militarization of local police forces, the brain washing of our children in public schools, the unionization of all government employees, the printing of worthless dollars, the unsustainable public debt, etc. We are no longer the country of our fathers and grandfathers.

I just joined "Oath Keepers" because our great republic is slipping away from us. We have to be aggressive in preserving our great Constitution and the Bill of Rights. Who is trying to take this all away? Our own government, that's who. It takes effort and pain to preserve our freedoms from the oppressors. I will do everything I can to keep America a free and sovereign country. I love the USA, and will fight to keep her free.[73]

Responding to the testimonial, another Oath Keeper followed the same format by providing his personal background before spelling out the existential threat to this country and recommending a course of action.

In 1968 I was full of piss and vinegar, I volunteered to join the Army and went to Vietnam. All of my Grandfathers had fought and bled to protect this country, the Greatest the world has ever seen. I swore and oath each time I re-enlisted to protect the Constitution from all enemies both foreign and domestic. I never in my wildest dreams to think that someday I or my children would have to fight to restore the Constitution to its former place of prominence. But now I find that we are on the threshold of have to do just that. Now I'm a lot older and wiser than in 1968, and a lot less able to do it the young men's way, but I can still shoot a rifle and hit what I'm shooting at every time. When I was born, I came into this world fighting and I intend to go out fighting.

We must all be vigilant in protecting our freedom and hold those, who are responsible for the loss thereof, accountable. They must be put on trial and executed if found guilty for treason. My forefathers are screaming from their graves at this insanity.[74]

Although the organization's mission statement claimed nonpartisanship, testimonials and comments on its website attested to the Oath Keepers' strongly held right-wing, conservative, and libertarian ideologies and a strong rejection of liberal and progressive ideas and policies. Most of the posts reflected their raw hate of Democrats in public offices, most of all President Obama and his administration. Thus, in one testimonial Jake wrote, "Although I am a registered democrat I have to admit that in the past nineteen months this President, his Administration and allies, with the help of the Main Stream Media, have been systematically eroding our Constitutional rights, as evidenced by their deplorable actions that are clearly outlined on my blog post site, which I adamantly believe will ultimately destroy this great country as we know it." A responder, GM, told Jake, "To my way of thinking MR. Obama is not the Commander in Chief. I will stand by ready protect the United States Constitution and Will Never accept an order from anyone that would defy it." Another Oath Keeper wrote, "I am a SWAT member and peace officer for the state which I live and my allegiance is to the US Constitution and my fellow Americans, not the socialist politicians we have attempting to take over our country and ruin our way of life and the way of life for future generations. God Bless."[75]

While the group was, on the one hand, a hotbed for extreme anti-Obama propaganda, there were also Oath Keepers who condemned both political parties for harming America. The arguments resembled those expressed by other Tea Partiers, especially within the Tea Party Nation e-community described earlier. Thus, one Oath Keeper wrote, "It is no longer about republican vs. democrat. There are patriots on both sides, however; both political parties are more intent on political power than the future of our freedoms." Responding to an anti-Obama tirade, another poster was far more critical of President George W. Bush's post-9/11 measures. "I can assure you that the destruction of our Constitutional Republic didn't start with President Obama," he explained. "It started decades ago. President Bush did a great job with the so-called 'Patriot' Act, the nullification of the Posse Comitatus Act and gun confiscation in New Orleans, wide open borders to the illegal invasion, the guting of American industry, the $500 billion operating deficit in 2008, lying us into two wars (There is probably no better way to destroy a republic than war.), ad infinitum. I left the Republican branch of The Democrat and Republican Party in 2000, decades too late."[76]

Similar sentiments were expressed in posts and responses publicized in the "Articles" section. Following the defeat of two Tea Party candidates in the Montana Republican primary in June 2012, a post signed by Elias Alias condemned those who convinced people to vote for the "electable" ticket that could defeat the Democratic candidates in the fall. He lamented that people did not understand that it does not make any difference whether mainstream Republicans or Democrats win. "So I am not surprised that a 'Bankster's Bitch'[Mitt Romney] won the Montana GOP gubernatorial primary even though two righteous Oath Keepers offered Montanans a real choice for freedom, prosperity, and independence," he wrote. In the same article, he condemned Senator Rand Paul for endorsing "the Banksters' Bitch, Romney, who draws his campaign war-chest from the likes of

Goldman-Sachs and J. P. Morgan and Citibank."[77] Commenters responding to this article attacked Romney as not really being "the free-market guy you think he is," as an interventionist like Obama and Bush, as the inventor of Obamacare, as having "a narcissistic personality disorder," and as "evil."

Oath Keepers' relentless rhetorical attacks on Romney were far more ferocious than on any other Tea Party site. Responding to another of several articles about Rand Paul's endorsement of Romney (his "betrayal"), one Oath Keeper wrote, "So now we are left to vote for 2 peas in a pod. The only difference is that one will destroy this Country faster than the other. I will no longer vote for the lesser of 2 evils. If the people want to protest the choices we've been left with, then don't vote."

Unlike the many posts in the "Testimonials" and "Articles" categories that were originally accessible by all site visitors, the "Forums" discussions were open only to registered Oath Keepers. By mid-2012, the group had also active Facebook and Twitter pages. In July 2009, only a few months after the founding of the group, one of the videos of "The Oath Keepers Declaration of Order We Will Not Obey" on YouTube had 405,000 views.[78]

In the run-up to the 2016 elections, Hillary Clinton became the most hated "enemy" of Oath Keepers. Steward Rhodes had attacked her when she was the early favorite in the 2008 presidential primaries as "Mr. Hitlery" and "dressed in her favorite Chairman Mao signature pantsuit."[79] When she ran in 2016 against Donald Trump, he and the Oath Keepers seemed at first more anti-Clinton than pro-Trump. But they heeded the claim that Democrats were trying to rig the election and called on members to watch the polls. One such appeal stated, "We are calling on our retired police officers, our military intelligence veterans, and our Special Warfare veterans (who are well trained in covert observation and intelligence gathering) to take the lead and apply their considerable training in investigation, intelligence gathering, and fieldcraft to help stop voter fraud. We ask that those most highly trained and experienced Oath Keepers members form up the intel gathering and crime spotting teams, and then lead those teams of Oath Keepers on election day."[80]

By the 2020 presidential election, Rhodes and the Oath Keepers had become part and parcel of the Trump movement, fanatic supporters of

Trump-related conspiracy theories and of the defeated president's lies about the stolen election. Rhodes repeatedly called on Trump to invoke the Insurrection Act and mobilize the militia, "including all of us veterans," to prevent the "attempted coup" by domestic and foreign enemies. (See Chapter 6 on the Oath Keeper's direct role in the violent breach of the U.S. Capitol on January 6, 2021.)

For years, Oath Keepers leader Rhodes and his leadership clique did not reveal the group's number of members. But when a hacker got access to their membership lists in 2021, it was revealed that the roster had "ballooned in recent years, from less than 10,000 members at the start of 2011 to more than 35,000 by 2020."[81] The annual membership fee of $50 and lifetime membership charge of $1,000 provided the Oath Keepers with ample financial resources for its disruptive antigovernment activities.

Summing up, our research found that from the birth of the Tea Party in early 2009 to the 2012 presidential election, the websites of the major Tea Parties and the Oath Keepers reflected, most of all, expressions of extreme anger and hate directed at President Obama, a preoccupation with anti-Obama conspiracy theories, and a determination to "take our country back" from un-American enemies within. Our findings confirmed the results of an analysis based on more than one thousand posts on Tea Party websites in 2009 and 2010 that concluded, "Almost one-in-four of the issues addressed on their websites entertains conspiracies that the president is a communist, socialist, or that the policies sought by the government Obama leads will ultimately result in the demise of America."[82]

Most importantly, social media was instrumental in enabling Tea Partiers to establish local communities. In their study of the Florida Tea Party movement, Deana Rohlinger and Leslie Bunnage found that "social media helped politically like-minded people locate one another and cultivate political communities that likely sustained activist commitment to changing the Republican Party over time."[83] Thus, especially in the early phase of the Tea Party, people who considered themselves members or supporters met virtually and physically to participate in political activities, as the case study (see box, "Tea Partiers in Wisconsin Governor . . .") attests to.

TEA PARTIERS IN WISCONSIN GOVERNOR SCOTT WALKER'S RECALL ELECTION CAMPAIGN

Before Wisconsin Governor Scott Walker, a Republican and Tea Party favorite, won his recall election in June 2012, the Tea Party movement's main websites urged members and supporters to work to advance Walker's campaign. The political organizers who obtained the signatures necessary for the recall election had opposed Walker's conservative agenda and especially his diminishing of the collective bargaining rights of state workers. A post on the Tea Party Nation site announced that the goal was "to make 100,000 calls from our 'Mobile Call Center' to Wisconsin voters." The same post publicized a call for strong conservative turnout at the polls issued not by Tea Party Nation but by the campaign-savvy Tea Party Express, which was a GOP-affiliated organization that focused on election campaigns. "With the news that the election is going to be too close to call," the Tea Party Express told Tea Partiers regardless of their group affiliation, "it is imperative that we make sure that conservatives show up to the polls to vote on Tuesday."[84]

Once Walker's victory was sealed, in thousands of social media posts, Tea Partiers celebrated his win as proof of their movement's enduring potency. "We have been on a 'roll' since the 2010 elections," Tammy Hyatt wrote on a Tea Party Patriots discussion board. "This just proves the lamestream media's claim that the tea party is dead could not be further from the truth." Signing with the initials Mc, another poster stated, "This battle [in Wisconsin] absolutely had to be won if we were to more effectively against the Progressive/Socialist forces arrayed against us. I believe the American people have awaked in part to the threat poised against them. This is shaping up to be our second American Revolution and second American Civil War."[85] On the TPN site, Country Girl responded to a blogger's post: "The Tea Party has made a big impact on what we're seeing now by making our voices heard and standing firm on our principles. It would be so great to see more people like Scott Walker take a stand knowing that they have an army of patriots behind him."[86] On Twitter, the hashtag #teaparty produced an endless stream of tweets, many of them posted by Tea Partiers. Top of Form

Tea Partiers were more than virtual activists. "I went to Wisconsin and helped with Gov. Walker's reelection," Dean Allen wrote in response to the post "Walkin' Tall: Walker Inspires an Army" on the TPN website. In Allen's judgment, "The tea party movement is definitely making a major difference in our country. Our movement was a big part of Gov. Walker's victory and he acknowledged that at a reception with some of us the Friday before the election."[87] Posters on the

Facebook site of Tea Party Express celebrated Walker and, even more so, their own group's on-the-ground activism. Nina Pellegrini wrote, "Congratulations Tea Party Express! You worked hard to get Governor Scott Walker elected! Keep rolling that bus across the country till Nov 2012! You're making a difference!"[88] On the Tea Party Patriot website, Jerry Phelps posted, "Thanks to all the hardworking Tea Party Patriots that paid their own way to Wisconsin and worked so hard to get out the vote for Scott Walker. You are to be commended for all your hard work and expense to support and win the fight against the union thugs and Communists that are trying to take over our country."[89]

Contrary to those who claimed that the Tea Party was over after President Obama's reelection in 2012, the movement was alive and well, before and after, thanks to an exemplary mixture of mass self-communication and old-fashioned on-the-ground activism, which also resulted in news coverage by print, broadcast, and cable news organizations.

THE TEA PARTY AND THE LEGACY PRESS

It has been suggested that "the formal broadcast and print media are so thoroughly penetrated and affected by the digital in terms of production, dissemination and consumption that they are no longer separable as institutions of mass media, for they exist and can only exist in the new media ecology."[90] The other side of the coin is that the "breaking news" topics on social media platforms are for the most part imported from the traditional print and broadcast media before being subjected to spin and falsification. Therefore, it is the interconnectivity among various media and communication types that matters most when it comes to understanding the ingredients that shape political debates and perceptions and misperceptions about public affairs.

Having examined the online communication hubs of major national Tea Party organizations and their content, we turn now to the traditional news organizations and their reporting on the Tea Party movement's formative phase. While some observers have identified websites, blogs, and social media as the most important factors in the formation and rise of the Tea Party,[91] others have argued that the conservative media—most of all radio and cable talk shows initially—and eventually the mainstream print and broadcast media were instrumental in "getting the word out."[92] In reality, both the new and the old media played important roles in the advent of the Tea Party movement and its stunning electoral success in the 2010 midterm elections. Based on her examination of the mass-mediated branding of the Tea Party, Costley White concluded as well that "the traditional and digital media have tended toward convergence."[93]

Barack Obama, whose rise to the presidency was a major motivational driver in the creation of the Tea Party, watched closely as the movement's publicity strategy very successfully exploited the interconnectivity between new and old media. In his memoir, Obama wrote that he had "a grudging respect for how rapidly Tea Party leaders had mobilized a strong following and managed to dominate the news coverage, using some of the same social-media and grassroots-organizing strategies we had deployed during my own campaign."[94]

GENEROUS COVERAGE OF TEA PARTIERS' PUBLIC DISPLAYS

In the past, the mainstream media rarely embraced social movements and protests as positive newcomers to the political process and instead emphasized the negative, disruptive nature of such movements, which has been reflected historically in the public's initial reactions to them.[95] But in the competitive media market of the twenty-first century, news organizations have covered and often highlighted sensational, shocking, and entertaining political actors and their actions as means to attract large reading, listening, and viewing audiences. Tea Party organizers (especially during the Tea Party's formative period and with the assistance of Fox News) were well versed in displaying what Tilly and Wood call a "social movement repertoire" of variable public performances, such as rallies, demonstrations, and media appearances.[96] While the websites of Tea Party groups were stunningly successful in creating strong online communities tied together by anger about the political status quo and hope for the return of the old order, they needed heightened mainstream media attention to reach mass audiences.

In September 2009, a few days after Glenn Beck's "Tax Payer March on Washington," Fox News paid for a full-page newspaper ad in the *Washington Post*, *Wall Street Journal*, and *New York Post* that tried to taunt media competitors with the image of protesters and the huge letters, "HOW DID ABC, CBS, NBC, MSNBC, AND CNN MISS THIS STORY?" The problem was that Fox's cable competition, CNN and MSNBC, had covered the event in Washington generously. During that whole month, CNN aired 134 news segments about or mentioning the Tea Party—significantly more than Fox News (52) and MSNBC (26).[97] While CNN typically aired the same news items repeatedly in various news programs and parts thereof, the evidence shows that all three cable channels covered the Tea Party extensively and thereby assured Tea Party activists the news attention they sought.

As we described earlier, Fox News promoted the Tea Party actively and continuously in the first weeks and months following its birth. Once the movement's public actions showcased its growing outbursts of rage, the other two cable networks, CNN and MSNBC first and, eventually, moderate mainstream print and broadcast media outlets decided to "join the party."[98] and receive the ratings bonanza that Fox News enjoyed from the outset of the Tea Party's activism. As table 2.1 shows, in 2009, the volume of Tea Party coverage was modest in the mainstream media except for Fox News and CNN and, to a lesser degree, MSNBC. The reporting volume increased significantly in 2010, especially in the run-up to the November midterm elections. CNN had by far the most expansive Tea Party coverage, significantly more than Fox News and the *New York Times*. In 2011, when a strong freshman class of Tea Party–endorsed GOP members of Congress flexed their muscles in their party's House and Senate conferences, news coverage remained high.

Some observers seemed to recognize that the high volume of Tea Party coverage contributed to the "electoral triumph" of the Republican Party in the 2010 midterm elections.[99] The following excerpt from CBS's *The Early Show* on November 3, 2010, the day after Election Day, was an affirmation of the news media's great attention to the Tea Party during the election campaign.

TABLE 2.1 Volume of stories about or mentioning the Tea Party

	NYT	CBS	CNN	FOX NEWS	MSNBC	NPR
2009	131	19	410	425	182	67
2010	1,083	278	2,539	1,428	853	623
2011	1,337	229	2,667	1,442	952	599
2012	148	106	50	95	119	192
Total	2,699	632	5,666	3,390	2,106	1,481

Source: Lexis Nexis News Archive, compiled by the authors.

It projected, correctly, the future clash between the Tea Party and mainstream Republicans in Congress.

> *Maggie Rodriguez (CBS)*: *We talked so much about the Tea Party during this election, inspired so much passion, so much discussion* [emphasis added]. And in the end, 40 percent of voters said that they support this Tea Party movement. Is the Tea Party, in your opinion, the future of the Republican Party?
>
> *John Dickerson (CBS)*: Well, it's the future and in a lot of ways it's the past. The Tea Party is the—the core of the Republican Party has gotten a new name and new message, certainly a lot of energy in this election. And absolutely, it was amazing to listen last night to various Tea Party representatives say the Republicans are on probation.
> We are watching . . .
>
> *Maggie Rodriguez*: Hm-Hm.
>
> *John Dickerson*: . . . we're going to hold their feet to the fire. They are as active in watching over the Republicans as they were in electing them.[100]

CNN, too, recognized the Tea Party's new influential role in American politics. After falling behind Fox News and MSNBC in the cable channels rating war, the cable network made a strong bid to expand its audience by joining forces with Tea Party Express to host the first primary debate among eight GOP presidential hopefuls for the 2012 election. Promoting this event in September 2011 and the Tea Party heavily, a CNN press release explained,

> The debate will focus on a wide-range of topics, including the role, size and scope of government with a specific emphasis on issue number one to tea party members and all Americans: the economy.
>
> In addition to questions from Blitzer, audience members inside the debate hall, made up in part by members from tea party groups in 31 states and the District of Columbia, will be invited to ask questions directly to the candidates. Questions will also be taken live from tea party members at debate watch parties in Phoenix, Ariz.; Cincinnati, Ohio; and Portsmouth, Virginia. Online, CNN will solicit questions via comments on CNNPolitics.com, the CNN Politics Facebook page, and by using the #CNNTeaParty hashtag on Twitter.[101]

Actually, the joint venture had been sealed several weeks after the Tea Party's stunningly successful influence in the 2010 midterm elections. At the time, CNN's political director, Sam Feist, called the Tea Party movement "a fascinating, diverse, grassroots force that already has drastically changed the country's political landscape."[102] That surely explained why CNN covered the Tea Party far more heavily than the other five news outlets we examined—including Fox News—especially in 2010 and 2011. The movement's coverage declined significantly in 2012, when the news focus switched to the GOP primaries and the general presidential campaign.

NEWS VOLUME AND GOOGLE SEARCHES

In an additional analysis, we examined the volume of Tea Party news in the *New York Times* and *Washington Post* from 2009 through 2020, searching the Factiva News Archive and Google Trends for the term "Tea Party" during this period. Figure 2.1 shows most of all how similar were the

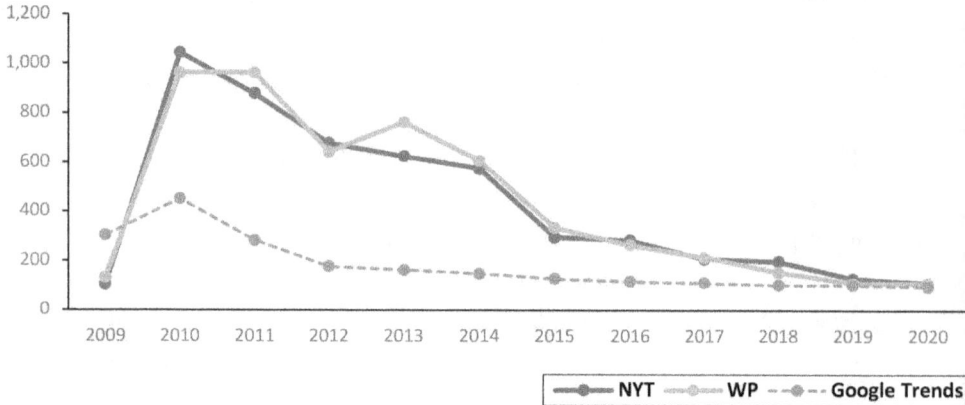

FIGURE 2.1 Tea-Party volume: NYT, WP, and Google Trends 2009-20.

Note: Trends in numbers of stories.

Source: Factiva/Google Trends, compiled by the authors.

trends in the volume of Tea Party coverage during the twelve-year period in the two leading newspapers (with an extraordinarily strong correlation, Pearson's r = 0.98). There were also similarities in the trends for the *Times* and *Post* coverage and the results over time for the "Tea Party" Google searches (r = 0.66). These results led us to assume that the volume of news coverage was reflected by or affected the number of "Tea Party" searches on Google's search engine.

THE CONTENT OF TEA PARTY NEWS

To assess media organizations' news coverage that did not have overt partisan leanings as (conservative) Fox News and (liberal) MSNBC, we selected four news organizations for a systematic content analysis of Tea Party news during two particular periods: August 2009, during the height of Tea Party–organized town hall protests against President Obama's health care reform proposals, and a fifteen-day period before and after the 2010 presidential election. We selected CBS as one of the TV networks and CNN as one of the cable networks as they did not yet display strong ideological dispositions in 2009 and 2010; and we selected the *New York Times* as one of the most influential newspapers and National Public Radio as a radio network devoted to substantive news coverage.[103]

News reporting is shaped in large part by the messages of sources who are quoted or cited in the coverage of particular events, developments, and issues. Typically, media outlets' anchors, correspondents, and reporters are in the driver's seat in explaining, evaluating, and framing the interpretations of issues and the statements and behavior of the actors involved in public affairs news.[104] As figure 2.2 shows, this was also the case in the coverage of the Tea Party, the movement's actions, and its policy preferences. Not surprisingly, media personnel made up 20 percent, or one-fifth, of the messages in relevant stories. At first glance, it was surprising that members of the general public accounted for 19 percent of news messages, nearly the same as media insiders and a far higher volume than usual.[105] But the angry outbursts during the Tea Party's public performances, including disruptions

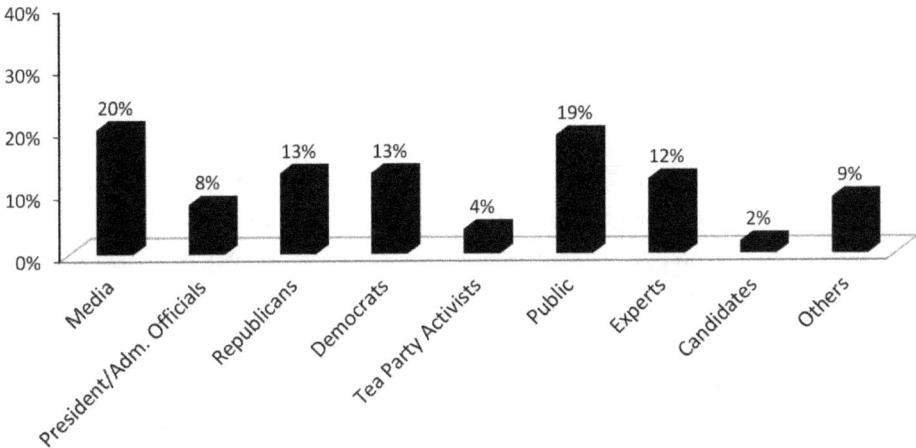

FIGURE 2.2 Sources mentioned or cited in Tea Party news coverage: CNN, CBS, NYT, NPR (August 2009 and midterm election period 2010).

Source: Compiled by the authors.

of town hall meetings held by congressional representatives of both parties, made participants in such events attractive sources for expressing their grievances and what they perceived as threats.

Without knowing whether those protesters were Tea Partiers, we coded them as members of the public, compared with directly identified Tea Party activists who were responsible for 4 percent of pertinent news messages. Democratic and Republican leaders or politicians each had a 13 percent share of news messages for the two periods. However, whereas Democrats had a 15 percent versus 7 percent advantage over Republicans in August 2009, Republicans dominated news messages during the 2010 midterm election period with 24 percent of all messages compared with Democrats' 14 percent of the message volume. The prominence of Republican sources in the latter period, when they outscored significantly even the media's own personnel sources, was the result of news coverage following the GOP's landslide election victory. The Republican Party picked up 63 seats in the House of Representatives and 6 seats in the Senate.

Republicans inside and outside Congress were by far the most supportive Tea Party sources interviewed or cited by the four mainstream news media outlets. Of these Republicans, 90 percent expressed support for the Tea Party, 8 percent were ambiguous, and only 2 percent offered critical views. Not surprisingly, of the messages attributed to Tea Party activists, 97 percent were supportive and only 3 percent ambiguous. A vast majority of the message sources that we coded as general public, 70 percent, were supportive of the Tea Party movement, 22 percent expressed opposition, and 8 percent were ambivalent. As for sources who were identifiable as Democratic actors, 70 percent of their messages were critical, 9 percent ambiguous, and 21 percent supportive of the Tea Party.

Although Tea Party leaders and followers attacked the alleged bias of the mainstream media relentlessly in their online communications after the emergence of the movement, coverage in the four mainstream media outlets was overwhelmingly positive during the two periods we examined. Our coding showed that 70 percent of news messages during the two periods were positive with respect to the Tea Party, 15 percent were negative, and 15 percent ambiguous or neutral, with the latter recognized as a balance between positive and negative messages. While messages attributable to media sources such as anchors and reporters were overwhelmingly neutral or ambiguous (72 percent), they were significantly more positive (20 percent) than negative (8 percent). Similarly, Jules Boykoff and Eulalie Laschever found in their content analysis of nine leading U.S. news organization, the Tea Party movement received "supportive frames more than twice as often as the deprecatory characterizations the activists opposed."[106]

The communications scholar W. Lance Bennett noted that such "high level of rather positive coverage given to the often rude and disruptive Tea Party differed from the often negative and dismissive coverage typically given to similar disruptive protest movements. This curious departure from coverage patterns suggests that indexing was operating at some level to get the Obama attack narratives into the news."[107] Indeed, our research shows that besides the overwhelmingly supportive media messages about the Tea Party, there was also a somewhat more positive than negative tenor in the characterization of the organization: 15 percent of news sources called the Tea Party "mainstream" and "not extreme," 14 percent called it a "grassroots or popular movement," and 3 percent deemed the organization "not racist." On the negative side, 8 percent labeled the Tea Party "racist," 7 percent "rightwing or extreme," and 5 percent "not a grassroots/popular movement." Most of the messages, however—48 percent—characterized the Tea Party in a neutral fashion, calling it simply a "movement."

Finally, news sources were somewhat more supportive (39 percent) than critical (32 percent) of President Obama's efforts to make affordable health insurance available to the uninsured, with 29 percent ambiguous. Those who spoke of "Obamacare" as a pejorative term were most hostile to the president's Democratic initiative.

THE TEA PARTY TRIUMPHS IN 2010
BUT NOT IN 2012

"The Tea Party is over," declared the Democratic Congressional Campaign Committee immediately after the 2012 election results were in. "The

2012 elections have been the undoing of the 2010 Tea Party tsunami that crashed upon Washington."[108] While less categorically, many partisan and nonpartisan voices spoke of the weakening of the Tea Party movement's influence inside and outside the Republican Party. The *Washington Post* reported, "Almost four years removed from its initial stirrings, the tea party movement finds itself riven by internal discord, without some of its most prominent leaders and faced with a party establishment that seems ready to abandon it—or at least buck its wishes—in the face of the 2012 election results."[109]

Such gloomy assessments seemed appropriate after President Barack Obama was reelected and the Democrats won additional seats in the Senate and House of Representatives, while four of the Tea Party's high-profile candidates lost their races for the Senate (Todd Akin, Richard Mourdock) and the House (Joe Walsh, Allen West). Other developments seemed to signal the movement's decline. Former House speaker Dick Armey resigned as head of FreedomWorks, the well-financed advocacy group most instrumental in the formation and organization of the Tea Party movement. Tea Party favorite Jim DeMint of South Carolina announced that he would resign from the U.S. Senate and become president of the Heritage Foundation, a conservative think tank. Finally, the GOP leadership in the House purged four recalcitrant Tea Party–affiliated members from two key congressional committees: Congressmen Justin Amash (Kansas) and Tim Huelskamp (Michigan) from the budget committee; Walter Jones (North Carolina) and David Schweikert (Arizona) from the financial services committee.

Obviously, the GOP's leadership trio of Speaker John Boehner, Eric Cantor, and Kevin McCarthy exploited the perceived weakness of the Tea Party movement to bolster their support in key committees at the expense of Tea Party loyalists. Even stalwart movement leaders seemed to accept the notion of a declining Tea Party. TPN founder Judson Phillips wrote that it would take a spark to ignite "Tea Party two"—just like it took a spark lit by "Rick Santelli's famous rant on CNBC" to ignite "Tea Party one" into a potent political force."[110]

In reality, Tea Party members of Congress continued to flex their muscles in the House Republican conference, and eventually they were powerful enough to challenge the GOP leadership. First, they were instrumental in Speaker Boehner's resignation and then in Cantor's stunning defeat in the 2014 midterm election by an unknown Tea Partier. They appeared to be boldly laying the groundwork for what they hoped would be a possible takeover of the GOP. Explicit Tea Party support among the electorate at large had been as high as 35 percent during the early part of the movement.

As shown in figure 2.3, while support fell off afterward, it held steady at around the 20 percent level into the 2016 election period and also, based on other polling (not shown), when it was last asked about in 2019 during the start of the 2020 campaign. It is very significant—and supportive of our claims—that election-related polling done at the start of the 2020 election season was concerned with the continuing influence of the Tea Party and its supporters.[111]

Most importantly, the 2012 election debacle taught Tea Party leaders a lesson that they kept in mind ahead of the 2016 presidential competition. According to one account, "The morning after President Obama's reelection, tea party activists and movement conservatives reacted with dejection,

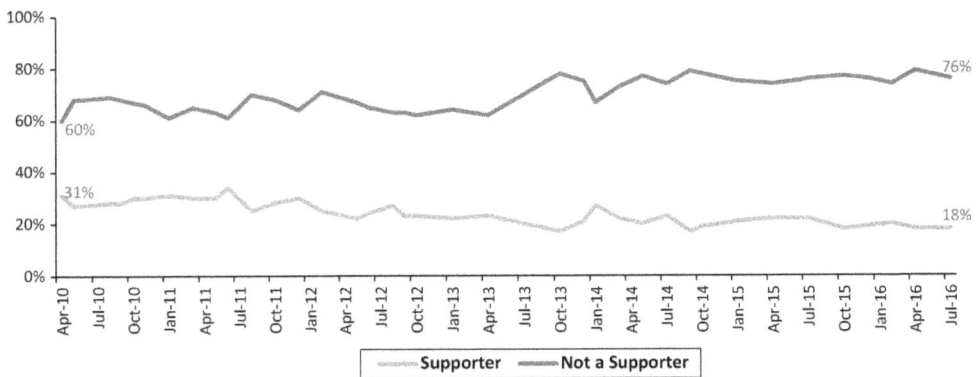

FIGURE 2.3 Support for the Tea Party movement.

Source: AP/Gfk.

rage and considerable resolve—saying "they just need *a better national candidate* [emphasis added] and a purer distillation of their anti-tax, small-government message to win the presidency in 2016."[112] They found their national candidate—and more—in Donald Trump. But the anti-Obama message that first drew broad attention to him was the birther claim that Obama was not born in the United States.

As we theorized at the outset of our research project, our findings underpin the crucial role of the two-directional communication links among the three corners of what we introduced in the introduction as the interconnectivity of political communication in the speedy rise of the Tea Party. This communication loop facilitated the communicative interactions among various forms of media, well-organized activists, and a significant number of anxious and angry citizens who became members or sympathizers of the movement. We also found a great deal of interconnectivity between the various media forms and symbiotic relationships within and between the traditional news media and the new digital social media platforms and websites; they fed off one another by reporting, supporting, or opposing messages originating in other forms of communication. In their assessment of media and movement interactions before the advent of digital media, William Gamson and Gadi Wolfsfeld found that "unlike public officials and heads of large established organizations, movement actors do not receive automatic standing in the media. They must struggle to establish it."[113] The opposite was true for the Tea Party movement.

3

ONLINE AND OFFLINE MEDIA AS SUPER-SPREADERS OF ANTI-OBAMA CONSPIRACY THEORIES

In July 2009, Delaware Republican Congressman Mike Castle held a town hall meeting for his constituents. It was a time of acrimonious debates triggered by President Obama's health care reform proposal, which was later passed as the Affordable Care Act and which opponents came to call Obamacare. During Castle's meeting with constituents, a woman held up what she described as her own birth certificate and attacked Delaware's sole congressman and other politicians for not addressing the issue of Barack Obama's allegedly missing birth certificate. A much-viewed YouTube video clip depicted the following exchange, which was accompanied by applause for the angry woman and jeers for the aristocratic congressman, who seemed shocked, if not intimidated, by the outburst and the crowd's reaction.

> *Woman*: I want to go back to January 20, and I want to know, why are you people ignoring his birth certificate? He is not an American citizen. He is a citizen of Kenya. I am American. My father worked—fought in World War II with the greatest generation in the Pacific theater for this country, and I don't want this flag to change. I want my country back!

Castle: If you're referring to the president there, he is a citizen of the
United States.

Woman: All the men and women who died for this country in 1776 'til
the present time. I think we should all stand up and give Pledge of
Allegiance to that wonderful flag and people that sacrificed their lives
for our freedom. Everybody, stand up![1]

As the video showed, everyone in sight stood up and recited the Pledge
of Allegiance. Soon thereafter, Tea Party activists backed one of their own,
Christine O'Donnell, to challenge Castle in Delaware's GOP primary for
a U.S. Senate seat. After her victory, O'Donnell thanked the 9–12 Delaware
Patriots and especially their leader, Russ Murphy, who "believes Obama
isn't an American."[2] According to Geoffrey Kabaservice, O'Donnell was
"unqualified for the nomination by any conventional measure."[3] Yet, she
beat Castle in a stunning upset—albeit losing decisively in the general
election to Democrat Chris Coons.

Tea Party organizers and rank-and-file movement supporters were
instrumental in mobilizing people across the country and dispatching them
to townhall meetings for rowdy protests against the federal government's
alleged malfeasance, such as overspending and planning the adoption of
"socialized medical care." Expressing unfounded anti-Obama rumors was
part and parcel of these Tea Party protests, which targeted Democratic and
selected Republican members of Congress.

The Delaware incident was not only a YouTube hit but also an outburst
that was much discussed on conspiracy websites and Tea Party discussion
boards. Not surprisingly, the mainstream media, too, reported prominently
and widely on the tumultuous event that foretold Representative Castle's
startling primary defeat by an inferior Tea Party candidate and anti-Obama
conspiracist. Moreover, the town hall spectacular and its aftermath provide
a window into the workings of interconnected political communication
among the three components: politicians—here involved in a nasty primary; ordinary people—here angrily expressing their belief in anti-Obama
rumors; and the essential role of the media—here bringing the news of the
Delaware incident to mass audiences.

In the next section, we explore the birth of anti-Obama rumors online, its initial growth, and the long history of political conspiracy theories in the U.S.—both showing the involvement of political activists and leaders as well as rank-and-file followers.

ANTI-OBAMA RUMORS AND THE LONG U.S. HISTORY OF CONSPIRACY THEORIES

The claim that Barack Obama was not born in the United States and therefore not eligible to run for and occupy the highest office in the land was first made by bloggers during the 2008 competition between Obama and Hillary Clinton for the Democratic Party's presidential nomination. Bloggers argued that Obama was born in Kenya and therefore constitutionally not qualified to become U.S. president. (What was ignored in the outcry about this assertion was that the interpretation itself was not correct, in that Obama's mother was a citizen who had resided in the United States the requisite number of years for Obama to be considered a citizen at birth according to the current law at the time.[4]) Obama's campaign reacted immediately by releasing a copy of his birth certificate.

But instead of stopping the rumor mill in its tracks, the document was challenged as a forgery. Fightthesmears.com, a website created by the campaign to counter false rumors and accusations, was equally unsuccessful in putting an end to birther rumors. As David Weigel noted, "Ironically, the 'birther' movement began in response to Obama's own efforts to debunk rumors."[5] What started as the far-fetched claim of a few bloggers exploded into an anti-Obama conspiracy theory, to which a growing circle of online activists contributed ever more fantastic pieces of what they labeled indisputable evidence on websites, blogs, and social media platforms.

This reaction to Obama's response followed the best tradition of conspiracy theories. According to Brian L. Keely, conspiracy theories are "the only theories for which evidence against them is actually construed as evidence in favor of them. The more evidence piled up by the authorities in favor of a given theory, the more the conspiracy theorist points to how badly 'They' must want us to believe the official story."[6] Similarly, based on a study of conspiracy theories from World War I through the terrorist attacks of September 11, 2001, Kathleen Olmsted concluded that "conspiracists come to believe in their theories as zealots believe in their religion: nothing can change their mind. When new evidence surfaces, or when experts insist that, say, towers can collapse if airplanes hit them and fires burn hot enough, the conspiracy theorists dismiss the experts as blinded by their own preconceptions at best, or as part of the conspiracy at worst."[7] According to Cass Sunstein and Adrian Vermeule, "Conspiracy theories generally attribute extraordinary powers to certain agents—to plan, to control others, to maintain secrets, and so forth. Those who believe that those agents have such powers are especially unlikely to give respectful attention to debunkers, who may, after all, be agents or dupes of those who are responsible for the conspiracy in the first instance."[8] In short, it is very difficult, if not impossible, to counter political rumors effectively.

Conspiracy theories have found true believers at all times in all parts of the world, but the United States in particular has a long history of persistent rumors and full-fledged conspiracy theories spanning from colonial times to the early twenty-first century. For Olmsted, the ethnic and religious mix of immigrants in America explains the perennial fears of subversion by alien conspirators. Nativist-isolationist rumors of alleged plots by the pope and Catholics aimed at gaining control over the United States were at the core of two political movements that for short but turbulent periods played major roles in nineteenth-century American politics.[9] The American, or Know Nothing, Party in the 1850s and the American Protective Association (APA) in the early 1890s gained significant support as anti-Catholic and anti-immigrant voices. Both had political traction during times of broad economic, political, and cultural discontent, so their causes came to transcend their original single-issue opposition to immigrants.

The Know Nothings and the APA, just like activists and supporters of the twenty-first-century Tea Party movement, spread rumors and promoted conspiracy theories in which American patriots were threatened by "others" whom they rejected as inferior races, ethnicities, and/or religions.

The pre– and post–Civil War years, and more recent American politics from the mid-1960s through the presidency of Donald Trump, were periods of heightened political conflict—partisan polarization, as we describe further in chapter 5. Persuasive data that track partisan conflict in the U.S. Congress show that these were long periods of partisan polarization compared with the years in between. Moreover, although it is difficult to make any definitive causal inference, trends in partisan conflict in Congress closely tracked the percentage of foreign-born in the United States.[10]

Further, the heightened emotions attached to the parties' divergence on major issues and the ideological nature of the political conflict have consequences for how people perceive—or, rather, misperceive—political reality and objective conditions, and these misperceptions may strongly persist and be difficult to correct.[11] In their persuasive study of how many Americans are receptive to conspiracy theories, Joseph Uscinsky and Joseph Parent show that the belief in such theories is greatest among those who have underlying receptive predispositions and are more ideologically extreme.[12] This receptivity, then, should be heightened in periods of ideological conflict, which should be highly pertinent to the three cases that we examine here of political movements, their right-wing ideologies, and their rumormongering.

To the extent that "belief in conspiracy theories is often fueled by group polarization,"[13] the Tea Party movement—which opposed government, progressivism, globalization, multiculturalism, elitism, and intellectualism,—provided fertile ground for birther rumors. Indeed, birthers seemed to understand that their outlandish claims resonated particularly well in Tea Party circles. The website birthers.org, for example, posted the following flyer, titled "Perfect for Tea Parties, ready to be printed and distributed": "Obama is not a natural born American citizen. His father was not a US citizen nor an immigrant. Barak [*sic*] Obama Jr. is a natural-born British subject. Ask yourself, could a true American president enslave three generations yet born with an inescapable debt, and could a true American president surrender our Constitution to international laws that mock our Constitution?"[14]

While not all Tea Partiers embraced birther rumors and related conspiracy theories, there was a natural overlap between Tea Partiers and birthers and those who believe rumors that Obama is a Muslim and/or that Obama sides with Muslims. Based on their meetings with Tea Party activists and supporters, Theda Skocpol and Vanessa Williamson concluded, "The son of an African father and a white American mother, Obama is perceived by many Tea Partiers as a foreigner, an invader pretending be an American, a fifth columnist."[15] Similarly, Christopher Parker and Matt Barreto found that the Tea Party and its sympathizers believed that President Obama was "a secret Muslim, or that he was not born in America" and that he "was out to destroy the country."[16]

Jonathan Kay, a Canadian journalist and self-described conservative, attended the 2010 National Tea Party Convention in Nashville, Tennessee, and was struck by the preponderance of conspiracy theories centered on Obama and his liberal allies, mostly in tune with the "established script of New World Order conspiracy theories, which have suffused the dubious right-wing fringes of American politics since the days of the John Birch Society." Kay also reported about the super-spreader of birther conspiracies, Joseph Farah, a political insider and founder of the right-extreme online "information" hub WorldNetDaily, who told the crowd at the Memphis convention, "My dream is that if Barack Obama seeks reelection in 2012 that he won't be able to go to any city, any town in America without seeing signs that ask, 'Where's the birth certificate?'"[17] Farah did not have to wait for the 2012 campaign to see this dream come true. Signs that raised this very question appeared regularly at Tea Party rallies throughout Obama's first term as president.

The birther conspiracy theory actually had several variations. The first and most persistent one held that Obama was not born in Honolulu but in Kenya, his father's homeland, and that his Hawaiian birth certificate was a falsification. Others claimed that even if born in Hawaii, Obama was a British subject because his father was a Kenyan with British citizenship at the time of his son's birth. In still another version, he was said to be an Indonesian citizen, since he was adopted by his Indonesian stepfather. Finally, there were several claims that Obama held dual citizenships—one American and the other Kenyan, British, or Indonesian.

Closely related was the claim that Barack Obama, the son of a Muslim father from Kenya and stepson of his mother's second husband, also a Muslim, was brought up in the Islamic faith and he secretly remained a Muslim. Surfacing shortly after Obama's electrifying speech at the 2004 Democratic National Convention in Boston, the rumor was first reported on the right-wing website FreeRepublic.com.[18] It was only during the 2008 presidential campaign, however, that the Obama-is-a-Muslim rumor gained momentum in the blogosphere. An anonymous chain email about Obama's alleged associations with radical Islam "spread with viral efficiency" in the months preceding the 2008 election campaign.[19]

PolitiFact.com, a site that reports the result of its fact-checking projects, published an article in June 2008 and reprinted in March 2011 that refuted anti-Obama conspiracy theories. With respect to the rumors that Obama is a Muslim and that he shed "Mohammed" from his name to cover up his true religion, the article stated,

> As a fact-checking news web site we went to extensive lengths to sort out the truth. We got a copy of his 1992 marriage certificate from the Cook County (Ill.) Bureau of Vital Statistics, His driver's license record from the Illinois Secretary of State's office, His registration and disciplinary record with the Attorney Registration & Disciplinary Commission of the Supreme Court of Illinois. Not to mention all of his property records. Not one of these documents shows a Muhammed (or Mohammed) in Obama's name. They all read "Barack H. Obama" or "Barack Hussein Obama.[20]

In the fall of 2008, when U.S. Senator John McCain, the GOP's nominee for president, held a campaign rally in Minnesota, a woman took the microphone and questioned Obama's biography, implying lies about his birthplace and religion. "I have read about him . . . he's an Arab," she said. McCain shook his head, took the microphone from her, and answered, "No, ma'am. No, ma'am. He's not. . . . He's a decent family man, citizen, that I just happen to have disagreements with on fundamental issues."[21]

Two weeks before the 2008 election, former secretary of state Colin Powell, a long-time Republican, debunked the Obama-is-a-Muslim conspiracy theory when he told NBC's Tom Brokaw,

> I'm also troubled by, not what Senator McCain says, but what members of the party say. And it is permitted to be said such things as, "Well, you know that Mr. Obama is a Muslim." Well, the correct answer is, he is not a Muslim, he's a Christian. He's always been a Christian. But the really right answer is, what if he is? Is there something wrong with being a Muslim in this country? The answer's no, that's not America. Is there something wrong with some seven-year-old Muslim-American kid believing that he or she could be president? Yet, I have heard senior members of my own party drop the suggestion, "He's a Muslim and he might be associated with terrorists." This is not the way we should be doing it in America.[22]

David Maraniss, whose Obama biography took issue with some of his subject's recollections of his early years, debunked birther and Obama-is-a-Muslim rumors point by point and characterized conspiracy theorists as "frauds and fabricators."[23]

But even when the mainstream media reported prominently on authoritative rebukes of anti-Obama rumors, conspiracy theories gained still further support. People are guided by what political psychologists call "motivated reasoning" (see also chapter 5), as "partisan goals trump accuracy goals so that individuals act as biased information processors who will vigorously defend their prior values."[24] When researchers examined why a significant number of Americans believed that President Obama was a Muslim, they found that ideology and partisanship (and race) are strong indicators for accepting misinformation and that the politically sophisticated are as susceptible to rumors as politically less knowledgeable people. As for Obama's religion, "Republicans, conservatives, and those with favorable feelings toward [Senator John] McCain were more likely to explicitly identify Obama as a Muslim than Democrats, liberals, and those with favorable feelings toward Obama."[25] Obviously, the movers and shakers in the anti-Obama rumor mill were well aware that "smear campaigns may be quite effective at creating implicit associations between targeted political figures and misinformation."[26]

Analyzing responses to public opinion survey questions concerning 9/11-related conspiracy theories, researchers found evidence of "robust positive associations between belief in conspiracy theories and higher consumption of non-mainstream media" and greater readership of blogs, sensational weeklies, and what they called "grocery store tabloids."[27] Noting that in the distant past, rumors were mostly transmitted by word of mouth, Adam Berinsky concluded that "the Internet has changed all that. Today, anyone can publish on the web, instantly acquiring a degree of credibility regardless of the quality of information they provide." Indeed, "given the speed with which information can disseminate through the Internet, the potential for the spread of fallacious information through rumors has increased greatly."[28] The sheer number and popularity of websites, blogs, and social media networks increased significantly from the time that strong links between the embrace of conspiracy theories and internet sites were first documented in the case of the 9/11 terrorist attacks.

As described in the following sections, we first examine websites and blogs most likely to disseminate birther and Obama-is-a-Muslim rumors, including those maintained by Tea Party organizations. Second, we explore how mainstream media (print, broadcast, and cable) reported on these conspiracy theories and the emergence of Donald Trump as a super-spreader of birther rumors in early 2011.

THE ONLINE HUB FOR CONSPIRACY THEORIES

In early June 2008, the conservative online news service WorldNetDaily (WND, https://www.wnd.com) published a story headlined "Is Obama's Candidacy Constitutional?" about rumors circulating in the blogosphere claiming that Barack Obama was born in Kenya and therefore not eligible for the presidency. Ten more stories were published before Election Day on the WND site that expressed growing doubt about the authenticity of the copy of Obama's birth certificate that his campaign had posted on its website. Two days before the November 4 election, WND expressed its own suspicion about Hawaiian officials' refusal to give the media access to the original document and declared it had interviewed Obama's uncle in Kenya, who was unsure where his nephew was born. Most of the articles chronicled efforts by birthers to have courts review Obama's eligibility for the highest office.

The pace of birther reporting intensified dramatically once the election results were in and Obama was declared president-elect. From the first birther story in June through Election Day, altogether 13 such posts appeared. WND itself published 13 pertinent items in the remaining days of November and 33 in December 2008. The frequency of birther stories fluctuated from month to month, but WND paid a great deal of attention to the rumors, with a total of 987 articles or short items publicized from June 2008 through December 2012. While reflecting a pro-birther tilt early on, WND became quickly the driving force in the birther movement in cyberspace. As one commenter on teapartynation.com noted, "The only media actively pursuing [Obama's eligibility] is WND."[29]

WorldNetDaily used its online platform to organize petition drives urging visitors to sign letters to be delivered to the U.S. Supreme Court and state electors chosen to cast the ultimate votes for Obama's election, alerting them to Obama's ineligibility for the presidency. In the first of these drives, WND claimed to have collected and delivered four hundred thousand signatures. WND created bumper stickers and yard and rally signs and launched a national billboard campaign asking the simple question, "Where's the birth certificate?"

WND Editor and Chief Executive Officer Joseph Farah offered a $10,000 reward to anyone able to prove that he or she witnessed Obama's birth. "Barack Obama claims to have been born in Honolulu Aug. 4, 1961," Farah stated. "His entire constitutional claim to the presidency rests on this premise. Yet, he refuses to release a copy of his long-form birth certificate—the only document that could possibly corroborate his claim. Therefore, in the interest of truth, justice and the Constitution, I am making the extraordinary offer to entice someone to come forward with the facts of his birth—whether it took place in Hawaii or elsewhere."[30]

In mid-April 2012, WND launched yet another petition drive in support of demands for the 112th Congress to "immediately undertake a full and impartial investigation into the constitutional eligibility of Barack Hussein Obama to serve as president of the United States." According to the petition, "every scientific survey shows that around half of American voters simply do not believe Barack Obama is telling the truth about his past—and specifically they remain unconvinced he is even legally qualified to occupy the presidency. Not to finally resolve this monumental and unprecedented constitutional issue would be intolerable, and would constitute the most extreme disrespect and contempt for the U.S. Constitution which every Congress member has sworn a solemn oath to defend."[31]

The WND website also pushed the Obama-is-a-Muslim rumors and linked them to the birther tale whenever the opportunity arose. From April 2008, when the first Muslim rumor was published, though December 2012, a total of 113 articles and short items were publicized on WND's main page—most of them in 2011 as time moved toward the 2012 election campaign. Once President Obama had been elected for a second term, the volume of both Obama-is-a-Muslim and birther rumors subsided. As table 3.1 depicts, the total volume of items questioning Obama's "true" birthplace and religion published by WND was significant.

Repeating the same disinformation, rumors, and fantastical theories over several years not only buttressed the convictions of the immediate

TABLE 3.1 Number of articles on birther and Obama-is-a-Muslim rumors in WND

	2008	2009	2010	2011	2012
Obama's birthplace	59	264	208	323	133
Obama's religion	22	12	23	18	38
Total	81	276	231	341	171

Note: For the birther conspiracy theory, all items posted on WND were counted; for alleged issues about Obama's religion, we counted only articles on WND's main page.
Source: WND website. Compiled by the authors.

community of anti-Obama conspiracy theorists, but over time it could affect a significant segment of the general public who were not among the theorists. WND was not simply one independent website but, rather, the information hub of an online network of anti-Obama blogs, websites, and social media accounts.

THE ONLINE RUMOR NETWORK

Other websites besides WorldNetDaily highlighted the birther or Obama-is-a-Muslim rumors or both. The blog *giveusliberty1776* was among the sites fully devoted to proving President Obama's noncitizenship and putting pressure on decision makers to restore "constitutional government." On June 12, 2012, shortly before noon, a counter located high up on the blog's home page displayed the "Time Since the Usurper Putative President Obama aka Barry Soetoro Unconstitutionally Took Office": 1,268 days, 23 hours, 39 minutes, 28 seconds. The radio podcasts available on the site were all-out attempts to frighten and convince listeners that the United States was experiencing "the greatest constitutional crisis in our country's history"; that America was under "daily assault from within"; that "our own government" was helping in destroying America; that "we" were "infiltrated by Socialists, Marxists, Communists, Bilderbergers, and One-World-Order Advocates"; that "we" were "led by a foreign-born, anti-American, anti-Christian fraud"; and that "corrupt political elites" were either part of this fifth column conspiracy or irresponsible bystanders to "them" and domestic enemies were taking our country down.[32]

The mission statement on this particular birther page was mostly a call for patriots to become active in the fight for the country's survival. "Whether you are currently active or if this [is] your first endeavor, we want you," the pitch stated. "We must unite now and fight back against the tyranny that is rapidly enveloping our country! We can be effective if we work together. However, we will never succeed unless we try! Do you have a telephone? Do you have an internet connection? Can you write letters, mail out postcards, hand-out flyers? Can you talk to neighbors and friends?

Can you get involved with us and brainstorm ideas?" The home page also urged patriots, "Fly Your American Flag Upside Down every weekend until Obama is removed from the White House."

The Birthers (birthers.org) website provided lengthy documents and articles relevant to questioning Obama's citizenship and linked to another frequently updated birther site (ObamaReleaseYourRecords.com), which contained headlines and short versions of the newest birther developments; the same information was also posted on the initiative's Twitter and Facebook pages. Typically, there were links to the sources of the original posts. At the end of July 2012, for example, a mouse click brought visitors to the WND site and an article about "a new national ad [that] has been playing on television—Fox News channel already has aired it—that takes the questions about Obama's background, eligibility, and qualifications directly to voters." The ad warned voters,

We know less about this man than any other president in American history. What's he hiding? His autobiography is full of fictional characters. But there's a lot more than that. If you tried to look into his past, you run into a brick wall.

His college records at Columbia. Sealed. His college records at Harvard. Sealed. We don't know what his thesis papers were about because those are sealed, too. His Selective Service record is sealed. His records as an attorney are sealed. He has a Massachusetts Social Security number and we can't get answers about that either and no one, I mean no one, has seen an actual physical copy of Barack Obama's birth certificate.

The fact is if we don't know who Barack Obama is, we shouldn't even have him as a candidate for president. Let's disqualify Obama before the Democratic National Convention.[33]

Other sites highlighted President Obama as anti-Christian, Antichrist, Muslim, and a tool of radical Islam. While declaring that the Obamaantichrist.org site offered visitors "an open forum" to discuss the issues surrounding Obama's religion, the articles on this site were devoted to convincing visitors that Obama was not a real Christian, that he was a Muslim and/or favored Islam over Christianity, and that he was or could be the Antichrist. "President Barack Hussein Obama is a demon sent from hell to extinguish the last remnants of virtue from the face of the earth. Barack Hussein Obama is the Antichrist," the anonymous poster of one article wrote. "'Beware of false prophets,' warns the bible, 'they come to you in sheep's clothing, but inwardly they are ferocious as wolves.' This quote has never been more relevant to humanity and perfectly describes Obama. He seduced the people with his slick, polished speeches, wearing out the saints with his eloquent blasphemy. Modern America faces a choice—freedom or enslavement, virtue or evil, Jesus or Satan. America will be the battleground for the greatest philosophical war ever waged: The final showdown between virtue and hedonism."[34]

The same site posted a video in which Bill Keller of Liveprayer.com made the case that Barack Hussein Obama was not a Christian and taking positions "in complete rebellion to Christ and the Bible," and that he is a Muslim whose goal is" the overthrow and destruction of the United States of America."[35]

The tease for a video on o.bamapost.com, put together from snippets of Obama's speeches, claimed to show "Obama admits that he is a Muslim. Obama bowing before a Muslim king. Obama talking about his Muslim family. Obama quoting from the Koran. Obama defending Islam. Obama visiting a Mosque. And many more clips of Obama and his Muslim connections." There was the admission that "of course," the tape "is edited, and "obviously he did not say all of this in one speech. However, does not the repetitive 'glory to Islam' message of this alarm you in the least?"[36]

TEA PARTIERS AND CONSPIRACY THEORISTS: TWO PEAS IN A POD

Besides those online sites exclusively devoted to anti-Obama conspiracy theories, there were also Tea party websites and blogs that spread birther rumors and questioned Obama's "real" religion. This close connection between Tea Partiers and anti-Obama conspiracists was recognized by

President Obama. In his memoir, *A Promised Land*, he wrote that after he took office, the Tea Party "resurrected an old rumor from the campaign: that I was not only Muslim but had actually been born in Kenya, and was therefore constitutionally barred from serving as President."[37]

Tea Party.org, was a hotbed of such conspiracy theories. Its home page displayed prominently a photograph of President Obama along with the caption, "See my Birth Certificate? Just as Fake as Me!"[38] Visitors who followed the invitation "Click Here" were first asked to donate money for the Tea Party, "to expose the 'Fraud President' to American households," since the "Blame Stream Media has consistently protected 'America's Fraud President' and buried Obama Frauds, such as:

- Forged Birth certificate issued by the White House!
- Multiple Social Security numbers!
- Sealed College records!
- Surrendered license to practice law!
- Missing birth records in Hawaii!
- Selective Service records sealed!
- Foreign Passports!
- Association with known Communists and subversives!
- Sworn testimonies by credible witnesses proving Obama was not born in America.
- America's top Sherriff threatened if he continues investigating the Obama Frauds!
- . . . and the list goes on!"

Hitting on all aspects of the birther conspiracy theory, these bullet points were followed by this call to action: "It's about time the Tea Party takes the bull by the balls and gives them a yank! Sound dangerous? You bet it is! So was facing the British over 236 years ago with a rag-tag Patriot Army. Just like we won then, we will win now!"[39] These words were quite similar to those used by the pro-Trump crowd who attacked the U.S. Capitol on January 6, 2021.

TeaParty.org had many visitors, perhaps because in response to the search words "Tea Party," search engines listed it ahead of distinct national

Tea Party organizations such as Tea Party Express and Tea Party Patriots. In blogs and forum discussions on this site, many Tea Partiers expressed their birther grievances and the belief that Obama was either a Muslim or had pro-Islamic and anti-Christian biases. At the end of August 2012, for example, the search words "Obama and birth certificate" produced 677 results on the "Forum" page. A post by "National Director, Dee" that was dated May 19, 2012, and claimed that President Obama's "true" birth certificate showed that he was born in Kenya, drew 23 comments.[40] One commenter wrote, "Everything is a lie when it comes from Obama." Another respondent noted, "The records cannot be checked, because the records for the week of Obama's birth are strangely missing. All other records are there, but only the records that can prove if mother was out of the country are missing? Obviously, Obama's stooges did their dirty deeds."

A March 3, 2012, post claiming that Obama's Hawaiian birth certificate was confirmed to be a forgery drew more than one thousand views and 129 comments. One Tea Partier commented, "This seems to be a conspiracy that goes as deep as the JFK assassination, which has never been fully explained. The conspirators would not have allowed Obama to run for President if they were not confident that their subterfuge could not be uncovered. You have to admit that so far they have been absolutely right. Someone even got to the Clintons early in the campaign and explained to them that Obama's eligibility was off bounds. Does anyone think Hillary would not find being Secretary of State more agreeable than a final resting place?"[41]

The Forum page showed also that Tea Partiers embraced rumors about Obama's "true" religion, his alleged support for Islamists—most of all the Muslim Brotherhood—and his support for the introduction of Sharia law into the American legal system. A search for "Obama is a Muslim" and "Obama is Muslim" produced 1,300 Forum results in late August 2012. Most of these items claimed that Obama was in bed with Muslims; others claimed that Obama is a Muslim now or was a Muslim in the past and therefore pushed Islamic interests at home and abroad. A post titled "Obama Administration Paves the Way for Sharia Law," which resulted in 990 views and 38 comments, claimed that "the most terrifying danger Americans face from a second Barack Obama term isn't the economy, which is scary enough. The most harrowing prospect is the Obama Administration's passivity in the face of attempts to introduce aspects of sharia law into our legal system. Now there is strong and open evidence of the Obama administration collaborating with Islamist activists to ensure the path toward sharia law is accelerated."[42] One commenter warned,

This is something I have been telling people since the beginning of oh'bummers usurpation of the oval office. It is so obvious that this is true I don't understand how it is that the pentagon which is supposed to be defending our constitution against all enemies hasn't put the traitor in prison. What is going on in our country? How deep is the infiltration? How corrupted have we become? I am very afraid when such obvious insanity as Islam is allowed to even be on our soil. I believe more every day that it's going to turn out that our only hope of salvation for our country is a very bloody civil war against our Muslim population.

While not as preoccupied with conspiracy theories as TeaParty.org, the posts and comments on the sites of major national Tea Party organizations facilitated rumormongering as well. Often short references to the various conspiracy strains were made in debates about completely different topics. Commenting on Obama's appeal among female voters, one female Tea Partier wrote on the Tea Party Nation site, "What in the world are those Obama worshipping females thinking or are they thinking—where have they been the past four years? Do they really believe this man who landed from no man's land in 2008, the person sent here from the Kenyan jungles came to save the female population in the USA?"[43] In the Tea Party Nation Forum discussion group "Islam: Enemy of Freedom," a male commenter gave female voters the following advice:

They are talking now that Obama is courting the women vote. The reason is he needs your votes to win. Women stand to lose the most if he continues due to the expansion of sharia law. Sharia dictates you and the children become as property and subservient to men. As property men can dispose of such at their whim. So a vote for Obama is not only a vote for the Muslim way but also a vote for sharia as this is their preferred law! So vote for Obama and you too can be the lead actress in another of America's honor killings. You ladies had best get busy!"[44]

In their responses to a recruitment appeal to the members of Tea Party Patriots, several commenters referred to anti-Obama birther and Muslim rumors. "We aren't sure if Oblahblah is an idiot or not since we've never seen his transcripts and with the teleprompter usage I wouldn't be so sure if this socialist can form an original or coherent thought," Penny wrote. Another woman stated, "Obama has had an agenda since he got elected. His whole idea was to transform America into an Islamic brotherhood nation. With the help of all the voters who put him in office he has done nothing but tear down the Constitution and eliminate the laws pertaining to the Constitution. Transformation is taking place under our noses and our beloved Congress is helping him."[45] Or take the following lead in a 2011 post on the Tea Party Patriots' site about an alleged administration plan to tax Christmas trees that pointed to Obama's anti-Christian attitudes and actions: "President Obama, who doesn't appear to care too much for Christmas, tried to impose a Christmas tree tax on those of us right-wing extremists who do. President and First Lady Obama do not give Christmas presents to their daughters. Also, the Obama White House Christmas (Holiday) tree last year was decorated with ornaments portraying the likeness of traditional Christmas figures such as Mao Tse Tung and drag queens."[46]

In the run-up to the 2012 presidential election, the Tea Party Express, the national Tea Party organization most closely associated with the GOP, posted an "Obama versus Jesus" article claiming that "Obama has been exposed as the most anti-Christian president in history." In an appeal to African-Americans, the post warned and admonished,

Black Christians who vote for Obama knowing his crimes against Christianity and biblical principles haven chosen to worship the idol of racial loyalty over their discipleship to Jesus Christ. Pure and simple.

"Thou shalt have no other gods before me." Exodus 20:3

Incredibly, some blacks have completely forsaken their Christianity for Obama.[47]

On August 15, 2012, Tea Party Nation founder Judson Phillips posted a lengthy Tea "Party Manifesto" in which he highlighted the importance of the birther movement.[48] Following his claim that few birthers believe Obama was born in Kenya, Phillips nonetheless endorsed all the other eligibility questions raised by birthers, when he wrote the following.

Why is eligibility so important?

Because if we prove that Barack Obama was not eligible to be President [emphasis added], all of his acts would be void. It would be as if they never happened.

Imagine a giant reset button that could take us back to 2009. This is what it would mean. All of Obama's appointees would not be appointed because Obama would not have been eligible to be President; therefor those appointments would have been void. All of the actions by those appointees would be void.

Two Supreme Court justices would be gone. Hundreds of federal judges would be gone.

Who knows what the odds are of proving that Barack Obama was ineligible to be President. One thing is certain. The rewards for proving him ineligible are huge and could be what it takes to save the nation.

Note, that Phillips wrote "if *we* prove," not if *birthers* prove. This was not a stylistic error. After all, the article ended with the wish or request, "We should all be birthers." Within two weeks, the article had attracted 6,655 views and 337 replies. A number of Tea Partiers identified themselves as long-time birthers or as buying in to the claim that important Obama documents were not made available. Some expressed their conviction that Obama was born in Kenya; others opted for Indonesia as his place of birth. Some voices cautioned against making Obama's eligibility a campaign issue and to concentrate instead on the economy. But almost all responders to Phillips's post supported one or the other or all birther claims, and they considered Obama's presidency a horrific threat to America. Many demanded drastic actions. One commenter posted a doctored picture showing Obama being manhandled by law enforcement officials who were in the process of arresting him. Still others added their own versions to the birther conspiracy theories.

Rumormongers feed off one another. While in the past misinformation of this kind was spread in large part by word of mouth (WOM), anti-Obama rumors and conspiracy theories were spread continuously online, first by the rumor hub WorldNetDaily and second by a network of extremist groups devoted to conspiracy theories and Tea Party websites. Electronic word of mouth, or eWOM, tend to be more effective than person-to-person WOM. As students of the new communication landscape pointed out, "Today's 'eWOM' from a mobile device can occur virtually anywhere and at anytime. Because the Internet allows for asynchronous communication, senders and receivers of eWOM do not need to worry about finding the right time to interact. In addition, eWOM that happens on websites such as blogs and customer review sites can reach millions of people at once. Those people then can post public feedback in ways that broaden and reinforce the comments they read on these sites."[49]

The WorldNetDaily rumor hub, which fed an expansive network of online sites and social media accounts, informed many Americans—most of all those associated with Tea Party groups—about the two most prominent anti-Obama conspiracy theories. We compared the monthly volume of birther "news" on the WND site with birther searches on Google from January 2009 through December 2012. We found a striking correlation over time between the two ($r = .73$), which is clearly reflected in the trend lines of figure 3.1. We also compared the monthly volume of stories about Obama's "true" religion on the WND website and the relevant Google searches from April 2008 (when the first such WND story was published) through the end of 2012. Here the correlation was not quite as strong ($r = .47$) as that for birther rumors but is still comparable, as figure 3.2 shows.

When a multitude of websites and blogs drew ever more attention to the rumors that Obama was not born in the United States and was not a Christian as he claimed, first radio talk shows, then mainstream television,

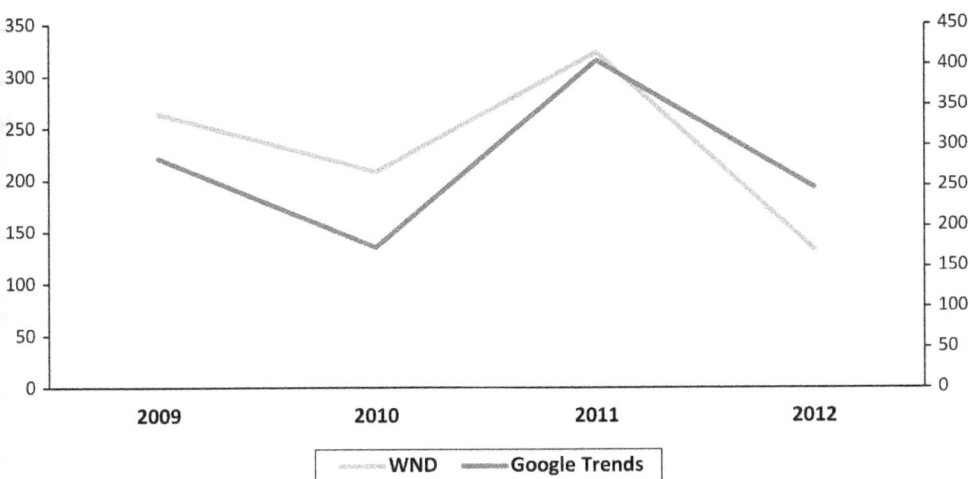

FIGURE 3.1 Birther conspiracy theory: WND volume and Google Trends 2009–12.

Note: The left axis shows News volume, number of stories, the right axis shows Google trends

Source: Lexis-Nexis and Google Trends, compiled by the authors.

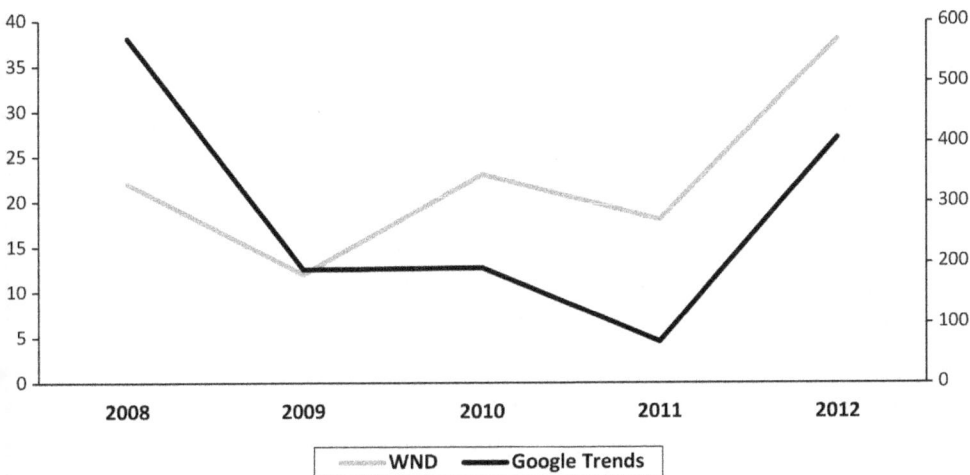

FIGURE 3.2 Obama-is-a-Muslim rumors: WND Volume and Google Trends.

Note: The left axis shows News volume, number of stories, the right axis shows Google trends

Source: Lexis-Nexis and Google Trends, compiled by the authors.

and eventually leading print news organizations paid attention to these political conspiracy theories, especially the birther tales.

BIRTHER-IN-CHIEF TRUMP

The flow of communication from the rumor hub WorldNetDaily and other like-minded online spreaders of conspiracy theories to the mainstream media did not escape President Obama. In a 2021 podcast interview to promote his memoir, Obama expressed criticism of the traditional media and especially the attention it paid to Donald Trump when the New York real estate developer and reality TV star made himself the spokesman-in-chief of the birther movement in early 2011. Obama told the *New York Times's* Ezra Klein, "The birtherism thing, which was just a taste of things to come, started in the right-wing media ecosystem. But a whole bunch of mainstream folks booked him all the time because he boosted ratings. . . . It was convenient for them to do, because it was a lot easier to book Donald Trump to let him claim that I wasn't born in this country than it was to actually create an interesting story that people will want to watch about income inequality. That's a harder thing to come up with."[50]

At the time Obama spoke of, Trump had raised his political profile by relentlessly attacking the president, flirting with the idea of running for president himself, and promoting birther rumors. His reality show, *The Apprentice*, had made him a national celebrity. Thus, Trump offered television and radio programmers what they wanted most in their quest for high ratings: entertainment with a mixture of shock jock attitude, drama, and conflict. As one observer noted, "Trump was one of the few people alive who could compete for ratings with the Kardashians."[51]

In his book *Amusing Ourselves to Death*, Neil Postman warned that even television news was "packaged as entertainment" and that therefore "we are deprived of authentic information" and "are losing our sense of what it means to be well informed. Ignorance is always correctable. But what shall we do if we take ignorance for knowledge?"[52] What Postman lamented in the 1980s came full circle in the twenty-first century when Trump began his metamorphosis from entrepreneur and TV reality star to celebrity politician with his eyes on the White House. As Trump won a successful primary campaign against his many GOP rivals in the spring of 2016, Andrew Sullivan recognized that "The Donald . . . emerged from the populist circuses of pro wrestling and New York City tabloids, via reality television and Twitter."[53] Thanks to those public venues, the shrewd New York real estate magnate had multimillions of fans across the United States who became his core support—first, when he flirted publicly with a presidential campaign in 2011 and even more so when he threw his hat for real into the presidential competition in mid-2015. As one observer noted about this celebrity politician, "many Trump supporters are more than just voters. They are political fans."[54] With fanatical supporters backing him, Trump was in a perfect position to demonstrate the triumph of ignorance over knowledge that Postman bemoaned. And this may best explain why there were so many believers in Trump's version of facts, post truths, conspiracy theories, and, finally, the Big Lie about the 2020 election results as justification for the insurrection of January 6, 2021.

The media spectacle of Trump as a celebrity politician with presidential ambitions and a purveyor of anti-Obama conspiracy theories began on March 23, 2011, when ABC's *The View* provided him fourteen minutes on a popular TV stage to introduce himself for the first time as the most visible and important pusher of birther falsities and demands for President Obama to show the original of his birth certificate. As she introduced Trump, media celebrity Barbara Walters asked whether the guest really wanted "to add president to his resume" and answered her own question with an enthusiastic, "A lot of people would like him to!" She told the applauding audience, "Let's welcome my friend, Donald Trump."

When he entered the stage, he first kissed each of the five female cohosts. After talking about his possible presidential run in 2012 and claiming repeatedly that he was the only person to tie President Obama in a recent public opinion poll, he got the opportunity to argue at length about alleged problems regarding the sitting president's birthplace. "There is something on that certificate that he does not reveal," he said. He also claimed that people "remember me since kindergarten" but "nobody remembers him [Obama]!" It was overall kind of a televised love-in, except for Whoopi Goldberg, who pushed back against his racially charged birther propaganda. "No White president has ever been asked to show his birth certificate," she said indignantly. But she, too, seemed quite accommodating, shaking Trump's outstretched hand at one point.

This first appearance as a birther opened the mainstream media gates for Trump, who was now considered the most energetic, entertaining, and shocking anti-Obama conspiracist. On NBC's *Today Show*, he told Meredith Vieira that he had sent people to Hawaii to investigate the birth certificate issue.[55] If the document turned out to be a fake, he said, the president "pulled one of the great cons in the history of politics. And beyond politics." He also said he considered himself a Tea Partier and was very proud to be.[56] Thus, Trump personified the convergence of Tea Partiers and birthers. At the end of March, he said on the Fox News *Laura Ingraham Show*, "I have a birth certificate. People have birth certificates. He doesn't have a birth certificate. He may have one but there is something on that birth certificate— maybe religion, maybe it says he's a Muslim, I don't know. Maybe he doesn't want that. Or, he may not have one."[57] On CNN's *State of the Union* Trump tried hard to convince viewers when he told a skeptical Candy Crowley,

> Well, it is not a birth certificate, Candy. And people are trying to figure out why isn't he giving his birth certificate? It is not a birth certificate. A certificate of live birth, and you can see that one that you have, and the one that I brought you, because that's the one that's on the Internet and all over the place, it doesn't even have a serial number. It doesn't have a signature, it doesn't have a signature, one that I saw on television has a stamp but that's not a signature.[58]

Why did even prestigious news organizations report prominently on Trump's birtherism campaign? CNN anchor Crowley explained, "There comes a point where you can't ignore something, not because it's entertaining— which he was on a lot of levels. The question was, 'Is he driving the conversation?' And he was."[59] The communication scholar Lance Bennett recognized "something of a prisoner's dilemma" for the gatekeepers of the traditional media when they "resist reporting thinly sourced information" spread by opinionated pundits elsewhere. According to Bennett, "It becomes difficult to avoid reporting the growing number of stories that are hyperbolic, sensational, distracting, or simply wrong. Indeed, avoiding such stories may mean that audiences will get them through other channels, making legacy news organizations irrelevant. The problem is that reporting such stories lends them credibility, while diminishing the hold of journalism on information quality."[60]

Nobody was more impressed by Trump's successful birther campaign in the mainstream media than Roger Ailes, chairman and CEO of Fox News. At the time, the network was fully anti-Obama and instrumental in the rise of the Tea Party movement (see chapter 2). While it is not clear whether Trump ever believed his lies about Obama's birthplace and religion, several credible sources attest to Ailes's conviction that "President Obama was a really sinister, bad guy. . . . He really did believe that the president was not born in the United States."[61] After a tense visit with Ailes in New York, then House speaker John Boehner reportedly said, "It was the most bizarre meeting I've had all my life. He had black helicopters fly all around his head that morning. It was every conspiracy theory you've ever heard. . . . Ailes believed in all this crazy stuff."[62]

Shortly after Trump's heavily reported appearance on *The View*, Ailes made Trump an offer the real estate mogul, TV reality star, and now leader of the anti-Obama conspiracy movement could not reject: Trump took a weekly call-in segment on Fox's morning program *Fox & Friends*. Ailes made sure that "Monday Mornings with Donald Trump" was widely promoted as "bold, brash, and never bashful, the Donald now makes his voice loud and clear every Monday on Fox." In Brian Stelter's assessment, "Through the weekly calls, he got to know Ailes' priorities. He got to know Fox's priorities. He got to know the people who became his voters. And they got to know him."[63]

Several weeks after Trump's birther offensive began, President Obama released his "long-form" birth certificate. Although Hawaii does not normally make these documents available, the authorities did so in response to the president's waiver request. But, again, the newly provided evidence fueled further birther suspicion that the latest White House move was merely another cover-up move. While Trump took credit for forcing the White House to release the birth certificate's long version, an immediate chorus arose from conspiracy theorists on blogs and websites calling the long-form certificate a fake. Birthers wanted more evidence. They demanded the release of Obama's immigration records and claimed that the president used a false Social Security number. Finally, rumors circulated that Obama had not earned his college degree at Columbia University and his law degree at Harvard and that he could only prove otherwise by releasing his transcripts.

While Trump opened his Twitter account, @realDonaldTrump, in March 2009 and posted his first tweet in early May, his personal 2011 birther campaign relied on appearances in and coverage by the mainstream media. But that changed the following year. Ninety-six of Trump's 116 tweets or retweets devoted to birtherism @realdonaldtrump were posted in the ten months leading up to Election Day 2012 in an effort to support GOP presidential candidate Mitt Romney and the entire slate of Republican candidates nationally. On March 12, 2012, Trump tweeted, "When I was 18, people called me Donald Trump. When he was 18, @BarackObama was Barry Soweto. Weird." Two months later, he retweeted, "In his own words, @BarackObama 'was born in Kenya, and raised in Indonesia and Hawaii,' This statement was made, (cont) http://tl.gd/hkim3j." Trump whipped his fellow conspiracists into another frenzy when he issued a multitude of tweets that demanded applications and transcripts as proof that Obama attended Columbia College and Harvard Law School. "Isn't it time that Obama release his college records and applications?" Trump asked in a tweet posted in October 2012. "Boy would that create a mess! He is not who you think."

More than 25 percent of all conspiracy-related tweets that year were devoted to Obama's allegedly missing records—besides the birth certificate that would allegedly prove his "questionable" past. More than 20 percent of these tweets were devoted to Trump's offer to pay Obama $5 million for his favorite charity on releasing all these documents. Trump lauded his "generosity" in exchange for Obama's "get clean" responses. In reality, his tweet storm revisited all aspects of anti-Obama conspiracy theories in the weeks before the November elections. "Obama has no problem leaking national security secrets. Why can't he release his records? Especially when $5M is going to charity," a tweet of October 24, 2012 stated. When it was clear that Obama did not respond to the offer, Trump tweeted (November 6, 2012), "Remember: Obama turned down $5M to charity which I said I would increase by 10X to $50M—just to show simple records. He's hiding lots!" In several tweets Trump used anti-Obama rumors in support of Romney. On July 12, 2012, for example, he tweeted, "President Obama wants @MittRomney to hand over even more past tax returns—he should when @BarackObama reveals his college applications."

Donald Trump used alternative media, mostly his Twitter account, to tweet and retweet ugly Obama rumors bolstering birther arguments. In this respect, he and the anti-Obama online network of political rumor-mongers followed the example of nationalist, anti-immigrant conspiracy theorists, especially those in the nineteenth century (see the boxed text).

THE PRESSES AND ANTI-CATHOLIC CONSPIRACY THEORIES IN THE NINETEENTH CENTURY

What Trump and most anti-Obama conspiracy theorists practiced in the early twenty-first century—the use of alternative media that they controlled—was also used by their predecessors in the nineteenth century when Catholic immigrants were the preferred targets of sinister conspiracy theories.

Beginning in the 1830s, in reaction to a large influx of immigrants and especially Catholics, leading nativists publicized a metaphorical call to arms by spreading threatening rumors and conspiracy theories. At the time, the newly emerging penny presses increased the numbers of people who could afford to buy a newspaper. Within a decade or so, the number of daily and weekly newspapers grew dramatically and became part of the early mainstream media. But according to Thomas C. Leonard, it was not the secular penny presses but the religious, evangelical newspapers that achieved the first mass circulation in the first half of

(continued on next page)

(*continued from previous page*)

the nineteenth century and became the greatest communication powerhouses.[64] A number of these religious presses were established as "No Popery" newspapers with the sole purpose of exposing the alleged Catholic menace. The titles of these papers, *The Downfall of Babylon, or the Triumph of Truth over Popery*, published by Samuel B. Smith, and *The American Protestant Vindicator and Defender of Civil and Religious Liberty against the Inroads of Popery*, published by the Reverend W. C. Brownlee, revealed their mission.

Candace A. Czernicki documented how Reverend Brownlee's paper "spawned countless imitators" and was thus instrumental in the advent of the No Popery press.[65] But it was Samuel F. B. Morse, best known as the inventor of the telegraph and Morse code, who, in the 1830s, became the public voice of an expansive anti-immigrant/anti-Catholic conspiracy theory. He influenced the later establishment of two anti-immigrant or nativist groups, The Order of Native Americans and The Order of the Star Spangled Banner, which were the pillars of the later Know Nothing Party, also called the American Party, in the 1850s.

In the *New York Observer*, a religious newspaper, Morse used the pseudonym Brutus to publish twelve letters that painted a dreadful picture of an existential threat to America's core values. When those lengthy missives were published as a book titled *Foreign Conspiracy Against the Liberties of the United States*, Morse summarized their alarming message in the preface: "It is a truth now no longer to be questioned, that Popery is so naturally the ally of Absolute government, that the diffusion of the former will result in producing the latter; and it is equally true, that the diffusion of Protestantism will result in the production of liberal institutions. What, then, is the duty of Americans, all who really love their own free system of government? There can be but one answer. They must unite in giving every facility to the spread of Protestant principles."[66]

Morse attacked what he called "the political press" for ignoring the Catholic takeover threat. For Morse this threat was "a matter not to be covered up by silence [on the part of what one might call the mainstream press of the time]." Instead, he wrote, "the political press has a fearful responsibility now resting upon it; it has a sacred duty to the country to perform, from which it cannot, must not shrink. It should be known, that there is a wider desire for knowledge on Popery, in its multifarious bearings upon society, than some seem to be aware of." Morse even suggested that the "enemy" was influencing the political press. He asked, "Is he [the Catholic enemy] not intriguing with the press? Is he not usurping the police of the country, and showing his front in our political councils?"[67]

In the last two decades of the nineteenth century, the United States was swamped with nativist newspapers and magazines—all devoted to spreading conspiracy rumors about an existential threat engineered by the Pope and his power over Roman Catholics in America. Not unlike Morse's antipopery tracts, the neonativist presses perpetuated rumors of a Catholic takeover of the U.S. government, claiming that the infiltration of decision-making institutions was already in place and threatened deep-seated American values. The latter part of the 1800s experienced high immigration levels, a severe economic downturn, and dislocations in the wake of rapid industrialization. It was a perfect storm for scapegoating religious minorities, especially Roman Catholics, for all the problems Americans were facing at the time.

The flagship of the nativist press was the monthly *A.P.A. Magazine* of the American Protective Association (APA), the most influential among secret anti-immigrant organizations that, at its peak in the mid-1890s, had an estimated membership of three million. As one scholar wrote about this particular press genre, "The hatred that the nativist press felt toward immigrants also came glaring through in their rhetoric the publications used, with word choices often communicating a sense of alarm and urgency. 'The people must be aroused to the dangers which are threatening our country, caused by the loose and liberal immigration laws,' read one item. 'Coming from the slumways and cesspools of ignorance, poverty and superstition, this foreign blood must be checked before our country is overflowed by a mighty torrent of alienism,' read another."[68]

Besides the APA magazine, the *American Standard* of San Francisco was a particularly vicious mouthpiece of APA extremism, demanding, for example, a stricter immigration system to prevent "criminals" from coming to America. "To hundreds and thousands of ignorant foreigners that have come to our shores," the *Standard* wrote in a typical commentary, "liberty means liberty to commit crime, freedom means freedom to the beastly and degraded. They contaminate everything they touch."[69]

Many mainstream presses were highly critical of the movement and its rumor-mongers. The *New York Times*, for example, wrote in an opinion article, "The A.P.A., by secretly circulating its lying literature, by spreading an 'anti-Romanist' alarm by word of mouth and by circular through newspapers devoted to their cause, and through its 'lecturers,' worked the people up to such a pitch of terror and panic that they were ready to believe anything."[70]

While the APA's hate was particularly directed at Catholics, especially newcomers, the organization's overall nativist propaganda was believed to have influenced public and elite hostility not just toward Catholic newcomers but immigrants in general. In short, alternative newspapers allowed nineteenth-century conspiracy theorists to communicate among themselves and to the masses and to spread their threatening narratives widely, although the speed and reach of this was far more limited than twenty-first-century electronic communication.

THE MAINSTREAM MEDIA AND
ANTI-OBAMA RUMORS

As noted earlier, some students of rumors have assumed that online sources and communications are the driving forces in the rapid and far-reaching spread of misinformation and conspiracy theories.[71] However, Brian Weeks and Brian Southwell concluded that with respect to anti-Obama rumors, the mainstream media "had an agenda-setting effect by raising the public's salience of the issue."[72] Thus, while we examined and documented the major roles of websites, blogs, and social media platforms, we also recognized the continuing importance of mainstream media as major information sources. Indeed, at the heights of anti-Obama rumors, both national and local television remained the preferred news sources of Americans. For that reason, it has been argued that the main driver of political polarization (which also breeds political conspiracy theories) "is not the web. It is more likely television . . . and in particular, the rise of partisan cable like Fox News and MSNBC."[73] The members of younger generations increasingly cite online sources as the source of their news in addition to other information. But this does not mean exclusively social media sources; it also includes the online offerings of print, radio, broadcast, and, yes, cable news. Thus, both alternative media controlled by promoters of rumors and conspiracy theories, for one, and mainstream media, for another, have been indispensable in alerting large numbers of people to allegedly existential threats and in influencing their views on those matters.

So, how much attention did the mainstream media, broadcast, cable, and print pay—or not pay—to birther and Obama-is-a-Muslim conspiracy theories? We selected a leading print media (*New York Times*), one of the TV networks (CBS), a radio network (National Public Radio), and the three leading cable networks (CNN, Fox News, and MSNBC) to examine and answer the question. We used the Lexis-Nexis archive to identify and count the text of articles and transcripts of those six media organizations for the period from 2008 through 2012 that were solely about birther rumors or mentioned them. As table 3.2 shows, the refuted

TABLE 3.2 Number of Media stories/aired segments about or mentioning birtherism, 2009–12

	NYT	CBS	CNN	FOX	MSNBC	NPR	TOTAL
2009	13	0	50	25	137	21	246
2010	30	2	73	33	137	14	289
2011	51	13	279	111	309	30	793
2012	19	7	99	35	176	20	356
Total	113	22	501	204	759	85	1,684

Source: Lexis-Nexis electronic archive. Compiled by the authors.

conspiracy theory received significant coverage in the mainstream media, most of all from the three cable networks. All together, the six media organizations publicized 1,684 articles or program segments either fully reporting on or mentioning birtherism. The three cable networks combined were responsible for 1,464 such segments and the three others for 220 such stories.

At first sight, it may be surprising that it was not the right-of-center Fox News network that publicized birther rumors most prominently but, rather, the left-of-center MSNBC and the more middle-of-the-road CNN, which was in second place. Stelter offered a plausible explanation for Fox's restraint in coverage of birtherism compared with the two cable rivals by pointing to Roger Ailes, who rejected excessive coverage of these conspiracy theories—even though he himself believed in them. Ailes knew, too, that "Fox was more powerful, when it was grouped with NBC and CBS [and not with the other cable networks]. Besides, Fox's base already suspected Obama was a foreigner. There was no need to say the obvious and racist part out loud."[74] The *New York Times*, representative of other prestigious daily newspapers, covered birthers and their beliefs not as intensively as cable television but still quite generously. Thus, MSNBC aired a whopping 759 segments about or mentioning birtherism, CNN 501, and Fox merely 204. Cable coverage was significantly greater than coverage in the *New York Times* (113 articles), National Public Radio (85 segments), and CBS with only 22 segments (table 3.2).

It was hardly surprising that 2011 was the year with the most intensive birther coverage. The six media organizations combined offered close to 800 stories that year, compared with 356 in 2012. As described earlier, 2011 was also the year Donald Trump launched his media blitz to promote birtherism. Actually, the bizarre conspiracy theory about Obama's birthplace got by far the greatest media attention in the early months of 2011. After Trump's debut on *The View* in March, his media appearances and interviews multiplied in April. There was also ample news coverage of whatever anti-Obama rumors and accusations he offered during his "Monday Mornings with Donald Trump" call-in show on *Fox & Friends*. Thus, in April 2011 alone, CNN had 149 segments about or mentioning birther rumors, Fox News aired 71, and MSNBC 66. The *New York Times* with 16, National Public Radio with 15, and CBS with 8 such stories upped their formerly very modest volume. In sum, Trump's campaign to promote the birther conspiracy theory—often in tandem with his hinted interest in the 2012 presidential campaign—resulted in substantial media attention.

Our content analysis of news coverage fully devoted to the controversial birther conspiracy theory and publicized by four mainstream news organizations (CBS, CNN, National Public Radio, and the *New York Times*) confirmed that Donald Trump was by far the single most publicly visible birther promoter during the nineteen months from January 1, 2009, through July 31, 2011. As figure 3.3 shows, with 12 percent, Trump was the most frequently covered individual in the mainstream media making assertions about President Obama's birthplace. Taken together, he and fellow birther conspiracists constituted 18 percent of the sources in these reports. As usual, media personnel (reporters, columnists, program hosts, etc.) dominated, with 40 percent, the largest share of sources expressing their views on the topic. It is also of interest that Republican sources accounted for 15 percent of the total compared with only 5 percent for Democrats, probably because Tea Partiers and Republicans were the most politically connected to—and had a stake in—the anti-Obama rumors.[75] This finding was confirmed by an investigation by staffers at the *Washington Post*, who

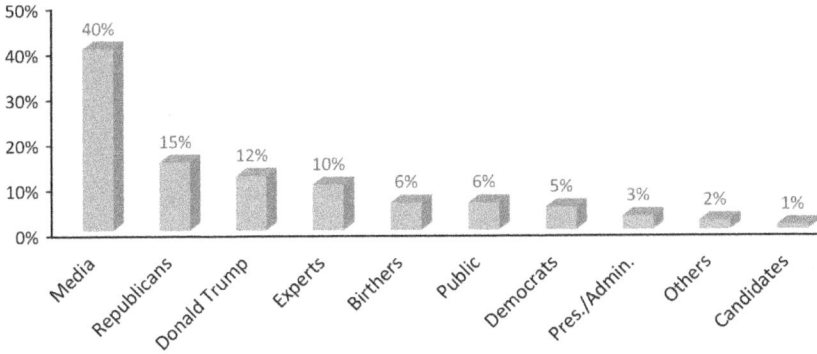

FIGURE 3.3 Sources in mainstream media birther coverage (CNN, CBS, NYT, NPR, January 2009–July 2011).

Source: Compiled by the authors.

found that the public spread of birther (and Obama-is-a-Muslim) rumors involved "a high degree of cueing from prominent Republican politicians, primarily members of Congress and or political candidates."[76]

What about the content of these birther messages in the media? Of the pertinent messages in the news, 64 percent were in fact critical of the conspiracy theory and of those who promoted these rumors. Media personnel provided the most, and the most critical, assessments and evaluations. Still, nearly one-third (30 percent) of all positions expressed in the news were supportive of the anti-Obama conspiracy theory, with the remaining 6 percent neutral or ambiguous. Assessing each full article and program segment, our content coders evaluated 70 percent as all or mostly negative, 29 percent as balanced or ambiguous, and only 1 percent as all or mostly supportive. What else would one expect when responsible news organizations report about unsubstantiated political rumors and an absurd partisan conspiracy theory?

Other rumors received attention as well; namely, questions about President Obama's "true" religion. But since Trump did not dwell on this controversy at the time, there was far less media attention. Nevertheless, in the four and a half years we examined, six leading media organizations

TABLE 3.3 Media stories/aired segments about or mentioning Obama's "true" religion, 2008–2012

	NYT	CBS	CNN	FOX	MSNBC	NPR	TOTAL
2008	31	4	91	22	42	30	220
2009	1	0	7	2	7	4	21
2010	9	4	47	17	23	6	106
2011	2	0	14	8	13	3	41
2012	12	1	17	13	40	5	88
Total	55	10	176	62	125	48	476

Source: Data compiled from Lexis-Nexis by the authors.

publicized a total of 476 articles or program segments about the controversy concerning Obama's religion (see table 3.3). Again, the three cable networks covered these rumors most often, with a combined volume of 363 segments, compared with 113 articles/segments for the *New York Times*, National Public Radio, and CBS. Among the cable networks, CNN aired 176, MSNBC 125, and Fox 62 such segments.

While the mainstream media repeatedly reported that Trump had questioned whether or not Obama was a Christian or implied that he was in reality a Muslim, this claim was not high on his attack agenda. Other nationally known figures got far more attention regarding this theory than the future forty-fifth President. Franklin Graham, a prominent evangelist and son of the influential Christian leader Billy Graham, received a great deal of news media coverage when he questioned Obama's religion early in 2012 at the beginning of the GOP's presidential primaries. The following is an excerpt from Graham's appearance on MSNBC's *Morning Joe* program.

> *Franklin Graham:* Under Islamic law, under sharia law, Islam sees him
> as a son of Islam because his father was a Muslim. His grandfather
> was a Muslim. Great-grandfather was a Muslim. And so under
> Islamic law, they—the Muslim world sees Barack Obama as a Muslim,

as a son of Islam. That's just the way it works. That's the way they see him. But of course, he says he didn't grow up that way. He didn't believe in that. He believes in Jesus Christ. So, I accept that. But I'm just saying the Muslim world, Muslim world, Islam, they see him as a son of Islam.

Willie Geist, Msnbc: But you do not believe he's a Muslim.

Graham: No. No.

Geist: Categorically not a Muslim.

Graham: Well, I can't say categorically . . .

Graham: Islam has gotten a free pass under Obama. Islamists are taking control of the Middle East. And people like Mubarak, who was a dictator, but he kept the peace with Israel—and the minorities, the Christian minorities in Egypt, were protected. Now those Christian minorities throughout the entire Arab world are under attack.

And in "Newsweek" magazine last week, cover story was the massacre of the Christians in the Islamic world from Europe all the way through the Middle East, Africa, into Asia and Oceania. Muslims are killing Christians. And we need to be forcing—and the president could come out and make a statement demanding that if these countries do not protect their minorities, no more foreign aid from the United States.[77]

Graham's remarks were prominently reported in print, radio, and television news, with the latter often playing video excerpts. More than nine years later, a rough Google search on Franklin Graham and questions related to Obama's religion produces well over one million results—many flagging news reports.

Rick Santorum, who competed in the 2012 GOP primaries, was also covered intensely after he appeared to leave open the question of whether President Obama was a Christian or Muslim at a campaign stop in Lady Lake, Florida. After a woman said, "Obama is a devout Muslim" and asked Santorum why he (Obama) was still president, the former U.S. senator did not correct her. He replied, "I am doing my best to get him out of the government right now. He uniformly ignores the Constitution."[78] This exchange was widely reported, as was another remark that Santorum made soon thereafter. In Ohio he told a crowd at a Tea Party event that President

Obama embraced "some phony theology. Oh, not a theology based on the Bible. A different theology." In response to a wave of criticism by pundits, Santorum quickly reversed course, telling CBS's Bob Schieffer, "I don't question the president's faith."[79]

Most Americans did not get the bulk of the relevant information here from Facebook, Twitter, or other social media, and less so from sites devoted to creating and/or perpetuating rumors and conspiracy theories. As noted earlier, television, cable, and the online news of mainstream newspapers, broadcast, and TV organizations remained the main sources of news. And as mainstream media report on controversial topics, including conspiracy theories, they do not simply inform their readers, listeners, and viewers; they also cue them to seek additional information from other internet sources, including search engines through Google.

Just as we found very strong correlations between the volume of birther and Obama-is-a-Muslim conspiracies on the WorldNetDaily site over time and the searches on Google about these conspiracy theories, we also found such relationships between the mainstream media volume of rumors concerning Obama's birthplace and religion and searches on Google for those two topics. As figure 3.4 shows, the correlation over time between the combined volume of segments about or mentioning birtherism on the three cable networks (CNN, Fox News, and MSNBC) was strong ($r = .85$) and nearly as strong a relationship ($r = .78$) between the volume of three print and broadcast media (CBS News, National Public Radio, and *New York Times*) and Google Trends, respectively. Taken together, the trends in the six media organizations' volume of coverage of the birther conspiracy theory were close to identical to the results for Google Trends search data for birther rumors ($r = .99$).

Turning to the mainstream media's yearly reporting on the rumors about Obama's "true" religion and Google searches on this topic during the same period (see figure 3.5), we find strong associations between the three cable networks (CNN, Fox News, and MSNBC) and Google searches on the same topic ($r = .88$). This correlation was even stronger for the three print and broadcast news organizations (CBS, National Public Radio, and *New York Times*; $r = .96$).

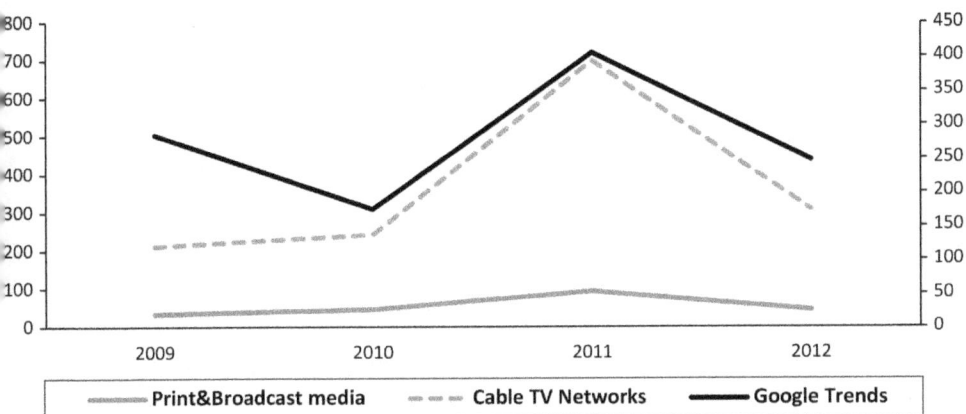

FIGURE 3.4 Mainstream media birther volume and Google Trends.

Note: The left axis shows News volume, number of stories, the right axis shows Google trends

Source: Lexis-Nexis and Google Trends, compiled by the authors.

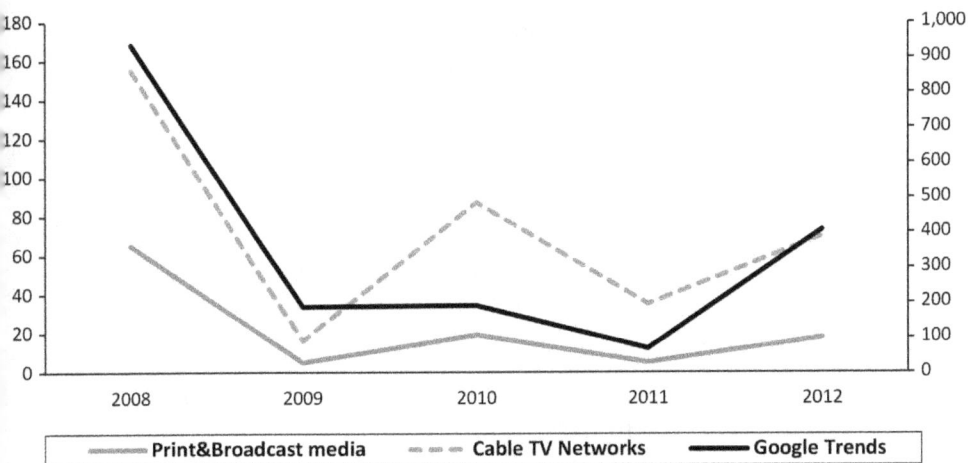

FIGURE 3.5 Mainstream media volume on Obama's rumored religion and Google Trends.

Note: The left axis shows News volume, number of stories, the right axis shows Google trends

Source: Lexis-Nexis and Google Trends, compiled by the authors.

It is noteworthy that the volume of coverage of the more partisan cable networks and the less partisan print and broadcast media organizations was more closely related to the trends of Google searches concerning the conspiracy theories about Obama's birthplace and religion than was WorldNetDaily, the more extreme-right online rumor mill when it came to such subjects.

PARTISANSHIP AND ANTI-OBAMA RUMORS

Research by Uscinski and Parent found that during more than a century worth of conspiracy theories, Democrats were just as susceptible as Republicans to becoming diehard conspiracists.[80] In the twenty-first century, both the overwhelmingly liberal 9/11 "Truthers" and the overwhelmingly conservative birthers were motivated by their conspiratorial predispositions and their ideological and partisan preferences. But after Barack Obama won the presidential election in November 2008, the dominant political rumors and conspiracy theories were tailor-made for diehard conservatives among Republicans. Based on their research, and as we consider further in chapter 5, Todd Hartman and Adam Newmark concluded that "predispositions such as ideology, partisanship, and race affect how citizens feel about Obama, which in turn motivates them to accept misinformation about the president. We also find that these implicit associations increase the probability of stating that Obama is likely a Muslim."[81] Thus, conservatives and, overwhelmingly, white Republicans were more inclined than liberals and Democrats to believe that Obama was a Muslim. The embrace of this conspiracy theory had nothing to do with the political sophistication of individuals. Although they identified Obama's religion correctly, when explicitly asked, politically sophisticated persons were "neither more nor less likely than unsophisticated individuals to automatically associate Obama with Islam."[82]

During Obama's second term, nearly half of "consistent conservatives" relied on Fox News as their major source for government and political news, with "local news" far behind in second place.[83] Not surprisingly, many

Republicans held the same or similar convictions on public affairs, rumors, and conspiracy theories as the network's most popular prime-time hosts. The conspiratorial predispositions and far-right ideological beliefs of the Republican Fox News audience were reinforced by voices in their favorite prime-time opinion shows.

As figure 3.6 displays, at the heights of the public debate about Barack Obama's true birthplace in the run-up to the 2010 midterm elections and Donald Trump's public promotion of birther rumors in early 2011, two in five Republicans believed that the president was born in another country, with Independents and Democrats far less inclined to express this view. Like other students of rumors and conspiracy theories, Sunstein and Vermeule found that "a central feature of conspiracy theories is that they are extremely resistant to correction."[84] But after Obama released his original long-form birth certificate at the end of April 27, 2011, there was a significant decrease among those Republicans who believed the false claims

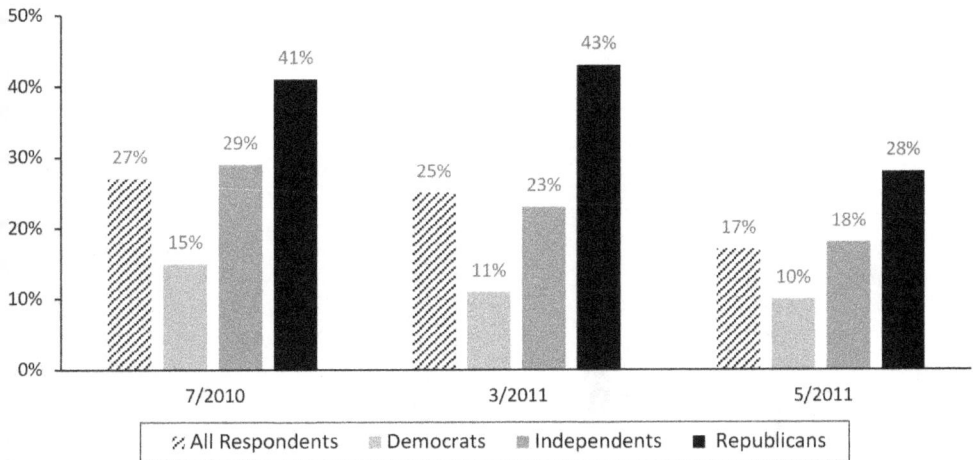

FIGURE 3.6 Percentage of Americans believing Barack Obama was born in another country.

Note: Percent Definitely/Probably born in another country.

Source: CNN/ORC.

about the president's birthplace. The survey, conducted immediately after the public had online access to the original certificate, showed a 15 percentage point decline in Republican birthers compared with the last poll before the release of the document.

The initial rumors about President Obama's "real" religion in 2008 and 2009 found more resonance among Republicans than Democrats and Independents. But the differences between partisans believing that Obama was a Muslim were quite modest. However, as figure 3.7 shows, during the 2010 midterm campaigns, there were significant upticks among Independents (from 10 percent in 2009 to 18 percent in 2010), even more so among Republicans (from 17 percent in 2009 to 31 percent in 2010) who believed that Obama was a Muslim. While there were no meaningful opinion changes during the 2012 presidential campaign, drastic increases occurred among all three partisan groups about three months after Donald Trump officially entered the race, with 15 percent of Democrats, 29 percent of Independents, and a striking 43 percent of Republicans expressing their belief that Obama was a Muslim, not a Christian, although there were no facts supporting these rumors.

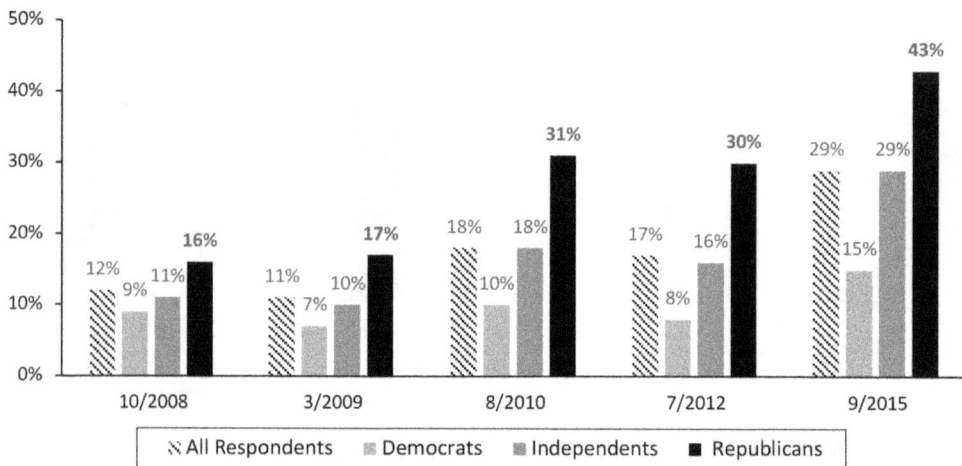

FIGURE 3.7 Percentage of Americans believing Obama is a Muslim.

Sources: Pew Research Center 2008–12, CNN/ORC 2015.

MEDIA SYMBIOSIS AND ANTI-OBAMA RUMORS

Our research into the dispersion of anti-Obama birther and Obama-is-a-Muslim conspiracy theories confirmed the interconnectivity within and between the various communication forms that we also established with respect to the rise of the Tea Party in the previous chapter. Right-wing extremist internet super-spreaders of anti-Obama rumors, digital discussion boards, and tweet productions by celebrities like Donald Trump were not relegated to a separate media space. Instead, they were part and parcel of the whole communication environment in which old and new media fed off each other. Even the most unlikely claims about President Obama's birthplace and religion made in cyberspace, right-wing radio, cable talk shows, or infotainment broadcast programs entered the gates of legacy media, which could not afford to ignore the cutthroat competition for audiences.

Anti-Obama rumors first gained traction on the internet, but they eventually got ample attention in cable, other broadcast, and print media, including the most respected news organizations. "When the origins of many influential news accounts fall little short of propaganda, the result is to invite popular self-selection of convenient truth," Bennett argued. "The outcome is a disorienting democratization of truth"[85] We found that public opinion trends concerning the two dominant anti-Obama conspiracy theories confirmed the dissonance between facts and misinformation within contemporary America's polarized public and private sphere.

In their compelling study of conspiracy theories in the second half of the twenty-first century, Nancy Rosenblum and Russell Muirhead examined the fast-spreading, ludicrous conspiracy claims that lacked any grounding in reality—among them the anti-Obama rumors that were closely tied to the Tea Party movement. When they started their research project, the authors anticipated that conspiracy theories would result in violence."[86] Their expectation was borne out by cases of political violence during Trump's presidency and, eventually, the political violence of January 6, 2021, when fanatic QAnon conspiracists were among the crowd that forcefully breached the U.S. Capitol.

4

DONALD TRUMP'S INCENDIARY RHETORIC AND POLITICAL VIOLENCE

On September 29, 2019, with his impeachment looming, President Donald Trump (@realDonaldTrump) retweeted a warning by the evangelical pastor Robert Jeffress: "If the Democrats are successful in removing the President from office it will cause a Civil War like fracture in this Nation from which our Country will never heal." Two days later, U.S. Representative Louie Gohmert, a Republican for Texas, warned Democrats that their "coup" was "pushing America into a civil war."[1] On far-right websites Trump supporters suggested drastic and even violent actions against the "enemy" within. Some warned that they may need to exercise their Second Amendment rights—in other words, take up arms against the traitors. Responding to one of Trump's Twitter attacks on Adam Schiff, the leading House member in the impeachment inquiry, his followers seconded the president's rhetorical assaults. One male commenter attacked Schiff as "a co-conspiratory in a coup attempt. This is treason." That same day, a fifty-two-year-old man in Tucson, Arizona, left a death threat on Schiff's voicemail. "I'm gonna f'ing blow your brains out," he warned.[2] The would-be attacker told police officers that "he watches Fox News and likely was upset at something that he saw on the news." He also stated "he strongly dislikes the Democrats, and feels they are to blame for the country's political issues."[3] The police found an AR-15 assault rifle, two pistols, and seven hundred rounds of ammunition in his residence.[4]

Although these examples of hate speech and threats of violence seemed shocking, they were merely iterations of Trumpian rhetoric and signposts for significant increases in right-extreme violence and school bullying in the United States. As demonstrated in the previous two chapters, activist Tea Party members and hardcore anti-Obama conspiracy theorists used angry, aggressive, and even violent rhetoric to push their causes.

We argue in this chapter, supported by evidence, that these uncivil speech patterns that Tea Partiers and conspiracists introduced into the political discourse foreshadowed and even paved the way for Donald Trump's more incendiary rhetoric once he became a presidential candidate and took office. Our research found, furthermore, that Trump's online and offline hate speech corresponded with his supporters' aggressive rhetoric, violent threats, and actual violence against his and their declared "enemies"—most of all, minorities, the news media, and oppositional politicians. As a key part of the interconnected political communication loop, the media conveyed the toxic public discourse and often amplified the most outrageous statements by Trump and his staunchest followers.

TRUMP'S DIVISIVE AND VIOLENT DEMAGOGUERY

Donald Trump has been characterized and criticized as a populist and autocrat. He can certainly, first of all, be called a demagogue who, like all demagogues, has distinguished between his loyal in-group on the one hand and disloyal out-group(s) on the other. This sharp demarcation allows demagogues to stir "hatred of the outgroup(s) . . . through scapegoating."[5] Trump proved himself a master at scapegoating others for all kinds of political, social, and cultural problems, with Barack Obama, the Democrats, the liberal "deep state," immigrants, and refugees high on his list. For example, when asked whether he would take responsibility for his administration's failure to provide an efficient national COVID-19 testing program, he first blamed his predecessor, Obama, and a particular set of circumstances. Then he said emphatically, "I don't take responsibility at all."[6]

According to one expert in this area, "demagoguery may be described as the process whereby skilled speakers and writers seek to influence public opinion by employing the traditional tools of rhetoric with complete indifference to truth."[7] This supports Patricia Robert-Miller's suggestion that "demagoguery is a subset of propaganda."[8] While demagogues love mass rallies to unleash their usually divisive rants and relish the waves of applause of "their" people, they also employ the most effective communication technologies to carry their propaganda.

Media scholars distinguish between communication as transmission, the technical dimension devoted to disseminating information further and faster, and communication as ritual, the most persuasive content of media. According to James Carey, ritual communication refers to the "sacred ceremony that draws persons together in fellowship and communality."[9] This assumes that at particular times, especially during natural or human-caused disasters, whole communities or whole nations can be drawn together by ritual communication, such as invoking shared values, patriotic sentiments, and showing of the flag. It is telling that the U.S. flag was by far the most often posted emoji in President Trump's tweets (33.2 percent) and in his followers' responses (29 percent).[10]

However, as Carey noted, there are also "rituals of excommunication" that pit groups against each other.[11] Trump used his spoken and tweeted words ceaselessly to draw his loyal followers together in perceived communality while excluding out-groups from those representing "we, the people." During the 2016 presidential campaign, he said, "the only important thing is unification of the people—because the other people don't mean anything."[12] In June 2020, he gave a televised speech in Tulsa, Oklahoma, that was labeled as the opening salvo of his reelection campaign. The following excerpts from this speech demonstrate how Trump celebrated his base of supporters as good Americans while simultaneously excommunicating the evil "others" from the community of real patriots:

> You are warriors, thank you.
>
> We had some very bad people outside; they were doing bad things. They got rid of a lot of bad people that were there for a long time [they were in fact peaceful "Black Lives Matter" protesters]. Sort of like me in Washington, draining the swamp. I never knew it was so deep. But it's happening. It's happening, I never knew it was so deep. It's deep and thick and a lot of bad characters.
>
> I stand before you today to declare the silent majority is stronger than ever before. They want to demolish our heritage.
>
> And when you see those lunatics all over the streets, it's damn nice to have arms. Damn nice. . . . The right to keep and bear arms, we'll protect your second amendment. Above all, we will never stop fighting for the sacred values that bind us together as one America, we will support, protect, and defend the Constitution of the United States.
>
> Our incredible success in rebuilding America stands in stark contrast to the extremism and destruction and violence of the radical left.
>
> We are one movement, one people, one family, and one glorious nation under God. . . . Together we will make America wealthy again, we will make America strong again, we will make America proud again, we will make America safe again, and we will make America great again.[13]

This was textbook demagoguery. By bringing up the right to bear arms, Trump issued a thinly veiled call to arms against the enemy within. As one student of rhetoric noted, "violence manifests itself in pinning labels on others and marking political, ethnic, racial, confessional, subcultural, sexist words. Violent speech emphasizes alienating differences between persons, social groups, or communities. Violent speech demarcates."[14]

An old children's rhyme claims, "sticks and stones may break my bones but words will never hurt me!" The rhyme's message is misleading because certain spoken and written words can have psychological and physical effects. As Justice Oliver Wendell Holmes, Jr., wrote in a Supreme Court opinion about one hundred years ago, "falsely shouting fire in a theater and causing a panic" would not be covered by free speech rights.[15] The sociologist Mary R. Jackman concluded that "verbal and written actions that derogate, defame, or humiliate an individual or group may inflict substantial psychological, social, or material injuries without being as conspicuous or flagrant as physical violence."[16] But the legal scholar Mari Matsuda speaks of "violence of the word," which, in the extreme, can inflict physical injury, in that "victims of vicious hate propaganda have experienced physiological symptoms and emotional distress ranging from fear in the gut, rapid pulse rate and difficulty in breathing, nightmares, post-traumatic stress disorder, hypertension, psychosis, and suicide."[17]

One form of such aggressive behavior is bullying, which is committed so often in American schools, places of work, and elsewhere that experts more recently began to warn of a bullying epidemic.[18] Bullying occurs in real and virtual spaces. Perpetrators and victims of verbal (and sometimes physical) bullying are children, adolescents, and adults, with the bully typically targeting weaker victims. When influential persons, such as political and religious leaders, engage in demagoguery that vilifies political opponents, journalists and whole news organizations, ethnic, racial, and religious groups, the consequences by far transcend the hate speech of the bully next door and of social media platforms. It is ironic that Donald Trump inspired bullying, whereas First Lady Melania Trump championed an antibullying campaign. Targets of hate speech are particularly vulnerable when the aggressive rhetoricians are powerful individuals in the public sphere with fanatical followers. As one scholar noted, "The linguistic violence executed by power is particularly dangerous and is manifested in purposeful confusion and temptation based on supremacy and predominance."[19]

An important device in the demagogue's linguistic toolbox is blemishing the humanity of groups who do not belong to the in-group. The goal is to reduce "an entire segment of the population into profligate, pernicious, and dastardly subhumans."[20] Trump repeatedly called immigrants "animals"— and not only when he singled out Latinos in the criminal MS-13 gang.

Demanding tougher immigration laws, President Trump said on one occasion , "We have people coming into the country or trying to come in, we're stopping a lot of them. . . . You wouldn't believe how bad these people are. These aren't people. These are animals."[21] He repeatedly labeled "Never Trump" Republicans as Democrats, alleged members of "the deep state," and journalists as "human scum" or "scum."[22] As Albert Bandura noted, "dehumanized persons are treated much more punitively than persons who have not been divested of their human qualities." Thus, by calling Hillary Clinton "the devil," Trump made it easier for his supporters to join forces in chanting, "Lock Her Up!" "Lock Her Up!" By attacking Adam Schiff as "human scum," Trump disengaged from moral norms and influenced some of his fanatical followers. When he unleashed tweet attacks on Black Lives Matter protesters and threatened them with "law and order" measures, he was echoed by devoted supporters with responses like these.

> @realDonaldTrump I don't say this lightly, Mr. President: But, people are acting like wild animals, victimizing whomever they please. And, wild animals only respect strength. It's time to be strong. Send in the military. Anyone being violent, make an example of them, with lead (June 3, 2020).
>
> @realDonaldTrump Please just deploy the military and take control of these animals who are ruining our cities! (June 3, 2020).
>
> @realDonaldTrump Please use the army against these treasonous animals (June 3, 2020).
>
> @realDonaldTrump please Mister kill all that's animals please (June 4, 2020).
>
> @realDonaldTrump So sad! These animals have no respect for human life and not fooling around (June 4, 2020).[23]

In fall 2020, during a campaign stop in Minnesota, President Trump invoked the pseudoscientific eugenics saga of white genetic superiority. "You have good genes. A lot of it is about the genes, isn't it, don't you believe? The racehorse theory. You think we're so different? You have good genes in Minnesota," he told his almost all-white audience. He warned his supporters that in case of rival Joe Biden's election victory, their state would become "a refugee camp" filled with "Islamic extremists"—an insult directed at Minnesota's more than 50,000 Somalian immigrants.[24]

Trump's branding slogan, "Make America Great Again," was a metaphor for a return to white Christian dominance of earlier times and the subjugation of racial, ethnic, and religious minorities. This was the ultimate division between "good" and "bad" groups. His promise to build a wall along the U.S. border with Mexico and the rallying screams of his followers, "Build the Wall! Build the Wall!," stood for stopping nonwhites from coming into the country. White nationalists understood Trump's dog whistles from the outset. One sure sign was that white supremacists and neo-Nazis like David Duke, a former Ku Klux Klan grand wizard, and Andrew Anglin, the creator of the racist website "Daily Stormer," endorsed Trump early in his run for the presidency.

RED MEAT FOR ANTI-SEMITES AND OTHER RACISTS

On October 13, 2016, three weeks before Election Day, Trump gave a speech in West Palm Beach that reiterated his major campaign topics. While never mentioning the Republican Party, which had nominated him, he did invoke the "movement" nine times. Twice he repeated the familiar campaign theme, "We will take back this country for you and we will make America great again." He attacked "immigration," "illegal immigration," and, not surprisingly, the "corrupt" political establishment, the news media in general, the "failing" *New York Times* in particular, and, reminiscent of Joe McCarthy, the State Department for engaging "in a massive coverup of widespread criminal activity."[25]

But whereas that rhetoric was a rehash of earlier campaign rants, at this particular rally, Trump threw red meat to racists as he had not done before, as in the following excerpt from his speech:

Hillary Clinton meets in secret with international banks to plot the destruction of U.S. sovereignty in order to enrich these global financial powers, her special-interest friends and her donors.

This election will determine whether we are a free nation or whether we have only the illusion of democracy, but are in fact controlled by a small handful of global special interests rigging the system. . . . The establishment and their media enablers will control over this nation through means that are very well known. Anyone who challenges their control is deemed a sexist, a racist, a xenophobe, and morally deformed.[26]

While many Americans may not have decoded these sentences, the white supremacy/neo-Nazi community heard Trump's messages clearly. His allegations smacked of these circles' doctrine; namely, that global banking and media elites, both controlled by Jews, are in cahoots with unpatriotic liberals like Hillary Clinton to destroy white American and Western civilization under the guise of multiculturalism.

The Daily Stormer's Andrew Anglin, whose website signaled its racist content with dashboard categories like "Jewish Problem" and "Race War," was euphoric. After announcing in the headline of his post that "Donald Trump is literally Hitler," he ended with a one-sentence summary of Trump's speech: "He said a lot of bad things about globalism, the media, the banks, and lobbyists, and those are all very J—Sheeeeit."[27] The responses by readers reflected Anglin's racism. A female commenter wrote, "They've tried and tried to break the bonds of white unity all over the globe, and they had us cornered for a few decades, but we see, every day, signs that our racial solidarity is coming back with a vengeance." Posting a swastika under his comment, one man rejoiced, "I was like, literally, tearing my eyes out watching Trump's speech! I literally exploded. It was like literally 1933. He's literally Hitler!"[28]

School bullies picked up on the rise of white supremacy voices and slogans. A teacher in Colorado reported that after Trump's election victory, "seventh-grade white boys [were] yelling, 'Heil Trump.'" Another teacher witnessed, for the first time in fifteen years of teaching, swastikas "appearing all over school furniture."[29] These incidents did not fade away during Trump's presidency. In the fall of 2018, a teacher in the state of Washington reported, "Student taped a piece of paper with a swastika on my classroom wall. This was a couple of days after the shooting at the Tree of Life Synagogue, and I am Jewish." An elementary school student in New York said, "I'm a fan of Hitler! God sent Hitler down to kill the Jews because they nailed Jesus to the cross."[30] In the days, months, and years following Trump's election victory, the words school bullies used most often were, according to one report, "the 'n-word,' various versions of 'build the wall' and 'go back to [insert foreign country name here, usually Mexico].' The most common hate symbol: swastikas."[31]

In August 2017, white nationalist leaders organized a two-day "Unite the Right" rally in Charlottesville, Virginia, in an effort to amalgamate various right-extreme groups under a strong alternative right or alt-right umbrella. Carrying arms, waving Confederate flags, and displaying Nazi symbols, the marchers chanted "Jews will not replace us!" and "blood and soil" (the translation of the racist Nazi slogan *Blut und Boden*"). In his speech, David Duke summarized American neo-Nazis' core belief. "The truth is," he said, "the American media, and the American political system, and the American Federal Reserve, is dominated by a tiny minority: the Jewish Zionist cause."[32]

After clashes between Unite the Right crowds and counterprotesters, among them Antifa (for "antifascist") members, one white supremacist deliberately drove his car at high speed into a crowd of peaceful protesters, killing one woman and injuring nineteen people. Two days later, reading from a teleprompter, President Trump condemned racism as evil and called out the KKK, neo-Nazis, and white supremacists. But a day later, during a press conference, he said unscripted, "You had some very bad people in that group, but you also had people that were very fine people, on both sides."[33] He added that "there was a group on one side that was bad, and you had a group on the other side that was also very violent." Alt-right leaders and followers liked what they heard.

For neo-Nazis, the American billionaire investor and philanthropist George Soros exemplified members of the alleged Jewish cabal poised to dominate U.S and global financial and political interests. Soros's generous donations to liberal causes at home and to prodemocracy forces abroad put him center stage in numerous conspiracy theories. In the weeks before the 2018 midterm elections, when President Trump warned voters of (nonexistent) huge caravans of Central American migrants moving toward America's southern border, conspiracy theorists claimed that Soros's Open Society Foundation paid migrants to join the caravans. During a reception for young Black conservatives in the White House, Trump attacked globalists for "cheating American workers." When his guests shouted "Soros" and "lock him up," the president responded, "lock him up!"[34] And at the height of the 2020 Black Lives Matter protests, which demanded the defunding of police departments, online conspiracy theorists accused Soros once again of financing the mass protests—again without any evidence.

President Trump retweeted anti-Soros claims, among them this item published originally by Breitbart.com: "RT @BreitbartNews REVEALED: An anti-deportation group partnering with George Soros's Open Society Foundation is one of the groups behind the 'defund the police' movement." Trump's followers seconded the allegation with a multitude of tweet responses, such as these.

#AntifaAreFascist #AntifaTerrorists #SorosForPrison #NoPurpleRevolution #noNWO #SorosForPrison #NoPurpleRevolution #noNWO

Is the call for the arrest of George Soros and freezing of all his assets coming up next? No mercy for terrorists! #Antifaterrorists #ArrestGeorgeSoros.

Neo-Nazi and white supremacy dogma was at home on the U.S. president's Twitter page. Around the same time, Trump posted a video of supporters in Florida shouting "White Power!" with the approving comment, "Thank you to the great people of The Villages. The Radical Left Do Nothing Democrats will Fall in the Fall. Corrupt Joe is shot. See you soon!!!"[35]

Starting with Trump's first election campaign through his presidency and beyond, anti-Semitic incidents, from assaults to harassment and vandalism, increased significantly in the United States (see figure 4.1)

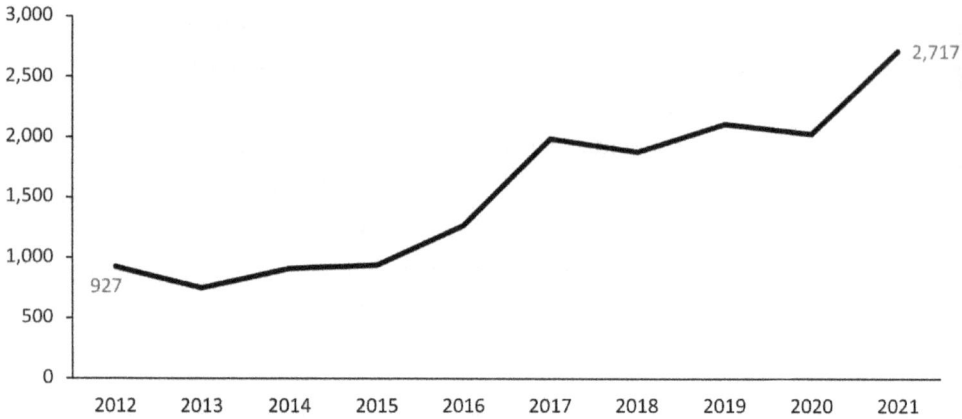

FIGURE 4.1 The rise of anti-Semitic incidents in the United States.

Source: Anti-Defamation League [ADL], 2022.

VILIFYING PRESIDENT OBAMA AND OTHER BLACKS

After Barack Obama won the presidential election in 2008, white Supremacists were devastated. The presence of a Black man in the Oval Office
meant for them the end of "their" America. The Aryan Nation's website displayed a tombstone with the inscription: "United States of America. Born:
July 4, 1776. Died: Nov. 4, 2008." During Obama's two terms in office and
thereafter, white supremacists' racist attacks against the first Black American president never subsided; they vilified and dehumanized him. And
nobody publicly poured more oil on the flames of racist hate against Blacks
than Donald Trump. First, as described in the previous chapter, he became
the public face of the so-called birther conspiracy theory, which depicted
Obama as an illegitimate president for allegedly been born not in the
United States but in Kenya. Second, as a presidential candidate and president, he accused Obama of being in bed with Islamic terrorists—an allusion
to many birthers' belief that Obama was not a Christian but a Muslim.

The fact that a Black man was the president of the United States of
America was unacceptable for racists, and it motivated them to invent

reasons to attack and dehumanize him as an illegitimate imposter. White nationalists' rhetorical assaults against President Obama were also metaphorical bouts against the Black race in general. And Donald Trump led the public charge as the head birther conspiracy theorist.

From late 2011, when he began to question Obama's birthplace, through mid-September 2015, when he was declared a presidential candidate, Trump devoted 116 tweets to promoting the absurd birther conspiracy theory. In addition to his tweet wave, he made this accusation in numerous appearances on cable television. Along the way, he also indicated that President Obama was a Muslim by calling him Barack Hussein Obama or tweeting, "When I was 18, people called me Donald Trump. When he was 18, @BarackObama was Barry Soweto." In another tweet @realDonaldTrump, he wrote, "Attention all hackers: You are hacking everything else so please hack Obama's college records (destroyed?) and check 'place of birth.'" The indication was that Obama had applied to college and law school as a foreign student. Trump's followers responded with tweeted comments like, "we all know he's hiding from the truth! He's a communist" and "This Barry is one shady individual," or worse. In late 2015, when on the campaign trail in New Hampshire, Trump said, "right," when a supporter screamed "We have a problem in this country. It's called Muslims. We know our current president is one."[36] And during a campaign stop in the summer of 2016, Trump told the crowd, "In many respects, you know, they [terrorists] honor President Obama. He is the founder of ISIS."[37]

After the death of Anthony Scalia in 2015, President Obama and the First Lady attended a memorial service for the Supreme Court judge but not his funeral. For Trump, it was an opportunity to once again question Obama's religion. "I wonder whether President Obama would have attended the funeral of Justice Scalia if it were held in a Mosque?" he tweeted. One of his followers answered his question, "Yes he would have attended if Judge Scalia's name was Mohammad Scalia."

Trump's obsession with attacking and denigrating Obama as president and ex-president is documented in his tweet history. In the six years before Trump announced his candidacy in June 2015, a stunning 50.8 percent of his tweets that we identified as rhetorical attacks denigrated President

Obama. During the four years of Trump's presidency, 2.8 percent of his attack tweets targeted his predecessor. Even during the presidential primaries and general campaign in the run-up to the 2016 election, when Trump competed first with fellow Republicans and then with Hillary Clinton, Obama remained one of Trump's top villains and was on the receiving end of 6.7 percent of candidate Trump's hateful tweets. Not surprisingly, during that same period, 9.1 percent of these attack tweets vilified "Crooked Hillary" and 7.7 percent, Hillary Clinton."[38]

In the spring of 2020, when polls revealed growing public dissatisfaction with Trump as the nation faced the deadly COVID-19 pandemic and a looming recession, the president invented a fake "Obamagate" scandal in an effort to distract the masses: The sitting president accused his predecessor of criminal wrongdoing. "OBAMAGATE makes Watergate look small time!" he tweeted. Those supporting #Obamagate tweeted a video showing America's first Black president being arrested by a smiling U.S. Attorney General William Barr with President Trump walking along as Obama is led to jail.

Perhaps all this was not surprising given that for years, Trump had left signposts that he equated Blacks with thugs and criminals. In 1989, after five teenagers of color were arrested for the brutal rape of a white woman in New York's Central Park, the then private businessman Trump took out full-page ads in four New York newspapers demanding the reinstatement of the death penalty. Even when another prison inmate confessed to the crime and the Central Park Five were exonerated, Trump attacked them as guilty. And after a documentary about the case was aired, Trump, by then birther-in-chief, tweeted, "The Central Park Five documentary was a one sided piece of garbage that didn't explain the horrific crimes of these young men while in the park."

Several weeks later he upped the ante by claiming that almost all crimes in New York City were committed by Blacks, tweeting, "According to Bill O'Reilly, 80 percent of all the shootings in New York City are blacks—if you add Hispanics, that figure goes to 98 percent. 1 percent white." A few minutes later, he generalized the "statistics" from New York City, tweeting, "Sadly, the overwhelming amount of violent crime in our major cities is committed by Blacks and Hispanics—a tough subject-must be discussed." These false numbers were propagated by white supremacists, who also claimed that most crimes in America were committed by criminals of color and almost all victims were white. In 2015, when a riot broke out in Baltimore in response to the violent death of a Black man in police custody, Trump tweeted, "Our great African American President hasn't exactly had a positive impact on the thugs who are so happily and openly destroying Baltimore!"

Nothing changed for the better during Trump's presidency. In early 2018, a day after he had received Norwegian Prime Minister Erna Solberg in the White House, President Trump met with Republican and Democratic senators to discuss the fate of young undocumented immigrants, or so-called dreamers. On this occasion he left no doubt about his distaste for Blacks and other people of color. Referring to Africa and countries like Haiti and El Salvador, the president asked, "Why are we having all those people from shitholes coming here? Why couldn't we just take in immigrants, say, from Norway?"[39]

When cities, towns, and counties all over America and in many other parts of the world experienced Black Lives Matter demonstrations, most of them peaceful, President Trump called the protesters killers, terrorists, arsonists, anarchists, thugs, hoodlums, looters, and ANTIFA in his Twitter feeds.

Three years into Trump's presidency, 65 percent of Black Americans told pollsters, "It is a bad time to be a black person in America."[40] According to the same survey, 80 percent of Black Americans believed that Trump was a racist. One respondent said, "He has taken hatred against people of color, in general, from the closet to the front porch."

Even the youngest Black Americans suffered from the increase of upfront racism. An elementary school teacher in Georgia recounted her experiences after Trump's election victory in sorrow. "This is my 21st year of teaching. This is the first time I've had a student call another student the n-word," she reported. "This incident occurred the day after a conference with the offender's mother. During the conference, the mother made her support of Trump known and expressed her hope that 'the blacks' would soon 'know their place again.'"[41]

HATE SPEECH AND HISPANICS

Among the groups that Donald Trump singled out as being existential threats to America's public safety and to "America as we know it" were Mexican Americans and others of Latino descent. He also badgered Latinos abroad, who, according to Trump, needed to be stopped from "invading" the country. Announcing his candidacy for the U.S. presidency in June 2016, Trump immediately went on the offensive. Aware that his announcement was reported as "breaking news," Trump wasted no time to attacking the undesirable "others" when he intoned, "When Mexico sends its people, they're not sending their best. They're not sending you. They're not sending you. They're sending people that have lots of problems, and they're bringing those problems with us. They're bringing drugs. They're bringing crime. They're rapists. And some, I assume, are good people."[42]

If elected president, he promised, "I would build a great wall, and nobody builds walls better than me, believe me, and I'll build them very inexpensively, I will build a great, great wall on our southern border. And I will have Mexico pay for that wall." These words were just the opening salvo in an election campaign and presidency full of vitriolic propaganda against Mexicans and other Latinos, including the people on the island of Puerto Rico, who—seemingly unknown to Trump—are U.S. citizens.

While Trump's aggressive written and spoken words evoked among Hispanics the perception of being ostracized and disrespected, the hateful discourse was accompanied by government actions and policies harmful to Latinos in America and those trying to seek asylum in the United States. After the unspeakable images of young Latino children held in caged areas in camps near the U.S.-Mexico border were reported in the news, President Trump defended his policy of separating asylum-seeking parents from their children as a deterrent to further border crossings. When asked by a White House reporter about the fate of "undocumented" children waiting in vain to be reunited with their parents, the president showed no compassion; instead, he warned, "Tell people not to come to our country illegally. That's the solution. . . . We have laws. We have borders. Don't come to our country illegally. It's not a good thing."[43]

Writing about anti-immigrant rhetoric in Europe at the end of the twentieth century, one scholar of violent discourse explained, "The increasingly overt but 'merely verbal' aggression against immigrants, refugees and minorities in political and media discourse may effectively curb immigration, encourage discrimination, legitimize inequality and generally violate the human rights of millions of people."[44] In Trump-speak, and in the perception of his followers, the terms "Mexico" and "Mexican(s)" became synonymous with undesirable people from Central America and the Caribbean. Thus, when a white high school teacher in New Jersey told his class of mostly Hispanic students that "he agreed with Donald Trump that Mexicans are bad for the country calling them 'pigs' and 'lazy' the day after the election in 2016," a student from the Dominican Republic "took the teachers' remarks on Mexicans as derogatory for all Latinos."[45] Similarly, words like "wall," "border," "deportation," "invasion," and "caravan" stood metaphorically for white Americans forcing illegal "intruders" back "behind the wall," preventing the invasion of "illegals" across the border into "our" country.

While Trump voiced his negative views about Hispanic immigrants before he entered the political arena as a presidential candidate, he amplified his often derogatory online and offline remarks during the campaign and during his presidency. In a typical tweet of this kind, he summarized his obsession with building a border wall to stop illegal immigrants (who in reality were asylum seekers): "More troops being sent to the Southern Border to stop the attempted Invasion of Illegals, through large Caravans, into our Country. We have stopped the previous Caravans, and we will stop these also. With a Wall it would be soooo much easier and less expensive. Being Built." In another tweet he wrote, "There are a lot of CRIMINALS in the Caravan. We will stop them. Catch and Detain!" One female supporter responded, "Thank you, Mr. President! It's comforting to know that we have a president with America in mind and the people in his heart! May God bless you and keep you safe!" Others simply wrote, "Build the Wall!"

As presidential candidate, Trump mentioned terms like "border," "wall," "border security," "Mexican(s)," "Mexico," "alien," "illegal immigrant," "caravan," and "invasion" in 5.6 percent of his attack tweets directed at Latinos inside or trying to enter the United States. He got even more aggressive in his rhetoric once he was president. During his four years in office, he used those terms in 9 percent of all his tweet attacks. After more than two years in office, Trump expressed ever more extreme ideas for stopping "aliens" from crossing the southern border. In one meeting he demanded that his aides completely close the two-thousand-mile border with Mexico by the next day. According to reports, he suggested illegal and inhumane measures, such as these:

- fortifying the border wall with a water-filled trench stocked with snakes or alligators;
- electrifying the border wall, "with spikes on the top that could pierce human flesh";
- soldiers shooting migrants if they were throwing rocks; or
- soldiers shooting migrants in the legs to slow them down.[46]

Whether made online or offline, Trump's relentless verbal attacks had consequences in the daily lives of Hispanics in America whether they had legal or illegal status.[47] Teachers across the country reported that following Trump's election victory, elementary, middle, and high school students used the terms "deportation" and "wall" more often than any other words when they taunted their Latino peers and other minority students. Thus, according to one teacher, "White high school students interlocked arms and walked together, chanting, 'Build a wall! Build a wall!' while making eye contact with students of color. Colleagues heard children saying, 'Trump won, you're going back to Mexico,' one student going around asking, 'Are you legal?' and another telling a teacher they no longer needed Spanish since Trump was sending all the Mexicans back."[48]

For many Latinos, verbal aggression and harsh government actions and policies against them and their ethnic brethren affected how members of the largest ethnic minority perceived their place in the country and the threat of being deported. Shortly after Trump's election victory, two in five (41 percent) Latinos in the United States told pollsters they were concerned "about their place in America."[49] Nearly two years into Trump's presidency, more than half of ethnic U.S. Hispanics (55 percent) feared that they themselves, a family member, or a friend could be deported. Not surprisingly, a strong majority of illegal Latinos (78 percent) had those worries; it was startling, however, that 65 percent of foreign-born legal residents and 58 percent of foreign-born U.S. citizens of Hispanic descent shared those concerns.[50] In mid-2019, 58 percent of Latinos in the United States said they had personally experienced discrimination based on their ethnicity or race, and 30 percent of those told pollsters they had "feared for their personal safety."[51]

ANTI-MUSLIM RHETORIC AND POLICIES

Similarly, Muslims in America were constantly attacked in Trump's tweets, at rallies, and in off-the-cuff remarks during ad hoc exchanges with the press. He repeatedly claimed that thousands of Muslim Americans living in New Jersey across from the World Trade Center in Manhattan celebrated the destruction of the famous twin towers on September 11, 2001—although there was no evidence for this. Trump retweeted several followers' claims that they saw militant Muslims celebrating the 9/11 attacks right here in America. By keeping his false accusations alive, Trump and his followers tagged Muslim Americans as traitors with allegiances to foreign enemies.

In late 2015, Trump called for prohibiting Muslims from traveling into the United States. In the "Statement on Preventing Muslim Immigration," posted on his official campaign website, he called for "a total and complete shutdown of Muslims entering the United States." The aggressive treatise claimed, "There is great hatred towards Americans by large segments of the Muslim population." Citing a survey of (American) Muslims conducted by a far-right organization, Trump's statement continued: "25 percent of those polled agreed that violence against Americans here in the United States is justified as a part of the global jihad" and 51 percent of those polled, "agreed that Muslims in America should have the choice of being governed according to Shariah." There were no other surveys at the time or thereafter showing that one of four Muslims in America supported Sharia law in the United States.[52]

The Trump-led anti-Muslim propaganda campaign was reminiscent of the verbal attacks on Japanese Americans and Japanese Canadians in the months and years following the Pearl Harbor attacks in 1941. According to Lynn Thiesmeyer, Japanese residents were "linguistically designated [by government officials] as 'enemy aliens,' although such labels or laws were never applied to resident Germans or Italians."[53] Many of them were incarcerated or deported. One U.S. general wrote at the time, "The Japanese race is an enemy race." He claimed that second- and third-generation "Japanese" may have become Americanized but that "the racial strains are undiluted."[54]

When under fire because of his statement, Trump defended his proposed Muslim ban as comparable to President Franklin D. Roosevelt's internment of Japanese Americans. In a television interview, Trump said, "What I'm doing is no different than FDR. I mean, take a look at what FDR did many years ago and he's one of the most highly respected presidents. I mean respected by most people. They named highways after him."[55] Trump compared Muslim Americans and Muslims abroad to the depiction of Japanese Americans and all Japanese after the Pearl Harbor attack—they all were "enemy aliens." In this view, being Muslim disqualified a person from enjoying the same rights other Americans were granted.

As for Trump's regular anti-Muslim rants, he threatened more than once that he was considering closing down all mosques in the United States. After several suicide attacks by jihadists in Brussels, Belgium, he recommended the surveillance of mosques in America, because we "have to deal with the mosques, whether we like it or not, I mean, you know, these attacks aren't coming out of—they're not done by Swedish people."[56] On another occasion he said "Islam hates us," making no distinction between the Islamic religion and extremist Islamic groups.[57] During Trump's election campaign, the conspiracy theorist and Trump propagandist Alex Jones and his Infowars team produced an anti-Muslim video that contained the following statement: "After every single Islamist terror attack we're subjected to the same BS from the media and the regressive left. 'This is just a tiny minority of radical extremists. This has nothing to do with Islam.' There's no such thing as moderate Islam. Islam is a violent, intolerant religion which, in its current form, has no place in supposedly liberal western democracies."[58] Appearing on Jones's radio show a few days later, Trump told the host, "Your reputation is amazing."[59] Many of the most outrageous rumors and conspiracy theories invented by Jones became part of Trump's propaganda and policy agenda.

One of his first acts as president was an executive order that banned citizens from seven Muslim majority countries from entering the United States. It was officially called a "travel ban," but a Muslim American lawyer described the measure more accurately as a "Muslim ban" and cause of great suffering by Muslims in the United States and abroad. She wrote, "This ban has split parents from children, wives from husbands, and extended family from each other and interrupted the lives of students, medical patients, and working professionals who cannot enter. There is fear that the ruling could create loopholes that our ruthless administration could use to re-define citizenship for all who are Muslim or perceived to be Muslim."[60] When Trump's move was widely criticized, his administration reworked the plan by singling out six Muslim countries plus Venezuela and North Korea and renaming it the "Foreign Terrorist Entry Act." Trump called it a watered-down politically correct policy. In her dissent from the 5–4 Supreme Court decision in favor of the Trump administration, Justice Sonia Sotomayor wrote, "The First Amendment stands as a bulwark against official religious prejudice and embodies our Nation's deep commitment to religious plurality and tolerance. . . . Instead of vindicating those principles, today's decision tosses them aside. In holding that the First Amendment gives way to an executive policy that a reasonable observer would view as motivated by animus against Muslims, the majority opinion upends this Court's precedent, repeats tragic mistakes of the past, and denies countless individuals the fundamental right of religious liberty."[61]

Trump's disregard for the civil and human rights of Muslim Americans was shared and applauded by his core supporters, whose responses to @realDonaldTrump tweets mirrored his "Islamophobia." When President Trump attacked Minnesota Governor Tim Walz for his refusal to loosen restrictions in the fight against COVID-19 and join heavily armed militias in their demand to "Liberate Minnesota," his supporters, well informed by Trump of Muslim communities in Minnesota and their Muslim representatives, reacted to @realDonaldTrump tweets with divisive demands like these: "Too many muslims! #StopImmigration"; "Americanize minnesota, too many muslims"; and "Make an ex. order so muslims can't hold office in our country."

The frequent verbal attacks on Islam and Muslims and the anti-Muslim measures implemented by Trump and blessed by a U.S. Supreme Court majority had psychological effects on Muslim Americans—and not only because of the travel ban. A few months after Trump's inauguration, 38 percent of Muslim Americans feared that their or family members' safety was threatened by white supremacy groups such as the Ku Klux Klan and neo-Nazis.[62] Muslim communities were aware of Trump's hate speech and his anti-Muslim policy proposals once he took office. At least Muslim American leaders knew, too, that Trump's campaign chief and White House adviser was Stephen Bannon, the former chief of Breitbart, a popular online right-wing media outfit. In his earlier position, Bannon had declared his site home of the racist alt-right.

Bullying incidents against Muslim boys and girls in schools increased across the country. According to one survey, "Teachers reported hearing Muslim students—or those perceived as Muslim—being called names such as 'terrorist,' 'bomber,' 'Osama' or 'ISIS.' One educator told us of classmates pressuring a student to translate the phrase 'Death of America' into Arabic."[63] A ten-year-old Muslim girl in a school in Massachusetts found a message in the cubby with the warning, "You are a terrorist. I will kill you."[64]

OPEN SEASON ON THE NEWS MEDIA

In Minneapolis, Minnesota, police arrested a CNN reporter and hit a Swedish journalist with a rubber bullet in the thigh while the two were reporting about protesters in the aftermath of the brutal killing of George Floyd, an unarmed Black man, at the end of May 2020. As peaceful and violent demonstrations spread like a wildfire through the United States, reporters seemed to be singled out by police officers in a host of cities, even when the reporters were in compliance with police orders. In Louisville, a female reporter and her camera operator were targeted by police and hit by pepper balls. "I'm getting shot!" screamed the reporter repeatedly. She suffered an eye injury. Two Australian journalists were assaulted near the White House by U.S. Park Police as they covered a peaceful Black Lives Matter demonstration, which was dispersed when the military shot rubber bullets and released tear gas.

Elsewhere, similar incidents of media hostility were displayed by police. During a three-day weekend of protests, at least one hundred incidents occurred of reporters being arrested, pushed around, shot at with pepper or rubber bullets, or buried in clouds of tear gas. According to the U.S. Press Freedom Tracker, "We're now investigating over **100** press freedom violations at the many #GeorgeFloyd protests around the country from the last few days. These include reporters arrested, pepper sprayed, tear gassed, hit with rubber bullets, and assaulted."[65]

If all this felt like open season on the press, it was not difficult to link frequent police interferences and violent attacks against the free press to President Trump's regular declarations of war against news organizations and individual journalists—except for his praises of his propagandists at far-right news organizations such as FOX News and One America News (OAN). In response to a documented jump of antimedia incidents at the height of this civil unrest, the president lashed out once again at what he frequently called the "enemy of the people." On May 31, 2020, he tweeted, "The Lamestream Media is doing everything within their power to foment hatred and anarchy. As long as everybody understands what they are doing, that they are FAKE NEWS and truly bad people with a sick agenda, we can easily work through them to GREATNESS!"

In his book *Time to Get Tough: Make America Great Again*, Trump wrote, "Politics and television are nasty businesses. When the two collide, things get even nastier."[66] This statement foreshadowed the hostile relationship between President Trump and the independent news media. He completely ignored that the country's leading print and TV media covered him far more extensively and, in fact, more positively than his GOP primary rivals and Democratic candidate Hillary Clinton during the preprimary season (January 1, 2015–December 31, 2015) and during the primary months (January 1, 2016–June 7, 2016).[67] Nearly three decades before he became a presidential candidate, Trump wrote, "If you are a little different, or a little outrageous, or if you do things that are bold or controversial, the press is going to write about you."[68]

In this, he was right. The more despicable his statements and behavior, the more media attention he got. It was far less important whether the coverage criticized or praised him. As a businessman Trump had embraced both positive and negative news about him as a net gain,[69] but as the GOP nominee and president, he attacked any journalistic criticism and the refusal of reporters to validate his and his administration's constant diet of "alternative facts" and "alternative truth."

The adjectives and nouns used most often in his tweet bombs dropped regularly on news organizations and individual reporters were "unhinged," "distorted," "unethical," "unpatriotic," "failing," "corrupt," "dishonest," "dumb," "crazy," "low-rated," "nasty," "obnoxious," "lightweight," "loser," and "psycho." His favorite put-downs of female journalists included the terms "stupid," "loser," "bimbo," "unattractive," "low IQ," and "third-rate."

Trump's obsession with the media was reflected in his tweet production. Of the 6,999 tweets that we coded as attacking particular targets during his presidency (January 20, 2017 to January 20, 2021), 24.1 percent were derogatory statements about "fake" or "lying" news organizations and individual journalists or hosts of political talk shows.

Toward the end of his term, Trump changed the cable network MSN-BC's name to "MSDNC," with the last three letters standing for Democratic National Committee and supposedly indicating that this cable channel was synonymous with the Democratic Party. It seemed that Trump borrowed his antipress tactics from past and present dictators by sowing doubts about the truthfulness of news organizations and media workers. Just as Hitler and his propagandists attacked the independent German news media as *Lügenpresse* ("lying press") before turning the press into a propaganda arm of the government, Trump set out to systematically undermine the American public's trust in the credibility of the mainstream media. Following his election victory in 2016, Trump had a telling encounter with the well-known TV reporter Lesley Stahl, which she described eighteen months later during a journalism award event, "At one point, he started to attack the press. There were no cameras in there. I said, 'You know, this is getting tired. Why are you doing it over and over? It's boring and it's time to end that. You know, you've won . . . why do you keep hammering at this?' And he said: 'You know why I do it? I do it to discredit you all and demean you all so that when you write negative stories about me no one will believe you'.[70]

Trump's supporters shared his obsession with the "bad, bad" news media. Comparing the president's tweets in the @realDonaldTrump account and responses by his followers during a five-week period (March, 27–May 1, 2020), we found the strongest word correlations for "news" and "fake" with "media" right behind "house" (for the U.S. House of Representative) in fourth place.

Trump supporters internalized his obsession with and war against all media that did not carry his propaganda. When their idol was confronted with the COVID-19 crisis and the concurrent Black Lives Matter uprising, his followers' verbal attacks on the media became more ferocious. There were a multitude of responses to Trump's antimedia tweets, such as the following.

> @nytimes @washingtonpost They're animals Trump, those newspapers, that is. Cheap rant fake media. Keep your iron hand work on many issues the country faces due to Obama mishandling of his responsibility with the country.
>
> President Trump is by far the best President this Nation has ever had, you scumbaggs are absolutely the dumbest group I have ever seen!
>
> They are the scum on top of the swamp protecting the creatures swimming just beneath the surface.

Besides selling his fake news scheme, the president appealed in tweets and speeches repeatedly for measures to curb press freedom, and he often followed up with proposed actions. Thus, he called for changes in libel law to make it easier for public officials to win defamation lawsuits. On September 5, 2018, for example, he tweeted in reaction to Bob Woodward's newly published book "Fear" and related articles, "Isn't it a shame that someone can write an article or book, totally make up stories and form a picture of a person that is literally the exact opposite of the fact, and get away with it without retribution or cost. Don't know why Washington politicians don't change libel laws?" There was no change in libel law during his term. However, in early 2020, the Trump campaign filed libel suits against the *New York Times*, *Washington Post*, and CNN. The plaintiffs knew they would ultimately lose those legal actions but were content to burden the three news organizations with substantial legal costs.

The president also threatened television networks with the withdrawal of their licenses. In a tweet from October 11, 2017, Trump wrote, "Network news has become so partisan, distorted and fake that licenses must be challenged and, if appropriate, revoked. Not fair to public!" While no broadcast licenses were rescinded, the president called repeatedly for the firing of TV executives. On one occasion (August 28, 2019), he even called for a boycott against Fox News because a few reporters did not support him fully. In one of his tweets he complained, "We have to start looking for a new News Outlet. Fox isn't working for us anymore." Yet, the morning show *Fox & Friends* and FOX's prime-time programs remained the president's favorites.

Opinion polls reflected the effectiveness of Trump's war against individual reporters and news organizations that did not slavishly praise his words and deeds. In late 2019, the vast majority of conservatives had the most trust in Fox News (75 percent), the network that was most distrusted by liberals (77 percent); liberals, on the other hand, had the most trust in CNN (70 percent), the cable network that 67 percent of conservatives distrusted.[71] When pollsters asked respondents in March 2017 whether or not they agreed with Trump's calling journalists and the media "the enemy of the American people," 34 percent agreed, 59 percent disagreed, and 7 percent were undecided.[72] In other words, one-third of the public viewed the media as an enemy of the people. When Trump was not mentioned, between 21 percent and 26 percent of survey respondents said they considered the news media the public's enemy.[73] The constant attacks on "fake" and "lying" news organizations and individual journalists affected Republicans to a degree that their trust in the mainstream media's reporting sank precipitously while it increased among Democrats and fluctuating among Independents.

Even more disconcerting was Trump's constant flogging of the press during his mass rallies before and after he became president. This angered his supporters to such an extent that they inevitably hurled insults and threats toward the press section. As he explained to Lesley Stahl of CBS, that was exactly what Trump's antimedia strategy and tactics were supposed to achieve.

RHETORICAL ATTACKS AGAINST
POLITICAL OPPONENTS

At the end of May 2020, some one hundred thousand Americans had succumbed to the COVID-19 pandemic, and cities across the country were dealing with social unrest in the wake of a Black man's brutal murder by police in Minneapolis. In the midst of this dual crisis, President Trump took the leisure to retweet a repugnant video posted by Cowboys for Trump (@RideWithC4T) that ended with one Trump supporter's exclamation: "The only good Democrat is a dead Democrat!"[74] This endorsement summed up Trump's bellicose speech and behavior toward political opponents. While America's partisan and ideological conflict had been deep before Trump came to power (see the next chapter), he made sure that it got much worse during his presidency. In their research on lethal partisanship, Nathan Kalmoe and Lilliana Mason mention the influence of opinion leadership and the example of Donald Trump, "who violates the norms of appropriate social and political behavior and frequently espouses views hostile to democracy, including the endorsement of low-level political violence at his campaign rallies."[75]

Democrats were collectively and individually the targets most often attacked in Trump's total output of attack tweets (before his candidacy, during the campaign months, during the transition period, and during his presidency), with 44.6 percent, surpassing the 22.4 percent targeting the media. As president, he devoted 47.6 percent of his attack tweets to Democrats compared with 24.1 percent to media organizations and individuals, with merely 2.8 percent of hate tweets reserved for Republicans, most of whom followed him blindly. The sole exception was the campaign period, when Republicans were put down in 33.2 percent of his attack tweets and Democrats in 31.9 percent. This high total for Republicans was the result of Trump's relentless and ruthless attacks on his GOP competitors during the 2015–16 primary season.[76]

In tweets and during his mass rallies or White House appearances, Trump vilified Democrats regularly. Bemoaning his impeachment in December 2019, the president tweeted, "The Radical Left, Do Nothing Democrats have become the Party of Hate. They are so bad for our Country!" Three months earlier, he wrote @realDonaldTrump, "I am so tired of hearing the rationalization of the Left in the country because they hate Donald Trump. Inexplicably and without foundation, they choose to hate America." These statements synthesized his attacks on Democrats as not loving but hating their country; as individually and collectively threatening the constitutional rights of patriotic Americans; and as the "Radical Left" harboring socialist and communist designs for this country. Thus his tweeted assurance, "We will never be a Socialist or Communist Country." At a rally in Louisiana in late 2019, Trump said, "Democrats are becoming increasingly totalitarian" and are "trying to overthrow American democracy to impose their socialism agenda." He accused Democrats of "trying to rip our nation apart."[77] In 156 posts of his total tweet production, Trump attacked the "Do Nothing Democrats" collectively or singled out particularly hated individuals for his tirades.

According to Jennifer Mercieca, "dangerous demagogues weaponize communication by tolerating or encouraging violence."[78] Thus, it seemed hardly a coincidence that the number of serious threats against members of the U.S. Congress increased sharply, from 902 in 2016 to 8,839 in 2021,

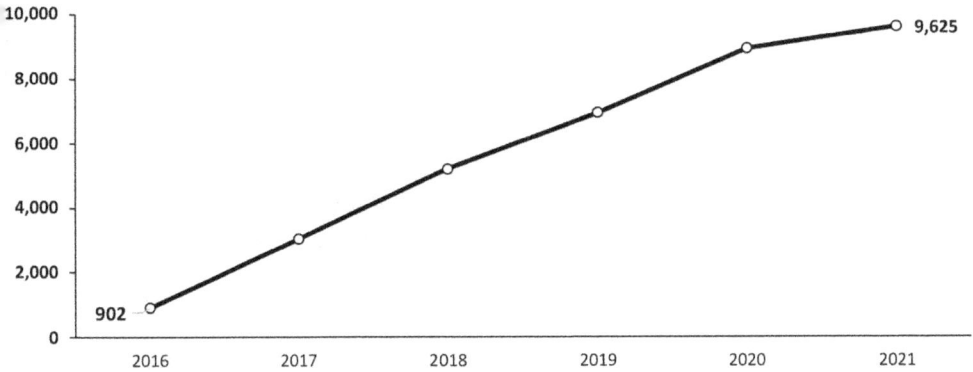

FIGURE 4.2 Rise in threats against members of Congress during the Trump years.

Source: Capitol Police.

Trump's last full year in office, and to 9,625 in 2021, when he left office (figure 4.2).

During the 2016 campaign, "Lock Her Up" became for Donald Trump and his supporters a rallying cry against Democratic nominee Hillary Clinton. Whenever Trump or one of his prominent supporters mentioned "Crooked Hillary," the "Make America Great Again" crowd demanded "Lock Her Up." But eventually this slogan, borrowed from Banana Republic strongmen, was used against other GOP "enemies" as well. After President Trump complained that House Speaker Nancy Pelosi had mumbled behind him during his 2020 State of the Union address, the crowd at his New Hampshire rally chanted, "Lock her up, lock her up."[79] At a rally in Iowa, Trump attacked U.S. Senator Dianne Feinstein for her role during the confirmation hearing for Supreme Court Justice Brett Kavanaugh and provoked the crowd to demand, "Lock her up!"[80]

As noted earlier, no other individual was as frequently and maliciously attacked as Barack Obama. Other male Democrats were on Trump's rhetorical hit list as well, among them "Sleepy Joe" Biden, who was mentioned 199 times in attack tweets; Adam "Shifty Schiff" (50 times); "Crazy Bernie" Sanders (46 times); and "Cry'in" Chuck Schumer (42 times).[81]

However, even as Trump singled out female reporters for his insults, he was particularly nasty in his rhetorical attacks on female politicians. He called Hillary Clinton a "total train wreck," Nancy Pelosi "crazy" and "an inherently dumb person," and Dianne Feinstein "another beauty." His most vicious attacks were reserved for a quartet of progressive congresswomen of color: Ilhan Omar of Minnesota, Alexandria Ocasio-Cortez of New York, Ayanna Pressley of Massachusetts, and Rashida Tlaib of Michigan. After the four, nicknamed "the Squad," criticized his policies, Trump tweeted (July 14, 2019), "So interesting to see 'Progressive' Democrat Congresswomen, who originally came from countries whose governments are a complete and total catastrophe, the worst, most corrupt and inept anywhere in the world (if they even have a functioning government at all), now loudly and viciously telling the people of the United States, the greatest and most powerful Nation on earth, how our government is to be run. Why don't they go back and help fix the totally broken and crime infested places from which they came." A female supporter tweeted her agreement: "The notion that you can't criticize these Anti-America fools by virtue of the amount of melanin they have in skin is utterly ridiculous." Ironically, three of the four politicians were born in the United States; only Ilhan Omar came in her youth (she was eight years old) as a legal immigrant from Somalia.

These rhetorical attacks had consequences. Representative Omar received death threats, as did her three colleagues. The owner of a gun shop in North Carolina, a Trump supporter, put headshots of the four congresswomen on a billboard with the message, "The 4 Horsemen Cometh," changing the words, after protests, into "The 4 Horsemen are Idiots."[82]

After Senator Kamala Harris was nominated as the Democratic Party's vice-presidential candidate, Trump attacked her in tweets and public statements as "mean," "horrible," "disrespectful," "awkward," and "a monster," claiming that "she doesn't meet the requirements [for vice president]" and "is going to be a big failure." As table 4.1 reveals, if anyone was horrible and disrespectful, it was Donald Trump in the way he labeled accomplished female politicians and tried to degrade them.

TABLE 4.1 Female politicians mentioned in Trump tweets

NAME OF POLITICIAN	CHARACTERIZED AS	NO. OF TWEETS
Hillary Clinton	"crooked"	709
Nancy Pelosi	"crazy"	362
Elizabeth Warren	"Pocahontas"	57
Kamala Harris	"phony"	44
Alexandria Ocasio-Cortez	"barely literate moron"	35
Ilhan Omar	"foul mouthed"	31
Maxine Waters	"low IQ person"	19
Dianne Feinstein	"disrespectful"	8
Gretchen Whitmer	"in over her head"	3
Muriel Bowser	"incompetent"	2

Source: @realdonaldtrump Twitter archive.

PRAISING AND ENCOURAGING VIOLENCE

Before and during his presidency, Trump's preferred words were those that project strength, toughness, and, most of all, wins. In his tweets he used "win" and "won" 1,468 times; also prominent were the terms "strong" (732 times), "tough" (367), "fight" (402), and "attack" (268). He degraded his opponents as "failing" or "failure" 363 times, "weak" 240 times, and "loser" or "losing" 322 times. According to his own account, Trump had showed his dominant traits even as a child. "Even in elementary school, I was a very assertive kid," he wrote in one of his books. "In the second grade I actually gave a teacher a black eye—I punched my music teacher because I didn't think he knew anything about music. It's clear evidence that even early on I had a tendency to stand up and make my opinion known in a very forceful way."[83]

On the campaign trail and during his presidency, Trump did not merely attack his opponents and "enemies" with aggressive and degrading language; he condoned, praised, and even encouraged physical violence against various "enemies." On August 9, 2016, at a campaign rally in Wilmington, North Carolina, Trump attacked Hillary Clinton and warned his supporters of the terrible things she would do if she were to win in November. Implying that she would end their constitutional right to bear arms, he warned, "Hillary wants to abolish—essentially abolish the Second Amendment. By the way, and if she gets to pick [CROWD BOOING] If she gets to pick her judges, nothing you can do, folks. Although the Second Amendment people, maybe there is. I don't know. But—but I'll tell you what. That will be a horrible day. If—if Hillary gets to put her judges—right now, we're tied. You see what's going on."[84] Many observers understood Trump's remarks as instigating violence in case of a Clinton victory. In response Clinton said, "If you are running to be president, or you are president of the United States, words can have tremendous consequences."[85]

In October 2018, after the congressional GOP candidate Greg Gianforte of Montana body-slammed and injured a reporter of *The Guardian* because he did not like to be questioned about his health care policy, President Trump praised Gianforte during a rally and mimicked a body-slamming motion. "Greg is smart," he said. "And by the way, never wrestle him. Never. Any guy that can do a body slam is my kind of guy. My kind. I shouldn't say that, but this is nothing to be embarrassed by."[86]

When his supporters roughed up protesters at his rallies, candidate and President Trump often supported these violent actions. Here are but a few examples of such incidents.

- After a Black Lives Matter protester at one of Trump's rallies in 2015 was kicked and punched by his supporters, candidate Trump supported the violent incident. "The man that was—I don't know, you say 'roughed up'— he was so obnoxious and so loud, he was screaming," he said. "He should have been, maybe he should have been roughed up."
- Allegedly informed by his security team that protesters were going to throw tomatoes at one of his 2016 campaign events, Trump told his supporters, "If you see somebody getting ready to throw a tomato, knock the crap out of them, would you? Seriously. Okay? Just knock the hell. I promise you I will pay for the legal fees. I promise."

- When another 2016 campaign rally was interrupted by protesters, Trump told his supporters, "I love the old days. You know what they used to do to guys like that when they were in a place like this? They'd be carried out on a stretcher, folks. It's true. . . . I'd like to punch him in the face, I'll tell you."

- President Trump encouraged police violence before police brutality resulted in social unrest in 2020. Addressing police officers in 2017, he said, "When you see thugs being thrown into the back of a paddy wagon, you just see them thrown in; rough. I said, please don't be too nice. Like when you guys put somebody in the car and you're protecting their head, you know, the way you put your hand over it. Like, don't hit their head, and they've just killed somebody. I said, you can take the hand away, O.K.?"[87]

- Four months after the MSNBC anchor Ali Velshi covered a peaceful Black Lives Matter demonstration and was hit by a rubber bullet, Trump recalled the incident at a campaign rally in September 2020 as he promoted a tough law-and-order stand. "They [law enforcement officers] threw him aside like he was a little bag of popcorn," the president said. "But I mean honestly, when you watch the crap that we've all had to take so long . . . when you see it, it's actually a beautiful sight."[88]

THE RISE OF POLITICAL VIOLENCE IN THE TRUMP ERA

Ultimately, the question is whether Donald Trump's frequent verbal attacks on minorities and his implicit and explicit calls to violence against singled-out groups and individuals resulted in political violence or what, by definition, could be acts of domestic terrorism.

An early study by the American Psychological Association concluded that "viewing [TV] violence increases viewers' appetites for becoming involved with violence or exposing themselves to violence."[89] To be sure, news consumers react differently to interpersonal and mass-mediated violent text and images. Thus, more recent experiments found that "citizens with aggressive personality traits expressed significantly greater support for political violence, and their support doubled when they were exposed to political messages infused with violent metaphors."[90]

Donald Trump declared his candidacy for the GOP presidential nomination on June 16, 2015. One day later, the nineteen-year-old white supremacist Dylann Roof shot to death nine African American worshippers at the Emanuel African Methodist Church in Charleston, South Carolina. In a "manifesto" Roof explained that he was radicalized by (right-extreme) online sites and their (false) information about the high number of incidents in which Blacks were killing whites. While then-candidate Trump did not cause Roof's violence, he had publicized the falsity that most violent crimes in the United States were committed by Blacks, the very same rumor that had motivated Roof to kill. Obviously, Roof was influenced by Trump's aggressive personality traits. "We have no skinheads, no real KKK, no one doing anything but talking on the internet," Roof wrote. "Well someone has to have the bravery to take it to the real world, and I guess that has to be me." He added mysteriously, "I am in a great hurry."[91]

One year later, ahead of the first anniversary of the Charleston massacre, South Carolina Governor Nikki Haley was the first public official to connect Trump's rhetoric and Roof's terrorist attack. According to a South Carolina newspaper, "Nikki Haley said Thursday she wishes Donald Trump communicated differently because bad things result from divisive rhetoric, as evidenced by last June's massacre in Charleston. The Republican governor said divisive speech motivated Dylann Roof to gun down nine black parishioners at historic Emanuel AME Church."[92] Indeed, Trump's racist speech before and during his presidential campaign and as president seemed to affect—clearly preceded—a significant number of like-minded individuals committing what the authorities labeled hate crimes. When asked by a reporter whether his rhetoric was dividing Americans, Trump answered, "I don't think my rhetoric does at all. My rhetoric is very—it brings people together."[93] Obviously, he counted only his supporters, his people united, and once again excluded the rest of the nation.

Examining whether correlations existed between counties that were venues of Trump's two hundred seventy-five campaign rallies in 2016 and subsequent hate crimes, three political scientists found that "counties that had hosted a 2016 Trump campaign rally saw a 226 percent increase in reported hate crimes over comparable counties that did not host such a rally." While cautioning that this "analysis cannot be certain it was Trump's campaign rally rhetoric that caused people to commit more crime in the host county," the researchers also found it "hard to discount a 'Trump effect' since data of the Anti-Defamation League showed "a considerable number of these reported hate crimes referenced Trump."[94]

Moreover, investigative reporting identified forty-one cases of domestic terrorism or hate crimes or threats thereof, in which the perpetrators invoked Trump favorably in manifestos, social media posts, police interrogations, or court documents. Almost all this violence was committed by white males against minorities, politicians singled out frequently by Trump for rhetorical attacks, and journalists.[95] The U.S. Press Freedom Tracker recorded a total of two hundred and two attacks on U.S. journalists from 2017, Trump's first year in office, through mid-2020.[96]

WHITE SUPREMACY AND THE GREAT REPLACEMENT

The three most lethal terrorist attacks during the Trump presidency—the mass shootings in the Tree of Life Synagogue in Pittsburgh, Pennsylvania; two mosques in Christchurch, New Zealand; and a Walmart supermarket in El Paso, Texas—were carried out by white supremacists who embraced racist "Great Replacement" conspiracy theories popular in their circles. The term "The Great Replacement" was coined by the French author Renaud Camus when he described the coming substitution of the native French majority by non-Western immigrants, many of them Muslims. Right-extreme conspiracy theorists expanded the alleged threat to whites in Western Europe and North America. Along with those beliefs came a multitude of similarly motivated attacks in the United States and elsewhere, in addition to foiled plots.

Pittsburgh, Pennsylvania. On the morning of October 27, 2018, forty-six-year-old Robert Bowers shot his way into the Tree of Life synagogue in Pittsburg, killing six worshippers and injuring six more. During his shooting spree and a stand-off with police, he screamed, "They have committed genocide to my people. I just want to kill Jews." Only minutes before rushing into the building, Bowers had logged on to his account on the Gab social media platform, telling his followers, "I can't sit by and watch my people get slaughtered." Bowers left a long trail of social media posts that revealed his admiration for Hitler, denial of the Holocaust, and extreme hate of African Americans, Muslims, and, most of all, Jews, whom he called "children of Satan." He posted conspiracy theories about George Soros and other globalists. He blamed the Hebrew Immigrant Aid Society, a Jewish prorefugee organization, for bringing "invaders in that kill our people."[97]

Five days before the Pittsburg massacre and less than three weeks before the midterm elections in early November, President Trump threw white supremacists the red meat they craved. At a campaign rally for U.S. Senator Ted Cruz in Houston, he said, "You know what a globalist is, right? A globalist is a person who wants the globe to do well, frankly, not caring about our country so much. You know what? I'm a nationalist. Use that word."[98] Some right-extremists rejoiced publicly. "Raise your hands if you are an American nationalist like Trump," tweeted a columnist for One America News. "Trump sounds like Breitbart," Ann Coulter posted on her Twitter feed.

Bowers seemed not to be appeased. He tweeted that he was not a Trump supporter, complaining that the president was "a globalist, not a nationalist." And, yet, his social media posts reflected Trump's divisive and hateful rhetoric toward minorities with terms like "caravan," "invaders," and "infestation." These similarities did not mean that Trump caused the bloody attack; however, they underscored that political rhetoric matters and that a leader like the president of the United States sets the tone.

Christchurch, New Zealand. On March 15, 2019, a twenty-eight-year-old Australian man entered Al Noor Mosque and, about twelve minutes later, the Linwood Islamic Centre in Christchurch during Friday prayers, killing fifty-one and injuring forty-nine worshipping Muslim men, women, and children with automatic weapons. With a camera mounted on his hat,

Brenton Tarrant streamed the massacre live on a social media account. In his lengthy manifesto, titled "The Great Replacement," the mass killer wrote, "We must crush immigration and deport those invaders already living on our soil. It is not just a matter of our prosperity, but the very survival of our people." He warned that the first such replacement in the United States would occur in and change Texas. "Soon the replacement of the whites within Texas will hit its apogee and with the non-white political and social control of Texas," he wrote. "And with this control, the electoral college will be heavily stacked in favor of a democratic victory so that every electoral cycle will be a certainty." He paid tribute to Donald Trump as "a symbol of renewed white identity and common purpose", emphasizing the importance of these words by underlining them in his text.[99]

El Paso, Texas. On August 3, 2019, a lone gunman armed with a semi-automatic civilian version of the AK-47 shot and killed twenty-three persons and injured twenty-three others at a Walmart supermarket in El Paso. The twenty-one-year-old, Patrick Crusius from Allen, Texas, selected this particular Walmart at the U.S.-Mexico border because he wanted to kill Mexicans and other Latinos. He was arrested shortly after the massacre.

"I support the Christchurch shooter and his manifesto," was the opening sentence in Crusius's own manifesto, which he posted online shortly before the horrific killing spree. "This attack is a response to the Hispanic invasion of Texas," he explained. "They are the instigators, not me. I am simply defending my country from cultural and ethnic replacement brought on by an invasion."

Repeating Tarrant's warning that the white race's replacement in Texas would cause a disastrous electoral shift, the El Paso terrorist wrote, "The heavy Hispanic population in Texas will make us a Democrat stronghold. Losing Texas and a few other states with heavy Hispanic population to the Democrats is all it would take for them to win nearly every presidential election."

Crusius's social media posts attested to his support of Donald Trump. Aware that the president's critics questioned Trump's attitudes toward white nationalists, the mass shooter tried to spare Trump such accusations. "Thus, at the end of his declaration he wrote that his ideology did not change 'for several years' and 'predate[d] Trump and his campaign for president.'" Like Trump, he attacked the "fake" media and predicted, "I know that the media will probably call me a white supremacist anyway and blame Trump's rhetoric."[100]

FAILED AND FOILED VIOLENCE

Homemade IEDs. In the second half of October 2018, sixteen homemade pipe bombs were mailed to Barack Obama, Joe Biden, Hillary Clinton, George Soros, the actor Robert De Niro, a number of other prominent Democrats, and the CNN headquarters in Atlanta. None of the improvised explosive devices detonated. Cesar Sayoc, age fifty-four, was arrested and eventually received a twenty-year prison term for building and mailing the devices. During his trial, defense lawyers described their client as a loner who "found light in Donald J. Trump," supported his idol "on social media and at rallies," and thereby found "the sense of community that he had been missing for so many years." Before his sentencing, Sayoc himself compared his obsession with Trump to an addiction.

Foiled plot of political violence. In early 2019, Coast Guard Lieutenant Christopher Hasson, age forty-nine, was arrested and charged with plotting terror attacks against a multitude of prominent Democrats in public offices and liberals in the news media. Police found seven rifles, two shotguns, four pistols, two revolvers, and two silencers, along with magazines and ammunition in his home. The search of his computers revealed that Hasson was a self-described white supremacist who idolized the Norwegian terrorist and mass shooter Anders Breivik, believed in the white genocide or great replacement conspiracy theory, and had compiled a list of targets. Shortly before he was arrested, his computer searches focused on the following topics:

- "what if trump illegally impeached,"
- "best place in dc to see congress people,"
- "where in dc do congress live,"
- "civil war if trump impeached."

THREATS OF POLITICAL VIOLENCE
ARE VIOLENCE

Many definitions of terrorism include threats of this sort of political violence and confirm John Galtung's categorical statement that "*threats of violence are also violence.*"[101] There were dozens of serious threats of violence against prominent Democrats, TV hosts, reporters, and members of minorities with references to Trump. Here are just three examples.

In the summer of 2019, police arrested thirty-five year old Eric Lin of Maryland for harassing a female Floridian with one hundred fifty pages of Facebook messages that threatened her with kidnapping and deadly attacks on her, her family, and other Latinos. According to the arrest warrant, the white supremacist made threats with the intent of the "extermination" of all Latinos. In one post he wrote, "I thank God every-day President Donald Trump is President and that he will launch a Racial War and Crusade to keep [derogatory names for African Americans and Latinos], Muslims, and any dangerous Ethnically or Culturally foreign group 'In Line.'" He spelled out that "In Line" meant concentration camps or forced military service.

In early 2019, the U.S Capitol Police arrested Stephen Taubert, a sixty-one-year-old veteran from Syracuse, New York, for threatening to kill two prominent Democrats, former President Barack Obama and Congress-woman Maxine Waters, both African Americans. According to prosecu-tors, Taubert used "overtly bigoted, hateful language" in his phone calls. After threatening to "hang" Obama in 2018, he called Representative Waters's Los Angeles office, warning that he would find her at public events and kill her and her staff. During his trial he explained that he got "riled up" when seeing negative comments about President Trump on social media and the news.

In August 2018, the *Boston Globe* published an editorial on its front page, declaring "We are not the enemy of the people" and asked other news organizations to join the resistance against President Trump's rhetorical assaults. In fourteen phone calls to the newspaper, a sixty-eight-year-old

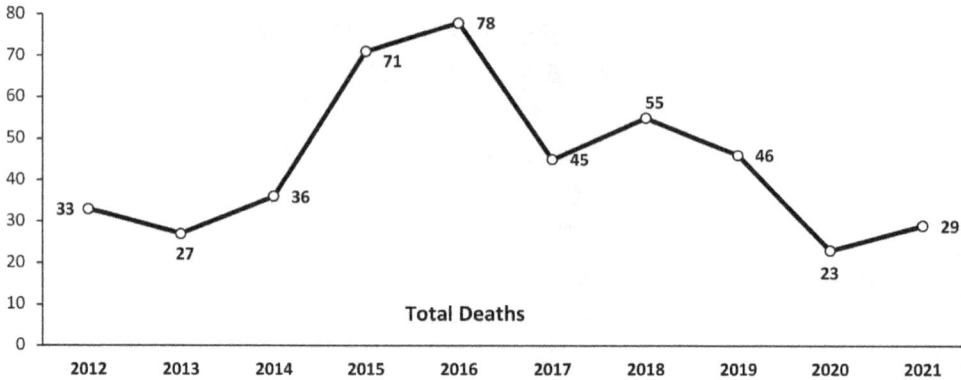

FIGURE 4.3 Rise in lethal political violence in the United States during the Trump years.

Source: ADL.

Californian, Robert Chain, repeated Trump's phrases "fake media" and "the media is the enemy of the people." He warned he would continue his threats as long as they were attacking President Trump. In one call he told a *Globe* staffer, "I'm going to shoot you in the f . . . head later today."

Figure 4.3 shows that deadly domestic extremism spiked in 2015 and 2016, when Donald Trump entered the presidential campaign and won the highest office in the land. The numbers remained high in 2017 and 2018. Far-right extremists were responsible for 75 percent of the 443 killings during the ten years from 2012 to 2021; far-left extremists for 4 percent, domestic Islamic extremists for 20 percent, and other extremists for 1 percent.[102]

VIOLENT RHETORIC AND VIOLENT CONSEQUENCES

Whereas the well-known children's rhyme mentioned earlier claims that unlike physical violence "words will never hurt me," our research demonstrates the opposite. Donald Trump's hate speech and demonization of nonwhites, mainstream media, and oppositional politicians, and his implicit and explicit praise of violence, resulted in many verbal and corporal attacks against members of the denigrated groups. School bullying increased, with many young bullies using hateful Trumpian terminology and/or referring to his discriminatory policies. Particularly in minority communities, there was heightened anxiety and fear. Just as important, Trump stirred fear, hate, and anger among his core supporters by warning them of dangerous "others," who allegedly threatened "America as we know it" in terms of history, culture, values, and racial dominance. Whether by dog whistle or bullhorn, online and offline, he voiced and spread a divisive propaganda that in many respects resembled right-extremists' ideologies.

Donald Trump did not invent racist and nativist hate speech. Racism and nativism are as American as apple pie. The reaction of right-extremists to Barack Obama, the first African American U.S. president , set off the latest wave of white nationalism and related hate speech. Trump, then best known as star of his own TV reality show, became the de facto spokesman of the anti-Obama birther conspiracy theory, embracing its racism along with anti-immigration nationalism as core components of his presidential campaign and presidency. Few observers recognized Trump's sympathies for violent actors as a warning sign for and prologue to the events of January 6, 2021—before it was too late.

Digital communication technology spreads propaganda instantly to huge audiences. Ultimately, however, it is the interconnectivity among all three mass media forms (the traditional news media, internet-based mass self-communication, and interpersonal communication) that assures the greatest public and elite attention and allows maximum manipulation within the triangle of political communication. Trump was a highly successful demagogic performer on all counts. His most malevolent tweets received the greatest attention not merely in the social media sphere but also in the mainstream media and during his frequent MAGA rallies, when he repeated his malicious slogans again and again.

In her examination of dangerous demagogues, among them Donald Trump, Jennifer R. Mercieca noted that these actors do "not only use weaponized communication as an authoritarian uses violence, but weaponized communication itself is a form of violence."[103] Molly McKew called right-extremists who systematically spread incendiary propaganda on social media platforms "information terrorists."[104] Whatever term one prefers, one cannot ignore a connection between the inciting tweets that President Trump posted after his defeat in the 2020 election and the violent breach of the U.S. Capitol by his supporters on January 6, 2021.

5

PARTISAN CONFLICT, ISSUES, AND EMOTIONS ON HIGH

"Since the 2020 election, millions of Republican voters have accepted former President Donald Trump's false claim that the presidential election was stolen from him. And now, here in 2022, many Republican politicians have capitalized on this lie and have won elections of their own."[1]

"I have a message for Joe Biden and Beto O'Rourke. If you want to take everyone's AR-15 in America, why don't you swing by my office in Washington, D.C., and start with this one." At this point, Buck reached for a stars-and-stripes-decorated rifle mounted on the wall. He brandished the weapon, smiled what he must have imagined was a tough-guy smile, and said, "Come and take it."[2]

"Then Jan. 6 happened. And next thing you know, I organized the whole thing, along with Steve Bannon. . . . I will tell you something, if Steve Bannon and I organized that, we would have won. Not to mention, it would've been armed."[3]

The level and lasting power of emotions attached to the 2020 election results and the issue of guns, as reflected in these remarkable quotes, had everything to do with partisan conflict that was covered widely in the mass media and spread over social media. This is closely connected to the January 6 assault on the U.S. Capitol (see chapter 1 and the follow-up in chapter 6) and what might have happened had the insurgents been better armed and if not for the metal detector screening and other measures in Washington that day.

President Donald Trump's claim that the Democrats stole the 2020 elections in one or more of the key states of Michigan, Wisconsin, Pennsylvania, Arizona, and Georgia was echoed by his Republican supporters. The repercussions of this claim are shown in figure 5.1, where we see that going forward, far fewer Republicans than Democrats—by fully forty-five percentage points (40 percent to 85 percent) in 2022—thought that votes would be accurately counted in the upcoming election.

These partisan differences were even starker regarding support for stricter laws covering the sale of firearms, as shown in figure 5.2. In 2022, support among Democrats exceeded that of Republicans by a stunning nearly sixty percentage points (86 percent to 27 percent), more than twice the difference compared with twenty years earlier.

These highly emotional partisan conflicts over elections and guns stand out because they are associated with a potentially violent threat

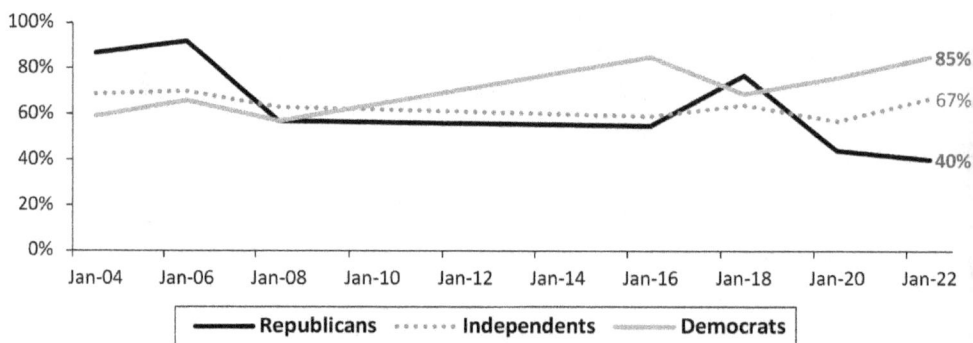

FIGURE 5.1 Americans' confidence in the accuracy of U.S. elections, by party.

Note: Percentage very/somewhat confident.

Source: Gallup.

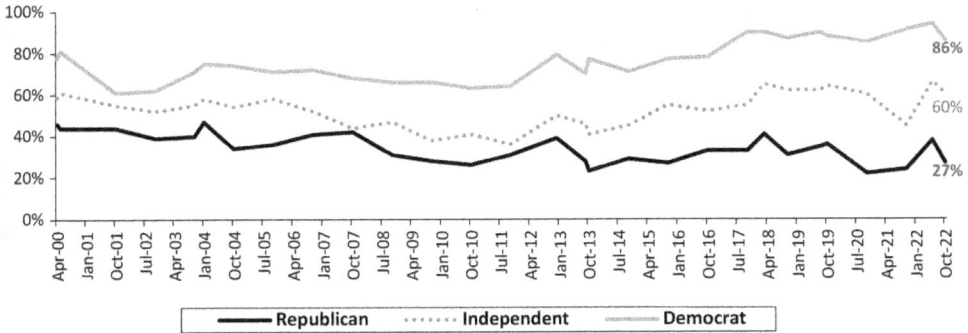

FIGURE 5.2 Partisans' preferences for stricter gun laws in the United States, 2001–22.

Note: Percentage more strict.

Source: Gallup.

to American democracy. But how and why did American politics reach this point? There was a broader context that led to this: partisan conflict and the anger that became attached to it were already on the rise before the elections of Presidents Trump in 2016 and Barack Obama in 2008. Their elections and presidencies inflamed further the existing animosity embroiling partisan politics.

It was, however, real-world partisan conflict and polarization that emerged over policy issues in American politics, along with tighter electoral competition between the Democratic and Republican Parties, which established the emotionally charged political environment for the weaponization of communication described in the previous chapters.

THE BROADER POLITICAL CONTEXT

The 2020 election battle royale, which was preceded by what happened from the 2016 election through the COVID-19 pandemic, which toppled Donald Trump, was a glaring display of the highly emotional partisan conflict that engulfed the United States. This conflict had clear attributes that contributed to the high level of political rancor. These included the rise of *affective partisanship*—the dislike of and anger toward the opposing party, its candidates, and its supporters; the stunning increase in *partisan divergence*, along liberal-conservative ideological lines, on virtually all major issues; *the closeness of elections*—the increase in competitiveness of the Democratic and Republican Parties for unified control of the national government; and partisan perceptual biases concerning facts, reality, and the spread of conspiracy theories that have accompanied these developments. And, at the end, came some indications of the greater acceptance of the political use of violence.

AFFECTIVE PARTISANSHIP

> February 17, 2022. SMETHPORT, Pa. (AP)—Some Democrats in rural Pennsylvania are afraid to tell you they're Democrats. . . . The party's brand is so toxic in the small towns 100 miles northeast of Pittsburgh that some liberals have removed bumper stickers and yard signs and refuse to acknowledge publicly their party affiliation. These Democrats are used to being outnumbered by the local Republican majority, but as their numbers continue to dwindle, those who remain are feeling increasingly isolated and unwelcome in their own communities. . . . "The hatred for Democrats is just unbelievable," said Tim Holohan, an accountant based in rural McKean County who recently encouraged his daughter to get rid of a pro-Joe Biden bumper sticker. "I feel like we're on the run."[4]

This news story shows how partisan conflict had not only penetrated to the level of individuals' disagreement over the counting of votes and firearms restrictions but also how Democrats and Republicans *feel* (thus "affect") toward those affiliated with the other party at the level of everyday life. This has been analyzed in research on the political and social psychology of individuals' "social identities," which have become embroiled in this conflict.[5] That is related to partisan differences that emerged and strengthened concerning the wide range of political issues, which we will examine at length in this chapter. But the conflict became personalized; it stemmed from emotions that have reached an "us against them" mentality starting with the behavior of political leaders and penetrating to result in increases in negative feelings among the public toward the opposition party and its leaders. This "negative partisanship" or "affective partisanship" is striking.[6] There is substantial evidence for the increase in dislike of and anger toward the opposition party in recent years.

Figure 5.3 shows the 0–100-degree feeling thermometer ratings of the Democratic and Republican candidates by the supporters among

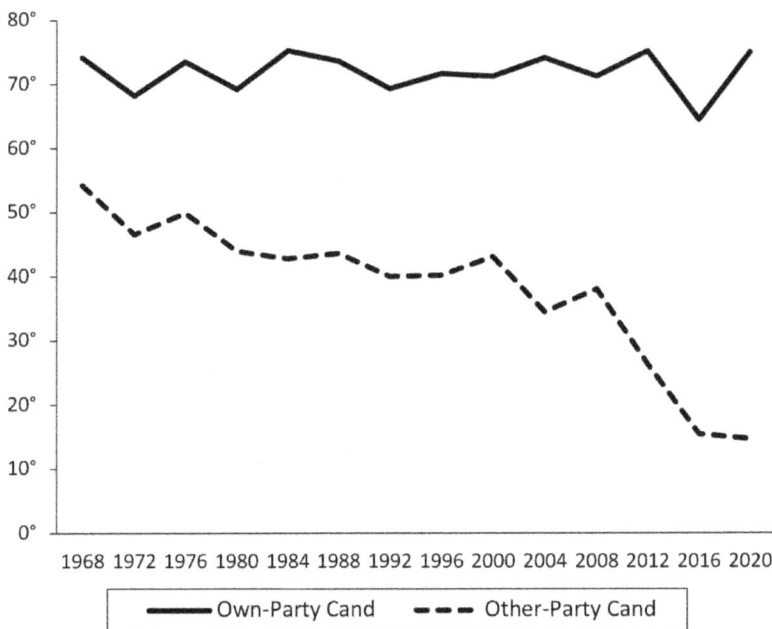

FIGURE 5.3 Partisans' feelings toward the parties' candidates.

Note: Average 0–100 feeling thermometer ratings.

Source: ANES.

the public who identify with each party—their fellow partisans. We find the same for ratings of each of the parties themselves. While the feelings toward individuals' own party and its candidates remained warm—at the 70-degree level—they dropped over time to 20 degrees for the opposition party and its candidates. This fall-off occurred sharply with the election of Obama in 2008, coinciding closely with the vehement anti-Obama sentiments that came with the rise of the Tea Party. There was increasing animosity—associated with affective polarization—in other ways (not shown): the extent to which the positive feelings toward one's own party are greater that the negative affect toward the other party, and the extent to which individuals both like their own party and dislike the opposition. After 2008, individuals disliked the opposition party more than they liked their own.

Based on different data, we also find that from 2016 to 2019, a twenty-point or more increase—to more than 70 percent—in the percentage of partisans feeling both warmly toward their party and coldly toward the opposition. There were also a large and increasing difference in partisans' feelings toward Trump, which only grew during the time he was elected until he left office—from fifty-nine to seventy-two percentage points. This reflected the increase that occurred over time in partisan differences in presidential approval, shown in figure 5.4. These differences reached and stunningly exceeded all-time highs: more than an eighty-point (!) partisan difference for President Trump and then, not far from that, for President Biden; these followed Obama's previously all-time high partisan gap in his approval rating.

These attitudes toward the parties, their leaders, and other candidates for office came to reflect increasing anger.[7] Figure 5.5 shows how Republicans' anger toward government increased with the election of Obama and a Democratic-controlled Congress, coinciding with the rise of the Tea Party, and reached a high of nearly 40 percent in 2014. The anger of Democrats was stoked to nearly as high a level (34 percent) with the election of Trump and a Republican-controlled Congress.

With these partisan emotions running high, it is not surprising to see in figure 5.6 that the percentage of voters who voted only for presidential

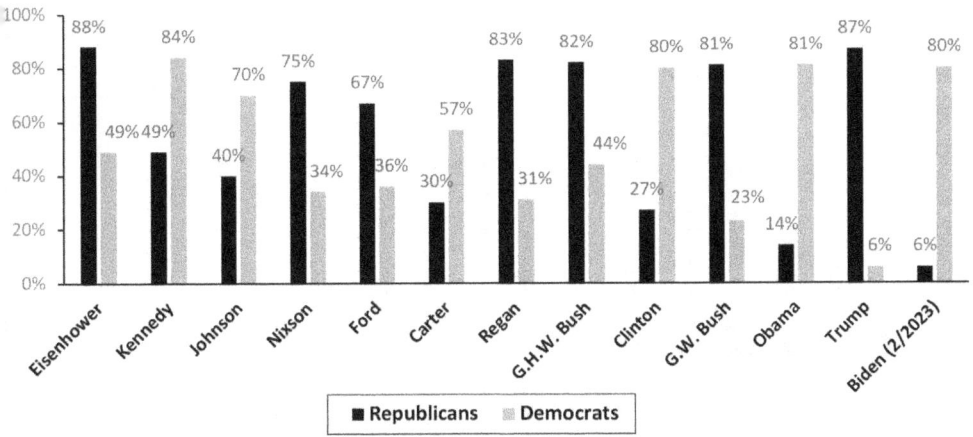

FIGURE 5.4 Partisan differences in presidential approval.

Note: Percentage approve.

Sources: Pew and Gallup.

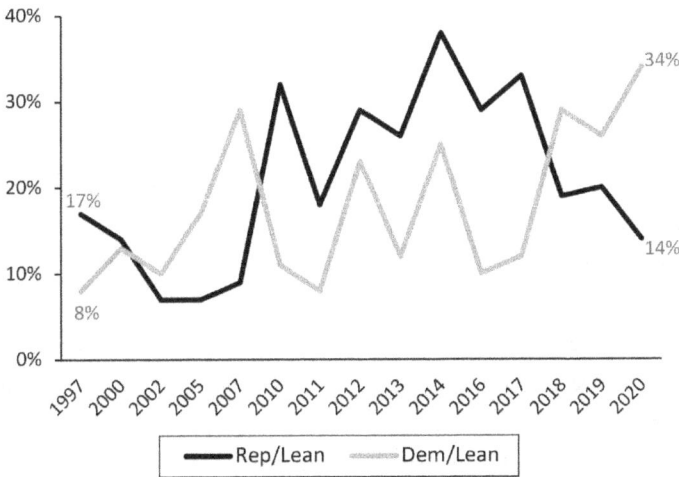

FIGURE 5.5 Anger toward government.

Note: Percentage feeling angry about the government.

Source: Pew.

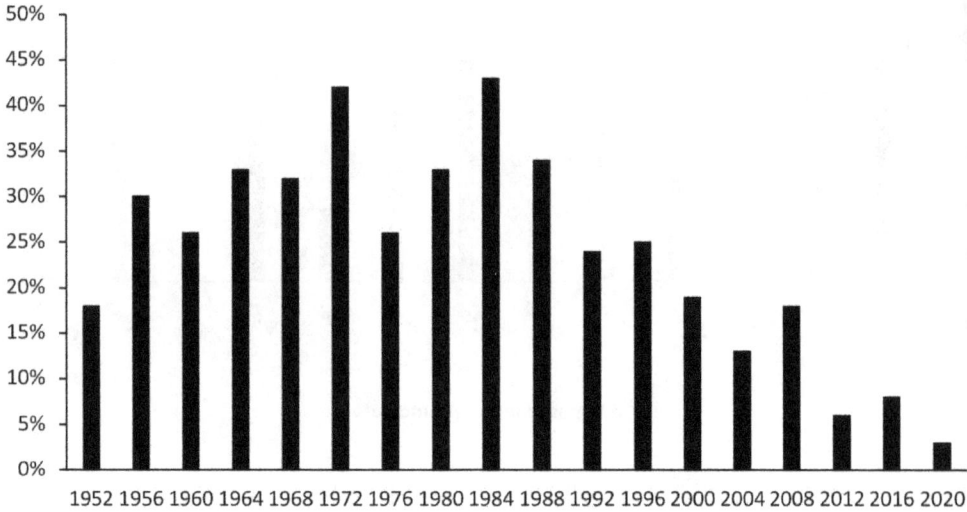

FIGURE 5.6 Split-ticket voting.

Note: Percentage splitting their party vote between presidential and House candidates 1952–2020.

Source: Robert Y. Shapiro, "Perspectives on Presidential Elections, 1992–2000: Introduction," in *Perspectives on Presidential Elections, 1992–2000*, ed. Robert Y. Shapiro (New York: Academy of Political Science, 2021), 16.

and congressional candidates of the same party reached an all-time high as well: a dramatic drop after 2008 in "split-ticket" voting (i.e., voting for presidential and congressional candidates of different parties), reaching a low of under 5 percent in 2020.

This increase in partisan animosity is clear. It reflected perceived—because they were real—striking differences between the parties and the parties' candidates. What were these differences? They did not just lie in personalities and styles of politicking and leadership. Democrats and Republicans increasingly disliked the opposition for what they stood for in terms of positions on political issues and in the ideology associated with those issues.

PARTISAN CONFLICT, POLICY ISSUES, AND IDEOLOGY

To assert in this century that the Democratic and Republican Parties had come to differ ideologically and on all manner of policy issues is to state the obvious. But that was not the case earlier in this American two-party system. It was clearly not so in the mid-twentieth century, for which there are data and studies of public opinion and voting that provide a frame of reference for examining the differences between the Democratic and Republican Parties.[8] Indeed, in 1950, the American Political Science Association (APSA) published "Toward a More Responsible Two-Party System: A Report," which took issue with this lack of difference between the two major parties.[9] The report lamented that the country's two parties did not offer voters clear choices so they could, as in parliamentary systems (theoretically, anyway), elect new governments that could change the direction of policies to deal with the nation's problems. This objective required competitive parties that could win elections, leading to unified party government.

How did this transformation of the parties come about? To answer that we must look at politics at the levels of both political leaders and American public opinion. At the time of the 1950 APSA report, which followed the nation's relative consensus during World War II and the Depression, the Democratic and Republican Parties were not divided on a wide range of issues. Liberal-conservative battle lines were drawn only on economic matters—on issues of economic welfare, regulation, labor, and, in general, the role of an activist "big government".[10]

The simplified view of this divide, which came out of the New Deal realignment of the parties, was that the Democrats were the party of the poor and working people up against conservative Republicans, who defended business interests and opposed an active, high-spending government. At the same time, the Republicans were more liberal than the Democrats when it came to civil rights and liberties: they were still the party of Abraham Lincoln, which had sided with the descendants of slaves against Southerners in the Democratic Party; and, often not well remembered, Republicans also had taken the side of women in the struggle for the right to vote and, later, with the proposed Equal Rights Amendment to the Constitution (until removing it from its party platform in 1980).[11]

In contrast, the Democrats were an uneasy alliance of northern liberals and anti–civil rights and antilabor Southerners. The alliance held together because both regional wings of the party were in agreement on economic welfare policies, for which the South had a great need and stake. In this uneasy union, issues bearing on the rights of Blacks in the Jim Crow South were kept off the political agenda.[12]

The Democrats' New Deal coalition endured for years, but it unraveled when the civil rights issue could no longer be suppressed. The political history is too long to do it justice here, but the issue began to gain momentum after World War II as the civil rights movement and its leaders—most notably Martin Luther King, Jr.—put civil rights on the political agenda. The role of Lyndon Johnson, both as president and the nation's leading Democrat, was crucial in what followed, culminating in the passage of the Civil Rights Act of 1964 and Voting Rights Act of 1965, with their bans against racial discrimination and segregation and against state actions that had prevented African Americans from voting in the South. In short, the northern liberal wing of the Democratic Party won out over its southern conservative, anti–civil rights wing, with support from pro-rights Republicans.

In response, the Republican Party began to change, moving away from the party of Lincoln. President Richard Nixon promoted a "Southern strategy" for the party, as the Democratic Party became a less welcome home for anti–civil rights white Southerners and sought to make up for this loss of political support by mobilizing in its favor Black voters, especially those who were newly enfranchised. With this change, the Republican Party became a conservative political force on racial issues and also on other issues, which, starting in the 1960s, became closely associated with race—especially law and order and "welfare" assistance for the poor.[13]

This transformation of the parties subsequently went far beyond civil rights issues. Over time, old and new issues rose in salience, which initially were not partisan. They came to include some highly emotional issues, such as rising rates of crime and violence, gun control, abortion, gay rights (and, later, gay marriage), the legalization of marijuana, and other matters connected to personal rights and religious values. Along with these issues were the ongoing and expanding partisan divide on the issues of economic welfare and inequality, health care, labor, regulation of business, environmental protection (later "climate change/global warming"), energy, and even national security and diplomacy in foreign affairs. New battle lines were drawn in these policy areas, and the parties consistently realigned internally or, as academics started calling it, "sorted" themselves along liberal-Democratic versus conservative-Republican lines.[14] Over time, party leaders diverged on these issues in predictable ideological ways. This conflict at the elite level became more pronounced and publicly visible, especially as the issues were covered by the media and became contentious in policy making and electoral politics. The conflict slowly penetrated to the level of mass opinion—to self-identified Democrats and Republican among the public.[15]

The data revealing this transformation of the parties are striking. The opinions of Democrats and Republicans diverged over time, just as the divide had played out first among political leaders and politicians in both parties. This is among the most stunning set of findings in the historical study of public opinion survey data.[16] We could have reported a great many more, perhaps hundreds, of partisan trends here. Many of these trends are reported in other works and online postings.[17] The trend data tell various stories about party politics and public opinion over periods since the 1970s, when the transformation of the parties became evident at the elite level.

IDEOLOGICAL DIFFERENCES

To start, we can readily see what happened for the parties and their leaders. Figure 5.7 captures the political leadership story in the House of Representatives, which is a common frame of reference among American political scientists. It and other closely related data show the divergence between politicians in both parties in both the House and the Senate. The divergence reached the point of partisan polarization at which there are fewer ideological moderates in the Congress than there used to be. The timing

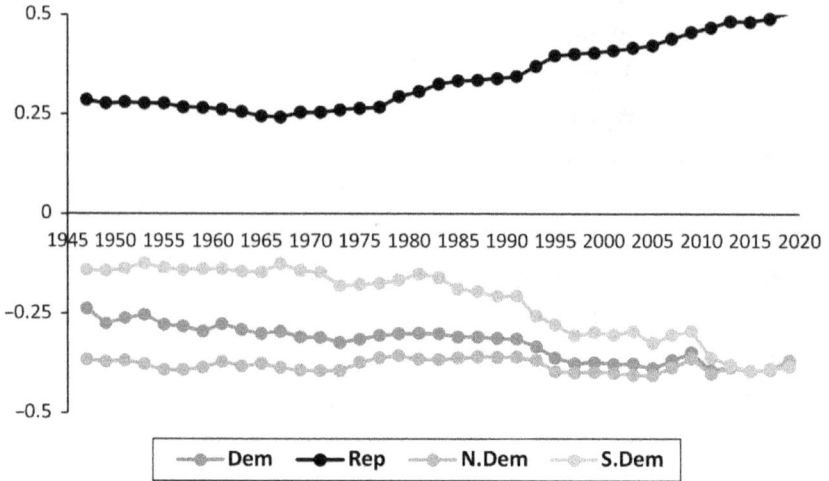

FIGURE 5.7 DW-NOMINATE (dynamic weighted nominal three-step estimation) scores, House of Representatives.

Note: Scores for Republicans versus Democrats, 1947–2019 (high values are conservative). N.Dem = Northern Democrats; S.Dem = Southern Democrats.

Source: Jeffrey B. Lewis, Keith Poole, Howard Rosenthal, Adam Boche, Aaron Rudkin, and Luke Sonnet, Voteview: Congressional Roll-Call Votes Database, 2023 https://voteview.com/data.

of the separation of the parties starts in the mid-1970s, when the effects of the transformation beginning with the civil rights revolution and turmoil of the 1960s became visible.

The increasingly liberal versus conservative ideological voting shown among members of the House of Representatives (figure 5.7) and the Senate (not shown) are an indication of the increase in partisan ideological disagreement among political leaders. These "DW Nominate Scores," as they are called and as developed by the political scientists Howard Rosenthal and Keith Poole, are a measure of liberal/conservative ideology (high values are conservative) based on roll call votes in Congress.[18] We see how Democratic and Republican House and Senate members diverged ideologically after the 1970s. The figure illustrates the high level of policy disagreement between leaders in the two parties and shows the extent to which the parties and their leaders offered clear choices to voters at the level of policy making.

To digress briefly, we note there is a positive aspect to the choices offered by this divergence among partisan leaders concerning policies and how to deal with national problems. It need not turn into animosity, uncivil behavior, and the inability to reach compromises. The partisan trends in DW-NOMINATE (dynamic weighted nominal three-step estimation) scores appear to show, overall, somewhat greater movement to the right by Republicans than to the left by Democrats. This is consistent with arguments that the partisan changes have been one-sided or "asymmetric," with Republicans driving the increase in partisan conflict.[19] The data for the public, however, do not show any decisive asymmetry, and Democrats in Congress did overall become somewhat more leftward oriented between 1970 and 2000 due to changes among Southern Democrats. In this respect, any blame directed toward either or both parties for the negative effects of polarization has more to do with other attitudes, perceptions, and behavior, discussed elsewhere.

The partisan divergence that occurred in Congress was reflected in political debates and in time occurred in public opinion as well among those who identified themselves as either Republicans or Democrats. They began to diverge along liberal and conservative lines, consistent with the rhetoric and behavior of their political leaders. Looking at public opinion concerning various policy issues, we do not see partisan divergence coinciding precisely with the timing of the trends in congressional voting. Rather, it varies by issue.[20] However, the trends in the public's overall self-reported liberal/conservative ideology tracked well what happened among partisan leaders.

Figure 5.8 shows the increase in the percentage of Republicans among the public who report they are conservatives and the decrease among Democrats. By the same token, there was an increase in the percentage of liberals among Democrats and the decline among Republicans (not shown). The increasing differences are striking beginning in the 1980s through 2020, widening threefold. The ideological conflict at the elite level clearly diffused—to put it mildly—into the public at large.

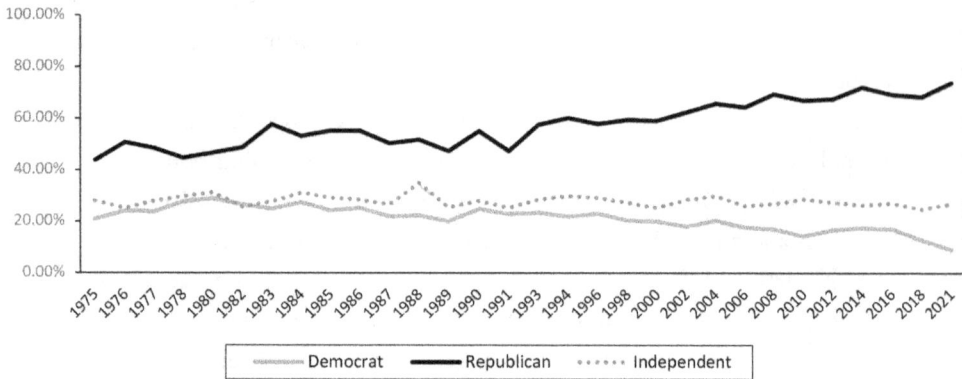

FIGURE 5.8 Conservative ideology.

Note: Percentage conservative, categories 5–7 (see appendix), by party.
Source: NORC-GSS.

PARTISAN CONFLICT ON ISSUES

What did this growing partisan conflict mean in terms of partisan disagreements in public attitudes and opinion concerning specific policy
issues? Here the conflicts that emerged, collectively, were more compelling. They occurred strikingly for a wide range of political issues. For a
great number of issues, we see how the public went from small or even
no partisan differences to an enormous level of disagreement. As a quick
overview, in tracking attitudes toward one set of issues, the Pew Research
Center reported how increases in partisan differences over time stood out
compared with constant differences for other subgroups based on demographic characteristics—race, age, gender, education, and religious attendance. This stability of differences indicated "parallel" trends for these
demographic subgroups.

In contrast, over the more than twenty years from 1994 to 2017,
partisan differences increased from fifteen to fully thirty-six percentage
points—a more than twenty-point increase on average, more than double
the difference—across a range of issues. This compared with increases

in differences by race, religious attendance, age, sex, and education of no more than five percentage points, if there was any change at all.[21] That partisan increases averaged twenty points meant that there were smaller increases for some issues but also substantially larger ones for others.

BIG GOVERNMENT AND SOCIAL WELFARE

Looking at a full range of issues and longer periods, we find even greater partisan conflict. To begin this whirlwind review of the data, there were partisan differences on issues dealing with "big government," regulation, economic well-being, and social welfare policy. This disagreement goes back to the New Deal–era realignment of the parties. The divide between the parties among the public widened on those issues, which came to include health care and the need to address economic inequality more broadly.

As noted earlier, partisan conflict expanded—and in a much more strident and emotional way—into issues of racial equality and civil rights. The debate over racial political and economic inequality were inexorably connected. While moving forward on civil rights legislation, President Johnson, with the benefit of consolidating a liberal political coalition in Congress, also led the nation with his War on Poverty programs and in expanding access to health care with the establishment of Medicare for the elderly and Medicaid for the poor. This extended the United States' social welfare programs that began with the New Deal. It also, along with Johnson's other Great Society legislation, increased the number and scope of issues over which the parties would do battle going forward.[22]

Figures 5.9 and 5.10 show the widening partisan differences regarding big government and regulation. These were long-standing partisan differences of around twenty percentage points, with Republicans preferring smaller government and feeling there was too much government regulation of business. This difference grew after the Tea Party emerged, reaching nearly fully fifty percentage points by the end of the Obama administration.

A significant part of the expansion of the American welfare state in the New Deal's response to the Great Depression and in the War on Poverty—along with the enactment of Social Security, Medicare, and Medicaid—was

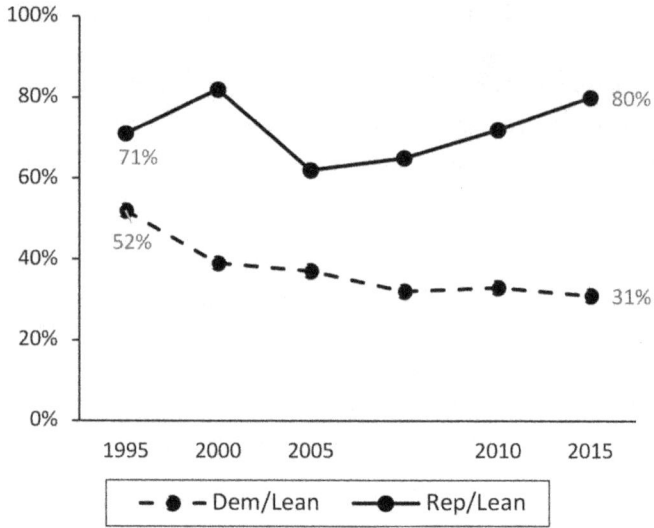

FIGURE 5.9 Support for small versus big government.

Note: Percentage who prefer a smaller government providing fewer services.

Source: Pew.

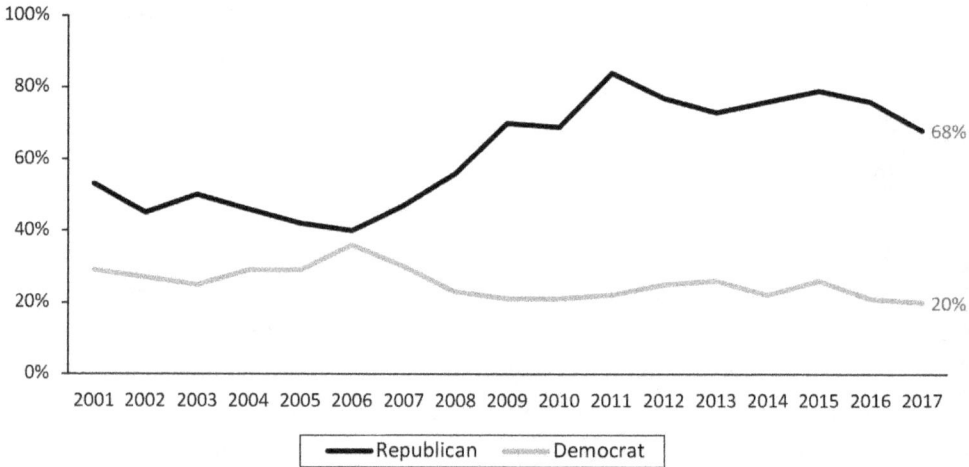

FIGURE 5.10 Opposition to government regulation of business.

Note: Percentage responding "too much" government regulation.

Source: Gallup.

economic assistance to the poor. In response to a well-known question on the General Social Survey of the University of Chicago's National Opinion Research Center (NORC-GSS), the twenty-point difference in the 1970s in the percentage of Republicans versus Democrats who said "we" were spending too much on "welfare"—the term most associated with assistance to the "undeserving poor" or those who defrauded the system—with Republicans more likely to claim "too much," grew into the 1990s and nearly doubled by the end of the Obama administration.[23]

In the case of health care policy, Medicare and Medicaid had been widely supported entitlement programs for the elderly and the poor. What followed them were more contentious efforts by the Democrats to expand the government's role in helping individuals get access to and afford health care. Efforts by Presidents Bill Clinton and Barack Obama to enact health care reforms were bitterly fought over.[24] While both Democratic presidents served during Democratic-controlled Congresses, Obama succeeded where Clinton failed because his party briefly benefited from a filibuster-proof Senate that enabled the Democrats to pass The Affordable Care Act ("Obamacare") with some clever legislative maneuvering.

The parties in Congress were deeply split in these cases, as was public opinion. Figure 5.11 exemplifies the partisan divide, which grew even further as Obamacare faced continued challenges by congressional Republicans, culminating in a shrill, unsuccessful legislative battle spurred on by President Trump, who had a deep and personal stake—his vendetta against Obama—in trying to terminate the Affordable Care Act.

In the 1970s, partisan differences in public support for government helping pay for medical care were not much more than ten percentage points (NORC-GSS survey data, not shown), but this gap widened substantially by the time Clinton fought his battle for reform; it broadened even further during the Obama presidency and reached more than thirty points as Trump persisted in attacking his predecessor's reforms. The increase in partisan conflict that ensued with the Tea Party's attack on Obama's reforms are shown more starkly in figure 5.11. In opinion surveys at the start of the Bush administration in 2001, Democrats more than Republicans, by a difference of thirty percentage points, responded that it

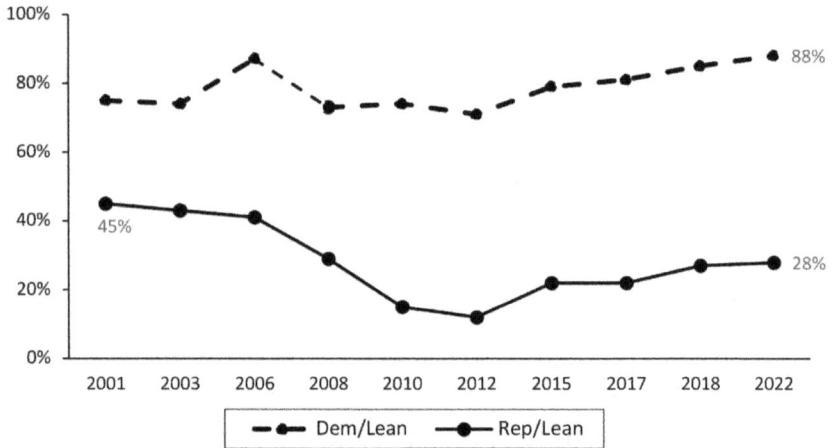

FIGURE 5.11 Support for government making sure all Americans have health care.

Note: Percentage saying it is the responsibility of the federal government to make sure all Americans have health care.

Source: Gallup.

was the "Responsibility of the Federal government to make sure all Americans have healthcare." This doubled to the fully sixty-point range by 2010 with the passage of the Affordable Care Act and the onslaught by the Tea Party—and where it remained thereafter (see figure 5.11).

CIVIL RIGHTS AND INEQUALITY

We see, then, how partisan conflict over the expansion of the role of government intensified for the public. The conflict went beyond that as the parties became divided in more sweeping ways—in the number of issues that divided the public as well as political leaders along liberal-conservative lines. This began with the highly divisive issues of civil rights and racial equality.

Figures 5.12 through 5.14 (and other data not shown) reveal the partisan differences that emerged strikingly after the party transformation occurred, putting Democrats and Republicans in conflict over the issue of racial inequality, with the Democrats unequivocally becoming the liberal defenders of civil rights. As noted earlier, the parties re-sorted themselves on this issue.

A key part of the sorting that contributed to this divide were Southern conservatives, who, over time, no longer self-identified as Democrats. By the 1970s, the battle lines had been redrawn, and they widened going forward, as shown in figures 5.12 to 5.14. There were more modest partisan differences in the 1970s concerning opinions toward the issues of giving Blacks preferential treatment, spending to improve their lives, and reducing racial discrimination. The differences between Democrats and Republicans doubled or tripled over the next forty or more years (see figures 5.12 and 5.13). Some of the later divergence occurred during the time of the Tea Party and ensuing conflict with the Obama administration, and some occurred with Trump's presidential candidacy and ascendance to office, with the differences reaching forty percentage points or more. There was a

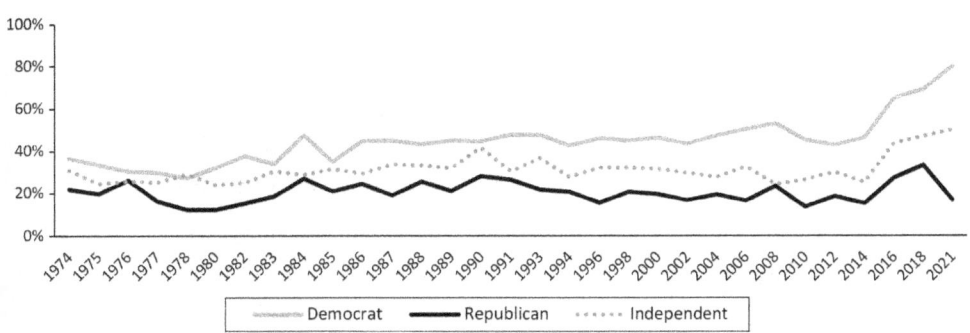

FIGURE 5.12 Support for national spending on improving the conditions of Blacks.

Note: Percentage responding "too little."

Source: NORC-GSS.

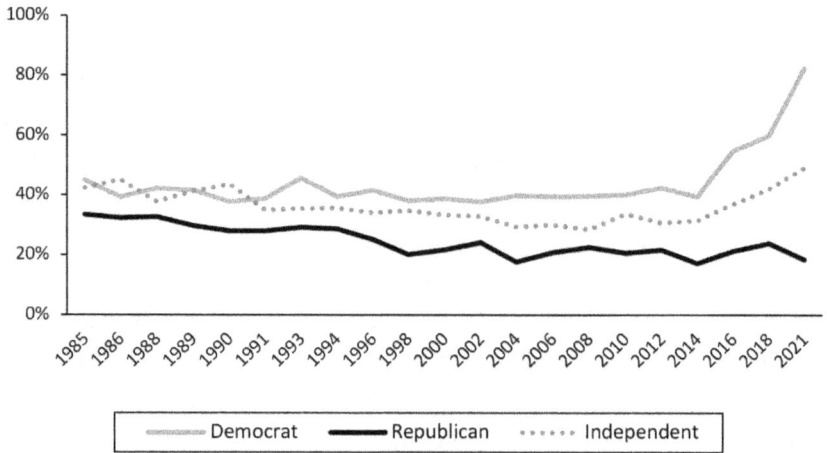

FIGURE 5.13 Racial differences due to discrimination.

Note: Percentage responding "Yes," non-Black respondents.

Source: NORC-GSS.

forty-five-point difference in opinions over the need to continue to pursue equal rights for Blacks (not shown).

These differences extended in 2021, as seen in figure 5.14, to issues about teaching about Black history and civil rights in the uproar over the teaching of critical race theory, in addition to continuing debates about the use of affirmative action in admission to colleges and universities and in employment (data not shown). The partisan difference here for approval of teaching about the history of racism is fully forty percentage points. Other data showed that from 2000 to 2018, the partisan gap regarding "not enough black history taught in schools" increased from twenty to fifty percentage points, with Democrats and Republicans moving in opposite directions.[25] This conflict over teaching about race fed into the far-right extremism described in other chapters.

Beyond racial equality, this interparty conflict expanded further as new issues arose and ongoing ones divided the parties and became more salient. Some were readily linked to interracial conflict. Assistance to the

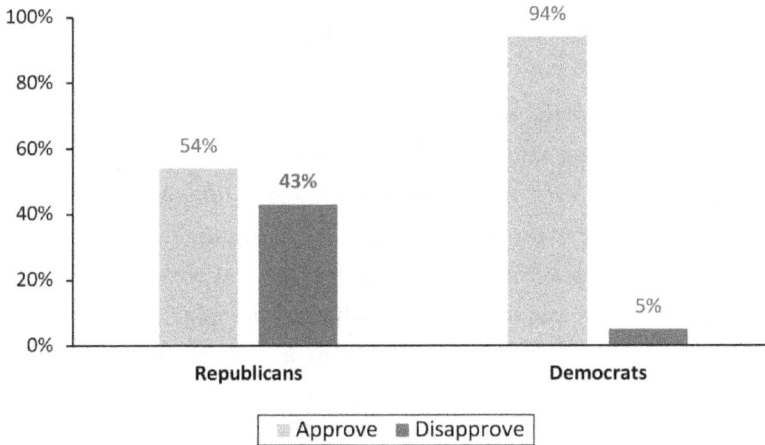

FIGURE 5.14 Support for teaching about the history of racism.

Source: Monmouth University, 11/2021.

poor—especially when framed not in terms of aid to those in desperate need, as Democrats were more likely to see it, but in terms of "welfare" associated with disincentives to work and possible fraud (Ronald Reagan's famous reference to "welfare queens"), the more common conservative Republican view—came to have a racial connotation because African Americans were more likely to be poor that whites.

Racial inequality and income inequality were interconnected, and it was hardly surprising to see an increase in partisan differences beginning in the 1970s in public support for government efforts to reduce income inequality. In response to a NORC-GSS question (not shown), Republicans became more supportive of "no action" and Democrats more likely to want government to act to reduce income differences. There was a spike in public support for no action coinciding with the early Obama administration and the rise of the Tea Party. Based on a Gallup question asking about support for redistributing wealth by raising taxes on the rich, partisan differences increased to fully fifty-five percentage points from 2008 to 2022 (79 percent among Republicans vs. 24 percent among Democrats).

LAW AND ORDER AND GUNS

Other major issues came out of the turmoil of the 1960s, the racial unrest in cities, rising crime rates, and debates over civil liberties. These had a racial dimension as well, with crime perpetrated in the African American community. This began on the Democrats' watch during the Johnson administration, and the Republican Party staked out "law and order" as its own partisan issue.[26] Partisans among the public diverged on opinions toward capital punishment for murder and the courts' treatment of criminals (see figure 5.15).

While support for capital punishment has remained solid as crime rates have risen and fallen, Democrats and Republicans have increasingly disagreed. What started as a fifteen percentage point difference in the early 1970s rose to a forty-point difference forty-five years later (not shown). Democrats since the 1990s have held less punitive attitudes (more likely to respond that the courts are "too harsh") toward criminals more generally, as figure 5.15 shows.

Opinion about firearms regulation is an anticrime attitude in terms of wanting to keep guns out of the hands of wrongdoers. In contrast, lessening restrictions on guns allows for their use for self-defense against would-be criminals. It is this latter perspective that, as we saw earlier, has been associated with Republicans' greater opposition to gun control or more severe restrictions compared with Democrats—and increasingly so, as shown earlier in figure 5.2.

The high level of support for requiring gun permits (NORC-GSS data not shown) has continued to have strong support but much less so for Republicans, by twenty percentage points, compared with essentially no partisan difference in the 1970s. This difference is starker when it concerns proposals for stricter gun laws: a partisan difference at the 60 percent level in 2022. This has made gun control a very divisive issue, as Republicans emphasized self-defense and the lawful use of weapons, while Democrats vehemently argued for the need to control guns to prevent shooting tragedies, as have occurred shockingly in recent years in schools and houses of worship.[27]

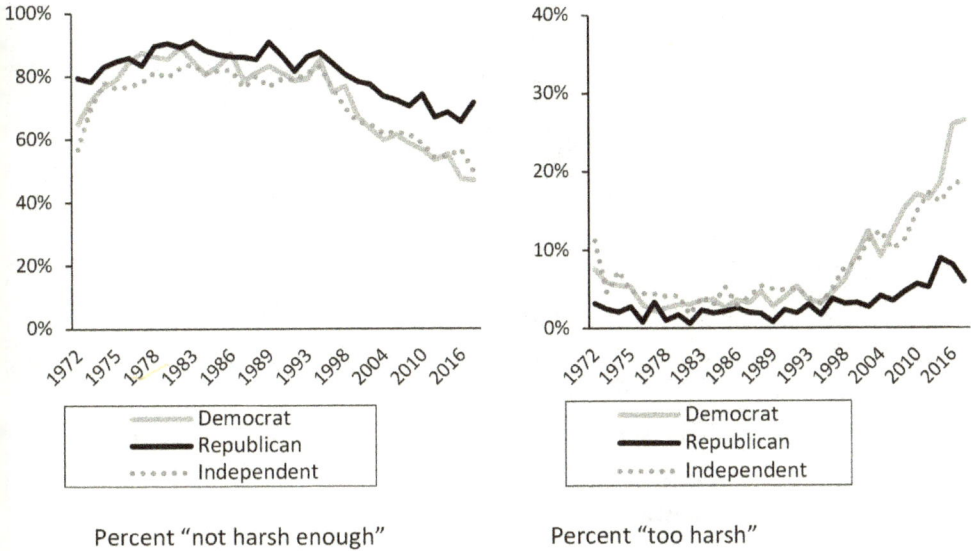

Percent "not harsh enough"   Percent "too harsh"

FIGURE 5.15 Courts too harsh or not harsh enough.

Source: NORC-GSS.

The legalization of marijuana has been a prominent issue, though less divisive than gun control and the other criminal justice concerns. While Democrats and Republicans have become more supportive of decriminalizing marijuana, Democrats have shifted more quickly in favor of legalization, so that the approximately five percentage point partisan difference in the 1970s grew to a twenty-five-point difference in later years (NORC-GSS data, not shown).

WOMEN, ABORTION, AND GAY RIGHTS

The issues just discussed from the 1970s going forward were accompanied by other new ones that emerged and have remained hot-button issues. The positions that the parties took came about through intraparty politics and competition. The parties' positions accordingly became defined as liberal Democratic versus conservative Republican. They often started out with little or no partisan divisions but subsequently became highly partisan, conflictual, and emotional.

For one, there were issues bearing on other individual rights and socio-religious values. Specifically, the role of women and especially abortion rights and, later, gay rights and gay marriage became the most emotionally charged issues.[28]

The most divisive issue concerning women was abortion rights. In is important to note that until sometime after the "pro-choice" (as opposed to "right to life") *Roe v. Wade* decision in January 1973, which legalized abortions nationwide, Republicans were, if anything, a bit more liberal than Democrats (NORC-GSS data, not shown). That, however, changed dramatically as the Republican Party became the party of conservative religious values and especially the right to life, compared with Democrats, who became substantially more pro-choice decades later (while Republicans' opinions became only somewhat more conservative regarding a woman wanting an abortion for "any reason"; NORC-GSS data, not shown).

By 2021, partisan differences had grown to the forty percentage point level or greater. In figure 5.16, based on responses to a question that asks directly about being pro-choice versus pro-life, we see a somewhat greater Republican movement in the pro-life direction (a decline in the "pro-choice" response) than Democrats in the pro-choice direction: the sixteen percentage point difference in the 1990s increased threefold to fully forty-eight points by 2021.

The size of the partisan gap reflected the bitterness of the political battle over abortion, much the same way that the political conflict over gun rights has played out, with the Republican Party representing support of restrictions on abortions for women but greater rights for gun owners. This conflict was front and center after the *Dobbs* v. *Jackson Women's Health Organization* (June 24, 2022) decision by the Supreme Court overturned *Roe* v. *Wade*, and it embroiled those on both sides of the issue even further at both

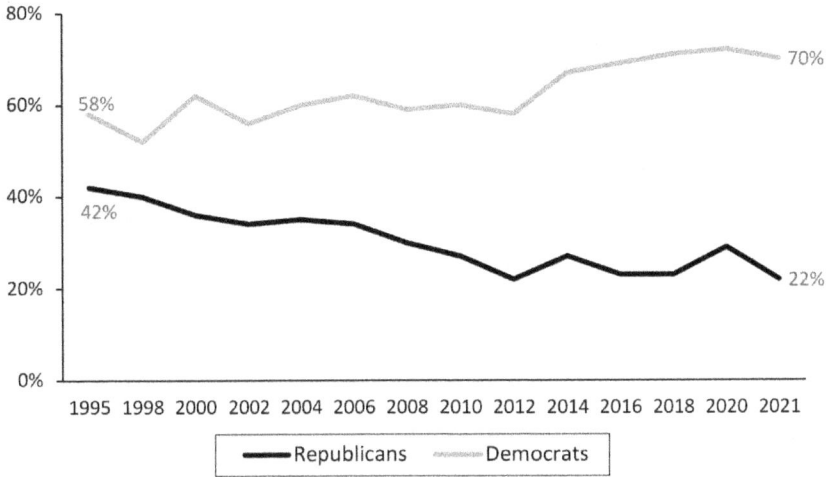

FIGURE 5.16 Abortion: pro-choice.

Note: Percentage responding "pro-choice."

Source: Gallup.

the national and especially the state level, the latter being where the legal status of abortions for individuals who seek to obtain them is determined.

Gay rights and gay marriage also became new and highly divisive issues in American politics. As in the case of abortion, Republicans and Democrats initially saw eye to eye in opposing homosexual behavior (few in the 1970s thought it was "not wrong at all" according to NORC-GSS data, not shown) and gay marriage (hardly anyone supported it at the time of the AIDS scare in the 1980s). The Republican Party thereafter remained the anti–gay rights party, as opposed to the Democratic Party, which increasingly supported these rights. While Republicans became more open on these issues, over three or more decades, the partisan gap nonetheless increased to twenty percentage points for homosexual behavior being not wrong at all and to thirty points regarding support for gay marriage, as shown in figure 5.17.

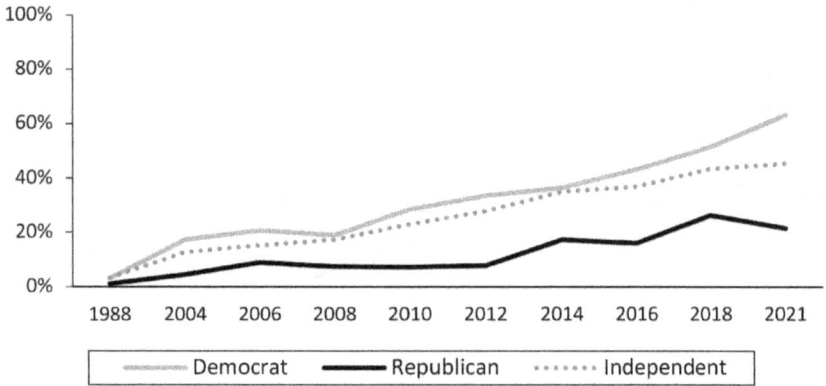

FIGURE 5.17 Gay marriage: homosexuals should have the right to marry.

Note: Percentage responding "strongly agree."

Source: NORC-GSS.

THE ENVIRONMENT

Beyond these rights of individuals, the new societal issues of environmental protection and energy policy grew in salience and importance and appeared in debates about "global warming" and "climate change." Clean air and water were issues at the time of Lyndon Johnson's presidency in the 1960s. Government became more active regarding the environment during the Republican Nixon administration, with the Endangered Species Act, the National Environment Policy Act, the creation of the Environmental Protection Agency, and passage of the Clean Air Act and a Clean Water Act, following up on government action in this area that had occurred much earlier. What was at first a bipartisan issue ultimately became increasingly partisan, related to differences regarding government regulation of business and the priority given to the economy.

Fast-forwarding into the twenty-first century, we see the battle lines drawn as environmental protection shift dramatically into the issue of

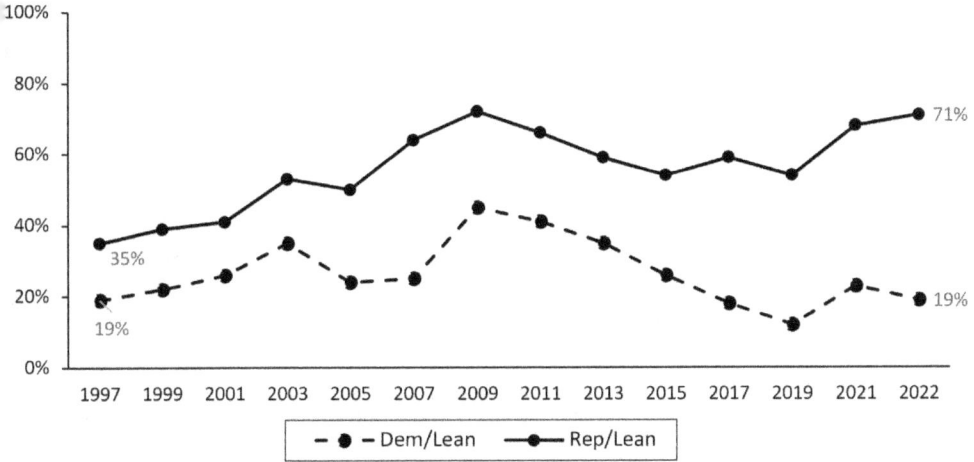

FIGURE 5.18 Economy versus environment.

Note: Percentage preference for prioritizing the economy over the environment.

Source: Gallup.

global warming and climate change. When NORC-GSS started asking about support for government spending to protect the environment a few years after the first Earth Day in 1970, a majority responded that government was spending too little. There was also a bit more than a ten percentage point difference between Democrats and Republicans. Forty-five years, later that difference rose to forty percentage points (data not shown).

Figures 5.18 and 5.19 show the trend that has ended with a more than forty-point difference. Figure 5.18 illustrates the differences in the percentage of Republicans compared with Democrats who prioritize the economy over the environment; a difference of sixteen points in 1997 reached a striking fifty-two points in 2022. Figure 5.19 presents a comparable trend over the last two decades in the Democrats worrying a "great deal" more (by forty-six points) than Republicans about the "quality of the environment."

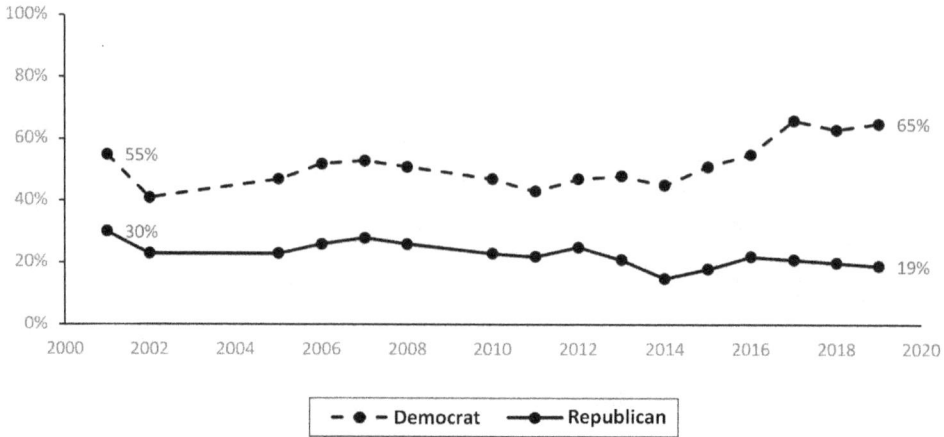

FIGURE 5.19 Concern for the environment.

Note: Percentage saying they worry a great deal about the quality of the environment.
Source: Gallup.

FOREIGN POLICY AND NATIONAL SECURITY

This increasing partisan divide not only covered a wide range of major domestic policies, but it occurred as well in the politics of foreign policy and national security issues. Politics no longer stopped at the water's edge, so to speak, but extended to the United States' interactions with the world and its defense of the nation. There was consensus after World War II about the U.S. role in the world—in its valuing diplomacy, international institutions, and the use of force abroad as necessary. There were partisan differences—as may be expected in politics—that reflected support for the policies of the president from one's party. That all changed in a fundamental way.

The Democratic Party became the one seen as more supportive of diplomacy and international institutions, whereas the Republican Party and, in turn, its supporters became more predisposed toward the unilateral use of military force. The terrorist attacks on September 11, 2001, the occupation of Afghanistan, followed by the invasion of Iraq in 2003 by the Bush administration, furthered the partisan divide that had emerged slowly after the Vietnam War. The increasing divide was related to differences in attitudes toward Muslims and the Muslim world and with respect to the Israeli-Palestinian conflict.

Political tensions increased during the Obama administration, with his rocky relations with Israel and Prime Minister Benjamin Netanyahu. Donald Trump took office and established better personal relations with the prime minister and voiced more support for Israel than Obama had. These trends are captured in figures 5.20 to 5.22.

After the end of the Cold War, majorities in both parties thought the best way to ensure peace was through diplomacy, though more Democrats than Republicans thought so. Figure 5.20 shows the extent to which that changed from 1994 to the September 11, 2001, terrorist attacks and the wars in Afghanistan and Iraq, which occurred under the watch and leadership of Republican President George W. Bush. Donald Trump's agenda, once he was elected president, was to pull the United States back from international diplomacy and support for international organizations, offering a stunning contrast to Democratic President Barack Obama, who was a proponent of diplomacy over the unilateral use of military force. This divergence in policy pulled the parties further apart, so that the sixteen-point partisan difference in 1994 more than doubled to more than forty points when Trump took office in 2017. (It remained at a thirty-seven-point difference in 2019.). Similarly, and surprisingly, given the Cold War consensus toward containing the Soviet Union, a partisan gap emerged with regard to the United States increasing or maintaining its commitment to NATO (the North Atlantic Treaty Organization), though there was still bipartisan majority support as Trump was leaving office (data now shown).

Figure 5.21 shows how the parties have differed since the end of the Cold War in their thinking that the United States was spending too little on national defense. There was no difference at the time of, and just after, the first Gulf War of 1990–91. Twenty years later, Republicans differed from Democrats by twenty percentage points or more in responding that too little was spent on defense, and this gap widened further thereafter.

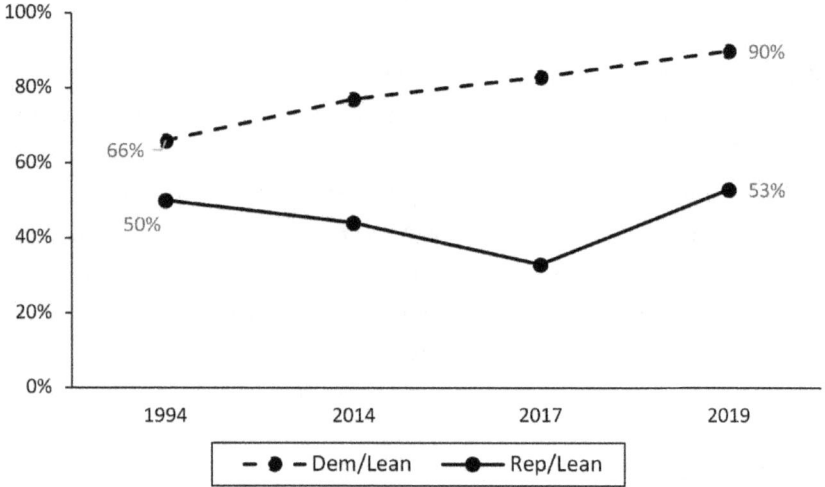

FIGURE 5.20 Public support for diplomacy.

Note: Percentage saying that good diplomacy is the best way to ensure peace.

Source: Pew.

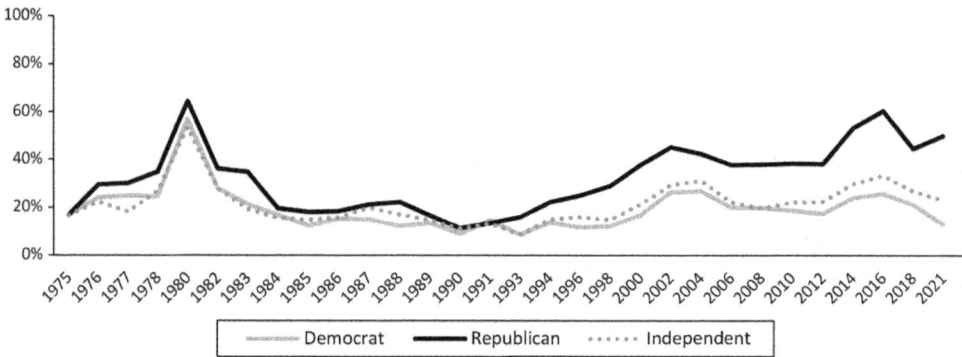

FIGURE 5.21 Public support for defense spending.

Note: Percentage responding "too little" national spending on military-armaments-defense/national defense.

Source: NORC-GSS.

In contrast, during the same period, Democrats compared with Republicans became less opposed to government spending on foreign aid. During the Trump administration, Democrats were less likely to think we were spending too much on foreign aid, by more than twenty percentage points versus Republicans, who much more consistently over time thought too much was being spent (not shown).

With the election of President Obama, a fissure between the parties regarding support for Israel that had emerged with anti-Muslim sentiment after the September 11 terrorist attacks solidified and grew wider. This is apparent in data (not shown) from 1978 onward from surveys by the Chicago Council on Foreign Relations (later renamed the Chicago Council on Global Affairs) and the Pew Research Center, in which respondents were asked whether they "sympathized" more with Israel or the Palestinians. Responses to a similar Gallup Poll question shows strikingly (see figure 5.22) that partisan differences in net sympathy for Israel versus the Palestinians increased from virtually no difference in 2001 to a stunning seventy-point difference after 2020 (the negative 11 represents the first time

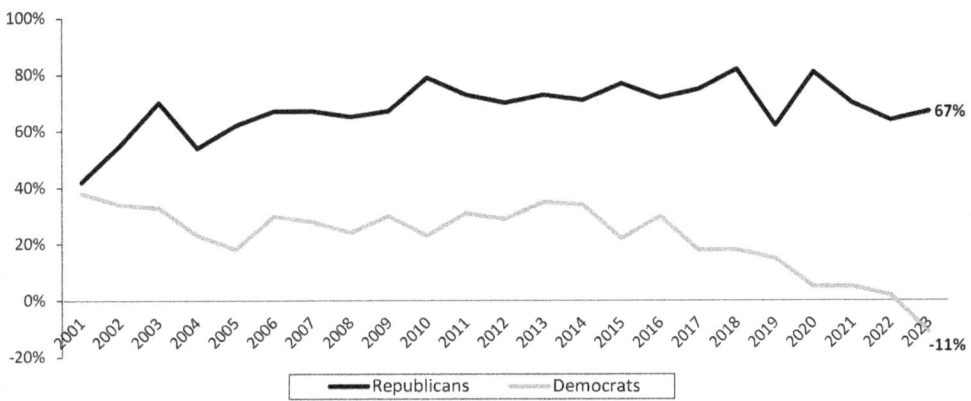

FIGURE 5.22 Net sympathy for Israelis (vs. Palestinians).

Note: Percentage more sympathetic to the Israelis minus the percentage more sympathetic to the Palestinians.

Source: Gallup.

more Democrats than Republicans sympathized more with the Palestinians than with the Israelis).

Other data (not shown) track how Democrats' support for "Palestinian Statehood" grew further, to 60 percent, after Obama became president and a twenty-nine-point partisan gap with Republicans remained until 2019, after Trump had been in office and had established more positive relations with Prime Minister Netanyahu. We see the same thing for the Democrats versus Republicans regarding support for putting more pressure on Israel in its conflict with the Palestinians: there was thirty-six-point partisan difference by the time Trump left office in 2021 (not shown).

TRADE AND IMMIGRATION

Foreign policy issues, then, became an additional touch point for partisan conflict, and they became highly charged at times, especially in the transition from Obama to Trump. This was particularly true for two types of issues that had foreign in addition to domestic policy aspects: policies concerning trade and immigration. International trade and immigration were hot-button issues in the 2016 election and after. They had not been highly partisan issues in the past, if distinctively partisan at all, but that changed significantly. For one, jobs in the manufacturing sector in particular were being lost due to foreign competition, and companies were moving jobs abroad that had been held by Americans. This issue was raised by the left wing of the Democratic Party, led by Senator Bernie Sanders, among others, challenging Democrats who had backed free trade orientation, especially in relations with Mexico and Canada.

It was President Bill Clinton's administration that had passed NAFTA (the North American Free Trade Agreement). Jobs were being lost to China and other countries in Asia. Meantime, the positive aspects of globalization were being touted by Democrats, among others, who did not want to put restrictions on the global economy at this stage. But the loss of jobs was affecting working-class Americans in the manufacturing and related sectors, especially reaching small town areas in addition to larger manufacturing centers, especially in the Midwest.

This shift gave Republicans an opportunity—which they took—to attract voters by emphasizing economic vulnerability and the need to protect American jobs. Democrats became vulnerable on trade and globalization. A new partisan conflict emerged, which was played up by the Tea Party and others on the political right after Obama took office during the Great Recession, which had begun in 2008. Trump emphasized and capitalized on this fact, stating he would end NAFTA and prevent further detrimental trade agreements such as the Trans-Pacific Partnership agreement (TPP).

We see the emergence of this political battle at the level of American public opinion. Partisan conflict widened regarding the NAFTA agreement, with fewer Republicans than Democrats (by thirty-six percentage points) seeing that treaty as a "good thing" by the time Trump took office (data not shown). While figure 5.23 shows that majorities of Democrats and Republicans still saw the effects of globalization as "mostly good" for

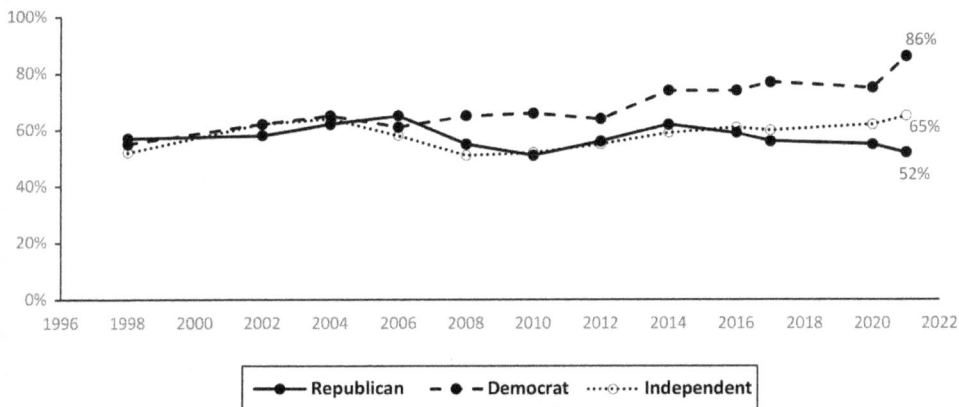

FIGURE 5.23 Public opinion regarding globalization.

Note: Percentage responding that the effects of globalization are mostly good for the United States.

Source: Chicago Council on Global Affairs.

the United States, the partisan difference grew to twenty points by the time Trump was elected, and it widened further after Biden replaced Trump as president.

While legal and undocumented immigrants also posed a threat to Americans' jobs, the Tea Party, Trump, and others framed immigration—especially from Mexico or through the Mexican border—as a threat to the nation, leading to more deadly crime and Latino gang activity. That these immigrants were largely nonwhite posed a racial as well as cultural threat to Americans' white identity. What had been a nonpartisan issue at the end of the twentieth century became a major, highly emotional one.

This is strikingly found in the opinion trend data. As late as 2002, there was no partisan difference in individuals seeing immigration as a "critical threat" to the United States (not shown), and in figure 5.24, no difference is found in viewing the need to control immigration as a major policy goal. Nearly twenty years later, these differences grew to fully forty-six and fifty-four percentage points, respectively.

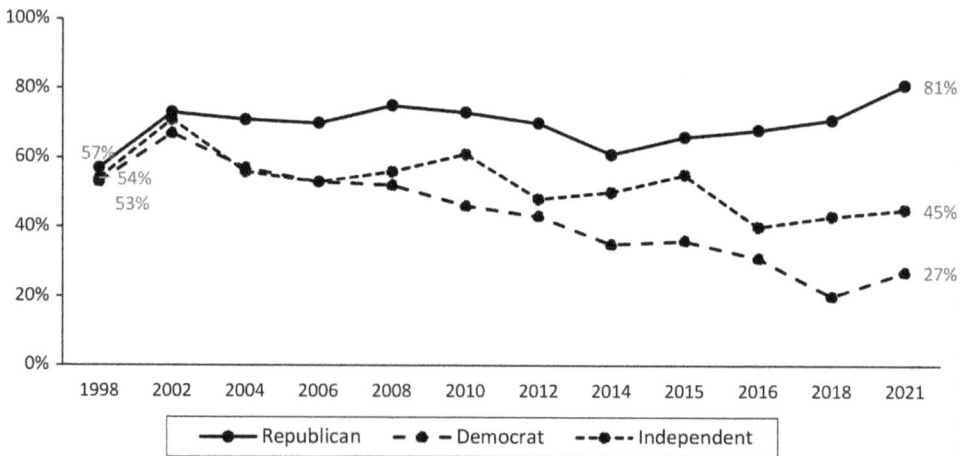

FIGURE 5.24 Controlling illegal immigration.

Note: Percentage responding that controlling illegal immigration is an important foreign policy goal.

Source: Chicago Council on Global Affairs.

Such differences concerning immigration have been politically important. They are at the core of the Make American Great Again (MAGA)/ America First movement, and they were radicalized by Donald Trump's hate speech against nonwhite minorities, as discussed in previous chapters.

THE COVID-19 PANDEMIC

Unlike the other issues we have described, the COVID-19 pandemic took everyone completely off guard. How all levels of American government responded to the pandemic became highly politicized, as well as the public's reaction to it.[29] COVID-19 got caught in and expanded the already high level of partisan conflict during the Trump administration. Populist rhetoric on the political right evoked powerful emotions—resentment and anger toward proponents of stringent government policies that attempted to control the spread of the coronavirus, including lockdowns of the economy and society writ large, testing requirements, social distancing, mask wearing, and other rules of (dis)engagement.

This conflict over the COVID-19 pandemic preceded the partisan fight over the outcome of the 2020 presidential election, both of which developments saw increasingly vehement partisan battling in American politics that had been catalyzed further by the Tea Party and then even further by Donald Trump. (Both are still more than lingering issues at this writing, April 2023.) The pandemic was a distinctive kind of issue, a global crisis for which one would expect a spirit of unity, not conflict. In the past, a national crisis or disaster of this sort may have led to some disagreement over how exactly to respond, but the major political parties would not normally become polarized over it.[30]

In the case of disastrous events like massive hurricanes, earthquakes, or fires, the federal government has provided assistance to states, localities, and their residents who have been harmed. Support for such emergency aid has typically been bipartisan. Public health crises involving diseases— most notably smallpox, the 1918 Spanish Flu, and polio—likewise have not become embroiled in partisan battles.[31] There have at times been disagreements over vaccine requirements for children and more generally in the United States, but opponents of vaccines—"anti-vaxxers"—who emerged in the past have come from both the political left and right—perhaps more so from the left.[32] These have not been partisan or even political issues. The COVID-19 pandemic, however, was different because it occurred during a particular time in American politics.

What happened with COVID-19 is too long to recount here, and its final history cannot be written yet. The virus posed too big a national and worldwide crisis to ignore, especially given the scope, speed, and overwhelming visibility of information communicated through the modern-day mass media. President Woodrow Wilson was able to ignore the Spanish Flu in day-to-day politics only because he had a bigger crisis to deal with: the ending of World War I and the international politics of establishing peace. In contrast, in 2020, President Trump had to take on COVID-19 much closer to an election, since his handling of it inevitably would have severe electoral consequences for him and his party. However, Trump did not at all see the pandemic as a national crisis of wartime magnitude threatening the lives of Americans—a crisis in which he could rise in stature the way Presidents Abraham Lincoln, Wilson, or Franklin Roosevelt had done during wartimes.

Rather, Trump saw COVID-19 mainly as a threat to the thriving economy that he had presided over—with modest economic growth and an all-time low unemployment rate along with low inflation. This strong economy would normally enable an incumbent president to glide through to reelection. Both political parties in Congress and Trump rallied to pass emergency legislation in response to the need to lock down parts of the country, including schools in a great many states. The emergency action especially replaced individual, family, and business incomes, which were lost as a large chunk of the nation's nonessential businesses and offices shut down, and it included funds for public health measures to deal with the pandemic. Trump's most significant accomplishment was to provide substantial support to fast-track the development of vaccines—in what was called "Operation Warp Speed."[33]

Beyond that, however, Trump did not use the public health crisis to rally the nation to deal more urgently and fully with the virus using all know prevention measures for which he could get bipartisan support. He could have done so: Democrats would have been receptive, and Trump's fellow Republicans in Congress and his base in the electorate would have almost certainly supported what their president proposed. Moreover, to deal with the economic problems most effectively, the widespread consensus among economists, liberal and conservative alike, was that the virus had to be dealt with first before the economy could rebound strongly.[34]

Still, the toll on the economy was enormous, and Trump saw it as a political threat. He proceeded to downplay the pandemic. That led directly to a partisan political conflict over the need to reopen the economy, and it led Trump, his Republican allies, and their base of supporters to challenge the judgments and recommendations of epidemiologists and other medical and public health experts. An increasingly vehement battle line was drawn over how serious to take the virus as it ran its course. Democrats saw the public's health and safety as paramount. Republicans were more concerned with the economic and other effects on individuals that shutting down the economy and social life was causing nationwide.

The available survey data and numerous studies quickly showed that opinions regarding the proposed public health measures in addition to governmental performance divided along partisan and ideological lines. There was a stark political conflict regarding the seriousness of the pandemic and the need for socially distancing, wearing masks, closing schools, and, when a vaccine became available, getting it into use most effectively to combat the virus—most controversially, by requiring individuals in all walks of life to be vaccinated.[35]

Partisan differences and increases in these differences in perceptions and attitudes toward the seriousness of the pandemic and responses to it are show in figures 5.25 to 5.28. Democrats more than Republicans saw COVID-19 as a "major threat," by twenty-six percentage points (59 to 33 percent, figure 5.25) at the outset of the pandemic in early 2020, and this increased to forty points or more into the summer and after. Further, at the start, Republicans more so than Democrats thought the coronavirus was

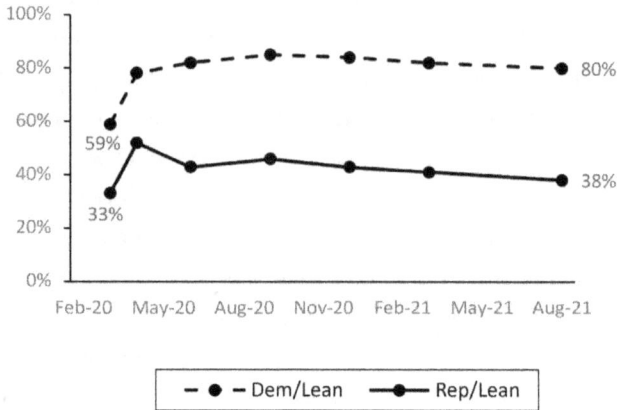

FIGURE 5.25 COVID-19 as a major threat.

Note: Percentage saying that the coronavirus outbreak is a major threat.

Source: Pew.

"made a bigger deal" than it really was, by thirty-three percentage points (47 to 14 percent; data not shown), which grew to nearly fifty points, where it remained into two years later (64 to 16 percent in early 2022; data not shown).

By the end of summer 2020, the Democrats had become, by nearly sixty percentage points (not shown), more critical of the government's inability to control the outbreak; the trend lines later converged to a twenty-seven-point gap by 2022 due to somewhat fewer Democrats expressing criticism of the now Democratic-controlled government and Republicans growing more likely to be critical of the opposition party's government. Figures 5.26 and 5.27 reveal the striking behavioral consequence of these increasingly partisan views of COVID-19: by summer 2020, Republicans were more than twenty points less likely to report wearing masks frequently, and this partisan difference increased to more than forty points a year later. Republicans were also much less likely to be vaccinated: by the fall of 2021, fully 92 percent of Democrats among adults surveyed reported being vaccinated fully or partially, compared with just 56 percent of Republicans.

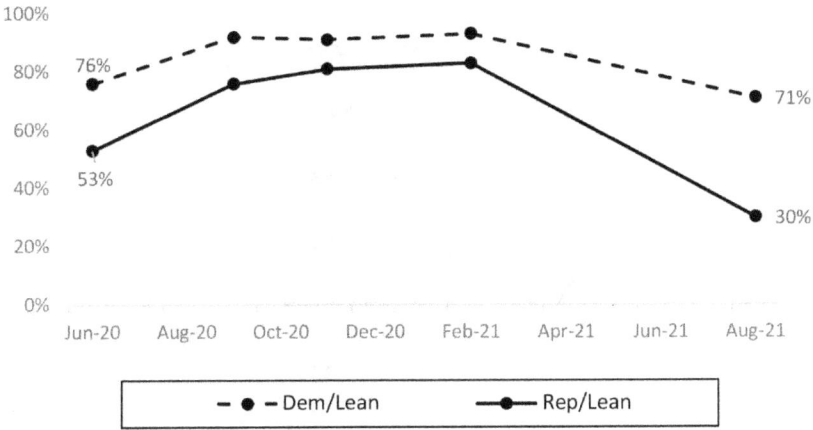

FIGURE 5.26 COVID-19 Mask Wearing.

Note: Percentage reporting frequent mask wearing.

Source: Pew.

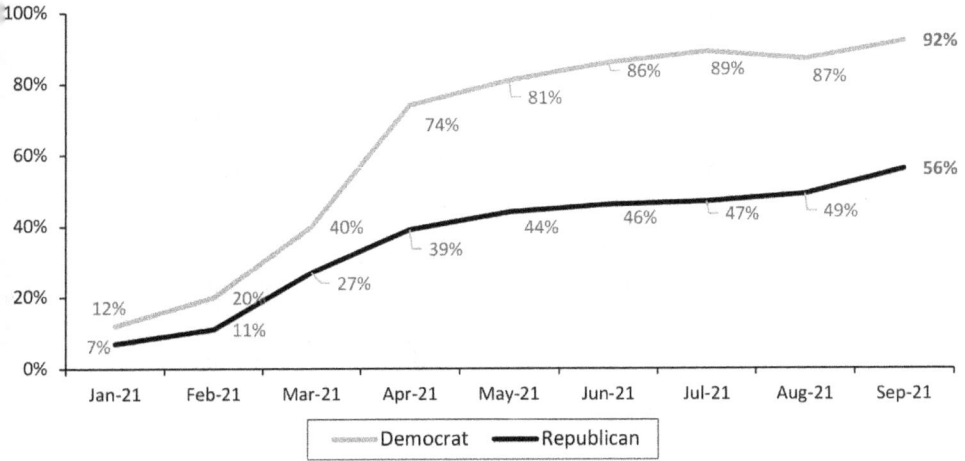

FIGURE 5.27 Vaccinations against COVID-19.

Source: Gallup 2021.

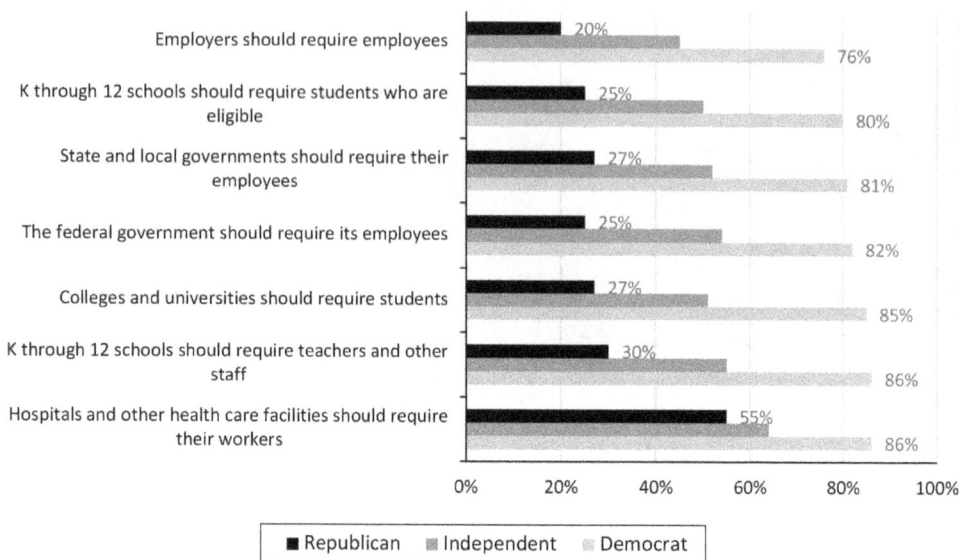

FIGURE 5.28 Support for requiring COVID-19 vaccinations.

Note: Each of the following should be required to get vaccinated for COVID-19 unless they have a medical exemption.

Source: Kaiser Family Foundation, 2021.

Figure 5.28 shows even more strikingly the overwhelming Republican opposition compared with Democrats to requiring people to be vaccinated—from private- and public-sector employees to students and staff in schools at all levels—by differences of well over fifty percentage points. The exception was the thirty-one-point difference for hospital and health care workers.

These conflicting partisan attitudes and behaviors were clearly associated with President Trump's attitudes and rhetoric regarding the pandemic and his treatment of scientific expertise, about which the mainstream media were reporting widely. Other data not shown here reveal corresponding partisan differences in attitudes toward science, expertise, higher education, and the media (see chapter 1).[36] The reality was that the United States had one of the greatest infection rates and the single largest number of deaths from COVID-19 of any country. That and the resulting harm done to the national economy contributed decisively to Trump's defeat in the 2020 election.[37]

The crisis continued after the election, with further partisan battling over public health measures, including, most prominently, controversial vaccine and mask requirements. Trump and other Republicans—continuing after the Biden administration took office and through this writing—were strongly opposed to aggressive restrictions and requirements in states and localities. These issues remained highly politicized along partisan lines, reaching a level of interpersonal conflict that was documented in news stories about threats and violent encounters over masking and other requirements.[38]

The conflicts over vaccines and mask requirements were deeply fraught with emotions and debates about the facts and reality of the health problems at hand, and these were reflected and amplified in the mass media and social media. The partisan struggle over COVID-19 stands out because of the nature and scope of the public health crisis, the deaths and injuries that came with it, and its further consequences for American politics.

LEADERS, THE MEDIA, AND ELECTORAL COMPETITION

This lengthy discussion of increases in partisan differences in public opinion could go further and cover even more issues. But the upshot is clear: public opinion trend data show that fundamental differences in policy preferences and ideology underlie the emotional dislike and anger that emerged. These long preceded the conflict over COVID-19 and the events of January 6, 2021.

American public opinion had changed psychologically since the 1970s, after shifts started occurring at the elite level in politics. Prior to this, when public opinion changed toward issues, partisans and all other subgroups largely changed in the same direction. What in the past had been parallel changes by Democrats and Republicans came to show striking divergence, with opinion differences widening between the parties across a broad range of government policies. This "partisan sorting" was highly emotional and strident on many matters of government policy. It was not benign—there was severe conflict here. The parallel changes that occurred in the past gave way to partisan divergence—on steroids. The information environment—events and social, economic, and political conditions, as communicated through the mass media—no longer had the same effect on all subgroups. The information and media content that individuals received no longer provided a common standard of judgment or framing for evaluating events and changes in real-world social and economic conditions and in politics—and for interpreting the debates about them among political leaders and others.[39] All that changed as partisan conflict increased.

The effect of this divergence was that Democrats and Republicans among the public were influenced to a greater extent by the information and standards of judgment provided by their partisan leaders, as communicated through the media[40] Moreover, the impact of this partisan conflict at the level political leaders was amplified by the media, because those organizations are businesses that are biased, if anything, toward content that attracts paying audiences; and it is conflict that attracts these audiences.[41]

What heightened the emotional level of politics even further was that as the partisan conflict grew, the parties were becoming more competitive electorally for control of all the levers of government. This created a new national politics in which the parties differed enormously and in which who wins elections can change the direction of government policies if either party can at the same time capture the presidency and gain control of both the House of Representatives and the Senate and who thereby also can determine appointments to the federal judiciary. That elections now mattered in this way raised the stakes and the level of conflict between the parties and between the supporters of the opposing parties. There was thus more conflict for the media to amplify.

Beginning in 1980, the parties became competitive for control of Congress, starting with the Senate. Since the 1930s, the presidency had alternated between the parties, but the Democrats held majorities and thereby control in the House and the Senate for most of the years between 1932 and 1980. That changed in 1980, when the Republicans gained control of the Senate on the coattails of Ronald Reagan's commanding defeat of Democratic President Jimmy Carter. The Republicans later, more stunningly, took majority control of the House as well as Senate in the 1994 midterm election fiasco for President Bill Clinton and the Democrats (so stunning that the Republicans and their House speaker, Newt Gingrich, became—and felt—enormously empowered).[42] A key part of this tighter competition was the political transformation in the South. The "Solid South"—the southern states that had elected Democrats to the House of Representative and the Senate for decades, began to elect and reelect Republicans.[43]

Figures 5.29 and 5.30 show clearly when the Republicans were able to start winning majorities in the House and the lion's share of southern seats

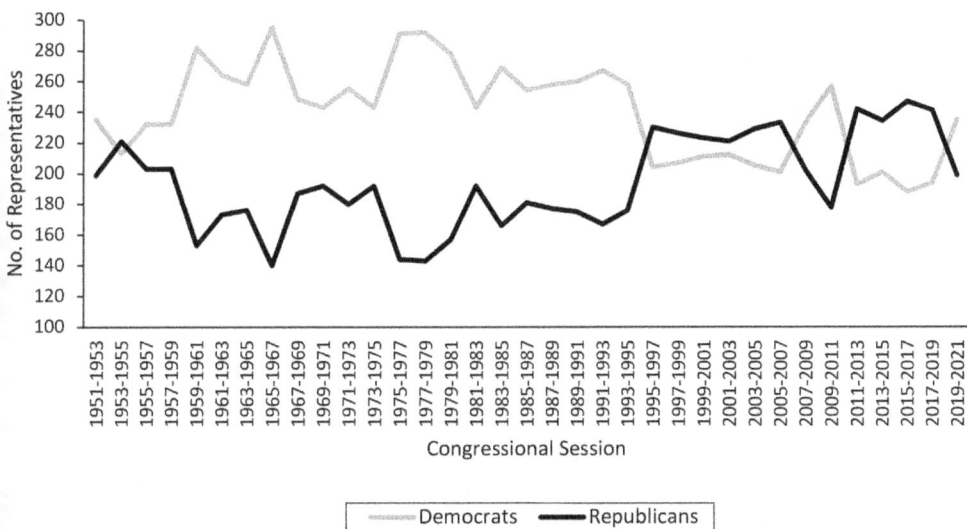

FIGURE 5.29 House of Representatives: partisan composition.

Source: Robert Y. Shapiro, "Perspectives on Presidential Elections, 1992–2000: Introduction," in *Perspectives on Presidential Elections, 1992–2000*, ed. Robert Y. Shapiro (New York: Academy of Political Science, 2021), 9.

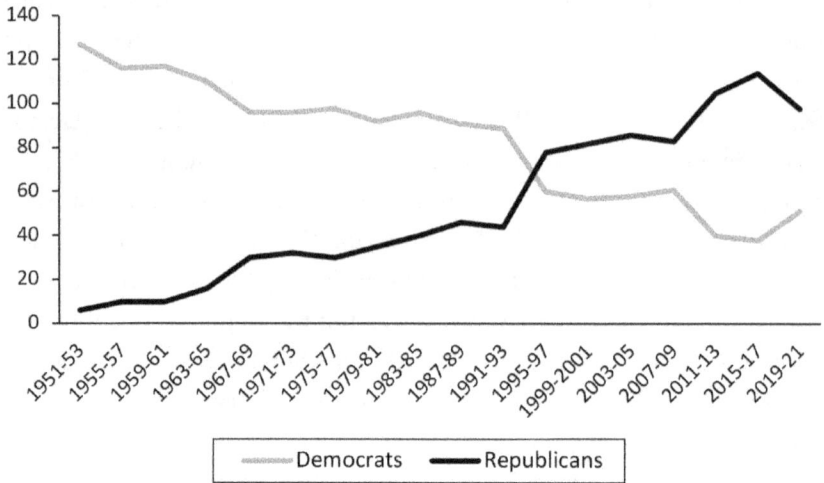

FIGURE 5.30 House of Representatives composition, 1951–2021: southern partisans.

Note: Number of Democratic versus Republican members of the House of Representatives from the South.

Source: Robert Y. Shapiro, "Perspectives on Presidential Elections, 1992–2000: Introduction," in *Perspectives on Presidential Elections, 1992–2000*, ed. Robert Y. Shapiro (New York: Academy of Political Science, 2021), 9.

in that chamber. The 1994 election result was pivotal. With this closer competition between the parties, it became increasingly possible for either party to sweep the national political races in a presidential election year and gain unified partisan control of the presidency and Congress. This also meant, again, control of all federal judicial appointments as proposed by the president and approved by the Senate.

This partisan power was further strengthened when Senate Democrats during Barack Obama's administration ended the Senate filibuster for federal appointments, including those for the judges below the U.S. Supreme Court. Senate Republicans later ended the filibuster for Supreme Court nominations when the election of Donald Trump gave them the opportunity to appoint conservative justices and thereby firmly change the ideological balance on the court. They had earlier used the filibuster in a spiteful partisan fashion to block President Obama's nomination, in his last year in office, of a successor to conservative Justice Antonin Scalia, who had died suddenly.

The very bitter politics of these Supreme Court nominations epitomized the heightened emotional level of partisan conflict during both the Obama and Trump administrations. And it continued when President Biden made his one nomination in 2022 (successful, but a close 53–47 Senate vote) to fill an opening on the Supreme Court.

Thus, elections had greater immediate consequences than before. Either party could obtain—and indeed has obtained—unified partisan control of all branches of government, which enables it to attempt to and succeed at changing the political agenda and ideological direction of government policy making. This has produced a politics that Morris Fiorina has called one of "unstable majorities."[44] Every president since 1992 has had, for a period, unified Republican or Democratic governments. This led to major policy changes: President George W. Bush's 2001 tax cuts and extension in 2003; President Obama's economic stimulus legislation and the enactment of the Affordable Care Act; President Trump's first-term tax reform legislation, his sweeping appointments to the federal courts, and his conservative transformation of the Supreme Court.

With Biden's victory in 2020 and the Democrats' assumption of control (albeit barely) of the Senate and control of the House, his administration was able to pass major spending legislation to deal with the pandemic and economic crisis—with the Democrats resorting to budget reconciliation bills, as needed, which require only a majority vote in the Senate. Biden was able to add many federal court judges as well. It is still the case that regular legislation can be filibustered, but there is the lingering threat that the party in control of the Senate could end that as well, which has raised considerably the stakes for Senate elections.

The battle for the presidency itself, of course, has also tightened and caused new tensions of its own. George W. Bush in 2000 and Trump in 2016 attained the presidency without winning the popular vote. Trump won the Electoral College vote by a total of fewer than eighty thousand votes from three states. Then, in 2020, although Biden won the popular vote handily, his Electoral College victory was by a total fewer than forty-five thousand votes, also from only three states. The Democrats then eked out runoff election victories in Georgia to gain control of the Senate (50–50 partisan split, with Vice President Kamala Harris providing the deciding vote). To say that emotions were high in these elections is another gross understatement. These emotions are reflected in the increase in affective polarization or negative partisanship described earlier.

PERCEPTUAL BIASES, CONSPIRACY THEORIES, AND POLITICAL VIOLENCE

The emotions tied to increased partisan conflict concerning issues and leaders and to close elections have pervaded attitudes beyond opinions on issues. These partisan emotions—especially anger—have affected individuals' perceptions of reality and factual information about political, societal, and economic conditions. From a psychological standpoint, these perceptions have affected political attitudes and opinions or, have been influenced by them after the fact, to achieve psychological consistency through processes of cognitive balancing or what has been called *motivated reasoning.*[45] Whether these perceptions are accurate or false, based on fact or fiction, or truth or lies does not matter. They become part of the emotional fervor—and anger—in politics. These emotions, as described earlier, are targeted toward the opposing parties, their leaders and candidates, and their supporters—extending even to how individuals interact with opposing partisans or avoid contact with them altogether. This pathological behavior not only involves perceptual biases regarding facts and realities, but it also pertains to the receptivity of individuals to conspiracy theories.

This behavior has reached the point, as many have claimed, that some Democrats and Republicans have come to reside in two different realities.[46] Evidence of this development preceded the COVID-19 pandemic, the debate about the results of the 2020 election leading to the events of January 6, and the two efforts to impeach and convict President Trump. That partisanship could lead to biases in perceptions goes back to the early voting studies,[47] which observed that partisan support or support for political leaders could lead to biases in perceptions of leaders' issue positions and even perceptions of economic conditions. But it was not apparent at the time of those studies that this would lead to widespread distortions. Figures 5.31 to 5.34 show some compelling examples of these distortions.

Figure 5.31 compares the perceptions of Democrats and Republicans regarding whether or not Saddam Hussein had weapons of mass destruction (WMDs)—the fact is that no WMDs were found. The results are the same concerning whether or not there was a connection between Iraq and al Qaeda in determining who was responsible for the September 11, 2001, terrorist attacks—the fact is that there was no connection. The differing partisan perceptions were tied to partisan conflict over Republic President Bush and his ordering of the invasion of Iraq in 2003, predicated on the existence of WMDs. (The argument about the al Qaeda connection to Iraq was dropped before the invasion.)[48]

Democrats and Republicans were more likely to acknowledge the "facts" that comported with their respective partisan views. Motivated reasoning was at work here, since this kind of reasoning hinges on individuals' ability to reason and argue against new information that is at odds with their existing attitudes and opinions. Partisanship and the emotions tied up with partisanship become motivating factors. In addition, when education is taken into account, as explored in figure 5.31, the most well-educated individuals are, on the one hand, expected to be more likely to be exposed to new information and discern the facts but, on the other, are better able to argue against information that contradicts their existing views. That is why the best-educated Republicans were more likely than less well-educated Democrats to dismiss the facts regarding Iraq, WMDs, and al Qaeda and the best-educated Democrats understood the facts most fully.

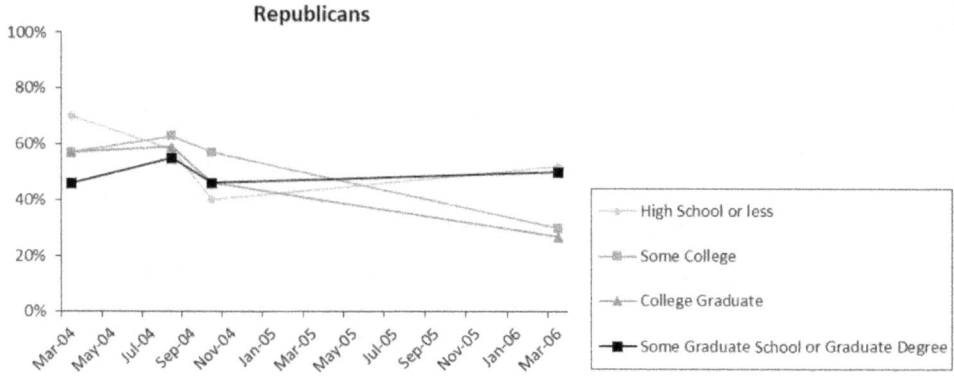

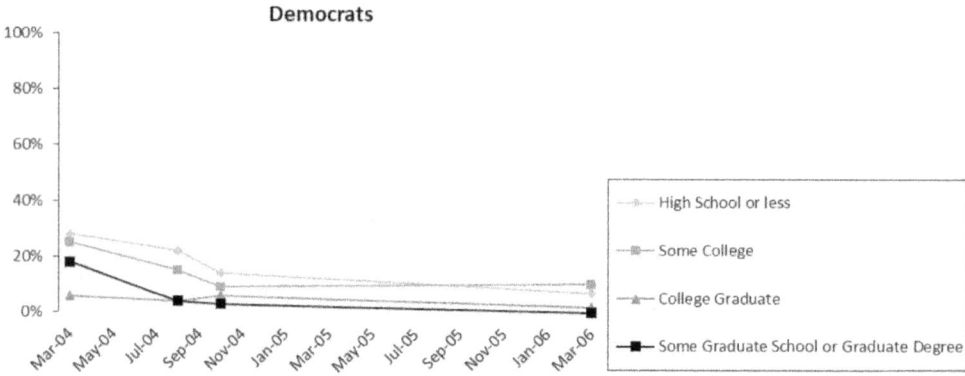

FIGURE 5.31 Public's belief about Iraq's WMDs, by partisanship and education.

Notes: A: Iraq had WMDs: perceptions of Republicans by education; B: Iraq had WMDs: perceptions of Democrats by education.

Source: PIPA surveys.

We see the same phenomenon at work in the example closely connected to the Tea Party and Donald Trump regarding the claim that Barack Obama was in some ways a deviant American—a Muslim (which he was not). Chapter 3 describes aptly the strong partisan differences in false perceptions about Obama's background (see figures 3.6 and 3.7). Figure 5.32 shows further that Republicans—including the best-educated—were

Republicans

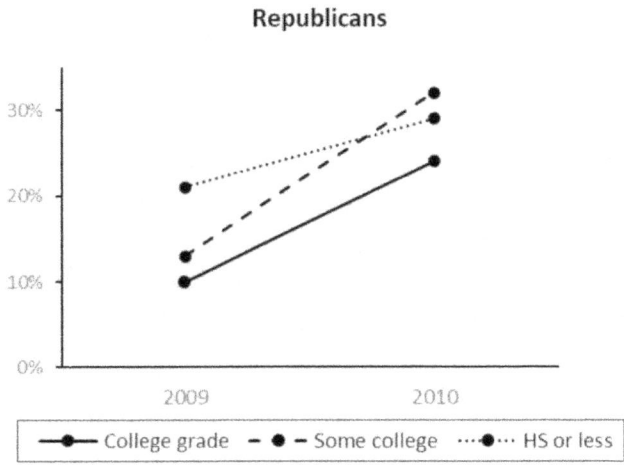

Democrats

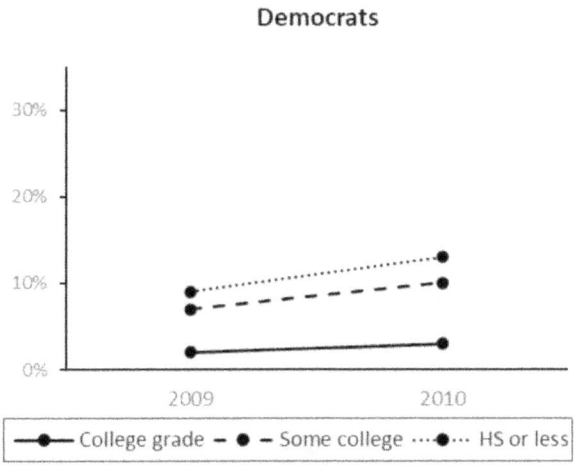

FIGURE 5.32 Belief that Obama is a Muslim.

Note: Percentage who believe Obama is a Muslim, by partisanship and education.

Source: John Sides, "Why Do More People Think Obama Is a Muslim?," Monkey Cage, August 26, 2010, https://themonkeycage.org/2010/08/why_do_more_people_think _obama/.

among the most likely to say they believed that Obama was a Muslim, in contrast to Democrats and especially compared with the most-educated Democrats, among whom virtually none accepted this falsehood.

A great many partisan attitudes are tied to differences in beliefs about the state of the world. Partisanship is associated with positive versus negative perceptions about the economy and even individuals' own economic circumstances, depending on whether the individuals' copartisans control the White House.[49] Democrats and Republicans have perceived differently the state of the environment and the threat of climate change. Figure 5.33 shows that this was very apparent by the time Barack Obama took office; at that time there was already a thirty-six percentage point partisan difference in perceptions that climate change was a major threat to the United States. That increased to nearly a sixty-point difference (fifty-seven points) when Trump took office, around which it stayed through the 2020 election year and beyond (a fifty-five point difference into 2022).

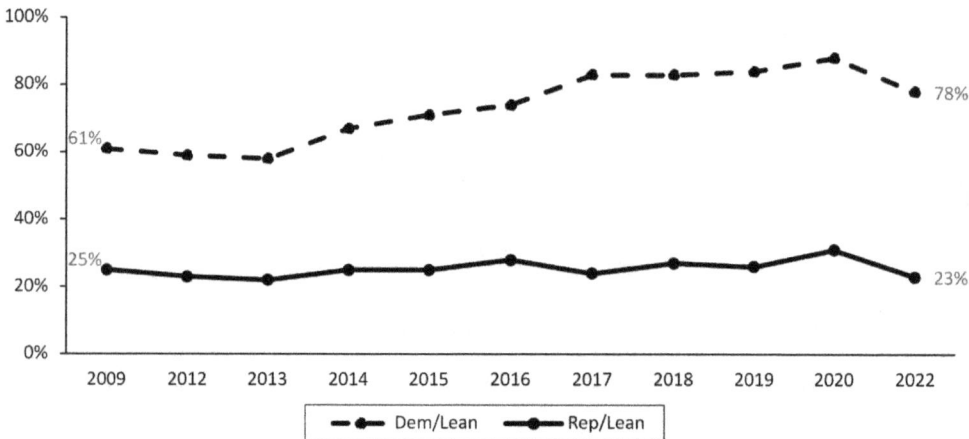

FIGURE 5.33 Perceptions of the threat of climate change.

Note: Percentage who perceive that global climate change is a major threat to the United States.

Source: Pew.

Conflict related to race, religion, and gender has fully pervaded American politics. This politics of social identities and the conflicts over policy issues related to them—which have been referred to as "tribal" politics—has been fueled by differing perceptions of the pervasiveness of inequalities and discrimination in how Blacks, Latinos, whites, Asians, women, men, gays and lesbians, Muslims, Jews, Christians, and other groups with possible social identities are treated in society. Individuals need to be able to justify their convictions with perceptions of the world that support them. The epitome of this tendency has been partisans' differing perceptions of unequal and unjust treatment of different types of people—leading to bitter identity politics.

Republicans and Democrats have perceived the reality of this treatment differently and increasingly so, with Democrats seeing more discrimination than Republicans against all the groups shown except for whites and evangelical Christians. Figure 5.34 and other data not shown reveal this quite clearly. From 2009 to 2019, the partisan difference in perceptions that there is a lot of discrimination against Blacks increased by thirty-six percentage points, for a gap of fully fifty points. For Latinos, the increase was thirty-four points, producing a gap of forty-two points in 2019. The gap was smaller for whites, with Republicans fifteen points more likely than Democrats to perceive discrimination against them in 2019.

For religious groups, the largest partisan differences were for Muslims, with a twenty-five-point variance in 2013, which increased to forty-one points in 2019, with 75 percent of Democrats perceiving a lot of discrimination against Muslims. Partisan differences concerning perceived discrimination against Jews was small, just six to eight points, and a twelve-point difference for evangelical Christians in 2016, which increased to twenty-two points in 2019, with 30 percent of Republicans perceiving a lot of discrimination against that group.

Finally, Republicans were strikingly less likely than Democrats to perceive a lot of discrimination against women and gays and lesbians. Regarding discrimination against women, an eight-point difference in 2009 increased to thirty-four points by 2019, after Trump's election and into his administration, with 44 percent of Democrats perceiving a lot

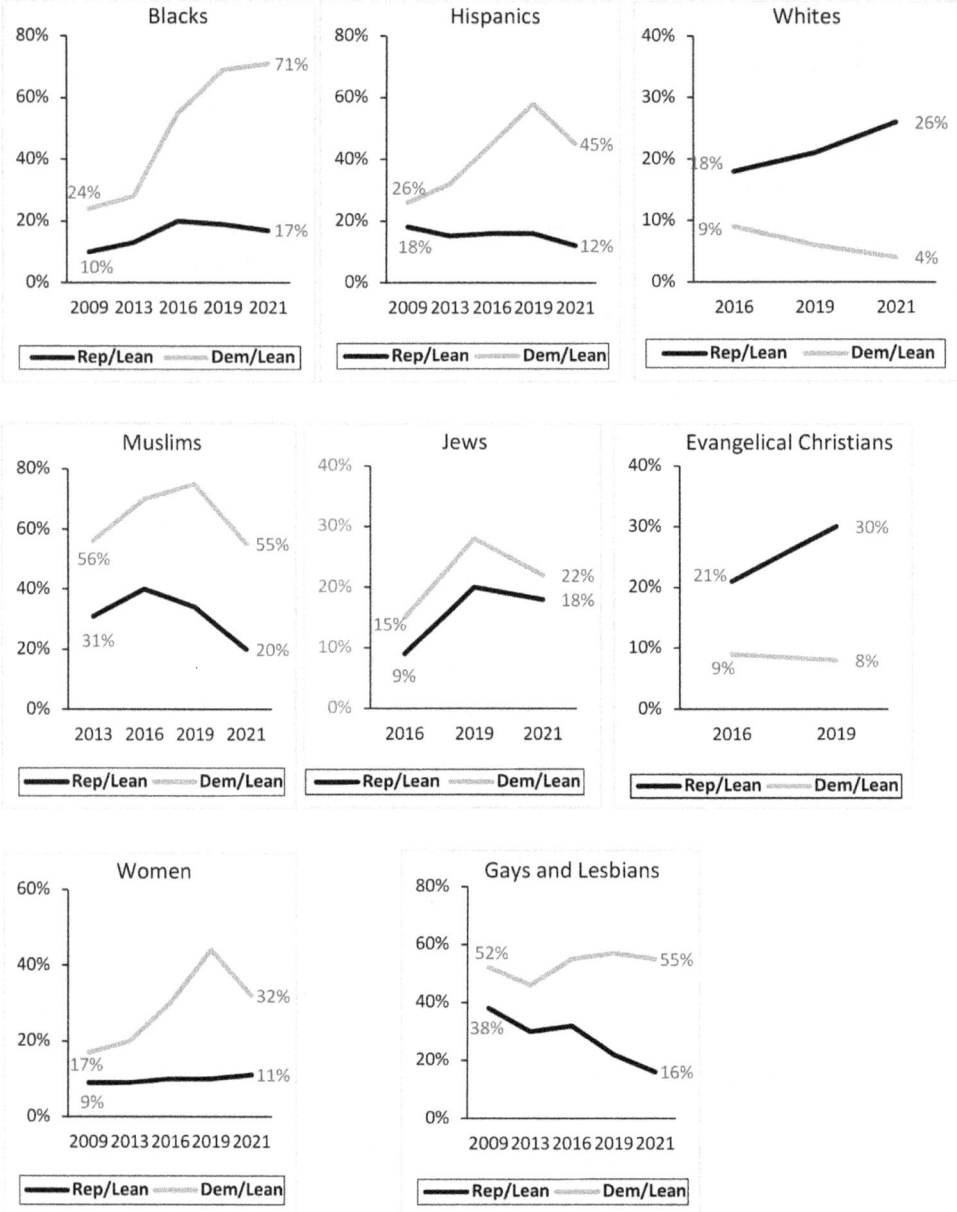

FIGURE 5.34 Perceptions of discrimination against groups.

Notes: Percentage of Republicans versus Democrats who say there is a lot of discrimination in our society against that group.

Source: Pew.

of discrimination at that time, up from 17 percent in 2009. A fourteen-point gap regarding gays and lesbians increased thirty-five points by 2019. This occurred as the percentage of Republicans perceiving discrimination against those groups dropped to 22 percent, while the proportion of Democrats rose a bit, to 57 percent. All these differences—and especially the substantially increasing partisan differences—increased the heat in the political conflicts involving social identities.

Partisan perceptual biases and the emotions associated with them are connected to how conspiracy theories have taken hold and to the threat of political violence that has been on the rise. This began with the Tea Party's populist rhetoric, propaganda, and the appearance of conspiracy theories, which provided the opening for Donald Trump's and his own populist rhetoric that evoked powerful emotions—further resentment and anger toward the established political parties and their leaders and followers. The assault on the Capitol on January 6, 2021, took the ongoing partisan conflict to a higher level.

This heightened conflict is reflected in partisan differences in perceptions and beliefs concerning conspiracy theories and in opinions toward the use of violence. Table 5.1 presents the significant partisan differences for a few of the most salient conspiracy theories: that Obama was not born in the United States, that there was a "deep state" of government officials working against Trump, that the COVID-19 pandemic was created by China, and that the Russian leader Vladimir Putin had damaging information about Trump. Republicans held to more conspiracies than Democrats in the first three cases, but the Democrats' belief about Putin was a big one.

In figure 5.35, we see that Democrats and Republicans held different theories about the actual number of COVID-19 deaths while Trump was president. Democrats thought the Trump administration and perhaps Republican governors were suppressing the numbers, whereas Republicans thought the deep state, in cahoots with the scientists and officials running public health agencies, was inflating them.

As to QAnon, the promoter of the most outrageous and far-fetched conspiracy theory, figures 5.36 and 5.37 show the partisan conflict in opinions.

TABLE 5.1 Conspiracies

CONSPIRACY STATEMENTS AND RESPONSES: COMPLETELY ACCURATE/MOSTLY ACCURATE	% DEMOCRATS	% REPUBLICANS
Unelected government officials, referred to as the "Deep State," have been working to undermine the Trump administration	10	59
COVID-19 was intentionally planned by China as part of a biological weapons program.	10	40
There is evidence that shows Barack Obama was born outside the U.S.	6	34
Vladimir Putin has damaging information about Donald Trump.	60	10

Source: American Perspectives, September 2020.

The third statement in figure 5.37 summarizes QAnon beliefs in a nutshell: that the nation is controlled by a cabal of Satan worshippers, pedophiles, and child traffickers. That close to a quarter (23 percent) of Republicans, as shown in figure 5.37, are believers is stunning, as is, as shown in figure 5.36, the mere 16 percent who reject as inaccurate the information promoted by QAnon.

Given that the conspiracy theories and differing perceptions of facts and reality had such traction, and given that emotions—especially anger—had risen to a threatening level, it is not surprising that the potential for violence became of increasing concern. The partisan differences regarding attitudes toward violence reflect this. As shown in figure 5.37, Republicans are two to four more times likely than Democrats—more than a quarter (28 percent) of Republicans—to agree that American patriots may have to resort to violence to save the country and that "a storm is coming" to "restore the rightful leaders." Our final chapter considers further the prospects regarding violence.

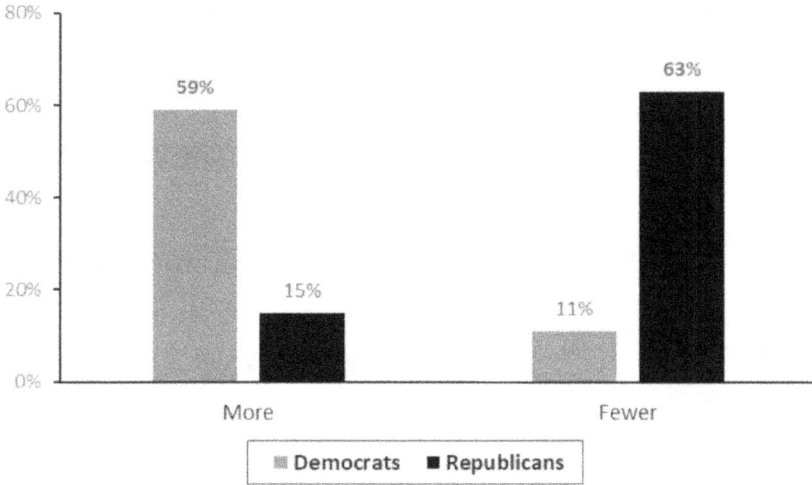

FIGURE 5.35 COVID-19 deaths.

Note: Percentage who say more versus fewer people have died than is reported.

Source: American Perspectives, September 2020.

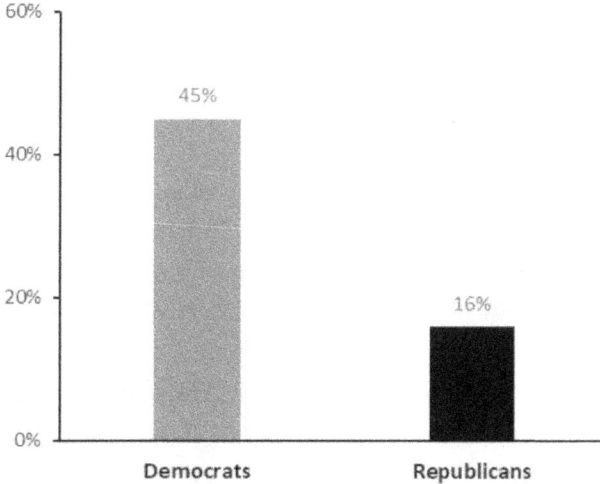

FIGURE 5.36 Perspectives promoted by QAnon, not accurate.

Note: Percentage who have heard of them believe they are not accurate.

Source: American Perspectives, September 2020.

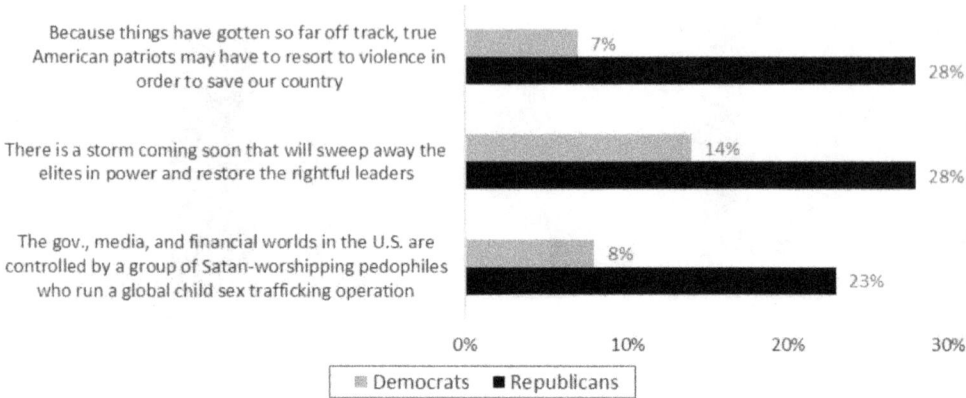

FIGURE 5.37 QAnon's beliefs about violence and conspiracy theories, by partisanship.

Note: Percentage who agree.

Source: PRRI-IFYC, March 2021.

PARTISAN OPINIONS, LEADERS, AND THE MEDIA

This chapter has focused on public opinion and attitudes bearing on political behavior—specifically, the longer-term elite-level and public polarization that has occurred and its intensification since the emergence of the Tea Party and the rise of Donald Trump. It has involved increasing partisan conflict on political issues, the heightened level of emotions in politics, and divergent partisan perceptions of reality and conspiracy theories. And here, at the end, as suggested at the beginning of the chapter, it involves the potential for violence.

To be sure, the media have been part of this story. Media reports and social media, as described in previous chapters, have conveyed information concerning what has happened and what has been involved in the conflict—and more. The media have amplified and helped fuel the conflict. The media have been used substantially by those engaged in the conflict to promote their side—through toxic political communication. These leaders and other political actors—not the media—have been the source of this toxicity. Both leaders and the media are part of the story of weaponized communication and its consequences.

We have made claims in this and earlier chapters about causal effects in the phenomena that we describe involving the mass media and social media.[50] We noted that partisan conflict over issues and ideology began at the level of party leaders and others. This had subsequent consequences for public opinion. We could say that this conflict, in tandem with increased electoral competition, led to heightened emotions related to the policy stakes of elections. These emotions and the content of media reports about political conflict led to more partisan perceptual biases and disagreements about facts and reality.

All this makes for a plausible causal story—up to a point. But perceptual biases and disagreement and the media's attention to them can feed back on affective partisanship and, in turn, on positions that individuals take on issues—especially new issues. While partisan leaders have influenced their partisan supporters, those supporters can in turn pressure these leaders. The media at the outset did not cause the divergence of the parties concerning issues and ideology, but by amplifying conflict, they can affect the extent to which leaders and the public stay the course and can make it difficult to reverse course. Thus, the politics here is filled with reverse or reciprocal influences—*endogeneity*.[51] For our purposes, disentangling causal effects is less critical than the finding that the trends discussed in this chapter are all part of the partisan conflict and emotional environment affecting the state of American democracy, of which toxic communication is a key part.

6

WEAPONIZED WORDS AND DEEDS
AGAINST DEMOCRACY

The first anniversary of the violent attack on the Capitol by supporters of then president Donald Trump confirmed the deep political cleavages in twenty-first-century America and the fragile state of the country's nearly two hundred fifty-year democracy. Whereas congressional Democrats commemorated the failed attempt to overthrow the legitimate election of President Joseph Biden with a moment of silence and a candlelight vigil, their Republican colleagues largely ignored these events and continued, in one way or another, to defend what happened on January 6, 2021. It was a startling demonstration of the partisan and ideological polarization we discuss at length in chapter 5 and a categorical clash of two sharply divergent views—one based on reality that can be seen on videotape or reviewed in the investigation of vote counts and court rulings on the states' administration of the 2020 election, and the other based on misinformation, distortions, and denial. In an op-ed piece published on the day of this anniversary, former President Jimmy Carter warned, "Our great nation now teeters on the brink of a widening abyss. . . . We are at genuine risk of civil conflict and losing our precious democracy."[1]

Franklin D. Roosevelt used the relatively new medium of radio to broadcast his popular fireside chats; John F. Kennedy was the first president who understood and embraced television to connect with the public; and Donald Trump was the first social media president, with his massive production of tweets. All three presidents were gifted rhetoricians who dominated the interconnected entities in the political communication loop—in the organized political, general public, and media realms. But whereas Roosevelt and Kennedy used the new and old communication forms of their times to appeal to the shared values of Americans and humankind, Trump misused the presidential bully pulpit to spew out hatred, chaos, and polarization—"us" versus "them" partisan conflict. Coming to power in the age of mediatized politics, what Angelos Kissas describes as "personalized, conversationalized, and dramatized politics,"[2] the former TV reality star Trump dominated the mass-mediated public spaces at the expense of all other politicians—supporters and opponents alike. Whereas FDR and JFK, also media stars, were promotors and defenders of democracy, Trump —during his presidency and persisting since then—was a threat to America's democratic system. As the former president began his third presidential campaign in the spring of 2023, he spoke kindly about Vladimir Putin while attacking President Biden and Washington's deep state as dangerous enemies within the nation. In one of his propaganda-like videos, Trump said, "The greatest threat to Western Civilization today is not Russia. It's probably, more than anything else, ourselves and some of the horrible, U.S.A. hating people that represent us. It's the abolition of our national borders. It's the failure to police our own cities. It's the destruction of the rule of law from within. It's the collapse of the nuclear family and fertility rates, like nobody can believe is happening. It's the Marxists who would have us become a Godless nation worshipping at the altar of race, and gender, and environment."[3]

Political polarization serves the selfish interests of authoritarian politicians. As Ruth Ben-Ghiat writes in her book *Strongmen: Mussolini to the Present*, "Authoritarians hold appeal when society is polarized, or divided into two opposing ideological camps, which is why they do all they can to exacerbate strife."[4] This particular behavior of authoritarian rulers helps explain the rise and lasting appeal of Donald Trump among many millions of Americans who were angry about, and blamed liberals and socialists for, growing multiculturism and other societal changes during recent decades. From the fateful day in June 2015, when he declared his candidacy, to his years as U.S. president and beyond, Donald Trump used demagogic rhetoric to draw a sharp line between "us," the real people, and "them," everyone outside his cultish and mostly white movement—regardless of whether those others were fellow Americans or foreigners. At a campaign rally in Tulsa, Oklahoma, in June 2020, for example, President Trump attacked the "out-group" and issued a stern warning:

> If Joe Biden were to become president an emboldened left will launch a full-scale assault on American life. . . . They want to crush religious liberty. They don't want religion. Silence religious believers, indoctrinate your children with hateful and vicious lies about our country, subsidize late term abortion and after birth execution.
>
> They want to take away your guns through the repeal of your Second Amendment, as sure as you're sitting there.

He then drew a sharp contrast between the threatening enemies and the virtuous patriots in the MAGA community.

> We are one movement, one people, one family, and one glorious nation under God. America will soon be thriving, like never before because, ladies and gentlemen of Oklahoma, the best is yet to come. Together we will make America wealthy again, we will make America strong again, we will make America proud again, we will make America safe again, and we will make America great again.[5]

The distinction between the good us and the evil them was also a hallmark of the Tea Party, which was "in fact, full of pseudo-conservatism . . . [and] marked by suspicion and resentment of out-groups."[6] The political ambitions of Trump and Tea Party activists had converged for the first time when Trump became the promoter of the birther conspiracy theory, which was popular among Tea Partiers. When Trump entered the GOP's competition for its presidential nomination, he was not the first choice of several Tea Party organizations. But once he stepped on the debate stage, trashed his opponents, and took the lead in public opinion polls—with the help of digital and mainstream media (see chapter 2), he became the favorite of Tea Party supporters and Christian evangelicals, many of whom also sympathized with the reactionary agenda of the Tea Party movement.

During his candidacy and continuing during his presidency, Trump appealed relentlessly to the emotions of his base and potential converts to his MAGA movement, which paid off in the more than ten million additional votes he received in 2020 compared with 2016. In an interview with the *Washington Post*'s reporters Bob Woodward and Robert Costa in March 2016, candidate Trump mentioned two powerful emotions: fear and rage. "Real power is—I don't even want to use the word—fear," he said. And, "I bring rage out. I do bring rage out. I always have."[7] Thus, the titles of Woodward's two books on Trump were *FEAR* and *RAGE*, and a third one, cowritten with Costa and titled *PERIL*—presumably short for democracy in peril as the dire result of stirring the emotions of fear and rage among his mass supporters.

Ultimately, emotions—not purely rational choices—can be the main drivers of people's political and policy preferences. And fear and anger or rage are the most potent ones, especially when persuasive messages succeed in arousing the deep-seated grievances of audiences. Here, Tea Party activists and Donald Trump were again on the same page. As one political analyst noted with respect to the roots of both the Tea Party and MAGA movements, "What's happening now isn't some transitory blip; it's the culmination of a 40-year campaign, an incessant drumbeat of grievance against minority rights, gun control, same-sex marriage, secularization, tax-and-spend Big Government, climate hoax, 'job killing' regulation, feminism and the rest of a sinister Liberal Agenda that amounts, of course, to tyranny."[8] (see Chapter 5 on the issues cited). Manuel Castells concluded that "people vote for the candidate that elicits the right feelings, not the candidate that presents the best arguments."[9] He, too, recognized the importance of fear and rage emotions in effective political appeals, whether in the context of social movements, election campaigns, or the political process in general. But Castells added a third and equally important emotion: hope. Propaganda experts have tested the fear appeal as a powerful persuasion technique. According to Anthony Pratkanis and Elliot Aronson, fear as a motivation works best when "it scares the hell out of people" and at the same time offers convincing recommendations for "overcoming the fear-arousing threat."[10] In other words, drastic fear appeals, often associated with entrenched grievances, are followed up by the possibility for hope.

In her study of earlier and contemporary fascist leaders, Ben-Ghiat defined propaganda as "a set of communication strategies designed to sow confusion and uncertainty, discourage critical thinking, and persuade people that reality is what the leader says it is."[11] She found that this propaganda scheme has by and large remained the same regardless of the advances in communication technology and types of mass media. At all times, strongmen staged frequent mass rallies to persuade their followers in person and to bathe in their supporters' unconditional devotion and loyalty. Robert O. Paxton attributed to early fascism "a new invention created afresh for the era of mass politics. It sought to appeal mainly to the emotions by the use of ritual, carefully stage-managed ceremonies, and intensely charged rhetoric."[12] In this respect there is a straight line from Benito Mussolini and Adolf Hitler to Vladimir Putin and, yes, Donald Trump.

Content analyses of Trump speeches and tweets confirm the frequency of emotional appeals. When he declared his candidacy in June 2015, for example, he began slowly trying to evoke fear and anger. "Our country is in serious trouble. We don't have victories anymore. We used to have victories, but we don't have them [anymore]," he warned. Then he spent most of his speech enumerating a multitude of alleged defeats and threats coming from Mexican criminals and rapists, Muslim terrorists, and foreign trade cheaters and their domestic enablers. He then ended with a strong message of hope: "If I get elected president, I will bring it [our country] back bigger and better and stronger than ever before, and we will make America great again!"[13] By and large, he stuck to this propaganda technique during his campaign and presidency.

Observers often wondered, why did Trump make the same appeals and the same often untrue statements again and again? Why did he never tire of repeating the same slogans? Whether by (his own) instinct or by design (on the part of his hired propagandists), he followed twentieth-century fascist playbooks, especially Adolf Hitler's propaganda formula. In his manifesto *Mein Kampf* ("My Struggle"), Hitler summarized the importance of repetition in propaganda directed at the masses.

> The purpose of propaganda is not to provide interesting distraction for blasé young gentlemen, but to convince, and what I mean is to convince the masses. But the masses are slow moving, and they always require a certain time before they are ready even to notice a thing, and only after the simplest ideas are repeated thousands of times will the masses finally remember them.
>
> When there is a change, it must not alter the content of what the propaganda is driving at, but in the end must always say the same thing. For instance, a slogan must be presented from different angles, but the end of all remarks must always and immutably be the slogan itself. Only in this way can the propaganda have a unified and complete effect.[14]

As candidate and president, Trump repeated the same grievances, the same attacks, the same promises, and the same fear, anger, and hope appeals—all the time, at every opportunity, including the "Make America Great Again" slogan. His followers remembered those repetitions, cited them, chanted them, believed them—big lies and small lies—as they waved Trump flags and displayed MAGA slogan on tee shirts, caps, coffee mugs, and tattooed biceps.

Just as the authoritarian brand of populism rejects pluralism and thus the existence of and cooperation with a loyal opposition, these populists "always want to cut out the middleman"[15]—and, first and foremost, an independent press that calls out their lies and destructive deeds. The Mussolini and Hitler movements early on established their own newspapers, and they attacked the mainstream media of their time—newspapers and radio—as fake press and "enemies of the people." After these dictators came to power, they quickly took control of their countries' entire press systems. As we described in the introduction and chapter 4, Trump relentlessly condemned and threatened the mainstream news media and individual broadcast hosts, reporters, and commentators while enjoying the way in which far right radio talk shows and cable channels served as his propaganda arms. President Trump's symbiotic relationship with Fox News TV hosts, such as Sean Hannity, Tucker Carlson, Lou Dobbs, Jeanine Pirro, and Laura Ingraham, benefited everyone involved. They served as his regular advisers, and he supplied them with breaking news tailored to the mood of his political base.

Apart from media outlets on the right, Trump went after the mainstream media at every opportunity, most of all through his constant stream of tweets. Commenting on Trump's mass self-communication through social media Jan-Werner Mueller noted, "'real Americans' can be done with the [mainstream] media and have direct access to (or the illusion of direct contact with) a man who is not just a celebrity; the self-declared 'Hemingway of 140 characters' uniquely tells it like it is."[16] However, research showed that the direct impact of Trump's tweet output was rather limited because less than 1 percent of his more than forty-five million Twitter followers read his tweets on his Twitter page. The real sway of his tweet production was facilitated by the mainstream media that covered his tweets regularly and prominently. Jim Anderson, the CEO of Social Flow, concluded that "[Trump] does have a platform and he is able to set the agenda and dictate what everybody is going to talk about over the course of the day, but it's the mainstream media that covers what he says that gives him the reach."[17]

We content-analyzed the *Washington Post* for three months from September 1 to November 30, 2016, to get a sense of the leading mainstream media's attention to, first, candidate and then president-elect Donald Trump's twitter posts. We found, not surprisingly, that the *Post* covered his tweet production regularly. His tweets, retweets, and other news sources' reactions to his Twitter posts were reported 265 times, an average of 88 times per month, in news reports, opinion pieces, and feature stories. Since other print, radio, and television outlets also reported on his tweets, the total media attention to Trump's Twitter posts added up to a potent echo chamber for this celebrity politician. The more aggressive, divisive, and outright false his tweets were, the more likely they were to be covered in the broader mass media. This led Twitter to close Trump's account shortly before the end of his presidential term and put an end to the steady flow of his repugnant and false tweets. The press could have accomplished the same much earlier by not slavishly repeating to the public, day in and day out, his most explosive tweet posts!

But the mainstream media never tired of starring Donald Trump in their coverage, even when Joe Biden, as presidential candidate and then the next president of the United States, should have had at least equal billing. From September 21, 2020, the Monday following Supreme Court Justice Ruth Bader Ginsberg's death, through February 14, 2021, the day after Donald Trump's acquittal in the U.S. Senate's impeachment trial, we selected and counted each day the number of times "Trump" and "Biden" were mentioned in the three most prominently featured headlines in five leading U.S. newspapers: the *New York Times*, *Washington Post*, *Wall Street Journal*, *Los Angeles Times*, and *USA Today*.[18] During this period, the presidential election, the appointment of a new Supreme Court justice, the challenges to Biden's election victory, the events of January 6, Trump's impeachment, and the impeachment trial itself took place.

As figure 6.1 shows, in every newspaper we examined, Trump was mentioned in the headlines of the most prominently featured stories far more than Biden, with the gap between the two greatest in the leading liberal newspapers, the *New York Times* and *Washington Post*. We examined further the content of the selected articles. What was signaled in the headlines was more negative for Trump than Biden, but the gap was greatest in the *New York Times* and *Washington Post*. With the exception of the *Los Angeles Times*, the positive sentiments were the same or similar in all the other newspapers (figure 6.2).

In general, television accommodated Trump generously—including the frequent live coverage of his mass rallies, which were carefully staged events. Referring to Benedict Anderson's "imagined communities" and Dayan and Katz's "media events" as rituals that emphasize and draw

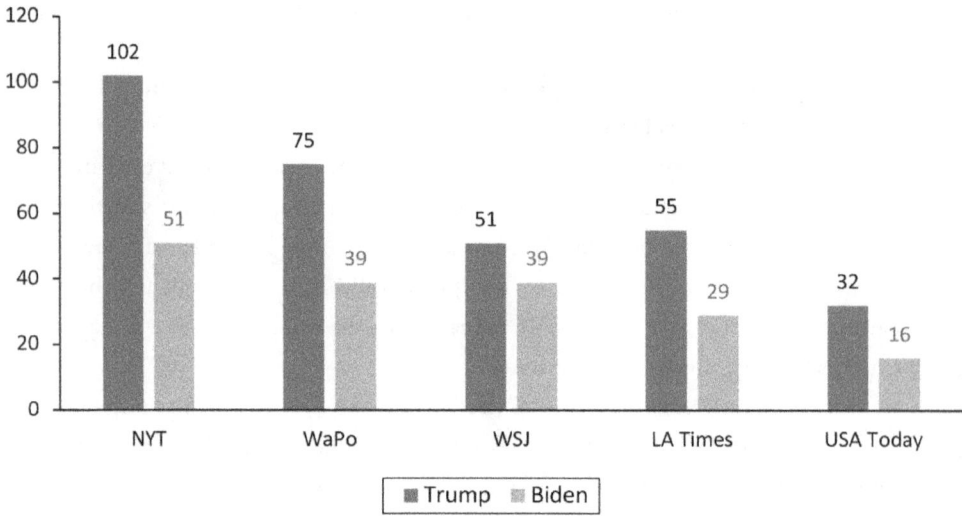

FIGURE 6.1 Frequency of "Trump" and "Biden" in Headlines of Leading Newspapers (September 21, 2020 to February 14, 2021).

(*Source*: Compiled by Authors)

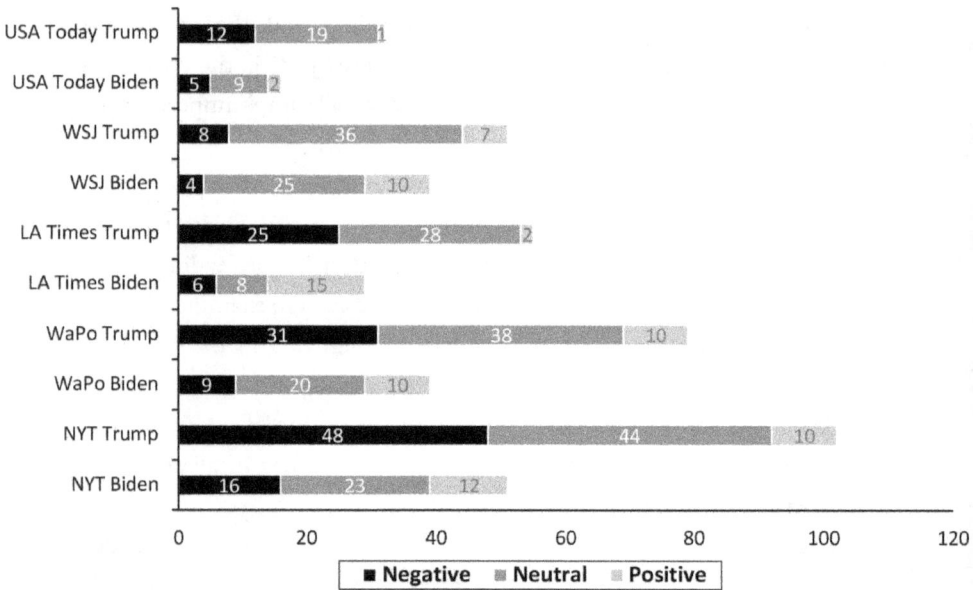

FIGURE 6.2 Frequency of "Trump" and "Biden" Sentiments in Newspaper Headlines (September 21, 2020–February 14, 2021).

(*Source*: Compiled by the Authors)

together national communality or resemble celebrations of consensus, James W. Carey contrasted those unifying features with televised events as rituals of degradation and excommunication. These were exemplified in the past by Senator Joseph McCarthy's televised "Red Scare" hearings in the 1950s and the U.S. Senate's confirmation hearings on Robert Bork's nomination to the U.S. Supreme Court in the late 1980s. According to Carey, "[Rituals of degradation] touch on core, sacred values but are episodes in the production of dissensus, episodes in the recreation, indeed redefinition, of the civil religion by social demarcation and exclusion. Rather than uniting the audience and the polity either in expectation or fact, they divide it ever more deeply. Their central element is not merely conflict but bitter discord and struggle. The event produces neither catharsis nor relief but ever widening and expanding ripples of civil disquiet."[19] Such rituals of division conveyed through the mass media were the norm at live televised events that starred a lavishly living billionaire named Trump attacking all types of real and imagined political opponents and minorities while promising all manner of benefits to the "real people" that he never delivered.

Shortly before the first anniversary of the January 6 violence, ex-President Trump released a written endorsement of Hungary's prime minister and strongman Viktor Orbán, whose self-described illiberal democracy was in reality an autocracy. Orbán and his party were in complete control of their country's institutions of government, the electoral system, and almost all the news media. Trump and influential right-wing conservatives inside and outside the Republican Party embraced Hungary's nondemocratic system and its leader as attractive models for effective governance. Fox News was part of Orbán's fan club. In the summer of 2021, one of the network's hosts, Tucker Carlson, beamed his show from Hungary for one week, praising the country's strongman and the stability of the illiberal system he created. Despite Orbán's regular clashes with the European Union and cozy relationship with Vladimir Putin, Hungary remained a member of the organization and the recipient of significant EU subsidies—probably because his iron-fisted rule did not include physical violence against remaining domestic dissidents.

Violence against domestic opponents, though, was condoned and even encouraged by Trump, especially during his raucous mass rallies (see chapter 4). Such incidents were common and reported in "breaking news" highlights. As one expert on the behavior of tyrants noted, "What was novel in 2016 was a candidate who ordered a private security detail to clear opponents from rallies and encouraged the audience itself to remove people who expressed different opinions. . . . This kind of mob violence was meant to transform the political atmosphere, and it did."[20] It was certainly new for a presidential candidate competing for and receiving the nomination of one of the two major parties in the United States. However, Trump's penchant for encouraging and praising violence, and his MAGA movement's real and threatened political violence, had precedents in the Tea Party movement.

In August 2009, barely six months after the speedy formation of the Tea Party, the new social movement's activists called on like-minded "patriots" to attend congressmembers' town hall meetings in their home states and home districts to voice their protest against President Obama's Affordable Care Act. In riotous town hall meetings across the country, many of them overcrowded, angry constituents and nonresident agitators shouted down members of the U.S. House and Sentae, often attacking them and their supporters verbally and physically. The following excerpts from news reports attest to the toxic nature of these meetings:

- In a townhall meeting held by Senator Arlen Specter (D-PA), a man screamed that someday God would judge Specter and his fellow "cronies on the Hill." Spector was being shoved and booed by other audience members and forced to leave the meeting.[21]
- An overcrowded town hall meeting with Representative Kathy Castor (D-FL) turned physical. Outraged protesters shouted "tyranny" and "you work for us."[22]
- Representative Bob Inglis (R-SC) was shouted down by his angry constituents despite the fact that he agreed with them. Protesters opposed to President Obama's health care reform shouted against "martial law" and "forced vaccinations" and, with respect to illegal immigrants, "Bus them home."[23]

- A protester hanged an effigy of Representative Frank Kratovil, Jr. (D-MD), at a rally opposing health care change. Representative Brad Miller (D-NC) said he had received a death threat about his support.[24]
- Members of Congress have been shouted down, hanged in effigy, and taunted by crowds. In several cities, noisy demonstrations have led to fistfights, arrests, and hospitalizations.[25]
- At a protest rally in Denver, demonstrators waved signs saying, "Don't Blame Me, I Voted for the American."[26]
- "The images were frightening. Obama with a Hitler mustache. Obama morphed to Heath Ledger's Joker. Obama, Parasite in Chief. Obama the Muslim, Obama the Marxist. Even Obama the Antichrist: Jesus is the Messiah, not Obama."[27]

As described in chapters 2 and 3, the threats issued on Tea Party websites were sharply critical of Barack Obama and often more extreme than the rhetorical attacks cited. Obama himself left no doubt that he was well aware of the hate speech of his critics affiliated with the Tea Party. In his memoir he wrote,

It became hard to ignore some of the more troubling impulses driving the movement. As had been true at Palin rallies, reporters at Tea Party events caught attendees comparing me to animals or Hitler. Signs turned up showing me dressed like an African witch doctor with a bone through my nose. Conspiracy theories abounded: that my health-care bill would set up "death panels" to evaluate whether people deserved treatment, clearing the way for "government-encouraged euthanasia," or that it would benefit illegal immigrants, in the service of my larger goal of flooding the country with welfare-dependent, reliably Democratic voters.[28]

The most fervent members of the Tea Party who became the most important part of the MAGA movement had shown years earlier a proclivity for actual and threatened violence in the service of political ends—even before they found their leader in Donald Trump.

Since the Tea Party movement and related anti-Obama conspiracy theories were Trump's backbone in his rise to power, it was hardly surprising that the most committed Tea Partiers in the Washington GOP lineup became the strongest Trump supporters once he became president. Several members of Congress left their elected offices to serve in the Trump administration. Mick Mulvaney (R. S.C.), who won a congressional seat in 2010 with Tea Party support, became Office of Management and Budget director and later acting White House chief of staff. Mark Meadows (R. N.C.) signed the Tea Party's "Contract from America" in his successful 2012 congressional campaign; he was leader of the Freedom Caucus, which replaced the Tea Party Caucus, before becoming White House chief of staff. Michael Pompeo (Kansas), another of the original Tea Partiers in the House, served as Trump's secretary of state.

Tea Partiers were also the strongest Trump cheerleaders in both chambers of the U.S. Congress, most of all Senators Rand Paul (Kentucky), Mike Lee (Utah), Ron Johnson (Wisconsin), Marco Rubio (Florida), Ted Cruz (Texas), and Tim Scott (South Carolina), along with Representatives Louie Gohmert (Texas), Steve Scalise (Louisiana), and Paul Gosar (Arizona).

Most of these men won their elections with Tea Party support and remained loyal to the Tea Party wing of the GOP; some won congressional offices under the Tea Party banner in subsequent elections. All served Donald Trump to substantial degrees and contributed to his propaganda team.

FAR-RIGHT VIOLENT EXTREMISTS AND HIGH GOVERNMENT OFFICIALS

Following Barack Obama's election victory in November 2008, the Aryan Nation, a white supremacy/neo-Nazi group with a history of violence, placed the picture of a tombstone on its website with the inscription, "United States of America. Born: July 4, 1776. Died: Nov. 4, 2008." The group issued the following call to arms: "Whitey is buying guns and ammunition at a record pace . . . no stop since the Marxist Communist Obama entered illegally (not a confirmed citizen) into the White House. . . . The United States will not see CIVIL WAR happen all at once across the country, but instead a gradual increase from area to area. . . . Stay focused all the times! Be prepared all the times."[29]

Following Joe Biden's election victory in November 2020, the Oath Keepers, a paramilitary group seen by some observers as the quasimilitary wing of the Tea Party (see chapter 2), urged Donald Trump in an "Open Letter to the President" to "Stop the Steal" by force. And two days before the breach of the U.S. Capitol on January 6, 2021, the group's leader, Stewart Rhodes, wrote in an urgent appeal on the group's website, "All Patriots who can get to DC need to be in DC. Now is the time to stand. It's not too late to go. Jump on a plane! Jump in your car! Just get there. Show the President you support him taking decisive action as both President and Commander-in-Chief. And show Congress that we the people will not stand for the election being stolen to plant an imposter Chicom [China Communist] puppet in the White House. Stand now, or kneel forever."[30]

These two episodes, separated by a dozen years, contextualized the stunning shift in the numerical strength of the far right's military-style groups and their relationship to high officials in the federal government. In late 2008, the tiny Aryan Nation group was a declared enemy of the first Black person to become president of the United States. In late 2020, the Oath Keepers had thousands of members and links to Donald Trump's inner circle. According to Rhodes, "Over the years, Oath Keepers have conducted hundreds of highly successful volunteer security operations all over the nation, protecting patriots from communist terrorist assault . . . including providing volunteer security escorts outside twelve Trump campaign rallies, and many PSD details for high profile VIPs, such as Roger Stone, as well as many elected officials and election fraud whistle-blowers and patriot office holders."[31]

Bragging about the group's links to elected officials in high places and mentioning President Trump and a member of his coterie were not cases of grandstanding by Rhodes. The group's connections to the highest places in Washington, D.C., were confirmed in news reports and mentioned by the House of Representatives select committee that investigated the events of January 6.[32] By early 2022, two dozen members of the group had been criminally charged, and most of them indicted, for their roles in the violent breach of Congress, along with members of the Proud Boys, another group of militant extremists with contacts to Roger Stone and other Trump confidants. Among the general public, the Proud Boys were better known than the older and far more numerous Oath Keepers because the former group was frequently and prominently covered by the press, whereas the latter received little news coverage before January 6.

During a live televised presidential debate in the fall of 2020, the moderator, Chris Wallace, asked President Trump whether he would condemn white supremacists and right-wing militias. Trump did not answer but demanded angrily, "Give me a name, give me a name, go ahead who do you want me to condemn." After Joe Biden named the Proud Boys twice, Trump answered, "Proud Boys. Stand back and stand by." Then he claimed that violent extremism "is not a right-wing problem. This is a left-wing problem."[33] The Proud Boys took notice. Enrique Tarrio, the national chairman of the males-only group, responded on Parler, "I will stand down sir!!! Standing by sir. So Proud of my guys right now."[34] On January 6, a contingent of the Proud Boys followed the presidential order, joining Oath Keepers and other white supremacist groups in the violent breach of the Capitol.

This change in the standing of white supremacists during President Trump's four years in office did not happen in the dark but mostly in broad daylight (see chapter 4). Like other white supremacist groups in the first decade of the twenty-first century, the Aryan Nation organization was an outcast hate group on the fringe. Its ruminations about the coming of an anti-Obama "civil war" were nothing but toothless threats. In stark contrast, the Oath Keepers in the twenty-first century's second decade had a large number of members who were active and retired members of the military, police, and other uniformed services. The Proud Boys had chapters across the United States and abroad, plus a record of violent offenses. Both had acquaintances in the highest circles of Washington politics. They were part of the far-right wing of the GOP.

The participation of these paramilitary groups in the storming of the Capitol in support of a sitting president fit the fascist playbook, not democratic laws and rules of the game. Timothy Snyder warned in his lessons on tyranny that men "marching with torches and pictures of a leader" were signals of democracy in peril.[35] On January 6, the Oath Keepers and Proud Boys did not carry torches, as the "Unite the Right" racists had done while marching in Charlottesville, Virginia, in the summer of 2017, among whom President Trump recognized "some very fine people." But the January 6 violence by those two groups—along with similar ones such as the Three Percenters, 1st Amendment Praetorians, and other self-claimed militia groups—was the strongest confirmation that far-right extremism had become part of the Trumpian power orbit.

Donald Trump, Jr., told his father's supporters shortly before the storming of the Capitol that the "Stop the Steal: rally "should be a message to all the Republicans who have not been willing to actually fight, the people who did nothing to stop the steal. This isn't their Republican Party anymore. This is Donald Trump's Republican Party."[36] After Capitol Police, D.C.'s Metropolitan Police, and National Guard units secured Capitol Hill, Trump wrote in one of his last tweets before his Twitter account was suspended, "These are the things and events that happen when a sacred landslide election victory is so unceremoniously & viciously stripped away from great patriots who have been badly & unfairly treated for so long. Go home with love & in peace. Remember this day forever!"

By praising the tightly organized far-right extremists who led the charge in the storming of the Capitol, and also the collective mass of his MAGA followers as "great patriots" and assuring them "love and peace," the sitting president confirmed a disquieting reality: in contemporary America "the most urgent threat to Americans' safety and security comes not from foreign terrorists but from the country's own citizens. And the threat is aimed at the future of democracy itself."[37] The radical ideas that once had a home in only a tiny fringe spread into the mainstream. And contemporary media and communication technology were instrumental in facilitating this shift from fringe to mainstream. As Rachel Kleinfeld put it, "Ideas that were once confined to fringe groups now appear in the mainstream media. White-supremacist ideas, militia fashion, and conspiracy theories spread via gaming websites, YouTube channels, and blogs, while a slippery language of memes, slang, and jokes blurs the line between posturing and provoking violence, normalizing radical ideologies and activities."[38]

JANUARY 6: A COUP, TERRORISM—OR WHAT?

In the wake of the January 6 events, news organizations searched for the most appropriate term or terms to describe the violence that unfolded on the ground and on live television. In the week following the attack, media outlets used "riot," "storm," "siege," "breach," and "attack," in that order, most often and without notable differences corresponding to their usual partisan and ideological preferences (see table 6.1). Notably, the term "insurrection," which means an uprising or revolt against the government, initially was rarely used by major news organizations, although what happened on January 6 was a violent attack on one branch of the American government—the U.S. Congress.

Missing completely in the media's early characterization of the event were the terms "coup" and "terrorism." Yet, when asked by pollsters immediately after January 6 whether or not they considered what happened at the United States Capitol a coup attempt, 47 percent of respondents answered yes, 43 percent said no, and 10 percent had no opinion or did not answer the question.[39] Eventually, a growing number of news sources characterized January 6 as a coup, and a few called the violent deeds on that day terrorism. Several weeks later, in the second half of February, the public's views on the nature of the attacks were mostly benign: 34 percent called the attacks "a protest," 31 percent "a riot," 14 percent "a demonstration," and 6 percent "a gathering"; only 5 percent called them an" insurrection," with 10 percent undecided.[40]

So, what would be the most appropriate way to describe what happened January 6? What happened on that day in the American capital of Washington, D.C., nearly two hundred fifty years after the American democracy was established?

TABLE 6.1 Media characterization of the events of January 6, 2021

EVENT	YAHOO	CNN	NYT	FOX	WP	BREITBART	BBC
Riot	6	9	9	10	9	9	10
Storm	9	7	6	6	5	7	10
Siege	6	1	7	–	7	1	5
Breach	4	6	3	3	2	2	3
Attack	3	1	6	1	3	4	3
Insurrection	3	3	1	1	1	–	–
Assault	5	1	1	1	–	–	1
Rampage	1	1	3	1	1	–	1
Invasion	–	–	–	–	–	–	3
Unrest	–	1	–	2	–	1	–

Source: Govind Bhutada, "How News Media is Describing the Incident at the U.S. Capitol," VisualCapitalist.com, January 16, 2021, https://www.visualcapitalist.com/how-news-media-is -describing-the-incident-at-the-u-s-capitol/.

We concluded that the violence was an amalgamation of (1) a coup d'état attempt by a circle of Trump insiders, presided over by the sitting president himself; (2) a terrorist attack by organized far-right groups, most of all Oath Keepers and Proud Boys; and (3) an insurrection by members of the MAGA movement and pro-Trump QAnon conspiracy theorists. While these three groupings or power hubs were distinct entities, there were linkages between and among them, including actual contacts between Oath Keepers and Proud Boys.

THE FAILED COUP D'ÉTAT

The most fervent loyalists among Trump's associates, who had failed to win support in the courts for their claim that Donald Trump and not Joe Biden had won the election, worked feverishly to pull off a coup. These people, among them Rudy Giuliani, John Eastman, Sidney Powell, and Stephen

Bannon, had conversations with the president in person and on the phone as they plotted to prevent the congressional certification of Biden's victory. The most prominent among them were the president's personal lawyer, Giuliani, and his former campaign and White House, adviser Bannon, the latter an ideologist of white nationalism and no friend of liberal democracy. While President Trump himself used his postelection speeches and tweets repeatedly to invite his supporters to the "wild" rally, Bannon's appeals were far more radical and precise. In his "War Room" podcast the night before January 6, Bannon said,

> It's not going to happen like you think it's going to happen. OK, it's going to be quite extraordinarily different. All I can say is, strap in. . . .
>
> You made this happen and tomorrow it's game day. So strap in. Let's get ready.

> All hell is going to break loose tomorrow. . . . So many people said, 'Man, if I was in a revolution I would be in Washington.' Well, this is your time in history.
>
> It's all converging, and now we're on the point of attack tomorrow.[41]

Giuliani did not hold back either. He told the crowd at the rally that fateful day, "Let's have trial by combat." The coup plotters, including the president, had direct lines to the most aggressive Trumpians in both chambers of Congress. One of those legislators, Representative Mo Brooks, was also present at the rally and used language to whip the crowd into a frenzy. "Today is the day American patriots start taking down names and kicking ass! Now, our ancestors sacrificed their blood, their sweat, their tears, their fortunes, and sometimes their lives, to give us, their descendants, an America that's the greatest nation in world history. So, I have a question for you: Are you willing to do the same? My answer is yes. Louder. Are you willing to do what it takes to fight for America? [cheers and applause] Louder! Will you fight for America?"[42]

Typically, coup d'états are plotted and attempted by the military or other elites to remove the highest leader or leaders from office and establish a new government. What happened on January 6 was different, in that it was an insider plot with the sitting president in a central and active role. As the investigations by the House Select Committee to Investigate the January 6th Attack on the United States Capitol found, Trump and a clique of outside advisers, most of them lawyers, pursued a multitude of illegal schemes to keep Trump in office. These unofficial advisers and the president himself tried to convince Republican officeholders in several states to falsify election results or the elector lineups in favor of the losing candidate—Trump. While most of the plotters worked behind closed doors, others—led by the president—promoted some of the schemes in public—at rallies, in social media, and on pro-Trump cable channels.

It was an assault on the constitution and the rule of law and an existential threat against the pillars of democracy.

THE TERRORIST ATTACK

"Terrorism" means deliberate violence or threats thereof by nonstate groups or individuals against civilians or noncombatants to achieve political goals. This definition and similar ones apply to both domestic and international terrorism. While the news media have been reluctant to use the "t-word"—especially in domestic cases—FBI Director Christopher Wray spoke of "domestic terrorism" in the months following the January 6 events. He was right. After all, Oath Keepers and Proud Boys and likely several other groups perpetrated premeditated violence against noncombatants— namely, uniformed police officers on duty to protect the Capitol—and threatened civilians—members of Congress, their staffs, and Vice President Mike Pence—for political ends. Still, it was not surprising that no person involved in the breach of the Congress was charged with or indicted for domestic terrorism. Although domestic terrorism is defined in the United States Code (18 U.S. Code § 2331), "there is no federal criminal provision expressly prohibiting 'domestic terrorism,' as the terms defining domestic terrorism are not elements of criminal offenses."[43]

One week after the first anniversary of January 6, a grand jury in Washington, D.C., charged the founder and leader of the Oath Keepers, Stewart Rhodes, and ten of the organization's members with a serious crime: seditious conspiracy (plus several other offenses). Except for Rhodes and one codefendant who had not been arrested and charged before, the other men and one woman were in custody and had been charged earlier with lesser crimes. In the forty-eight-page indictment, the prosecution detailed its seditious conspiracy charges based on the clear and precise definition in U.S. Code (18 U.S. Code § 2384-Seditious Conspiracy). According to the indictment, "From in and around November 2020, through in and around January 2021, in the District of Columbia and elsewhere, the defendants . . . did knowingly conspire, confederate, and agree, with other persons known and unknown to the Grand Jury, by force to prevent, hinder, and delay the execution of any law of the United States. The purpose of the conspiracy was to oppose the lawful transfer of presidential power by force."[44]

Given the realities of the code, the criminal charge of seditious conspiracy was the right choice for this circle of Oath Keepers. The former leader of the Proud Boys, Henry "Enrique" Tarrio, and four other members of the group were also charged with seditious conspiracy and a multitude of other crimes.[45] Among the other indicted participants in the January 6 violence were fanatic believers in the pro-Trump QAnon conspiracy theory. In his remarkable study of the QAnon phenomenon, James Fitzgerald provides the following succinct description of the conspiracy theory's core beliefs:

The world is run by a shadowy cabal of Satan-worshipping paedophiles and this cabal includes top-level democrats such as Joe Biden, Hilary Clinton, Barack Obama and George Soros, as well as a number of high-profile (liberal/democrat-leaning) celebrities including Oprah Winfrey and Tom Hanks. In addition to running a global paedophile ring, members of this cabal execute and eat their child victims to extract the chemical compound 'adrenochrome', which is used to keep the politicians and celebrities unnaturally young. US President Donald Trump is (still) the saviour and is acting to expose this cabal, although he is hamstrung by the (liberal/democrat) deep state. The moment of triumph will arrive when Trump finally succeeds in his crusade against the deep state, exposing the cabal in an event known as "the Storm"2, which ultimately ends with the mass incarceration of the paedophilic Satan-worshippers on Guantanamo Bay.[46]

In the out-of-control crowd on January 6, a number of persons displayed the letter "Q" on flags, signs, or clothes—although the picture of one of them, the so-called QAnon Shaman, who wore horns, was one of the most-publicized images during and after the incident. He and other QAnon conspiracists were members of a virtually organized group that advocated violence to keep Donald Trump in office. While the QAnon online community differed from the more traditional far-right extremists, such as Oath Keepers and Proud Boys, a number of its most fanatical members had records of violence based on their conspiracist beliefs well before January 6.[47]

More than four in ten Republicans (at least a quarter or more based on responses to various questions in the previous chapter's figures 5.36 and 5.37) but also a significant number of Independents and Democrats believed in the QAnon conspiracy theory. In other words, many millions of Americans embraced this most bizarre tale. Donald Trump, too, embraced the QAnon conspiracy theorists because, as he said, "I understand they like me very much, which I appreciate."[48] This association was hardly surprising since, as Thomas B. Edsall put it, "Donald Trump deploys conspiracy theory as a political mobilizing tool designed to capture anger at the liberal establishment, to legitimize racial resentment and to unite voters who feel oppressed by what they see as a dominant socially progressive culture."[49] Trump did so when he promoted the anti-Obama conspiracy theories (see chapter 3) before he entered electoral politics and later, as president, when he had kind words for QAnon.

Many among the millions of QAnon conspiracy theorists believed that God had sent Trump to punish the unpatriotic enemies and lead the nation back to glory. And this glorification was shared by members of his inner circles. On April 30, 2019, for example, Trump's campaign manager, Brad Parscale, tweeted, "Loved watching the crowd fill up for the 547th Rally in Green Bay. There has never been and probably never will be a movement like this again. Only God could deliver such a savior to our nation and only God could allow me to help. God bless America!" As White House press secretary Sarah Huckabee Sanders told the Christian Broadcast Network News, "I think God calls all of us to fill different roles at different times, and I think that he wanted Donald Trump to become president. And that's why he's there, and I think he has done a tremendous job in supporting a lot of the things that people of faith really care about."[50]

This kind of worship is quite common among the coteries of authoritarian leaders. Comparisons to the inner circle of Adolf Hitler in Nazi Germany are instructive: Hermann Goering, the second most powerful man in the Nazi leadership, wrote, "How shall I give expression, O my Führer, to what is in our hearts? How shall I find words to express your deeds? Has there ever been a mortal as beloved as you, my Führer? Was there ever belief as strong as the belief in your mission. You were sent us by God for Germany!" Hitler's propaganda chief, Joseph Goebbels, claimed that "Germany has been transformed into a great house of the Lord where the Fuehrer as our mediator stands before the throne of God."[51] And another henchman, Rudolf Hess, told fellow Germans in a speech, "With all our powers we will endeavor to be worthy of the Führer thou, O Lord, has sent us!"[52] There are valuable lessons to be learned from the past, but too often, those lessons and warnings have been ignored by open worshippers and silent enablers of strongmen, as January 6 once again demonstrated.

In the months after the January 6 attacks, thousands of U.S. Department of Justice documents that charged and indicted members of organized groups revealed how these men and women used social media and other advanced communication technologies to communicate with each other. The indictments of Rhodes and ten other Oath Keepers charged, for example, that the defendants were "using websites, social media, text messaging, and encrypted messaging applications to communicate with co-conspirators." In this particular indictment, as in almost all January 6 cases against members of organized far-right groups, many pages were filled with the transcripts of written and spoken communications among group members as well as descriptions of streamed videos that captured and often celebrated their violence near and in the Capitol.

However, the very means of communication that enabled violent extremists to plot their actions before January 6 contained powerful evidence of their offenses, which led eventually to the arrests and indictments of dozens of group members.

THE INSURRECTION BY TRUMP SUPPORTERS

The political scientists Suzanne Mettler and Robert Lieberman warned in the aftermath of the violent events of January 6, 2021, "This year the insurrectionists failed, but we would do well to heed the ominous words one scrawled on a paper on a desk in Speaker Nancy Pelosi's office: 'WE WILL NOT BACK DOWN.' As long as Republican Party leaders continue to trade in falsehoods, deceiving their supporters about the election results, their followers will persist in trying to reverse the outcome, and next time, they may prevail."[53] Contrary to the members of well-organized white supremacy/neo-Nazi groups, these insurrectionists were individuals who traveled alone, with a family member, a close friend, or a colleague to Washington, D.C., to answer the call of the president they loved. In the weeks and months after January 6, whenever more participants in the violence around and in the Capitol were arrested, the news media reported about the background of a number of these people, many of whom were charged with criminal offenses. Mostly, they were described by relatives, friends, and neighbors as nice and peaceful persons devoted to their families, communities, and churches. They were seen as ordinary citizens caught up in a mass rally gone out of control.

There was the forty-year-old mother of eight children, who "sold cheese and yogurt at local farmers' markets and used Facebook mostly to discuss yoga, organic food, and her children's baseball games."[54] That was before she embraced extreme political views during the COVID-19 crisis and Donald Trump's reelection campaign. As videos showed, she used "a battering ram to smash a window and a bullhorn to issue orders" during the breach of the Capitol.[55] Her mother expressed surprise when she learned about her daughter's violent behavior.

In a lengthy *New York Times* portrayal of seven men, all perpetrating violence that day, the reporters explained that "doing so provides a close-up view of how seemingly average citizens—duped by a political lie, goaded by their leaders and swept up in a frenzied throng—can unite in breathtaking acts of brutality."[56] Again, those who knew these men claimed they were not extremists turned criminals but caring members of their families and communities. However, in published letters to the editor, some readers of the *Times* took issue with the notion of "average" or "ordinary" citizens simply making bad decisions that fateful day. One reader wrote, "The article notes that prosecutors and congressional investigators are looking into how 'seemingly average citizens—duped by a political lie, goaded by their leaders and swept up in a frenzied throng—can unite in breathtaking acts of brutality.' This statement evokes Kristallnacht and the horror that followed. Donald Trump did goad this group. What these 'ordinary citizens' are capable of in the thrall of a demagogue is frightening."[57]

Another reader objected to describing violent insurrectionists as "ordinary" people and issued a warning: "We should not be distracted by the attempts to portray these participants as just ordinary folk. Some of them brought or used other items as weapons, as well as communication devices for coordinating their efforts. These participants engaged in a violent attempt to subvert our democracy and injure or kill our elected officials, as well as the police protectors of our nation's democratic process and buildings."[58]

The reference in one of these letters to *Kristallnacht*, the unspeakable 1938 anti-Jewish pogroms throughout Germany, was an appropriate comparison. While the paramilitary Nazi *Sturmabteilung* (SA) led the attacks, many civilians joined in killing and maiming their fellow Germans who were Jews. After Germany's defeat in World War II and the end of the

Hitler regime, the term *Mitläufer* was used as an excuse by and for people who joined the actions of organized Nazis during the Third Reich period. The claim was that these people were not the driving forces; they were merely going along with what organized Nazis said and did. In reality, they were participants—not only during *Kristallnacht* violence. The *Mitläufer* of January 6, too, followed the example of organized white supremacist/neo-Nazi squads moving toward the U.S. Capitol, attacked officers, and used force to enter congressional buildings. They were not ordinary citizens who reacted out of the blue to a sudden burst of rage. Most, if not all, were radicalized before they made the trip to Washington, D.C.

In the weeks and days before January 6, the most extreme versions among pro-Trump online forums were full of violent appeals in support of Trump's Stop the Steal efforts and brutal threats against those supporting Joe Biden as president-elect. These were not the online sites of organized groups but discussion boards for individuals who were attracted to the communicative rituals of degradation and excommunication that Carey recognized in certain "media events" of the twentieth century.[59] By the end of the twenty-first century's second decade, certain far-right sites had become online versions of the (mainstream) media events of the previous century—along with pro-Trump cable networks, the audience sizes of which were tiny in comparison with those of far-right social media platforms. Among those online sites, thedonald.win was "a furiously pro-Trump forum that became an online staging ground for the Capitol assault [and] a cautionary tale about the Internet's dark side."[60] According to the site's owner, its forum attracted one million visitors daily in December 2020, the critical weeks before the insurrection in early January 2021.[61]

Comments posted just before January 6 in the moderated threads "trump-tweet-daddy-says-be-in-dc" and "Good Luck Patriots, the Eyes of the World Look Upon You Now" on the thedonald.win site seem to have been posted by nonorganized individuals, many of whom mentioned they were traveling alone to Washington, D.C., or looking for others to carpool with. They seemed obsessed with arms and violence and total devotion to Donald Trump. Responding to a posted reminder that carrying guns was not legal in Washington, one man wrote, "yes, it's illegal, but this is war and we're clearly in a post-legal phase. . . . LIVE AS A FREE AMERICAN AND BRING YOUR ARMS." Another commenter stated, "To all our enemies high and low you want a war? Well your asking for one. . . . To the American people on the ground in DC today and all over this great nation, be prepared for anything. . . . Now we are here. Now they get what they want."

One poster advised rally participants that they should travel in groups and "not let [someone] disarm someone without stacking bodies." This was seconded by a responder who recommended, "Those coming armed should meet outside the city and then move en masse. Too easy to get picked off moving onesies and twosies. Wish I owned land in Virginia but I don't. Need to find a patriot land owner in Virginia with a hundred acres or so." There were special appeals to those who "are active-duty law enforcement or possess retired law enforcement credentials" and who "are allowed to carry concealed [guns] in D.C."

And there were repeatedly testaments of allegiance to Donald Trump and support for the president's fight against Biden's "illegal" election in posts like the following.

We The People, will not tolerate a Steal. No retreat, No Surrender. Restore to my President what you stole or reap the consequences!!!

Well, shit. We've got marching orders, bois.

LET'S MAKE THIS MARCH BIBLICAL PATRIOTS!

I'm gonna grab my plane ticket. This needs to be an absolute monster.

VP Pence has tremendous Constitutional authority in the proceeding on January 6, if he decides to use it. The RINOs will provide very little support, but it does not change this fact.

Imagine a congress where Jim Jordan was House Majority Leader and Lauren Boebert was Senate Majority Leader? Then we can actually have a chance of getting back our country, putting the democrat traitors to task.

Donald has been a better dad to me than the piece of shit that got my mom pregnant with me and my brother. Donald Trump is my dad.[62]

Presumably, a number of these online posters were among the thousands at Trump's January 6 rally and the several hundred enraged people who stormed the U.S. Capitol immediately after the president spoke. More than one thousand of the latter were criminally charged that year and later. Some expressed regrets and even shame for their actions, particularly in the face of indictments and prison terms. For hardcore MAGA followers, these men and women were not criminals or terrorists but ordinary citizens held as political prisoners by far-left communists and other evildoers.

Among the far larger number of rally attendees who did not participate in the violent acts and did not enter the Capitol, many, if not most, continued to believe in the Big Lie about the 2020 election and a multitude of other old and new conspiracy theories. One year after January 6, one of the nonviolent rally participants told reporters that "his status as a Jan. 6 attendee had become 'a badge of honor' with fellow conservatives."[63] For this man and millions of Americans, the events of January 6, 2021, did not end with the failure to restore President Trump; on the contrary, it strengthened their activism and fortified the Trump movement, which had taken over the GOP. Mettler and Lieberman wrote about the critical role of leaders in these sorts of crises and warned, "Accepting defeat squarely and honestly is a mark of leadership, and it is what we should insist on from our leaders, in both parties No one likes to lose an election, but democracy requires adults, leaders who can face losses themselves and break the news to their supporters, and citizens who can accept the outcomes. When people cease to accept losses in elections, democracy is over."[64]

But Republican leaders, too, did not let up in spreading the Big Lie about the 2020 election results, and only one-third of rank-and-file Republicans considered Joe Biden to be legitimately elected, whereas almost all Democrats (95 percent and 97 percent in two polls) and two-thirds of Independents deemed him a legitimately elected president (figure 6.3). Given that, overall, just two-thirds of the American public believed Biden to be a legitimate president, it was not surprising that some ten months

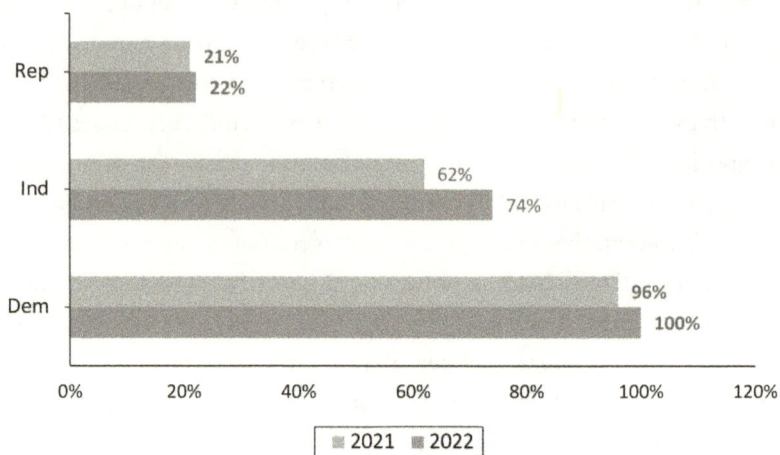

FIGURE 6.3 President Biden was Legitimately Elected.

Percent yes

(*Source*: NBC)

after January 6, fewer than half the American public condemned the persons involved in the breach of the Capitol as criminals: 40 percent said "they went too far, but they had a point"; 7 percent thought "they acted appropriately"; 5 percent were undecided; and 2 percent refused to answer.[65] In other words, the majority of Americans did not categorically criticize the insurrectionists.

More troublesome was that the number of Americans who believed it was justified for citizens to take violent actions against the government grew significantly, from 16 percent in 2010 to 23 percent during the 2016 presidential campaign periods and 34 percent in 2021 (figure 6.4). That was precisely the decade in which first the Tea Party and then Donald Trump entered the political stage.

In her analysis of far-left violence of the 1960s and 1970s in the United States, Hannah Arendt concluded, "The danger of [political] violence . . . will always be that the means overwhelm the end. If goals are not achieved

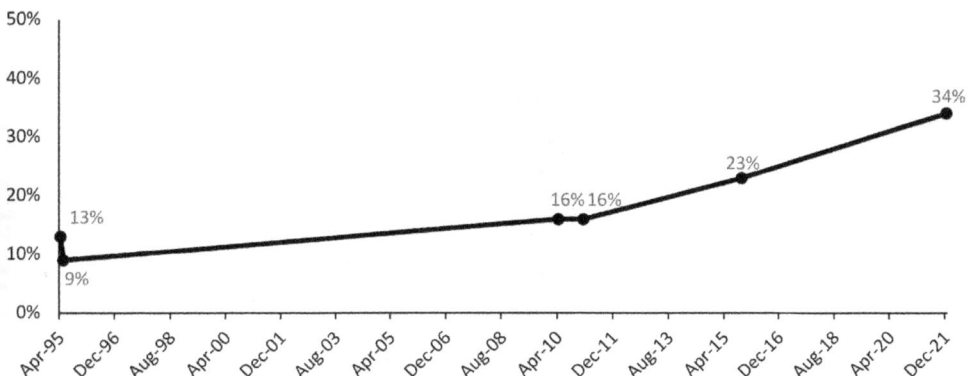

FIGURE 6.4 Political Violence is Justified.

Percent yes

(*Sources:* 4/95, 4/10, 1/11, 10/15—CBS/NYT, CBS; 5/95—WP/ABC, 12/21—WP-UMD)

rapidly, the result will be not merely defeat but the introduction of the practice of violence into the whole body politic. . . . The practice of violence, like all actions, changes the world, but the most probable change is to a more violent world."[66]

Arendt's warning of political violence metastasizing into "the whole body politic" once this practice has been introduced seemed borne out by the partisan breakdown of the poll conducted eleven months after January 6. When asked whether violence against the government is ever justified, Republicans (40 percent) did not reveal greater acceptance of political violence than Independents (41 percent). While Democrats (23 percent) were substantially less likely than Republicans and Independents to justify violence, their acceptance rate was still high for the democratic setting of the United States (figure 6.5). The reasons for validating violence in the three partisan groups were most likely very different, but taken together, the poll results indicate that the acceptance of violence spread across the whole American body politic.[67]

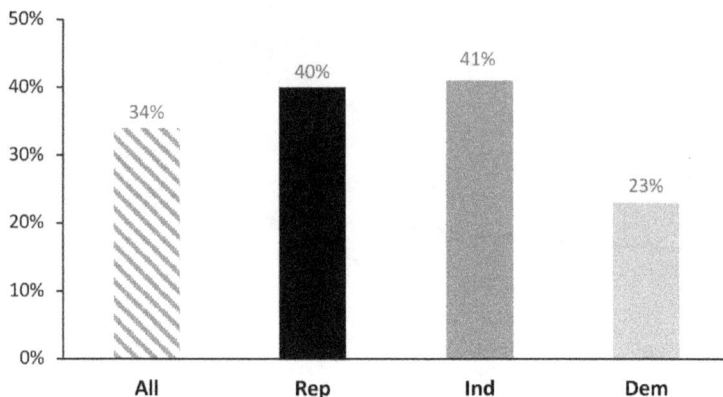

FIGURE 6.5 Violence Is Justified—by Party.

Percent yes

(*Source*: WP/UMD, 12/2021)

WHO WERE THE JANUARY 6 TERRORISTS AND INSURGENTS?

Contrary to far-right Republicans' characterization of violent January 6 intruders as overenthusiastic tourists, among those arrested were several dozen organized terrorists and hundreds of insurrectionists. We analyzed FBI and U.S. Department of Justice court documents along with news reports to gather information about the backgrounds of persons charged with crimes committed during the storming of the Capitol.[68]

We found that 87 percent of those charged were men and 13 percent were women. This included Ashli Babbitt, the thirty-five-year-old Air Force veteran who was killed as she tried to break into the House chamber—a threatening act to be sure. We also found that 6.7 percent of those criminally charged participated as couples (married, engaged, or boyfriend and girlfriend); the average age of the whole group was forty; 9.4 percent were military veterans or were serving in the military; the most represented home states were Florida with 10.9 percent, followed by Texas (9.3 percent) and Pennsylvania (9.0 percent); and 50.1 percent of those arrested were charged with violent crimes. Of all those charged, 45.5 percent mentioned Donald Trump before, during, or after the violence of January 6.

In addition, 16.8 percent of the accused were members of extreme right-wing groups with histories of violence or were part of the QAnon online community. Of the one hundred eleven persons in this cohort, 15 (13.5 percent) were females, a surprisingly large number for far-right reactionary groups, which traditionally excluded women from participation in militant activities. In this case, more than a dozen women were among the most aggressive strata of January 6 attackers. Among them was Jessica Watkins, a thirty-eight-year-old Army veteran and leading Oath Keeper, who posted a selfie on her Parler account from inside the U.S. Capitol with the caption, "Yeah. We stormed the Capitol today. Teargassed, the whole, 9. Pushed our way into the Rotunda. Made it into the Senate even. The news is lying (even Fox) about the Historical Events we created today."[69]

DEMOCRACY IN PERIL

Addressing the newly established United Nations in June 1945, President Harry Truman praised the UN Charter's dedication to fundamental freedoms. "Unless we can attain those objectives for all men and women everywhere— without regard to race, language or religion—we cannot have peace and security."[70] In the same speech, he warned of the lasting threat to democracy by lingering fascist ideas: "All Fascism did not die with Mussolini. Hitler is finished—but the seeds spread by his disordered mind have firm root in too many fanatical brains. It is easier to remove tyrants and destroy concentration camps than it is to kill the ideas which gave them birth and strength. Victory on the battlefield was essential, but it was not enough."

During the Cold War, which followed World War II, the United States of America was the leader of the free world and the model of an enduring, stable democracy. Nearly seventy-five years after Truman's forewarning of the enduring threat of fascism, the American model was in decline. According to Freedom House, from 2010 through 2020, "the United States' aggregate *Freedom in the World* score dropped by 11 points, placing it among the 25 countries that suffered the largest democratic declines in this period. The drop was driven by several factors, including: political corruption and conflicts of interest, lack of transparency in government, and punitive immigration and asylum policies."[71] Rated on the scale of 0 to 100, the U.S.'s score was 94 in 2010 and declined to 83 at the end of 2020. Even more alarming was a similar evaluation, the so-called polity score. That score rates countries around the world on a 21-point scale, from +10 to −10, with a democracy rating +6 to +10), an anocracy −5 to +5, and autocracy −1- to −6. Anocracy signals that a country's system of governance ranks between democracy and autocracy and is particularly susceptible to political instability and even civil war.

At the end of 2020, the polity score for the United States fell to a shocking +5, moving the country, for the first time since the measurement was introduced, from a democracy into the anocracy range.[72] At that point the United States was, according to Barbara Walter, an expert on civil wars, no longer a democracy but "an anocracy for the first time in more than two hundred years . . . [and] no longer the world's oldest continuous democracy."[73] Despite the violence during the events of January 6, the score was raised in 2021 to +8, back into the democracy range. Still, more than one year after the democratic guardrails prevented the attempts to overturn the 2020 presidential election, Walter continued to warn Americans in an interview with the *Washington Post*, "What we're heading toward is an insurgency, which is a form of a civil war. That is the 21st-century version of a civil war, especially in countries with powerful governments and powerful militaries, which is what the United States is. And it makes sense. An insurgency tends to be much more decentralized, often fought by multiple groups. Sometimes they're actually competing with each other. Sometimes they coordinate their behavior."[74]

As discussed in chapter 5, during the formative years of the Tea Party movement, and particularly during the Trump presidency, partisan conflict widened even further in the United States. And the question that became even more pressing was whether or not the deep rift could be repaired. In his book *The Next Civil* War, Stephen Marche gives a pessimistic answer. "One way or the other, the United States is coming to an end. . . . The icons of national unity are losing their power to represent."[75] And in a sobering opinion piece published in the *Washington Post* a few weeks before the first anniversary of January 6, three retired U.S. Army generals—Paul D. Eaton, Antonio M. Taguba, and Steven M. Anderson—urged the military to prepare now for a 2024 insurrection, warning that "the potential for a total breakdown of the chain of command along partisan lines—from the top of the chain to squad level—is significant should another insurrection occur. The idea of rogue units organizing among themselves to support the 'rightful' commander in chief cannot be dismissed."[76]

The research presented in this volume supports the glum conclusions of the military and civilian experts cited here. The significant number of current and former members of the armed forces among the violent participants in the January 6 storming of the Capitol, the open support for Donald Trump's Stop the Steal lies, the vilification of the Democratic Party by a large number of retired admirals and generals,[77] and the mainstreaming of violent far-right extremist groups with military training and equipment at their disposal were dangerous warning signs for an unsettling future. The incomprehensible pro-Putin rhetoric by ex-president Donald Trump, the extreme wing of Republican politicians, and Fox News' far-right mouthpieces during Russia's assault on neighboring Ukraine in 2022 and 2023 were distressing stress tests for America's democracy.

By late 2022, there were some glimpses of encouragement for those fearing the continued rise of antidemocratic ideas and actors—most of all what seemed a waning influence of ex-president Trump and the enablers around him. Many of the Republican candidates whom Trump endorsed in the midterm elections were defeated by their Democratic rivals. Two of the former president's handpicked GOP contenders in the swing states of Pennsylvania (Mehmet Oz) and Georgia (Herschel Walker), who were utterly unqualified to serve in the Senate, lost and cost the Republican Party the majority in the upper chamber of Congress. On the other hand, the GOP won a thin majority in the House of Representatives, which turned a small number of far-right members—all extremist supporters of Trump—into powerbrokers within the Republican conference in the House.

It took an embarrassing fifteen rounds of voting for Kevin McCarthy to be elected speaker of the House, because the extreme faction of his party refused to vote for him without concessions to its members, which included giving them influential committee assignments. For the members of this powerful faction, the January 6 violence was a nonevent. They called the indicted and sentenced lawbreakers "political prisoners" and "patriots." Supremacist and neo-Nazi groups increased their propaganda and recruitment activities in public venues and online. Donald Trump did not hide or apologize for his close relationship with well-known anti-Semites, among them the rapper Kanye West. Anti-Semitic hate crimes increased to a record level; according to the Anti-Defamation League (ADL), there were 3,697 anti-Semitic incidents throughout the United States in 2022, the highest number since the organization began tracking such incidents in 1979. "This is the third time in the past five years that the year-end total has been the highest number ever record," the ADL stated in its report.[78]

After Trump declared his third presidential candidacy in late 2022, his approval among Republicans declined. But that was merely a temporary blip. In spring 2023, Trump outpolled his declared and potential rivals for the GOP's nomination. He also got back the social media privileges that he lost following the January 6 violence. After Elon Musk's Twitter reactivated Trump's account in November 2022, Facebook, Instagram, and YouTube followed suit a few months later. Whether during his public appearances, interviews with sufficiently right-wing TV personalities, or on social media, Trump did not hide his contempt for the rule of law. He hinted repeatedly that he would pardon convicted January 6 lawbreakers on his return to the White House. In his speech at the 2023 Conservative Political Action Conference (CPAC), he said, "I am your warrior. I am your justice. And for those who have been wronged and betrayed, I am your retribution."[79]

As Trump himself faced multiple criminal indictments, he intensified his verbal attacks on the whole law enforcement system and threatened individual prosecutors and judges. Predicting upcoming criminal charges against him in New York City, he urged his followers to stage protest demonstrations against the Manhattan district attorney's office. On his social media platform truthsocial.com, he raged against his detractors, calling them "human scum" and threatening "death & destruction" that "could be catastrophic for our Country" in case of his indictment and arrest."[80] In a disturbing visual, Trump held a baseball bat close to the head of Alvin Bragg, the first Black Manhattan district attorney, indicating a violent attack in progress. The offensive post was removed quickly. In another deleted rant, Trump called the district attorney an "animal." Among the many threats received in Bragg's office was a letter with the warning, "Alvin, I am going to kill you."[81]

With very few exceptions, Republican leaders did not criticize the former president, if only because they feared the power of Trump's base in primary elections.

It was no coincidence that Trump chose Waco, Texas, to stage his first mass rally of the 2024 presidential campaign cycle. After the confrontation between the Branch Davidians cult and federal law enforcement agents there, Waco became the holy grail for far-right antigovernment extremists. Militia groups and other Second Amendment fanatics consider the events of 1993 a blatant example of the government's overreach that justifies antigovernment violence. In 1995, Timothy McVeigh perpetrated the horrific Oklahoma City bombing on the second anniversary of the events at Waco. Three decades later, Trump stood at the sacred ground of the far right, depicting himself and his MAGA movement as the victims of the America-hating deep state. He promised to make America free again, "if you put me back into the White House."[82]

In the cheering crowd, many wore T-shirts and waved flags with the inscription "JESUS IS MY SAVIOR, TRUMP IS MY PRESIDENT."

The sociologists Philip S. Gorski and Samuel L. Perry have argued that the principles of white Christian nationalism, which has much in common with traditional white supremacy, became the driving ideological forces in the Trump-dominated GOP. In their book *The Flag and the Cross* they warn, "These forces have not disappeared. On the contrary, they are building again. A second eruption would likely be larger and more violent than the first [on January 6, 2021]. Large enough to bury American democracy for at least a generation."[83]

Based on our research, we agree with their risk assessment that January 6 might have been merely a rehearsal for a much greater threat to America's liberal democracy.

POSTSCRIPT

Trumpism With and Without Trump

The end of the final chapter raised the specter that the insurrection of January 6, 2021, could be a prelude to a far greater threat to American democracy as 2024 presidential candidate Trump faced multiple criminal indictments and intensified his verbal attacks on the nation's law enforcement system, individual prosecutors and judges, as well as President Joseph Biden. Since that and the partisan conflict chronicled in the book are still ongoing as we are writing, we can only close with a brief update and reflect on what lies ahead (as of July 1, 2023).

Where the rubber will hit the road, so to speak, will be the outcome of the 2024 election—who wins, who loses, and, once again, any controversy about the voting that determines the election results. We discuss here what has happened and what to watch for regarding the future of Donald Trump and Trumpism—with and without Trump.

WHAT'S HAPPENING

The broader context, as chapter 5 emphasized, is that the two parties are ideologically divided and evenly matched, with tempers aflame. In the 2024 election, a unified Republican or Democratic government is once again a real possibility, which can push government policies sharply to the right or the left.[1] Both sides aspire to win big: the Democrats coming out of the 2022 midterms, doing better than expected and Biden optimistic that he can defeat Trump again—assuming Trump will be the Republican nominee. He defeated Trump in 2020, and Trump has been damaged by the January 6 violence, his endless election denial, and ongoing or impending indictments.

The Republicans see the election differently. First, because they picked up House seats in both 2020 and 2022, gaining control of that chamber (they picked up fewer than expected in 2022, since, surprisingly, they had netted several despite losing the presidency in 2020). Second, they believe they can take back the Senate from the Democrats, who are defending many seats, by running better conservative Republican candidates than the tarnished ones they ran in 2022. And third, they believe the presidency should be theirs because of Biden's low approval rating (43 percent, according to the latest realclearpolitics.com average) due to dissatisfaction with inflation, the overall economy, and perceptions of Biden's failure on illegal immigration at the southern border and on the increase in crime nationally.

This hotly battled election may be embroiled, as in 2016, by conflict over voting, questions about election administration, and the status of how electors may be chosen (though the power of state legislatures has now been constrained by the Supreme Court decision in *Moore v. Harper*). Trump himself is *the* Republican campaign issue that a crowded field of candidates has struggled to take on. The candidates have been dividing support without peeling off any from Trump, just like what occurred in the 2016 election. At this writing, his opponents include Ron DeSantis, Mike Pence, Nikki Haley, Tim Scott, Chris Christie, Asa Hutchinson, Vivek Ramaswamy, Larry Elder, Doug Burgum, Francis Suarez, and Will Hurd. Trump has led his closest challenger, Florida Governor Ron DeSantis, by a very wide margin.[2] The logic for all these candidates can only be that while behind in the national polls, they aspire to defeat Trump or run close enough in the early caucus and primary states of Iowa and New Hampshire to pick up momentum into the next races.

The Trump issue has to do with the consequences of his unfounded denial of the 2016 election results and the set of major legal, including criminal, proceedings against him. At this writing, he has been indicted in federal court in Miami for mishandling classified government documents, and there are indictments pending related to the January 6 attack on the U.S. Capitol and his alleged interference in the presidential election in Georgia. Trump has also been indicted in New York on charges of allegedly falsifying business records to hide payments for sex, which could have damaged his 2016 presidential campaign, and he has also lost a civil case in which he was found to have committed sexual abuse and defamation (but not rape). These indictments have thus far (and this could change) not negatively affected his support and even solidified it among his core supporters. While Hutchison, and especially Christie and Hurt, have directly attacked Trump on his indictments, his other challengers have still been deterred from confronting him so fully head on for fear of alienating Trump's electoral base, whose support they have been desperately trying to attract.

HATE SPEECH AND THE THREAT OF POLITICAL VIOLENCE ARE ALIVE AND WELL

In the wake of Trump's federal indictment, the level of hate speech spiked; it came from Trump, his fans among GOP officials inside and outside Congress, and his MAGA base in the electorate. Although a group of previous Republican administration officials—among them Trump's own attorney general, William Barr—condemned his illegal handling of highly classified documents, his approval among Republicans rose further, and his hard-core supporters threatened violence, saying of the indictment, "this is war" and threatening an "eye for an eye."[3]

Trump's own response to the legal proceedings was to attack both the individuals spearheading the cases and the criminal justice system. He claimed that the federal justice system has been the "weaponized" against him, and his supporters among Republican leaders and followers have amplified this claim through the media. That included most of the Republican presidential candidates, who preferred to attack Trump's attackers—and the weaponization of the federal justice system—and not him. This occurred foremost with the federal indictment on June 8, 2023, on thirty-seven charges of mishandling classified government documents, which Trump had taken on leaving office and then proceeded to obstruct the government's efforts to get them back.

Two things happened. First, Trump called for his supporters to protest at the federal court where he was being arraigned in Miami, raising the possibility of violence in the spirit of the January 6 attack on the Capitol. Nothing on any scale happened. Score one for cooler heads prevailing.[4] Second, in attacking the federal justice system, some Trump supporters in Congress hearkened back to January 6, 2021, by glorifying the violent attackers.

> During the very same hour in which the former president surrendered to federal authorities in Miami, his Republican allies in the House were, in their most visible and official way yet, embracing as heroes and martyrs the people who sacked the Capitol on Jan. 6, 2021, in hopes of overturning Trump's election defeat. . . . In the Capitol complex, Rep. Matt Gaetz (R-Fla.), with sidekick Rep. Marjorie Taylor Greene (R-Ga.) and four other far-right lawmakers, held a "hearing" that honored participants in the riot, family members of Jan. 6 rioters and organizers of the attempted overthrow of the 2020 vote.[5]

True to form, as described comprehensively throughout the book, Trump lashed out on social media regarding his prosecution and the conspiracy against him and the nation. In response to reports about the strength of Special Counsel Jack Smith's case against him, including more than one interview with Trump and grand jury transcripts, Trump promptly begged in all caps on social media for Congress to "investigate the political witch hunts against me"[6]

This response by Trump and his supporters was not surprising in the context of what this book has described, as echoed in the language of initial reports after the announcement of Trump's indictment:

> The federal indictment of former President Donald J. Trump has unleashed a wave of calls by his supporters for violence and an uprising to defend him, disturbing observers and raising concerns of a dangerous atmosphere ahead of his court appearance in Miami on Tuesday.
>
> In social media posts and public remarks, close allies of Mr. Trump — including a member of Congress — have portrayed the indictment as an act of war, called for retribution and highlighted the fact that much of his base carries weapons. The allies have painted Mr. Trump as a victim of a weaponized Justice Department controlled by President Biden, his potential opponent in the 2024 election.[7]

Trump fell back, as he had in the past and during his presidency, on attacking Democrats as communists, and his supporters joined in. "It is noteworthy that in his post-indictment speech he linked what was happening to him with a litany of familiar, polarizing, conservative culture war issues. If they get me, he suggested to supporters, they will soon be after you. And that message seemed to get through, with some of his MAGA allies quickly joining Trump in blaming communists for his legal troubles. Georgia Rep. Marjorie Taylor Greene, for instance, said the indictment was the product of 'CORRUPT AND WEAPONIZED COMMUNISTS DEMOCRAT CONTROLLED DOJ.'"[8] This echoes what Trump wrote on Truth Social (his social medium of choice, which he owned, after leaving Twitter) as part of his Easter Holiday greeting: "TO ALL OF THOSE WEAK & PATHETIC RINOS, RADICAL LEFT DEMOCRATS, SOCIALISTS, MARXISTS, & COMMUNISTS WHO ARE KILLING OUR NATION, REMEMBER, WE WILL BE BACK!"[9] And in a later Truth Social post, Trump asserted without any evidence that the FBI planted the top-secret documents in boxes he brought to his

Mar-a-Lago resort, "Congress will hopefully now look at the ever continuing Witch Hunts and ELECTION INTERFERENCE against me
on perfectly legal Boxes, where I have no doubt that information is being
secretly 'planted' by the scoundrels in charge, the Perfect Phone Calls
(Atlanta), the illegal DOJ/Pomerantz/Manhattan D.A. Hoax, where virtually EVERYONE agrees THERE IS NO CASE, and the NYSAG
SCAM, where I have proven beyond a doubt that there is no case, but have
a hostile Judge who should not be on this case!"[10]

Trump's supporters among the public rallied around him, as reflected
in opinion poll results showing they bought Trump's and Republican leaders' claims that he was being prosecuted for political reasons and that the
Justice Department had been weaponized against him, while Democratic
leaders Hillary Clinton and Biden were not indicted for similar mishandling of government documents.[11]

WHAT TO WATCH FOR: TRUMP
AND TRUMPISM?

This book has emphasized the communication of hate speech on the far
right, from the Tea Party to Trump. Trump and Trumpism have posed a
threat to democracy. Trumpism involved Trump's reshaping or refocusing
of the Republican Party in opposition to the liberal Democratic elite establishment on issues concerned with taxes, regulation, racism, crime, immigration, trade, women, labor, education, rights issues related to "political
correctness" or "wokeness," how judicial appointments can move policies to
the right, elections and voting, and truth versus misinformation. It has also
strikingly involved an authoritarian style of politics against all opponents,
including mainstream Republicans who have opposed him. Trumpism has
been a movement involving the further transformation of the base of the
Republican Party to include, in particular, voters without college degrees
and from small towns and rural areas who can pressure the party to adhere
to Trumpist positions. Such movements, by one compelling account, have

interacted with political parties and have been central to "democratiza-tion" or democratic backsliding in American history, depending on the movement.[12]

What, then, is the future of this threat to democracy? Trump has been the direct threat in his denial of the 2020 election results and his authori-tarian outlook on political power. The weaponization and interconnectivity of political communication have been part of this story.

What happens with the threat from Trump will be decided by the 2024 election. It would take too much space here to go through the scenarios resulting from the different possible primary and general election results. The existential threat to democracy that occurred with the shenanigans involving Trump's putting pressure on Vice President Pence to discount the electors from key states and the threat of state legislatures to select the electors themselves has been mitigated by the passing of the Elec-toral Count Reform Act of 2022 and the Supreme Court decision in late June 2023 constraining the independence of state legislatures in establish-ing election procedures. Those actions have not, however, ended threats to rules promoting democratic elections and voting that have occurred. While the GOP has begun to recognize the usefulness of mail voting, in literally all red states measures have been adopted or been considered to maximize Republican votes—gerrymandering that reduces the number of congres-sional and state legislative districts with Black majorities, cutting back on the numbers of voting sites, and implementing particular residency, voter ID, and other requirements. There is the continuing threat of Republicans knowing that they cannot win in fair elections and resorting to undemo-cratic means.

Trumpism poses a comparable threat as Trump himself but without his screaming about fraudulent votes, wrongful counts, and voting machine hacking. Election denial is not a winning issue, and Republican leaders nationally have been winning elections as they have ascended politically (see chapter 5).

But we have been seeing the passing of the torch from Trump to Trump-ism. In the shadow of additional indictments in the Georgia case and the violent breach of the Capitol, Trump's support has remained strong and at times increased. The only other candidate with consistently double-digit numbers—Ron DeSantis—will be first in line should something unforeseeable happen to Trump's candidacy.

To compare these two candidates, consider the following. Right after his criminal indictment, in his campaign speech in Georgia on June 10, 2023, Trump made the up to then most threatening apocalyptic statements: "This is the final battle." "Either the Communists win and destroy America, or we destroy the Communists."[13] At the same time, DeSantis has said that he can and will defeat "leftism" and "woke ideology."[14] In a way, he goes further than Trump: whereas Trump warns of an existential battle, DeSantis says up front he is the one who will win that battle—as he has been trying to do in Florida.

Both candidates have declared that after winning in 2024, they will claim much more executive power. Trump has attacked the deep state and especially the "weaponized" Department of Justice and FBI. DeSantis has repeatedly said that instead of Trump's chaos, he will implement his Florida Blueprint in the federal government swiftly. DeSantis has rejected the idea that a president should view the Department of Justice and the FBI as independent and plans to use Article II of the U.S. Constitution to "remake the government" and use his power "for conservative ends."[15] Democracy in this way, too, could continue to erode from the top as it has elsewhere.[16]

In other words, Trumpism can prevail with either Trump or DeSantis, in that there will be an all-out battle against Democrats. Indeed, Trumpism seems stronger than even Trump. Two cases in point. Called out by evangelicals for claiming that states should decide what happens on abortion issues, Trump quickly switched positions and endorsed federal legislation to restrict abortion rights nationally. Similarly, Trump has hesitated to praise his role in the development of COVID-19 vaccines—a real accomplishment of his presidency—that his MAGA and QAnon fans have decisively rejected.

The other threat from Trumpism that remains after Trump is the way he himself, to be polite, made falsehoods and misinformation acceptable. Hyper-partisan conflict and affective polarization contributed to this.[17]

Describe it as you like, but as Thomas Edsall has written, "The Politics of Delusion Have Taken Hold."

> In other words, the irrational element of partisan hostility has seemingly created a political culture resistant to correction or reform. If so, the nation is stuck, at least for the time being, in a destructive cyclical pattern that no one so far has found a way to escape.
>
> The embodiment of delusional politics is, of course, Donald Trump, with his false, indeed fraudulent, claim that the 2020 election was stolen from him. The continuing willingness of a majority of Republican voters to tolerate this delusion reflects the difficulty facing the nation as it struggles to restore sanity to American politics—if it's not too late.[18]

With this state of political hostility has come vindictiveness. The escalation of partisan conflict that came with the Republicans taking control of the House in 2023 led them to censure Adam Schiff (who was running for the Senate) for misleading the public over the Trump-Russia investigations. In addition, Republican House members have been seeking to impeach Biden administration officials—including Biden himself. Trump has threatened to take revenge against his foes if he is elected in 2024.

To what extent and for how long will this delusion and accompanying rhetoric and threat to American democracy from the right remain? Will Trump and his claims about elections being stolen be cast aside? Will Trumpism remain? At this point, the closing of our last chapter stands—the threat against democracy has not diminished and may have increased.

ABBREVIATIONS

(See Appendix for survey questions)

ABC: American Broadcasting Company

ADL: Anti-Defamation League

American Perspectives: Survey Center on American Life

ANES: American National Elections Studies

AP/Gfk: Associated Press-Growth from knowledge

Capitol Police: United States Capitol Police

CBS: Columbia Broadcasting System

CCGA: Chicago Council on Global Affairs (formerly the Chicago Council on Foreign Relations)

CNN: Cable News Network

DW Scores: DW-NOMINATE scores, estimated roll call vote scores for the House of Representatives and Senate. See chapter 5 text. Source: https://voteview.com/about.

Factiva/Google Trends: Global News Monitoring & Search Engine, DOW JONES

Gallup: Gallup Organization

Investmentwatchblog: investmentwatchblog.com (moved to citizen-watchreport.com) Traffic Analytics & Market Share

KFF: Kaiser Family Foundation

Lexis Nexis News Archive: Global Information & Analytics Company

Monmouth University: Monmouth University Polling Institute

The Monkey Cage: a website covering political science and politics

NBC: National Broadcasting Company

NORC-GSS: General Social Survey (GSS), National Opinion Research Center, University of Chicago

NYT: *New York Times*

ORC: Opinion Research Corporation

Pew: Pew Research Center

PIPA: Program on International Political Attitudes/Knowledge Networks

PRRI-IFYC: Public Religion Research Institute

WP: *Washington Post*

WP-UMD: *Washington Post*-University of Maryland Poll

APPENDIX

Further Information About Figures

CHAPTER 1

Figure 1.4

Q: In general, how much trust and confidence do you have in the mass media—such as newspapers, TV and radio—when it comes to reporting the news fully, accurately and fairly—a great deal, a fair amount, not very much, or none at all? (% Great deal/Fair amount).

Source: Gallup.

CHAPTER 2

Figure 2.3

Q: Do you consider yourself a supporter of the Tea Party movement, or are you not a supporter of the Tea Party movement?

Notes: From June 2011 to January 2013, if the answer was "support," the responses included the options "Strongly" or "Moderately," and from

December 2014 onward, the support category was divided into "Support-Strongly" and "Support-Somewhat." Categories were collapsed. When there was more than one time point per month, an average is displayed.

Source: AP/Gfk.

CHAPTER 3

Figure 3.6

Q: Do you think Barack Obama was definitely born in the United States, probably born in the United States, probably born in another country, or definitely born in another country? (% Definitely/Probably born in another country).

Source: CNN/ORC.

Figure 3.7

Q: Do you happen to know what Barack Obama's religion is? Is he Christian, Jewish, Muslim, Buddhist, Hindu, atheist, agnostic, or something else? (Pew); Do you happen to know what religion Barack Obama is? Is he Protestant, Catholic, Jewish, Mormon, Muslim, something else, or not religious? (CNN/ORC).

Sources: Pew Research Center 2008–12; CNN/ORC 2015.

CHAPTER 5

Figure 5.1

Q: How confident are you that, across the country, the votes will be accurately cast and counted in this year's election—very confident, somewhat confident, not too confident, or not at all confident? (% Very/Somewhat confident).

Source: Gallup.

Figure 5.2

Q: In general, do you feel that the laws covering the sale of firearms should be made more strict, less strict, or kept as they are now? (% More strict).

Source: Gallup.

Figure 5.3

Q: I'd like to get your feelings toward some of our political leaders and other people who are in the news these days. I'll read the name of a person and I'd like you to rate that person using something we call the feeling thermometer. Ratings between 50 degrees and 100 degrees mean that you feel favorable and warm toward the person. Ratings between 0 degrees and 50 degrees mean that you don't feel favorable toward the person and that you don't care too much for that person. You would rate the person at the 50 degree mark if you don't feel particularly warm or cold toward the person.

Source: ANES, weighted.

Figure 5.4

Q: Do you approve or disapprove of the way _____ is handling his job as president?

Sources: Pew and Gallup.

Figure 5.5

Q: Some people say they are basically content with the federal government, others say they are frustrated, and others say they are angry. Which of these best describes how you feel? (% feeling angry about the government).

Source: Pew.

Figure 5.8

Q: We hear a lot of talk these days about liberals and conservatives. I'm going to show you a seven-point scale on which the political views that people might hold are arranged from extremely liberal—point 1—to extremely conservative—point 7. Where would you place yourself on this scale? (% Conservative, 5–7, by party).

Source: NORC-GSS.

Figure 5.9

Q: If you had to choose, would you rather have a smaller government providing fewer services, or a bigger government providing more services? (% who prefer a smaller government providing fewer services).

Source: Pew.

Figure 5.10

Q: In general, do you think there is too much, too little, or about the right amount of government regulation of business and industry? (% Too much).

Source: Gallup.

Figure 5.11

Q: Do you think it is the responsibility of the federal government to make sure all Americans have healthcare coverage, or is that not the responsibility of the federal government? (% saying it is the responsibility of the federal government to make sure all Americans have health care).

Source: Gallup.

Figure 5.12

Q: We are faced with many problems in this country, none of which can be solved easily or inexpensively. I'm going to name some of these problems, and for each one I'd like you to name some of these problems, and for each one I'd like you to tell me whether you think we're spending too much money on it, too little money, or about the right amount. . . . Are we spending too much, too little, or about the right amount on . . . improving the conditions of Blacks? (% Too little).

Source: NORC-GSS.

Figure 5.13

Q: On the average (Negroes/Blacks/African-Americans) have worse jobs, income, and housing than white people. Do you think these differences are . . . mainly due to discrimination? (% Yes, non-Black respondents). Source NORC-GSS.

Figure 5.14

Q: Do you approve or disapprove of public schools teaching about the history of racism?
Source: Monmouth University, November 2021.

Figure 5.15

Q: In general, do you think the courts in this area deal too harshly or not harshly enough with criminals?
Source: NORC-GSS.

Figure 5.16

Q: With respect to the abortion issue, would you consider yourself to be pro-choice or pro-life? (% responding Pro-choice).
Source: Gallup.

Figure 5.17

Q: Do you agree or disagree? Homosexual couples should have the right to marry one another. (% responding Strongly agree).
Source: NORC-GSS.

Figure 5.18

Q: With which one of these statements about the environment and the economy do you most agree—protection of the environment should be given priority, even at the risk of curbing economic growth (or) economic growth should be given priority, even if the environment suffers to some extent? (% preference for prioritizing the economy over the environment).
Source: Gallup.

Figure 5.19

Q: Next, I'm going to read a list of problems facing the country. For each one, please tell me if you personally worry about this problem a great deal, a fair amount, only a little, or not at all? First, how much do you personally worry about . . . the quality of the environment? (% saying they worry a great deal about the quality of the environment).

Source: Gallup.

Figure 5.20

Q: I'm going to read you some pairs of statements that will help us understand how you feel about a number of things. As I read each pair, tell me whether the FIRST statement or the SECOND statement comes closer to your own views—even if neither is exactly right. The best way to ensure peace is through military strength/Good diplomacy is the best way to ensure peace. (% saying that good diplomacy is the best way to ensure peace).

Source: Pew.

Figure 5.21

Q: We are faced with many problems in this country, none of which can be solved easily or inexpensively. I'm going to name some of these problems, and for each one I'd like you to name some of these problems, and for each one I'd like you to tell me whether you think we're spending too much money on it, too little money, or about the right amount. First (READ ITEM A) . . . are we spending too much, too little, or about the right amount on (ITEM)? The military, armaments and defense. (% responding Too little national spending on military-armaments-defense/national defense).

Source: NORC-GSS.

Figure 5.22

Q: In the Middle East situation, are your sympathies more with the Israelis or more with the Palestinians? (% more sympathetic to the Israelis minus the % more sympathetic to the Palestinians).

Source: Gallup.

Figure 5.23

Q: Do you believe that globalization, especially the increasing connections of our economy with others around the world, is mostly good or mostly bad for the United States? (% mostly good).

Source: Chicago Council on Global Affairs.

Figure 5.24

Q: Below is a list of possible foreign policy goals that the United States might have. For each one, please select whether you think that it should be a very important foreign policy goal of the United States, a somewhat important foreign policy goal, or not an important goal at all . . . Controlling and reducing illegal immigration. (% responding that controlling illegal immigration is an important foreign policy goal).

Source: CCGA.

Figure 5.25

Q: How much of a threat, if any, is the coronavirus outbreak for . . .? (% saying that the coronavirus outbreak is a major threat).

Source: Pew.

Figure 5.26

Q: In the past month, how often, if ever, have you worn a mask or face covering when in stores or other businesses (because of the coronavirus outbreak)? All or most of the time, some of the time, hardly ever, never, have not gone to these types of places? (% reporting frequent mask wearing).

Source: Pew.

Figure 5.27

Q: Have you been fully vaccinated against the coronavirus/COVID-19? By fully vaccinated, this means receiving all required doses of the vaccine (there may be one dose or two, depending on which vaccine you received).

Source: Gallup 2021.

Figure 5.28

Q: In general, do you think _____ should require their employees to get vaccinated for COVID-19 (coronavirus) unless they have a medical exemption, or not?

Source: Kaiser Family Foundation, 2021.

Figure 5.31

Q: Is it your belief that, just before the war, Iraq: Had actual weapons of mass destruction; Had no weapons of mass destruction but had a major program for developing them; Had some limited activities that could be used to help develop weapons of mass destruction, but not an active program; Did not have any activities related to weapons of mass destruction; No answer?

Source: PIPA.

Figure 5.32

Q: Now, thinking about Barack Obama's religious beliefs . . . Do you happen to know what Barack Obama's religion is? Is he Christian, Jewish, Muslim, Buddhist, Hindu, atheist, agnostic, or something else?

Source: John Sides, "Why Do More People Think Obama Is a Muslim?," *Monkey Cage*, https://themonkeycage.org/2010/08/why_do_more _people_think_obama/, August 26, 2010.

Figure 5.33

Q: I'd like your opinion about some possible international concerns for [survey country]. Do you think that each of the following is a major threat, a minor threat, or not a threat to [survey country]?—Global climate change. (% who perceive that global climate change is a major threat to the U.S.).

Source: Pew.

Figure 5.34

Q: Please tell us how much discrimination there is against each of these groups in our society today. (% who say there is a lot of discrimination in our society against each group).

Source: Pew.

Figure 5.35

Q: Do you believe that more people have died of COVID-19 than is being reported by the news, fewer people have died than is being reported, or do you think news reports of COVID-19 deaths are generally accurate? (% who say more or fewer people have died than is reported).

Source: American Perspectives, September 2020.

Figure 5.36

Q: How much, if anything, have you heard or read about QAnon? (IF A LOT OR A LITTLE) Do you think the information shared by QAnon has generally been shown to be accurate or would you say has been generally shown to be inaccurate? (% who have heard of it and believe it is NOT accurate).

Source: American Perspectives, September 2020.

Figure 5.37

Q: How much do you agree or disagree with each of the following? (Completely agree, mostly agree, mostly disagree, completely disagree): The government, media, and financial worlds in the U.S. are controlled by a group of Satan-worshipping pedophiles who run a global child sex trafficking operation.; There is a storm coming soon that will sweep away the elites in power and restore the rightful leaders.; Because things have gotten so far off track, true American patriots may have to resort to violence in order to save our country. (% of agree . . .).

Source: PRRI-IFYC, March 2021.

CHAPTER 6

Figure 6.3

Q: Do you think that Joe Biden won the presidency legitimately? (% yes).

Source: NBC.

Figure 6.4

Q: Do you think it is ever justified for citizens to take violent action against the government, or is it never justified?

Sources: CBS/NYT, CBS: April 1995, April 2010, January 2011, October 2015; WP/ABC: May 1995; WP-UMD: December 2021.

Figure 6.5

Q: Do you think it is ever justified for citizens to take violent action against the government, or is it never justified?

(Source: WP/UMD, 12/2021)

NOTES

1. INTRODUCTION: FROM THE TEA PARTY AND DONALD TRUMP'S MAGA EXTREMISM TO JANUARY 2021

1. "Sen. Romney: 'This Was an Insurrection Incited by the President of the United States,'" CNN, January 7, 2001, https://edition.cnn.com/videos/politics/2021/01/07/mitt-romney -riot-violence-reaction-capitol-certification-sot-vpx.cnn. To put this stunning event into a historical context, Suzanne Mettler and Robert C. Lieberman pointed to the violent overthrow of the 1898 local election in Wilmington, North Carolina, by white supremacists in the Democratic Party who thereby nullified the victory of a multiracial alliance. "The flagrant takeover by party leaders in North Carolina occurred more quietly all over the South during the 1890s, as Democrats in each state seized power," they wrote. Thus, while unprecedented on the federal level, there were precedents in southern states, albeit more than one hundred years ago. See Suzanne Mettler and Robert Lieberman, "Democracy Means Accepting Loss," *Bipartisan Policy Review*, January 2023, 14–15, https://cpb-us-e1.wpmucdn.com/blogs.cornell.edu/dist/1/8955/files/2019/09/bipartisan review2021-final.pdf.

2. Amy Sherman, "Time Line of What Trump Said Before Jan. 6 Capitol Riot," *Politifact*, January 11, 2021, https://www.politifact.com/article/2021/jan/11/timeline-what-trump-said -jan-6-capitol-riot/.

3. "Transcript of Trump's Speech at Rally Before U.S. Capitol Riot," *U.S. News & World Report*, January 13, 2021, https://www.usnews.com/news/politics/articles/2021-01-13 /transcript-of-trumps-speech-at-rally-before-us-capitol-riot.

4. "Transcript of Trump's Speech."

5. On Trump's rhetoric more broadly, see the excellent study by Roderick P. Hart, *Trump and Us: What He Says and Why People Listen* (New York: Cambridge University Press, 2020).

6. Carol Leonnig and Philip Rucker, *I Alone Can Fix It: Donald J. Trump's Catastrophic Final Year* (New York: Penguin, 2021), chap. 21.

7. Timothy Snyder, *On Tyranny*, graphic edition (New York: Ten Speed, 2021), 56.

8. Tim Alberta, *American Carnage: On the Front of the Republican Civil War and the Rise of President Trump* (New York: Harper, 2019), 6.

9. See Matt A. Barreto et al., "The Tea Party in the Age of Obama: Mainstream Conservatism or Out-Group Anxiety?," *Political Power and Social Theory* 22 (2011): 105–36; Theda Skocpol and Vanessa Williamson, *The Tea Party and the Remaking of Republican Conservatism* (New York: Oxford University Press, 2012); Christopher S. Parker and Matt Barreto, *Change They Can't Believe In: The Tea Party and Reactionary Politics in America* (Princeton, NJ: Princeton University Press, 2013); Robb Willer, Matthew Feinberg, and Rachel Wetts, "Threats to Racial Status Promote Tea Party Support Among White Americans," SSRN, April 28, 2016, https://papers.ssrn.com/sol3/papers.cfm?abstract_id=2770186; Bryan T. Gervais and Irwin L. Morris, *Reactionary Republicanism: How the Tea Party in the House Paved the Way for Trump's Victory* (New York: Oxford University Press, 2018).

10. Jill Lepore, *The Whites of Their Eyes: The Tea Party's Revolution and the Battle Over American History* (Princeton, NJ: Princeton University Press, 2010), 137.

11. Elizabeth Price Foley, *The Tea Party: Three Principles* (New York: Cambridge University Press, 2012).

12. Skocpol and Williamson, *The Tea Party*, 27, 32–34.

13. Parker and Barreto, *Change They Can't Believe In*, 2–3.

14. See Kate Zernike, *Boiling Mad: Behind the Lines in Tea Party America* (New York: St. Martin's, 2010); Scott Rasmussen and Douglas Schoen, *Mad as Hell: How the Tea Party Movement Is Fundamentally Remaking Our Two-Party System* (New York: Broadside, 2010); Paul Street and Anthony DiMaggio, *Crashing the Tea Party: Mass Media and the Campaign to Remake American Politics* (Boulder, CO: Paradigm, 2011); Jules Boykoff and Eulalie Laschever, "The Tea Party Movement, Framing, and the US Media," *Social Movement Studies* 10, no. 4 (2011): 341–66; David A. Weaver and Joshua M. Scacco, "Revisiting the Protest Paradigm: The Tea Party as Filtered Through Prime-Time Cable News," *International Journal of Press/Politics* 18, no. 1 (2013): 61–84; Vincent Raynauld, "The Perfect Political Storm? The Tea Party Movement, the Redefinition of the Digital Political Mediascape, and the Birth of Online Politicking 3.0" (PhD diss., Carleton University, 2013); Khadijah Costley White, *The Branding of Right-Wing Activism: The News Media and the Tea Party* (New York: Oxford University Press, 2018); and Jennifer Mercieca, "Dangerous Demagogues and Weaponized Communication," *Rhetoric Society Quarterly* 49, no. 3 (2019): 264–79.

15. Yochai Benkler, *The Wealth of Networks: How Social Production Transforms Markets and Freedom* (New Haven, CT: Yale University Press, 2006).

16. Yochai Benkler, Robert Farris, and Hal Roberts, *Network Propaganda: Manipulation, Disinformation, and Radicalization in American Politics* (New York: Oxford University Press, 2018).

17. Jamie Settle, *Frenemies: How Social Media Polarizes America* (New York: Cambridge University Press, 2018); Richard Hasen, *Cheap Speech: How Disinformation Poisons Our Politics—and How to Cure It* (New Haven, CT: Yale University Press: 2022).

18. W. Lance Bennett and Steven Livingston, "A Brief History of the Information Age: Information Wars and the Decline of Institutional Authority," in *The Disinformation Age: Politics, Technology, and Disruptive Communication in the United States*, ed. W. Lance Bennett and Steven Livingston (New York: Cambridge University Press, 2021), 3–40.

19. See William H. Westermeyer, "Local Tea Party Groups and the Vibrancy of the Movement," *Political and Legal Anthropology Review* 39, no. S1 (2016): 121–38; Sheetal D. Agarwal et al., "Grassroots Organizing in the Digital Age: Considering Values and Technology in Tea Party and Occupy Wall Street," *Information, Communication & Society* 17, no. 3 (2014): 326–41; W. Lance Bennett and Alexandra Segerberg, "The Logic of Connective Action," *Information, Communication & Society* 15, no. 5 (2012): 739–68; Joshua D. Atkinson and Suzanne Valerie Leon Berg, "Narrowmobilization and Tea Party Activism: A Study of Right-Leaning Alternative Media," *Communication Studies* 63, no. 5 (2012): 519–35.

20. See Nancy L. Rosenblum and Russell Muirhead, *A Lot of People Are Saying: The New Conspiracism and the Assault on Democracy* (Princeton, NJ: Princeton University Press, 2020); J. Eric Oliver and Thomas J. Wood, *Enchanted America: How Intuition and Reason Divide Our Politics* (Chicago: University of Chicago Press, 2018); Rachel M. Blum, *How the Tea Party Captured the GOP: Insurgent Factions in American Politics* (Chicago: University of Chicago Press, 2020); Stanley B. Greenberg, *R.I.P. G.O.P.: How the New America Is Dooming the Republicans* (New York: Thomas Dunne,2019); Hart, *Trump and Us*.

21. John Sides, Chris Tausanovitch, and Lynn Vavreck, *The Bitter End: The 2020 Presidential Campaign and the Challenge to American Democracy* (Princeton, NJ: Princeton University Press, 2022).

22. Manuel Castells, *Communication Power* (New York: Oxford University Press, 2011).

23. Daniel Dayan and Elihu Kath, *Media Events: The Live Broadcasting of History* (Cambridge, MA: Harvard University Press, 1994).

24. Parker and Barreto, *Change They Can't Believe In*.

25. Castells, *Communication Power*, 194.

26. White, *The Branding of Right-Wing Activism*, 14.

27. From a survey conducted June 9, 2011–June 13, 2011, for NBC News/*Wall Street Journal* by Hart and McInturff Research Company.

28. From an Axios survey conducted May 29, 2020–June 1, 2020, by Ipsos.

29. Gervais and Morris, *Reactionary Republicanism*, 171.

30. Mercieca, "Dangerous Demagogues," 275.

31. Adam Carlson and Tal Axelrod, "Former Vice President Mike Pence Speaks About Capitol Riot in Exclusive Interview with ABC News," ABC News, November 14, 2022, https://www.abc15.com/news/national/former-vice-president-mike-pence-speaks-about-capitol-riot-in-exclusive-interview-with-abc-news.

32. Thomas E. Patterson, *How America Lost Its Mind: The Assault on Reason That's Crippling Our Democracy* (Norman: University of Oklahoma Press, 2019); Alberta, *American Carnage*; Greenberg, *R.I.P. G.O.P.*

33. Sophia Moskalenko and Clark McCauley, "QAnon: Radical Opinion Versus Radical Action," *Perspectives on Terrorism* 15, no. 2 (2021): 142.

34. Rosenblum and Muirhead, *A Lot of People Are Saying*, xi.

35. Isabel Wilkerson, *Caste: The Origins of Our Discontents* (New York: Random House, 2020), 17–18.

36. Nathan Glazer and Daniel Patrick Moynihan, *Beyond the Melting Pot* (Boston: MIT Press, 1963), 315.

37. Geoffrey Kabaservice, *Rule and Run: The Downfall of Moderation and the Destruction of the Republican Party, from Eisenhower to the Tea Party* (New York: Oxford University Press, 2012), xviii.

38. Richard Hofstadter, *The Paranoid Style in American Politics* (1952; repr., New York: Vintage, 2008), 23.

39. Baker was interviewed by Fareed Zakaria, the host of CNN's program *GPS*, on April 10, 2011.

40. The text of Buchanan's August 17, 1992, speech is available at Voices of Democracy: https://voicesofdemocracy.umd.edu/buchanan-culture-war-speech-speech-text/.

41. McKay Coppins, "The Man Who Broke Politics," *The Atlantic*, November 2018, https://www.theatlantic.com/magazine/archive/2018/11/newt-gingrich-says-youre-welcome/570832/; Greenberg, *R.I.P. G.O.P.*, 3.

42. Kabaservice, *Rule and Run*, 376–77.

43. Alberta, *American Carnage*, 3.

44. Coppins, "The Man Who Broke Politics."

45. Coppins, "The Man Who Broke Politics."

46. Chris Christie, *Republican Rescue: Saving the Party from Truth Deniers, Conspiracy Terrorists, and the Dangerous Policies of Joe Biden* (New York: Threshold Editions, 2021), 175.

47. "Speech by Joseph McCarthy, Wheeling, West Virginia, February 9, 1950," George Mason University, History Matters, http://historymatters.gmu.edu/d/6456/.

48. Hofstadter, *The Paranoid Style*, 25.

49. Daniel T. Rodgers, "What We Get Wrong About a City on a Hill," *Washington Post*, November 13, 2018, https://www.washingtonpost.com/outlook/2018/11/13/what-we-get-wrong-about-city-hill/.

50. Kathryn S. Olmsted, *Real Enemies: Conspiracy Theories and American Democracy, World War I to 9/11* (New York: Oxford University Press, 2009), 178.

51. Patrick J. Buchanan, *The Death of a Superpower* (New York: Thomas Dunne, 2011), 400.

52. Jason Schwartz, "55 Years Ago—The Last Press Conference," Richard Nixon Foundation, November 14, 2017, https://www.nixonfoundation.org/2017/11/55-years-ago-last-press-conference/.

53. John Tebbel and Sarah Miles Watts, *The Press and the Presidency: From George Washington to Ronald Reagan* (New York: Oxford University Press, 1985), 501.

54. Tebbel and Watts, *The Press and the Presidency*, 506.

55. Katharine Graham, "The Watergate Watershed: A Turning Point for a Nation and a Newspaper," *Washington Post*, January 28, 1997, https://www.washingtonpost.com/wp-srv/national/longterm/watergate/stories/graham.htm.

56. Nancy Benac, "Remember Nixon? There's History Behind Trump's Press Attacks," Associated Press, February 14, 2014, https://apnews.com/article/donald-trump-media-newspapers-richard-nixon-douglas-brinkley-8b2919563if44033ad94d8b2b74048co.

57. Patterson, *How America Lost Its Mind*, 59.

58. Snyder, *On Tyranny*, 65.

59. A transcript of Trump's October 13, 2016, speech is made available by NPR: https://www.npr.org/2016/10/13/497857068/transcript-donald-trumps-speech-responding-to-assault-accusations.

60. Liz Halloran, "Culture War Brewing Within Tea Party?," NPR, November 22, 2010, https://www.npr.org/2010/11/22/131512631/culture-war-brewing-within-tea-party.

61. Robert O. Paxton, *The Anatomy of Fascism* (New York: Vintage Books, 2004), 219–20.

62. Brigitte L. Nacos, *Terrorism and the Media* (New York: Columbia University Press, 1994).

63. Gianpietro Mazzoleni and Winfried Schulz, "Mediatization of Politics: A Challenge for Democracy?," *Political Communication* 16, no. 3 (1999): 247–61; Peter van Aelst et al., "Political Communication in a High-Choice Media Environment: A Challenge for Democracy?," *Annals of the International Communication Association* 41, no. 1 (2017): 3–27; Markus Prior, "Conditions for Political Accountability in a High-Choice Media Environment," in *The Oxford Handbook of Political Communication*, ed. Kate Kenski and Kathleen Hall Jamieson (New York: Oxford University Press, 2017): 897–910.

64. The American Society of News Editors, founded in 1922, ceased to exist in 2019. Its successor organization, News Leaders Association, does not publicize the "Statement of Principles" on its website.

65. Snyder, *On Tyranny*, 56.

66. See Thomas E. Patterson, "Pre-Primary News Coverage of the 2016 Presidential Race: Trump's Rise, Sander's Emergence, Clinton's Struggle" (Harvard Kennedy School, Shorenstein Center on Media, Politics, and Public Policy, 2016); and Thomas E. Patterson, "News Coverage of the 2016 Presidential Primaries: Horse Race Reporting Has Consequences" (Harvard Kennedy School, Shorenstein Center on Media, Politics, and Public Policy, 2016).

67. Sides, Tausanovitch, and Lynn Vavreck, *The Bitter End*, 8.

68. From May 4, 2009, when he posted his first tweet, through January 8, 2021, when Twitter suspended his account, Donald Trump posted a total of 56,571 tweets according to the @realdonaldtrump Twitter archive. We identified 14,807 tweets of his total tweet production as "attack tweets" and identified for those tweets the targets of his rhetorical attacks. For all our content coding, unless otherwise noted, the intercoder agreement was 90 percent or better.

69. Jeffrey M. Berry and Sarah Sobieraj, "Understanding the Rise of Talk Radio," *Political Science and Politics* 44, no. 4 (2011): 764.

70. Berry and Sobieraj, "Understanding the Rise of Talk Radio"; Anne Nelson, *Shadow Network: Media, Money, and the Secret Hub of the Radical Right* (New York: Bloomsbury, 2019).

71. Berry and Sobieraj, "Understanding the Rise of Talk Radio," 764.

72. Source of radio ownership information at http://www.insideradio.com/resources/who _owns_what/, accessed October 22, 2021.

73. Nelson, *Shadow Network*, 38, 56.

74. Nelson, *Shadow Network*, 56.

75. Sidney G. Tarrow, *Power in Movement: Social Movements and Contentious Politics*. (New York: Cambridge University Press, 2011), 98.

76. Blum, *How the Tea Party Captured the GOP*; Parker and Barreto, *Change They Can't Believe In*.

77. Blum, *How the Tea Party Captured the GOP*, 25.

78. Michael Kazin, *The Populist Persuasion* (Ithaca, NY: Cornell University Press, 1995), 1.

79. Claes H. de Vreese et al., "Populism as an Expression of Political Communication Content and Style: A New Perspective," *International Journal of Press/Politics* 23, no. 4 (2018): 423–38.

80. Tyler Branson, "Steeped in Rhetoric: Digital Populism and the Tea Party Movement" (master's thesis, American Studies and the Graduate Faculty, University of Kansas, 2011), 93–94.

81. Castells, *Communication Power*, 55.

82. The term *newsroom populism* was coined by Gianpietro Mazzoleni, Julianne Steward, and Bruce Horsfield, *The Media and Neo-Populism* (Westport, CT: Praeger, 2003).

83. Jesper Stroembaeck, "Four Phases of Mediatization: An Analysis of the Mediatization of Politics," *International Journal of Press/Politics* 13, no. 3 (2008): 240. For mediatization of politics, see also Angelos Kissas, "Three Theses on the Mediatization of Politics: Evolutionist, Intended, or Imagined Transformation," *Communication Review* 22, no. 3 (2019): 222–42.

84. Paxton, *The Anatomy of Fascism*, 220.

2. THE TEA PARTY MOVEMENT, THE MASS MEDIA, AND CONTENTIOUS POLITICS

1. Santelli's rant was widely reported in the news media writ large.

2. The Rush Limbaugh Show, February 19, 2009, accessed March 26, 2011, http://www .rushlimbaugh.com/home/daily/site_021909/content/01125106.guest.html.

3. Glenn Beck radio show, February 20, 2009, accessed March 26, 2011, http://www .glennbeck.com/content/articles/article/198/21756/.

4. Geoffrey Kabaservice, *Rule and Run: The Downfall of Moderation and the Destruction of the Republican Party, from Eisenhower to the Tea Party* (New York: Oxford University Press, 2012), 387.

5. Paul Street and Anthony DiMaggio, *Crashing the Tea Party: Mass Media and the Campaign to Remake American Politics* (Boulder, CO: Paradigm, 2011), 33.

6. Michael Levenson, "Ron Paul Backers Stage Boston Tea Party, Raise Millions," *Boston Globe*, December 17, 2007.

7. In December 2011, Paul's campaign manager, John Tate, told supporters, "Four years ago, the Tea Party Money Bomb launched the modern Tea Party movement. This weekend's Tea Party Money Bomb can launch Ron Paul's presidency." See "Ron Paul's 'Tea Party' Money Bomb Approaches $4 Million Goal," Thestatecolumn.com, December 17, 2011, http://www.thestatecolumn.com/texas/ron-pauls-tea-party-money-bomb-approaches -4-million-goal/.

8. Khadijah Costley White, *The Branding of Right-Wing Activism: The News Media & the Tea Party* (New York: Oxford University Press, 2018), 2.

9. John Avlon, *Wingnuts: How the Lunatic Fringe Is Hijacking America* (New York: Beast, 2010), 26.

10. Quotes are from the transcript of the Fox News show *Hannity* on April 15, 2009, accessed in the Factiva data base (Document SHAN000020090416e54f00001).

11. MSNBC.com, *The Ed Show with Ed Schultz*," April 15, 2009.

12. Scott Rasmussen and Douglas Schoen, *Mad as Hell: How the Tea Party Movement Is Fundamentally Remaking Our Two-Party System* (New York: Broadside, 2010); Street and DiMaggio, *Crashing the Tea Party*; Kate Zernike, *Boiling Mad: Behind the Lines in Tea Party America* (New York: St. Martin's, 2010).

13. Avlon, *Wingnuts*; Rasmussen and Schoen, *Mad as Hell*.

14. Mark Ames and Yasha Levine, "Exposing the Rightwing PR Machine: Is CNBC's Rick Santelli Sucking Koch?," *The Exiled*, February, 27, 2009, https://exiledonline.com /exposing-the-familiar-rightwing-pr-machine-is-cnbcs-rick-santelli-sucking-koch/.

15. Ames and Levine, "Exposing the Rightwing PR Machine."

16. For the full list, see http://www.freedomworks.org/blog/bstein80/how-to-organize-your -own-%E2%80%9Ctea-party%E2%80%9D-protest, accessed June 6, 2012.

17. For Steinhauser's guidance and other information about the February 27, 2009, Tea Party protests, see http://www.freedomworks.org/blog/bstein80/atlanta-tea-party-protest, accessed June 8, 2012.

18. John H. Parmelee and Shannon L. Bichard, *Politics and the Twitter Revolution: How Tweets Influence the Relationship Between Leaders and the Public* (Lanham, MD: Lexington: 2012), 12.

19. The blogger David Sarno was quoted by Parmelee and Bichard, *Politics and the Twitter Revolution*, 12.

20. The full message is available at http://www.freedomworks.org/petition/iamwithrick/index .html, accessed June 10, 2012.

21. Street and DiMaggio, *Crashing the Tea Party*.

22. Ryan Powers cited Pelosi on the ThinkProgress blog, accessed January 1, 2012, http:// thinkprogress.org/politics/2009/04/15/37578/pelosi-astroturf/?mobile=nc.

23. Francis Fukuyama, "The Future of History," *Foreign Affairs* 91, no. 1 (2012): 59.

24. Theda Skocpol and Vanessa Williamson, *The Tea Party and the Remaking of Republican Conservatism* (New York: Oxford University Press, 2012), 10.

25. Sidney Tarrow, *Power in Movement: Social Movements and Contentious Politics* (New York: Cambridge University Press, 2011), 6, emphasis added.

26. Charles Tilly and Lesley J. Wood, *Social Movements, 1768–2008* (Boulder, CO: Paradigm: 2009), 7.

27. Manuel Castells, *Communication Power* (New York: Oxford University Press, 2011), 301.

28. Armey made these remarks during an appearance in the PBS *News Hour* on September 9, 2010, accessed January 7, 2012, http://www.pbs.org/newshour/bb/politics/july-dec10/armey _09-09.html.

29. Elizabeth Price Foley, *The Tea Party: Three Principles* (New York: Cambridge University Press, 2012), xiii.

30. Gianpietro Mazzoleni, Julianne Steward, and Bruce Horsfield, *The Media and Neo-Populism* (Westport, CT: Praeger, 2003), 4–5.

31. Michael Kazin made those remarks during his appearance on National Public Radio's *Weekend All Things Considered*, February 6, 2010, https://www.npr.org/templates/story /story.php?storyId=123447238.

32. Sophia Rosenfeld, *Common Sense: A Political History* (Cambridge, MA: Harvard University Press, 2011), 254.

33. Michael Kazin, *The Populist Persuasion* (Ithaca, NY: Cornell University Press, 1995), 1.

34. Michael J. Lee, "The Populist Chameleon: The People's Party, Huey Long, George Wallace, and the Populist Argumentative Frame," *Quarterly Journal of Speech* 92, no. 4 (2006): 357–62.

35. Ben Stanley, "The Thin Ideology of Populism," *Journal of Political Ideologies* 13, no. 1 (2008): 106.

36. Richard Hofstadter, *The Paranoid Style in American Politics and Other Essays* (New York: Alfred A. Knopf, 1965), 23.

37. Neil King Jr., "Rick Perry, in First Negative Ad, Calls Obama a Socialist," *Wall Street Journal*, November 16, 2011, http://blogs.wsj.com/washwire/2011/11/16/rick-perry-in-first -negative-ad-calls-obama-a-socialist/.

38. *Huffington Post*, "Newt Gingrich's 2012 Campaign," December 7, 2011, http://www .huffingtonpost.com/2011/12/07/newt-gingrich-2012-campaign 1133454.html.

39. Sara Sorcher, "Michele Bachmann Gives Closing Speech, Calls Obama a Socialist," *National Journal*, updated January 3, 2012, https://news.yahoo.com/michele-bachmann -gives-closing-speech-calls-obama-socialist-195717797.html?fr=sycsrp_catchall.

40. Christopher S. Parker and Matt Barreto, *Change They Can't Believe In: The Tea Party and Reactionary Politics in America* (Princeton, NJ: Princeton University Press, 2013), 3.

41. Santorum's remarks were widely reported by the news media. See, for example, Daniel Politi, "Santorum Stands by Calling Obama a 'Snob,'" *Slate*, February 26, 2012, http:// slatest.slate.com/posts/2012/02/26/santorum_calls_obama_a_snob_and_says_jfk_speech _made_him_want_to_throw_up.html, and William Selway and Timothy R. Homan, "Santorum 'Snob' Attack on College Collides with Wage Gains," Bloomberg, February 29, 2012, http://www.bloomberg.com/news/2012-02-29/santorum-snob-attack-on-obama -s-college-pitch-collides-with-wage-gains.html.

42. Aldemaro Romero Jr., "Anti-Intellectualism Cast Shadow Over Higher Ed.," theintelligencer.com, November 21, 2016, https://academicworks.cuny.edu/cgi/viewcontent .cgi?article=1086&context=bb_pubs.

43. The quotes are from Adolf Hitler, "A Reckoning," chap. IV, pt. One in *Mein Kampf*, online English translation, accessed June 27, 2023, http://www.hitler.org/writings/Mein_Kampf /mkv1ch06.html.

44. The citation is from Goebbels's speech, "Knowledge and Propaganda." A transcript is available at https://research.calvin.edu/german-propaganda-archive/goeb54.htm, accessed June 27, 2023.

45. Leonie Bershidsky, "Trump's Anti-Intelligencia Revolution," Bloomberg Opinion, November 14, 2016, https://www.bloomberg.com/opinion/articles/2016-11-14/trump-s-anti -intelligentsia-revolution.

46. Skocpol and Williamson, *The Tea Party*, 37.

47. David E. Campbell and Robert D. Putnam, "God and Caesar in America: Why Mixing Religion and Politics Is Bad for Both," *Foreign Affairs* 91, no. 2 (March/April 2012): 38.

48. For DeMint's speech, see "'The Great American Awakening': Senator DeMint's Shares His Vision," MSNBC, July 11, 2011, http://today.msnbc.msn.com/id/43709768/ns/today -books/t/great-american-awakening-senator-demint-shares-his-vision/#.Tw9Hlvn2lcA.

49. Drew Westen, *The Political Brain: The Role of Emotion in Deciding the Fate of the Nation* (New York: Public Affairs, 2008), 388–89.

50. Palin's speech of February 6, 2010, accessed June 27, 2023, http://www.americanrhetoric. com/speeches/sarahpalin2010teapartykeynote.htm.

51. Palin's speech.

52. Jane Mayer, *Dark Money* (New York: Doubleday, 2016), 182, 183.

53. Mayer, *Dark Money*, 183.

54. Skocpol and Williamson, *The Tea Party*, 13.

55. Lloyd Marcus, "Obama Going Rogue," Tea Party Express, accessed June 27, 2023, http://www.teapartyexpress.org/4818/obama-going-rogue.

56. Lloyd Marcus, "America's Divine Intervention," Tea Party Express, accessed June 27, 2023, http://www.teapartyexpress.org/5051/america-and-divine-intervention.

57. Kabaservice, *Rule and Run*; Skocpol and Williamson, *The Tea Party*.

58. Stephanie Mencimer, "How a Feud Between Two Tea Party Leaders Helped Lay the Groundwork for the Capitol Insurrection," *Mother Jones*, April 19, 2021, https://www .motherjones.com/politics/2021/04/how-a-feud-between-2-tea-party-leaders-helped-lay -the-groundwork-for-the-capitol-insurrection/. Mark Meckler was the third cofounder; he resigned from the group in 2012. Because of a clash between Martin and Kremer, the latter left Tea Party Patriots and joined Tea Party Express and took a leading role.

59. See CNN video excerpt of the January 6, 2021, insurrection, in Casey Tolan, "The Operative," accessed June 27, 2023, https://edition.cnn.com/interactive/2021/06/us/capitol -riot-paths-to-insurrection/amy-kremer.html.

60. Tea Party Patriots, "National News," accessed July 4, 2012, http://www.teapartypatriots .org/groups/national-news/.

61. Amy Gardner, "Gauging the Scope of the Tea Party Movement in America," *Washington Post*, October 24, 2010, https://www.washingtonpost.com/wp-dyn/content/article/2010/10/23/AR2010102304000.html.

62. Devin Burghart and Leonard Zeskind, *Tea Party Nationalism: A Critical Examination of the Tea Party Movement and the Size, Scope, and Focus of Its National Factions* (special report, Institute for Research and Education on Human Rights, Kansas City, MO, Fall 2010), 41, https://www.irehr.org/wp-content/uploads/2012/09/images_pdf_TeaPartyNationalism.pdf; Skocpol and Williamson, *The Tea Party*, 108.

63. Mencimer, "How a Feud."

64. Jenny Beth Martin, "The Tea Party Movement Is Alive and Well—And We Saw Trump Coming." *Politico*, November 19, 2016, http://www.politico.com/magazine/story/2016/11/the-tea-party-movement-is-alive-and-well-and-we-saw-trump-coming-214469.

65. Mencimer, "How a Feud."

66. Eventually, Martin's TPP group worked with evangelical groups in joint political actions. According to Stephanie Mencimer, "How a Feud," TPP cooperated, for example, with Concerned Women for America and Heritage Action and "the joint Council for National Policy, a secretive network of powerful religious conservatives."

67. See Lawrence R. Jacobs and Robert Y. Shapiro, *Politicians Don't Pander: Political Manipulation and the Loss of Democratic Responsiveness* (Chicago: University of Chicago Press, 2000).

68. Tea Party Nation, "Should the Republican Party Survive?," accessed June 20, 2012, http://www.teapartynation.com/forum/topics/should-the-republican-party-survive.

69. Tea Party Nation, "Should the Republican Party Survive?"

70. Tea Party Nation, "Obama's Rapid Decline," accessed June 21, 2012, http://www.teapartynation.com/profiles/blogs/obama-s-rapid-decline.

71. Tea Party Nation, "Trump You Are Hired," accessed July 5, 2016, http://www.teapartynation.com/profiles/blogs/trump-you-re-hired.

72. "The Tea Party's Military Wing" was the slogan in the tease for Justine Sharrock, "Oath Keepers and the Age of Treason," *Mother Jones*, March/April 2010, https://www.motherjones.com/politics/2010/02/oath-keepers/.

73. The Oath Keepers, "Testimonials," accessed July 8, 2012, http://oathkeepers.org/oath/category/oathkeeper-testimonials/.

74. The Oath Keepers, "Testimonials." The original spelling and grammar left intact in this quote and all citations from these sorts of posts.

75. The Oath Keepers, "Testimonials."

76. The Oath Keepers, "Testimonials."

77. Alias's post and the following responses were published on the Oath Keepers site as "Articles," accessed July 7, 2012, http://oathkeepers.org/oath/category/oathkeeper-articles/.

78. See https://www.youtube.com/watch?v=Zztaj2AFiy8, accessed July, 17, 2012.

79. Stewart Rhodes's reprint of the 2008 article was published on the Oath Keepers' website, http://oath-keepers.blogspot.com/2009/05/keeping-your-oath-not-just-following.html, accessed November 9, 2016.

80. The Oath Keepers, "Call to Action," accessed November 3, 2016, https://oathkeepers
    .org/2016/10/oath-keepers-call-action-spot-document-report-vote-fraud-intimidation
    -election-day-2016/.

81. Isaac Arnsdorf, "Oath Keepers in the State House: How a Militia Movement Took Root
    in the Republican Mainstream," *ProPublica*, October 20, 2021, https://www.propublica
    .org/article/oath-keepers-in-the-state-house-how-a-militia-movement-took-root-in
    -the-republican-mainstream.

82. Matt A. Barreto et al., "The Tea Party in the Age of Obama: Mainstream Conservatism or
    Out-Group Anxiety?," *Political Power and Social Theory* 22 (2011): 21.

83. Deana A. Rohlinger and Leslie Bunnage, "Did the Tea Party Movement Fuel the Trump-
    Train? The Role of Social Media in Activist Persistence and Political Change in the 21st
    Century," *Social Media + Society* (April–June 2017): 1.

84. The Tea Party Nation, "Forum," accessed June 20, 2012, http://www.teapartynation.com
    /forum/topics/our-goal-is-to-make-100-000-calls-from-our-mobile-call-center-to.

85. Tea Party Patriots, "National News."

86. Tea Party Nation, "Profiles," accessed June 11, 2012, http://www.teapartynation.com/profiles
    /blogs/walkin-tall-walker-inspires-an-army.

87. Tea Party Nation, "Profiles."

88. Tea Party Express, accessed June 27, 2023, https://www.facebook.com/ourcountrypac.

89. Tea Party Patriots, "Tonight We Saved Wisconsin, Tomorrow We Continue Saving the
    Country," accessed June 12, 2012, http://www.teapartypatriots.org/news/tonight-we-saved
    -wisconsin-tomorrow-we-continue-saving-the-country/.

90. Akil N. Awan, Andrew Hoskins, and Ben O'Loughlin, *Radicalization and Media: The
    Connectivity and Terrorism in the New Media Ecology* (London: Routledge, 2011), 6.

91. Zernike, *Boiling Mad*; Street and DiMaggio, *Crashing the Tea Party*.

92. Skocpol and Williamson, *The Tea Party*, chap. 4.

93. Costley White, *The Branding*, 177.

94. Barack Obama, "A President Looks Back on His Toughest Fight," *New Yorker*,
    October 26, 2020, https://www.newyorker.com/magazine/2020/11/02/barack-obama-new
    -book-excerpt-promised-land-obamacare.

95. Todd Gitlin, *The Whole World Is Watching: Mass Media in the Making and Unmaking of the
    New Left* (Berkeley: University of California Press, 1980); Benjamin I. Page and Robert Y.
    Shapiro, *The Rational Public: Fifty Years of Trends in Americans' Policy Preferences* (Chicago:
    University of Chicago Press, 1992), 350–54.

96. Tilly and Wood, *Social Movements*.

97. We researched the news archive Lexis Nexis for segments about or mentioning
    "Tea Party."

98. Skocpol and Williamson, *The Tea Party*, 138.

99. Stanley Greenberg, *RIP GOP: How the New America Is Dooming the Republicans* (New York:
    Thomas Dunne, 2019), 77.

100. CBS, *The Early Show*, November 3, 2010. The transcript is available at the Factiva media
    archive, accessed July 8, 2023.

101. The full text of the press release is at "CNN, Tea Party Express to Host First-Ever Tea Party Debate, Sept. 12," September 8, 2011, https://cnnpressroom.blogs.cnn.com/2011/09/08/cnn-tea-party-express-to-host-first-ever-tea-party-debate-sept-12/.

102. Shannon Travis, "CNN and Tea Party Express to Host First-of-Its-Kind Tea Party Presidential Primary Debate," CNN, December 17, 2010, https://politicalticker.blogs.cnn.com/2010/12/17/cnn-and-tea-party-express-to-host-first-of-its-kind-tea-party-presidential-primary-debate/.

103. For the first research period (August 2009) and the second research period (October 26, 2010, through November 9, 2010, which included seven days before, on, and seven days after Election Day, November 2, 2010), we used the search word "Tea Party" to access the relevant news items in the Lexis Nexis News Archive. We coded and analyzed all stories about and mentioning the Tea Party aired or published by CBS News, the *New York Times*, and National Public Radio. Because of the large number of Tea Party segments aired by CNN, we coded and analyzed the cable network's Tea Party coverage every fifth day. The focus of the Tea Party protests in August was President Obama's health care reform plan. To assess news coverage of this particular policy, we also examined news items about this issue. The intercoder reliability was just under 90 percent agreement.

104. See Thomas E. Patterson, *Out of Order* (New York: Vintage, 1994); Joseph N. Cappella and Kathleen Hall Jamieson, *Spiral of Cynicism: The Press and the Public Good* (New York: Oxford University Press, 1997); and Jacobs and Shapiro, *Politicians Don't Pander*.

105. See Brigitte L. Nacos, Yaeli Bloch-Elkon, and Robert Y. Shapiro, *Selling Fear: Couterterrorism, the Media, and Public Opinion* (Chicago: University of Chicago Press, 2011), 41.

106. Jules Boykoff and Eulalie Laschever, "The Tea Party Movement, Framing, and the US Media," *Social Movement Studies* 10, no. 4 (2011): 341.

107. W. Lance Bennett, "Press-Government Relationship in Changing Media Landscape," in *The Oxford Handbook of Political Communication*, ed. Kate Kensi and Kathleen Jamieson (New York: Oxford University Press, 2017).

108. Democratic Congressional Campaign Committee, "The Tea Party Is Over," accessed December 6, 2012, http://dccc.org/blog/entry/the_tea_party_is_over/.

109. Chris Cillizza, "Is the Tea Party Dead? Or Just Resting?," *Washington Post*, December 4, 2012, https://www.washingtonpost.com/news/the-fix/wp/2012/12/04/whither-the-tea-party/.

110. Tea Party Nation, "Forum," accessed December 12, 2012, http://www.teapartynation.com/forum/topics/what-should-happen-what-will-happen-what-must-happen.

111. Greenberg, *RIP GOP*; Democracy Corps, Carville|Greenberg, Greenberg Research, "Trump Mobilizes His Tea Party Observant Base, But at High Cost," December 2019, https://democracycorps.com/wp-content/uploads/2019/12/Dcorps_December-National-GOP-Poll_Slide-Deck_121819.pdf

112. James Rainey, "Republicans Mourn 'the Day America Died' and Plot Path Ahead," *Los Angeles Times*, November 4, 2012, https://www.latimes.com/politics/la-xpm-2012-nov-07-la-pn-republican-reaction-obama-reelection-20121107-story.html.

113. William Gamson and Gadi Wolfsfeld, "Movements and Media as Interacting Systems," *Annals of the Academy of Political and Social Science* 528 (July 1993): 117.

3. ONLINE AND OFFLINE MEDIA AS SUPER-SPREADERS OF ANTI-OBAMA CONSPIRACY THEORIES

1. YouTube, "Mike Castle Confronts Right-Wing Hatred," accessed June 29, 2023, https://www.youtube.com/watch?v=lbQKry5Z_ok.

2. George Zornick, "Prominent O'Donnell Backer Has Extremist Ties, Believes Obama Isn't an American," Thinkprogress, October 21, 2010, accessed May 21, 2012, http://thinkprogress.org/politics/2010/10/21/125795/odonnell-extremist-birther/.

3. Geoffrey Kabaservice, *Rule and Run: The Downfall of Moderation and the Destruction of the Republican Party, from Eisenhower to the Tea Party* (New York: Oxford University Press, 2012), 390.

4. J. Gordon Hylton, "What the Birthers Have Taught US About Obama and the Constitution," Marquette University Law School Faculty Blog, October 13, 2009, https://law.marquette.edu/facultyblog/2009/10/what-the-birthers-have-taught-us-about-barack-obama-and-the-constitution/.

5. David Weigel, "'Birther' Movement Dogs Republicans," *Washington Independent*, July 30, 2020, http://washingtonindependent.com/51489/birther-movement-picks-up-steam. The original article was published July 30, 2009.

6. Brian L. Keeley, "Of Conspiracy Theory," *Journal of Philosophy* 96, no. 3 (1999): 120.

7. Kathryn S. Olmsted, *Real Enemies: Conspiracy Theories and American Democracy, World War I to 9/11* (New York: Oxford University Press, 2009), 11.

8. Cass R. Sunstein and Adrian Vermeule, "Conspiracy Theories" (University of Chicago Public Law & Legal Theory Working Paper no. 199, 2008).

9. Olmsted, *Real Enemies*, 3.

10. Nolan McCarty, Keith T. Poole, and Howard Rosenthal, *Polarized America: The Dance of Ideology and Unequal Riches* (Cambridge, MA: MIT Press, 2006). For graphs on polarization by the same authors, see https://legacy.voteview.com/political_polarization_2014.htm and https://legacy.voteview.com/Polarized_America.htm, accessed June 29, 2023.

11. Robert Y. Shapiro and Yaeli Bloch-Elkon, "Do the Facts Speak for Themselves? Partisan Disagreement as a Challenge to Democratic Competence," *Critical Review* 20, nos. 1–3 (2008); Brendan Nyhan and Jason Reifler, "When Corrections Fail: The Persistence of Political Misperceptions," Political Behavior 32, no. 2 (2010).

12. Joseph E. Uscinski and Joseph M. Parent, *American Conspiracy Theories* (New York: Oxford University Press, 2014), 18–19.

13. Sunstein and Vermeule, "Conspiracy Theories," 13.

14. From the flyer "Perfect for Tea Parties," which was posted for years at the Birthers movement's website, http://birthers.org/, accessed February 3, 2012.

15. Theda Skocpol and Vanessa Williamson, *The Tea Party and the Remaking of Republican Conservatism* (New York: Oxford University Press, 2012), 77.

16. Christopher S. Parker and Matt Barreto, *Change They Can't Believe In: The Tea Party and Reactionary Politics in America* (Princeton, NJ: Princeton University Press, 2013), 253.

17. Charles Johnson, "Jonathan Kay: The Tea Party Movement Is Full of Conspiracy Theories," Littlegreenfootballs.com, February 10, 2010, accessed June 29, 2023, http://littlegreenfootballs.com/article/35758_Jonathan_Kay-_The_Tea_Party_Mo.

18. Jim Rutenberg, "The Man Behind the Whispers About Obama," *New York Times*, October 12, 2008, https://www.nytimes.com/2008/10/13/us/politics/13martin.html.

19. Matthew Mosk, "An Attack That Came out of the Ether," *Washington Post*, June 28, 2008, https://www.washingtonpost.com/wp-dyn/content/article/2008/06/27/AR2008062703781.html?sid=ST2008062703939&pos=.

20. Amy Hollyfield, "Obama's Birth Certificate: Final Chapter," *Tampa Bay Times*, June 27, 2008, updated March 2011, http://www.politifact.com/truth-o-meter/article/2008/jun/27/obamas-birth-certificate-part-ii/.

21. The incident was captured on video and posted on YouTube, AP, McCain Counters "Obama 'Arab' Question," accessed June 29, 2023, https://www.youtube.com/watch?v=jrnRU30cIH4.

22. Powell was a guest at NBC's *Meet the Press* on October 19, 2008, https://www.nbcnews.com/id/wbna27266223.

23. David Maraniss, "What Drives the Obama Doubters and Haters?," Opinion, *Washington Post*, July 27, 2012, https://www.washingtonpost.com/opinions/what-drives-the-obama-doubters-and-haters/2012/07/27/gJQAIbImDX_story.html?itid=sr_1.

24. Todd K. Hartman and Adam J. Newmark, "Motivated Reasoning, Political Sophistication, and Associations Between President Obama and Islam Hartman," *Political Science and Politics* 45, no. 3 (2012): 449.

25. Hartman and Newmark, "Motivated Reasoning," 451–52.

26. Hartman and Newmark, "Motivated Reasoning," 454.

27. Carl Stempel, Thomas Hargrove, and Guido H. Stempel III, "Media Use, Social Structure, and Belief in 9/11 Conspiracy Theories," *J&MC Quarterly* 84, no. 2 (2007): 366, 362.

28. Adam Berinsky, "Rumors, Truths, and Reality: A Study of Political Misinformation," 2011, early draft, 3, 4.

29. See http://www.teapartynation.com/forum/topics/the-birther-manifesto?id=3355873%3ATopic%3A2156901&page=3#comments, accessed August 30, 2012.

30. WorldNetDaily, "Farah's $10,000 Birth Certificate Challenge," June 22, 2009, http://www.wnd.com/2009/06/101892/.

31. WorldNetDaily, http://www.wnd.com/wnd_petition/petition-urging-congress-to-investigate-obamas-eligibility/, accessed July 12, 2012.

32. The home page displayed the counter of President Obama's remaining time in office, links to podcasts, and a mission statement; see http://giveusliberty1776-thepowerof1oproject.blogspot.com/, accessed June 12 and July 23, 2012.

33. The ad content was available on WorldNetDaily's website, http://www.wnd.com/2012/07/ad-campaign-blasts-eligibility-question-at-voters/print/, accessed July 30, 2012.

34. See http://www.obamaantichrist.org/obama-antichrist-evidence/, accessed July 26, 2012.

35. See http://www.obamaantichrist.org/does-obama-fufill-muslim-prophecy/, accessed July 28, 2012.

36. See http://o.bamapost.com/Video_proof_Obama_is_Muslim.html, accessed July 28, 2012.

37. Barack Obama, "A President Looks Back on His Toughest Fight," *New Yorker*, October 26, 2020, https://www.newyorker.com/magazine/2020/11/02/barack-obama-new-book-excerpt-promised-land-obamacare.

38. See http://www.teaparty.org, accessed June 29, 2023.

39. See http://www.teaparty.org/AFPInfo.html, accessed August 30, 2012.

40. The post and all comments were accessed August 30, 2012, http://teapartyorg.ning.com/forum/topics/obama-campaign-responds-to-breitbart-kenya-booklet-story?commentId=4301673%3AComment%3A733548.

41. The post and comments were accessed on August 30, 2012, http://teapartyorg.ning.com/forum/topics/investigators-now-in-hunt-for-forger?id=4301673%3ATopic%3A590209&page=5#comments.

42. Post and comments were accessed August 30, 2012, http://teapartyorg.ning.com/forum/topics/obama-administration-paves-the-way-for-sharia-law?id=4301673%3ATopic%3A871520&page=2.

43. Tea Party Nation, "Obama's Campaign Against Women," accessed September 17, 2012, http://www.teapartynation.com/profiles/blogs/obama-s-campaign-against-women.

44. Tea Party Nation, "Islam: Enemy of Freedom," accessed August 30, 2012, http://www.teapartynation.com/group/islam-enemy-of-freedom/forum/topics/back-to-islam-enemy-of-freedom.

45. Tea Party Patriots, "Recruit for the Republic . . .", accessed July 30, 2012, http://www.teapartypatriots.org/2012/07/recruit-for-the-republic-reach-out-to-your-friends-today/#comments.

46. See http://www.teapartypatriots.org/2011/11/bah-rack-humbug-will-the-grinch-tax-christmas/, accessed July 15, 2012.

47. See Lloyd Marcus, "Obama Versus Jesus: Black Christians Must Decide," accessed June 29, 2023, http://www.teapartyexpress.org/5264/obama-versus-jesus-black-christians-must-decide.

48. See http://www.teapartynation.com/forum/topics/the-birther-manifesto, accessed August 30, 2012.

49. John H. Parmelee and Shannon L. Bichard, 2012. *Politics and the Twitter Revolution: How Tweets Influence the Relationship Between Leaders and the Public* (Lanham, MD: Lexington, 2012), 72.

50. Ezra Klein, "Obama Explains How America Went from 'Yes, We Can' to 'MAGA.'" *Ezra Klein Show* (podcast), *New York Times*, June 1, 2021, https://www.nytimes.com/2021/06/01/opinion/ezra-klein-podcast-barack-obama.html?action=click&module=Opinion&pgtype=Homepage.

51. Tim Alberta, *American Carnage: On the Front of the Republican Civil War and the Rise of President Trump* (New York: Harper, 2019), 98.

52. Neil Postman, *Amusing Ourselves to Death: Public Discourse in the Age of Show Business* (New York: Penguin, 1985), 107–8.

53. Andrew Sullivan, "Democracies End When They Are Too Democratic. And Right Now, America Is a Breeding Ground for Tyranny," *New York* magazine, May 1, 2016, https://nymag.com/intelligencer/2016/04/america-tyranny-donald-trump.html.

54. Simon Kuper, "The Rise of the Political Fan," *Financial Times*, July 22, 2017, 5.

55. There was never any proof that Trump had dispatched investigators to Hawaii; it was just another fake statement that fellow birthers believed.

56. Trump made these remarks in an interview with Meredith Vieira on NBC's *Today Show* on April 14, 2011.

57. Glynnis MacNicol, "Trump: Maybe Obama's Missing Birth Certificate Says He's a Muslim," *Business Insider*, March 30, 2011, https://www.businessinsider.com/trump-birther-obama-muslim-video-2011-3.

58. Trump appeared on CNN's *State of the Union* program on April 10, 2011.

59. Jim Rutenberg, "Trump Bows Out, But Spotlight Barely Dims," *New York Times*, May 16, 2011, https://www.nytimes.com/2011/05/17/us/17trump.html?_r=3&hp=&pagewanted=all.

60. W. Lance Bennett, "Press-Government Relationship in Changing Media Landscape," in *The Oxford Handbook of Political Communication*, ed. Kate Kensi and Kathleen Jamieson (New York: Oxford University Press, 2017).

61. Brian Stelter, *HOAX: Donald Trump, Fox News, and the Dangerous Distortion of Truth* (New York: One Signal, 2020), 39.

62. Alberta, *American Carnage*, 190.

63. Stelter, *HOAX*, 45.

64. Thomas C. Leonard, *The Power of the Press: The Birth of American Political Reporting* (New York: Oxford University Press, 1986), 58.

65. Candace A. Czernicki, "The Catholic Press Response to Nativism in the 1850s AND 1920s" (master's thesis, Marquette University, 1990), 22.

66. Samuel F. B. Morse, *Foreign Conspiracy Against the Liberties of the United States* (New York: Chapin & Co., 1841), 18–19. The book is available online, https://www.google.com/books/edition/Foreign_Conspiracy_Against_the_Liberties/cbcTAAAAYAAJ?hl=en&gbpv=1&dq=entitled+Foreign+Conspiracy+against+the+Liberties+of+the+United+States&pg=PA29&printsec=frontcover.

67. Morse, *Foreign Conspiracy*, 26, 100.

68. Rodger Steinmatter, "The Nativist Press: Demonizing the American Immigrant," *Journalism and Mass Communication Quarterly* 76, no. 4 (1999): 675.

69. Steinmatter, *The Nativist Press*, 677.

70. "Degrading Warfare of A.P.A.," *New York Times*, June 1, 1894. The article was accessed in the ProQuest archive of historical newspapers.

71. Berinski, "Rumors, Truths, and Reality" Stempel, Hargrove, and Stempel, "Media Use."

72. Brian Weeks and Brian Southwell, "The Symbiosis of News Coverage and Aggregate Online Search Behavior: Obama, Rumors, and Presidential Politics" *Mass Communication and Society* 13 (2010): 357.

73. Levi Boxell, Matthew Gentzkow, and Jesse M. Shapiro, "Is Media Driving Americans Apart?," Opinion, December 6, 2017, *New York Times*, https://www.nytimes.com/2017/12/06 /opinion/is-media-driving-americans-apart.html. See also Levi Boxell, Mathew Gentzkow, and James M. Shapiro, "Greater Internet Use Is Not Associated with Faster Growth in Political Polarization Among US Demographic Groups," *Proceedings of the National Academy of Sciences* 114, no. 40 (2017): 10612–17, https://doi.org/10.1073/pnas.1706588114.

74. Stelter, *HOAX*, 39, 40.

75. Our two research assistants' intercoder agreement was just under 90 percent.

76. Bennett, "Press-Government Relationship."

77. Excerpt from an exchange on MSNBC's *Morning Joe*, February 21, 2012.

78. Shushanna Walshe, "Santorum Says It's Not His Job to Correct a Woman on Obama's Religion," ABC News, January 23, 2012, https://abcnews.go.com/blogs/politics/2012/01 /santorum-says-its-not-his-job-to-correct-a-woman-on-obamas-religion.

79. Andre Tartar, "Santorum Says Obama's Not a Real Christian, Then Grudgingly Admits He Is," *New York* Intelligencer, February 19, 2012, https://nymag.com/intelligencer/2012/02 /santorum-implies-hes-the-only-real-christian.html.

80. Uscinski and Parent, *American Conspiracy Theories*.

81. Hartman and Newmark, *Motivated Reasoning*, 449.

82. Hartman and Newmark, *Motivated Reasoning*, 449.

83. Amy Mitchell, Jeffrey Gottfried, Jocelyn Kiley, and Katerina Eva Matsa, *Political Polarization & Media Habits*" (report, Pew Research Center, Washington, D.C., October 21, 2014), https://www.pewresearch.org/journalism/2014/10/21/political-polarization-media -habits/.

84. Sunstein and Vermeule, "Conspiracy Theories," 210.

85. Bennett, "Press-Government Relationship," 256.

86. Nancy L. Rosenblum and Russell Muirhead, *A Lot of People Are Saying: The New Conspiracism and the Assault on Democracy* (Princeton, NJ: Princeton University Press, 2020), x.

4. DONALD TRUMP'S INCENDIARY RHETORIC AND POLITICAL VIOLENCE

1. Kelen McBreen, "Rep. Gohmert: Democrat 'Coup' About to Push America 'Into Civil War,'" Infowars.com, October 31, 2019, https://www.infowars.com/rep-gohmert-democrat -coup-about-to-push-america-into-civil-war/?commentId=19ccc4d1-9581-4585-a19d -6741edecee3e.

2. Nick R. Martin, "Threat Against Adam Schiff," The Informant, February 4, 2020, https://www.informant.news/p/threat-against-adam-schiff.

3. Kyle Cheney and Andrew Desiderio, "Arizona Man Facing Charges of Threatening Adam Schiff," Politico, February 4, 2020, https://www.politico.com/news/2020/02/04 /arizona-man-threatening-schiff-110682.

4. Schiff and members of his staff had earlier received death threats, as had the whistleblower whose information eventually led to the impeachment.

5. Patricia Roberts-Miller, "Democracy, Demagoguery, and Critical Rhetoric," *Rhetoric and Public Affairs* 8, no. 3 (2005): 459–76.

6. Caitlin Oprysko, "'I Don't Take Responsibility at All': Trump Deflects Blame for Coronavirus Testing Fumble," POLITICO, March 13, 2020, https://www.politico.com/news /2020/03/13/trump-coronavirus-testing-128971.

7. Charles W. Lomas, "The Rhetoric of Demagoguery," *Western Speech* 25 (1961): 161.

8. Roberts-Miller, "Democracy, Demagoguery, and Critical Rhetoric," 466.

9. James W. Carey, *Communication as Culture: Essays on Media and Society* (New York: Routledge, 1992), 17.

10. According to our content analysis of Trump tweets and responses by his supportive Twitter followers.

11. Carey, *Communication as Culture*, 19.

12. Carey, *Communication as Culture*, 22.

13. The full transcript is available at "Donald Trump Tulsa, Oklahoma Rally Speech Transcript," Rev, June 21, 2020, https://www.rev.com/blog/transcripts/donald-trump-tulsa -oklahoma-rally-speech-transcript.

14. Ruben G. Apressyan, "Violent Speech," *Peace Review: A Transnational Quarterly* 10, no. 4 (December 1998): 590.

15. *Schenck v. United States* 249 U.S. 47 (2019).

16. Mary R. Jackman, "Violence in Social Life," *Annual Review of Sociology* 28 (2002): 396; Robert L. Holmes, ed., *Nonviolence in Theory and Practice* (Belmont, CA: Wadsworth, 1990), 1–2.

17. Mari J. Matsuda, "Public Response to Racist Speech: Considering the Victim's Story," *Michigan Law Review* 87, no. 8 (1989): 2320–36, https://doi.org/10.2307/1289306.

18. Julie Peirano, "The Bullying Epidemic: Here's Everything You Need to Know," Showbiz CheatSheet, March 2, 2018, https://www.cheatsheet.com/health-fitness/everything-you -need-to-know-about-bullying.html.

19. Apressyan, "Violent Speech," 589.

20. Alexander Tsesis, "Destructive Messages: How Hate Speech Paves the Way for Harmful Social Movements," in *Destructive Messages: How Hate Speech Paves the Way for Harmful Social Movements* (Rochester, NY: New York University Press, 2002), 89.

21. Gregory Korte and Alan Gomez, "Trump Ramps Up Rhetoric on Undocumented Immigrants: 'These Aren't People. These Are Animals,'" *USA TODAY*, updated May 17, 2018, https://www.usatoday.com/story/news/politics/2018/05/16/trump-immigrants-animals -mexico-democrats-sanctuary-cities/617252002/.

22. According to Trump's Twitter account's archive, up to the end of February 2020, he used these terms eight times in his tweets, URL: also see Julie Peirano, "The Bullying Epidemic."

23. These were some of the responses to President Trump's tweet on June 2, 2020: "Our highest respect to the family of David Dorn, a Great Police Captain from St. Louis, who was viciously shot and killed by despicable looters last night."

24. Christopher Wilson, "Trump Tells White Audience in Minnesota They Have 'Good Genes,'" News.yahoo.com, September 21, 2020, https://news.yahoo.com/trump-minnesota-good-genes-eugenics-dog-whistle-202828480.html.

25. A transcript of the speech is available at NPR, October 26, 2016, https://www.npr.org/2016/10/13/497857068/transcript-donald-trumps-speech-responding-to-assault-accusations.

26. Speech transcript, NPR, October 26, 2016.

27. Andrew Anglin, "This Time (((We))) Really Mean It: Donald Trump Is Literally Hitler,'" Daily Stormer, October 14, 2016, accessed June 20, 2020, https://dailystormer.su/this-time-we-really-mean-it-donald-j-trump-is-literally-hitler/.

28. Anglin, "This Time."

29. Southern Poverty Law Center, "The Trump Effect: The Impact of The 2016 Presidential Election on Our Nation's Schools," November 28, 2016, https://www.splcenter.org/20161128/trump-effect-impact-2016-presidential-election-our-nations-schools.

30. Southern Poverty Law Center, "Hate at School," November 2019, https://www.splcenter.org/20161128/trump-effect-impact-2016-presidential-election-our-nations-schools.

31. Francisco Vara-Orta, "Hate in Schools," *Education Week*, August 6, 2018, Leadership, School Climate & Safety, https://www.edweek.org/leadership/hate-in-schools/2018/08.

32. Yair Rosenberg, "Perspective | 'Jews Will Not Replace Us': Why White Supremacists Go After Jews," *Washington Post*, August 14, 2017, https://www.washingtonpost.com/news/acts-of-faith/wp/2017/08/14/jews-will-not-replace-us-why-white-supremacists-go-after-jews/.

33. Angie Drobnic Holan, "In Context: Donald Trump's 'Very Fine People on Both Sides' Remarks," POLITIFACT, April 26, 2019, https://www.politifact.com/article/2019/apr/26/context-trumps-very-fine-people-both-sides-remarks/.

34. Mary Papenfuss, "Trump Chuckles at Suggestion to 'Lock Up' George Soros After Calling for Harmony," *Huffington Post*, October 26, 2018, https://www.huffpost.com/entry/donald-trump-lock-george-soros-up_n_5bd38ba1e4b0d38b583368d7.

35. After Trump's tweet was widely reported in the mainstream media, it was deleted from @realDonaldTrump.

36. Katie Rogers, "Donald Trump Does Not Correct a Man Who Called Obama a Muslim," *New York Times*, September 18, 2015, U.S., https://www.nytimes.com/2015/09/19/us/politics/donald-trump-obama-muslim.html.

37. "Trump Charges Obama with Being 'Founder of ISIS,'" Fox News, August 11, 2016, https://www.foxnews.com/politics/trump-charges-obama-with-being-founder-of-isis.

38. From May 4, 2009, when he posted his first tweet, through January 8, 2021, when Twitter suspended his account, Donald Trump posted a total of 56,571 tweets, according to the @realdonaldtrump twitter archive. We identified 14,807 tweets of his total production as "attack tweets" and identified the targets of his rhetorical attacks for different periods: pre-candidacy, candidacy, transition (from his election victory to his inauguration), presidency, and post-2020 elections.

39. Philip Bump, "Analysis | Haiti and Africa? No, Thanks. Trump Prefers Immigrants from Some of the Least Diverse Countries on Earth.," *Washington Post*, January 11, 2018,

https://www.washingtonpost.com/news/politics/wp/2018/01/11/haiti-and-africa-no
-thanks-trump-prefers-immigrants-from-some-of-the-least-diverse-countries-on-earth/.

40. Cleve R. Wootson, Jr., et al., "Black Americans Are Deeply Pessimistic About the Country Under Trump, Whom More Than 8 in 10 Describe as 'a Racist,' Post-Ipsos Poll
Finds," *Washington Post*, January 17, 2020, https://www.washingtonpost.com/politics
/black-americans-deeply-pessimistic-about-country-under-president-who-more-than
-8-in-10-describe-as-a-racist-post-ipsos-poll-finds/2020/01/16/134b705c-37de-11ea-bb7b
-265f4554af6d_story.html.

41. Southern Poverty Law Center, "The Trump Effect," 12.

42. For a transcript of the speech, see CBS News, June 16, 2015, https://www.cbsnews.com
/news/transcript-donald-trump-announces-his-presidential-candidacy/.

43. Maegan Vazquez and CNN, "Trump on Immigrant Family Separation Crisis: 'Don't
Come to Our Country Illegally,'" July 10, 2018, https://www.cbsnews.com/chicago/news
/donald-trump-immigration-family-separation-dont-come-illegally/.

44. Teun A. van Dijk, "The Violence of Text and Talk," *Discourse & Society* 6, no. 3 (July 1,
1995): 307–8, https://doi.org/10.1177/0957926595006003001.

45. Vara-Orta, "Hate in Schools."

46. Michael D. Shear and Julie Hirschfeld Davis, "Shoot Migrants' Legs, Build Alligator
Moat: Behind Trump's Ideas for Border," *New York Times*, October 1, 2019.

47. Thirty-seven months into Trump's presidency, on February 28, 2020, a Google search
for "Trump and wall" produced 492 million results, "Trump and border" 306 million, and
"Trump and deport" 5.9 million. While using the terms "border" and "wall" very frequently
in his tweets, Trump used the words "deport" and "deportation" less frequently. However,
he spoke frequently of "deport(ing)" and "deportation" in his public appearances.

48. Southern Poverty Law Center, "The Trump Effect."

49. Pew Research Center Staff, "State of Hispanics in the U.S. Today," in *Latinos and the
New Trump Administration* (report, Pew Research Center, Washington, D.C., February 23,
2017), https://www.pewresearch.org/hispanic/2017/02/23/state-of-hispanics-in-the-u-s
-today/.

50. Mark Hugo Lopez, Ana Gonzalez-Barrera, and Jens Manuel Krogstad, *More Latinos Have
Serious Concerns About Their Place in America Under Trump* (report, Pew Research Center,
Washington, D.C., October 25, 2018), https://www.pewresearch.org/hispanic/2018/10/25
/more-latinos-have-serious-concerns-about-their-place-in-america-under-trump/.

51. Ana Gonzalez-Barrera, "Hispanics with Darker Skin Are More Likely to Experience
Discrimination Than Those with Lighter Skin," Pew Research Center blog, July 2, 2019,
https://www.pewresearch.org/fact-tank/2019/07/02/hispanics-with-darker-skin-are
-more-likely-to-experience-discrimination-than-those-with-lighter-skin/.

52. The statement was posted on December 7, 2015, and removed from the website on May
8, 2017. For the full text, see Christine Wang, "Trump Website Takes Down Muslim Ban
Statement After Reporter Grills Spicer in Briefing," CNBC, May 8, 2017, https://www
.cnbc.com/2017/05/08/trump-website-takes-down-muslim-ban-statement-after-reporter
-grills-spicer-in-briefing.html.

53. Lynn Thiesmeyer, "The Discourse of Official Violence: Anti-Japanese North American Discourse and the American Internment Camps," *Discourse & Society* 6, no. 3 (1995): 319.

54. Thiesmeyer, "The Discourse of Official Violence," 332.

55. Meghan Keneally, "Donald Trump Cites These FDR Policies to Defend Muslim Ban," ABC News, December 28, 2015, https://abcnews.go.com/Politics/donald-trump-cites-fdr -policies-defend-muslim-ban/story?id=35648128.

56. Jenna Johnson and Abigail Hauslohner, "'I Think Islam Hates Us': A Timeline of Trump's Comments About Islam and Muslims," *Washington Post*, May 20, 2017, https://www .washingtonpost.com/news/post-politics/wp/2017/05/20/i-think-islam-hates-us-a -timeline-of-trumps-comments-about-islam-and-muslims/.

57. Theodore Schleifer, "Donald Trump: 'I Think Islam Hates Us,'" "CNN Politics, March 10, 2016, https://www.cnn.com/2016/03/09/politics/donald-trump-islam-hates-us/index.html.

58. Paul Joseph Watson, "The Truth About Islam," Infowars.com, November 23, 2015, https://www.infowars.com/the-truth-about-islam/.

59. Eric Hananoki, "A Guide to Donald Trump's Relationship with Alex Jones," Media Matters for America, May 3, 2017, https://www.mediamatters.org/donald-trump/guide -donald-trumps-relationship-alex-jones.

60. Namira Islam, "An Anti-Muslim Narrative Has Shaped Policy for Decades. The Travel Ban Will Make It Worse," VOX, June 27, 2018, https://www.vox.com/first-person/2018 /6/27/17510560/travel-ban-muslim-trump-islamophobia.

61. Trump v. Hawaii, 565 U.S. (2018).

62. Dalia Mogahed and Youssef Chouhoud, "American Muslim Poll 2017: Muslims at the Crossroads" (Institute for Social Policy and Understanding, Dearborn, MI, 2017), available at SSRN, https://doi.org/10.2139/ssrn.3454205.

63. Southern Poverty Law Center, "Hate at School."

64. Southern Poverty Law Center, "Hate at School."

65. This message was tweeted by U.S. Press Freedom Tracker on June 1, 2020.

66. Donald J. Trump, *Time to Get Tough: Make America Great Again!* (Washington, D.C.: Regnery, 2015), 173.

67. The Shorenstein Center at Harvard University conducted extensive content analyses of the news media. The reports on preprimary and primary coverage are available: Thomas E. Patterson, "Pre-Primary News Coverage of the 2016 Presidential Race: Trump's Rise, Sanders' Emergence, Clinton's Struggle," June 13, 2016, https://shoren steincenter.org/pre-primary-news-coverage-2016-trump-clinton-sanders/, and Thomas E. Patterson, "News Coverage of the 2016 Presidential Primaries: Horse Race Reporting Has Consequences," July 11, 2016 https://shorensteincenter.org/news-coverage-2016 -presidential-primaries/.

68. Donald J. Trump and Tony Schwartz, *Trump: The Art of the Deal* (New York: Ballantine, 2015), 56.

69. Trump, *Trump: The Art of the Deal*, 57.

70. Dan Mangan, "President Trump Told Lesley Stahl He Bashes Press 'to Demean You and Discredit You So . . . No One Will Believe' Negative Stories About Him," CNBC, updated

October 29, 2018, https://www.cnbc.com/2018/05/22/trump-told-lesley-stahl-he-bashes-press-to-discredit-negative-stories.html.

71. Mark Jurkowitz et al., "*U.S. Media Polarization and the 2020 Election: A Nation Divided*," (report, Pew Research Center, Washington, D.C., January 24, 2020), https://www.pewresearch.org/journalism/2020/01/24/u-s-media-polarization-and-the-2020-election-a-nation-divided/.

72. The poll was conducted on March 1–5, 2017, by Suffolk University and *USA TODAY*.

73. According to seven surveys conducted by Quinnipiac in 2018 and 2019.

74. The exact date of the retweet was May 29. A day later Trump warned Black Lives Matter protesters in a tweet, "When the looting starts, the shooting starts."

75. Nathan P. Kalmoe and Lilliana Mason, "Lethal Partisanship: Prevalence, Correlates, & Electoral Contingencies" (paper prepared for presentation at the January 2019 NCAPSA American Politics Meeting); Nathan P. Kalmoe and Lilliana Mason, "A Holistic View of Conditional American Support for Political Violence," *Proceedings of the National Academy of Sciences* 119, no. 32 (January 25, 2022): e2207237119, https://doi.org/10.1073/pnas.2207237119.

76. The data presented in this paragraph are from our extensive content analysis of @realDonaldTrump tweets before his candidacy, during his candidacy, the president-elect period, and his presidency (June 16, 2015–January 8, 2021, when his Twitter account was suspended in the aftermath of the breach of the U.S. Capitol on January 6, 2021).

77. Lauren Egan, "Trump Attacks Democrats as 'Totalitarian,' 'Doing Illegal Acts,'" NBC News, November 6, 2019, https://www.nbcnews.com/politics/donald-trump/trump-attacks-democrats-totalitarian-doing-illegal-acts-n1078001.

78. Jennifer R. Mercieca, "Dangerous Demagogues and Weaponized Communication," *Rhetoric Society Quarterly* 49, no. 3 (May 27, 2019): 273, https://doi.org/10.1080/02773945.2019.1610640.

79. Kenneth Garger, "Trump Rally Chants 'Lock Her Up' After Nancy Pelosi Mention," *New York Post*, February 10, 2020, https://nypost.com/2020/02/10/trump-rally-crowd-chants-lock-her-up-at-nancy-pelosi/.

80. William Cummings, Sen. Dianne Feinstein Becomes New Target of Trump Supporters' 'Lock Her Up' Chant," *USA TODAY*, October 10, 2018, https://www.usatoday.com/story/news/politics/onpolitics/2018/10/10/dianne-feinstein-lock-her-up-chant-donald-trump-rally/1587135002/.

81. Based on all attack tweets we identified.

82. Caitlin O'Kane, "Gun Shop Billboard Mocks 'the Squad,' Calling Four Congresswomen 'Idiots,'" CBS News, July 31, 2019, https://www.cbsnews.com/news/gun-shop-billboard-mocks-the-squad-calling-four-congresswomen-idiots/.

83. Trump, *Trump: The Art of the Deal*, 69–70.

84. The complete transcript is available at *TIME* Staff, "Read the Full Transcript of Donald Trump's 'Second Amendment' Speech," *TIME* Politics, August 9, 2016, https://time.com/4445813/donald-trump-second-amendment-speech/.

85. The video of Hillary Clinton's response to Donald Trump's Second Amendment remarks is available at "Hillary Clinton Says "Words Matter" While Talking Trump in Des Moines," CBS News, August 10, 2016, cbsnews.com/video/full-video-hillary-clinton-says-words-matter-while-talking-trump-in-des-moines/.

86. Trump made the remark on October 18, 2018, at a rally in Montana. See AP Archive, "Trump Praises Congressman for Assaulting Reporter," YouTube, https://www.youtube.com/watch?v=71mhO2eq4-Y.

87. These few examples of many occasions when Trump publicly praised and encouraged violence are based on press reports.

88. Inae Oh, "Trump Gleefully Praises Violence Against Journalists as a 'Beautiful Sight,'" *Mother Jones* (blog), September 23, 2020, https://www.motherjones.com/politics/2020/09/trump-ali-velshi/.

89. American Psychological Association, Commission on Youth and Violence, *Report of the APA Commission on Violence and Youth* (Washington, D.C.: American Psychological Association, 1993).

90. Nathan P. Kalmoe, "Fueling the Fire: Violent Metaphors, Trait Aggression, and Support for Political Violence," *Political Communication* 31, no. 4 (October 16, 2014): 556, https://doi.org/10.1080/10584609.2013.852642.

91. See "Full Text of Charleston Suspect Dylann Roof's Apparent Manifesto," June 20, 2015, https://talkingpointsmemo.com/muckraker/dylann-roof-manifesto-full-text.

92. Seanna Adcox, "Haley Talks of Trump, Confederate Flag Ahead of Anniversary," *Post and Courier*, June 1, 2016, updated November 2, 2016, https://www.postandcourier.com/politics/haley-talks-of-trump-confederate-flag-ahead-of-anniversary/article_07eaac6c-8b80-53f3-8214-6be8321efff5.html.

93. Jordan Fabian, "Trump Defends Rhetoric After Critics Point Finger Over Mass Shooting," *The Hill* (blog), August 8, 2019, https://thehill.com/homenews/administration/456519-trump-i-think-my-rhetoric-brings-people-together/.

94. Ayal Feinberg, Regina Branton, and Valerie Martinez-Ebers, "Counties That Hosted a 2016 Trump Rally Saw a 226 Percent Increase in Hate Crimes," *Washington Post*, March 22, 2019, https://www.washingtonpost.com/politics/2019/03/22/trumps-rhetoric-does-inspire-more-hate-crimes/.

95. Mike Levine, "'No Blame?' ABC News Finds 54 Cases Invoking 'Trump' in Connection with Violence, Threats, Alleged Assaults," ABC News, May 30, 2020, https://abcnews.go.com/Politics/blame-abc-news-finds-17-cases-invoking-trump/story?id=58912889.

96. Because unprecedented attacks on the news media began during Trump's election campaign, the database began to gather and confirmed physical violence against the media in 2017. Thus, comparable pre-2017 data do not exist. The database is accessible at U.S. Press Freedom Tracker, https://pressfreedomtracker.us/physical-attack/?categories=10&date_lower=2018-01-01&date_upper=2018-12-31&tags=74, accessed June 30, 2023.

97. In this and the following section, we used media accounts and police and court documents to describe incidents of political violence with references to Donald Trump.

98. Jason Le Miere, "Donald Trump Says 'I'm a Nationalist, Use That Word' at Texas Rally for Ted Cruz," *Newsweek*, October 22, 2018, https://www.newsweek.com/donald -trump-nationalist-texas-rally-1182223.

99. The full text of the manifesto is available at https://tsaoutofourpants.files.wordpress.com /2019/03/nz-shooter-manifesto.pdf, accessed June 30, 2023.

100. News Division, "Here's the El Paso Shooter's Full Manifesto: Read It Before You Believe the News," Pulpit & Pen, August 5, 2019, https://pulpitandpen.org/2019/08/05 /heres-the-el-paso-shooters-full-manifesto-read-it-before-you-believe-the-news/.

101. Johan Galtung, "Cultural Violence," *Journal of Peace Research* 27, no. 3 (August 1, 1990): 292, https://doi.org/10.1177/0022343390027003005, emphasis added.

102. According to the Anti-Defamation League; see *Murder and Extremism in the United States in 2021* (report, Anti-Defamation League, New York, February 10, 2022), https://www.adl .org/murder-and-extremism-2021.

103. Mercieca, "Dangerous Demagogues and Weaponized Communication," 270.

104. Molly McKew, "Brett Kavanaugh and the Information Terrorists Trying to Reshape America," *WIRED*, October 3, 2018, https://www.wired.com/story/information-terrorists -trying-to-reshape-america/.

5. PARTISAN CONFLICT, ISSUES, AND EMOTIONS ON HIGH

1. Nathaniel Rakich and Kaleigh Rogers, "At Least 120 Republican Nominees Deny the Results of the 2020 Election," July 18, 2022, FiveThirtyEight, https://fivethirtyeight .com/features/at-least-120-republicans-who-deny-the-2020-election-results-will-be-on -the-ballot-in-november/.

2. Video message from March 2020 by Republican member of the U.S. House of Representatives Ken Buck of Colorado's Fourth District while standing in his Capitol Hill office. David Frum, "Only the GOP Celebrates Political Violence,", *The Atlantic*, October 29, 2022, https://www.theatlantic.com/ideas/archive/2022/10 /pelosi-republicans-partisan-political-violence/671934/.

3. Ed Pilkington, "Marjorie Taylor Greene: Capitol Attack 'Would've Been Armed' If I Was in Charge," *The Guardian*, December 12, 2022, US news, https://www.theguardian .com/us-news/2022/dec/12/marjorie-taylor-greene-jan-6-capitol-attack-armed-speech.

4. Steve Peoples, "'The Brand Is So Toxic': Dems Fear Extinction in Rural US," AP News, February 17, 2022, https://apnews.com/article/joe-biden-elections-pennsylvania-lifestyle -election-2020-fc79679ef54d850c0245f96dac37456c.

5. Henri Tajfel and John Turner, "The Social Identity Theory of Intergroup Behavior," in *Psychology of Intergroup Relations*, ed. Stephen Worchel and William G. Austin (Chicago: Nelson-Hall, 1986); Shanto Iyengar, Gaurav Sood, and Yphtach Lelkes, "Affect, Not Ideology: A Social Identity Perspective on Polarization," *Public Opinion Quarterly* 76, no. 3 (2012): 405–31; and Lilliana Mason, *Uncivil Agreement: How Politics Became Our Identity* (Chicago: University of Chicago Press, 2018).

6. See Alan Abramowitz, *The Great Alignment: Race, Party Transformation, and the Rise of Donald Trump* (New Haven, CT: Yale University Press, 2018); Abramowitz, "The Polarized American Electorate: The Rise of Partisan-Ideological Consistency and Its Consequences," *Political Science Quarterly* 137, no. 4 (Winter 2022): 645–74, https://doi .org/10.1002/polq.13388; Alan I. Abramowitz and Steven W. Webster, "Negative Partisanship: Why Americans Dislike Parties But Behave Like Rabid Partisans," *Political Psychology* 39, no. S1 (2018): 119–35, https://doi.org/10.1111/pops.12479; Thomas B. Edsall, "Is Politics a War of Ideas or of Us Against Them?," *New York Times*, November 6, 2019, Opinion, https://www.nytimes.com/2019/11/06/opinion/is-politics-a-war-of-ideas-or-of -us-against-them.html; Shanto Iyengar and Sean J. Westwood, "Fear and Loathing Across Party Lines: New Evidence on Group Polarization," *American Journal of Political Science* 59, no. 3 (2015): 690–707; Mason, *Uncivil Agreement*; Thomas E. Patterson, *How America Lost Its Mind: The Assault on Reason That's Crippling Our Democracy*, Julian J. Rothbaum Distinguished Lecture Series, vol. 15 (Norman: University of Oklahoma Press, 2019); Iyengar, "Affective Polarization or Hostility Across the Party Divide," in *New Directions in Public Opinion*, ed. Adam J. Berinsky, 3rd ed. (New York: Routledge, 2019), 99–117, https://doi .org/10.4324/9781351054621-5; and James N. Druckman and Jeremy Levy, "Affective Polarization in the American Public," in *Handbook on Politics and Public Opinion*, ed. Thomas J. Rudolph (Cheltenham, UK: Edward Elgar, 2022), https://www.elgaronline.com/display /book/9781800379619/book-part-9781800379619-30.xml.

7. See Steven W. Webster, *American Rage: How Anger Shapes Our Politics* (Cambridge: Cambridge University Press, 2020).

8. Bernard R. Berelson, Paul F. Lazarsfeld, and William N. McPhee, *Voting: A Study of Opinion Formation in a Presidential Campaign* (Chicago: University of Chicago Press, 1954); Angus Campbell, Philip E. Converse, Warren E. Miller, and Donald E. Stokes, *The American Voter* (Chicago: University of Chicago Press, 1976).

9. American Political Science Association, "Toward a More Responsible Two Party System: A Report," supplement to *American Political Science Review* 44, no. 3, pt. 2 (September 1950).

10. For example, see Costas Panagopoulos and Robert Y. Shapiro, "Big Government and Public Opinion," in *The Oxford Handbook of American Public Opinion and the Media*, ed. George C. Edwards, Lawrence R. Jacobs, and Robert Y. Shapiro (Oxford: Oxford University Press, 2011), https://doi.org/10.1093/oxfordhb/9780199545636.003.0039.

11. Jane J. Mansbridge, *Why We Lost the ERA* (Chicago: University of Chicago Press, 1986) .

12. Eric Schickler, *Racial Realignment: The Transformation of American Liberalism, 1932–1965* (Princeton, NJ: Princeton University Press, 2016); Edward G. Carmines and James A. Stimson, *Issue Evolution: Race and the Transformation of American Politics* (Princeton, NJ Princeton University Press, 1989).

13. Carmines and Stimson, *Issue Evolution*.

14. Matthew Levendusky, *The Partisan Sort: How Liberals Became Democrats and Conservatives Became Republicans* (Chicago: University of Chicago Press, 2009); Morris P. Fiorina, Samuel J. Abrams, and Jeremy Pope, *Culture War? The Myth of a Polarized America* (New York: Pearson Longman, 2005).

15. See, e.g., Abramowitz, *The Great Alignment*; Joshua N. Zingher, *Political Choice in a Polarized World: How Elite Polarization Shapes Mass Behavior* (New York: Oxford University Press, 2022); Joseph Bafumi and Robert Y. Shapiro, "A New Partisan Voter," *Journal of Politics* 71, no. 1 (January 2009): 1–24, https://doi.org/10.1017/S0022381608090014; Marc J. Hetherington, "Resurgent Mass Partisanship: The Role of Elite Polarization," *American Political Science Review* 95, no. 3 (2001): 619–31; Geoffrey C. Layman and Thomas M. Carsey, "Party Polarization and Party Structuring of Policy Attitudes: A Comparison of Three NES Panel Studies," *Political Behavior* 24, no. 3 (2002): 199–236; and Geoffrey C. Layman and Thomas M. Carsey, "Party Polarization and 'Conflict Extension' in the American Electorate," *American Journal of Political Science* 46, no. 4 (2002): 786–802, https://doi.org/10.2307/3088434.

16. See and compare Benjamin I. Page and Robert Y. Shapiro, *The Rational Public: Fifty Years of Trends in Americans' Policy Preferences*, (Chicago: University of Chicago Press, 1992).

17. See Pew Research Center, *Partisan Polarization Surges in Bush, Obama Years. Trends in American Values: 1987–2012* (report, Pew Research Center, Washington, D.C., June 4, 2012), http://www.people-press.org/2012/06/04/partisan-polarization-surges-in-bush-obama-years/; Pew Research Center, *Political Polarization in the American Public: How Increasing Ideological Uniformity and Partisan Antipathy Affect Politics, Compromise and Everyday Life* (report, Pew Research Center, Washington, D.C., June 12, 2014), https://www.pewresearch.org/wp-content/uploads/sites/4/2014/06/6-12-2014-Political-Polarization-Release.pdf; Pew Research Center, *The Partisan Divide on Political Values Grows Even Wider* (report, Pew Research Center, Washington, D.C., October 5, 2017), http://www.people-press.org/2017/10/05/the-partisan-divide-on-political-values-grows-even-wider/; Robert Y. Shapiro, "Essay: Liberal Internationalism and Partisan Conflict," in H-Diplo/ISSF Policy Roundtable 1–6: Is Liberal Internationalism Still Alive? (Robert Jervis International Security Studies Forum, March 14, 2017), https://issforum.org/roundtables/policy/1-6-liberal-internationalism; Shapiro, "The Evolution and Nature of Partisan Conflict in the United States" (presentation at Virtual Days on Campus, Columbia University, New York, April 15, 2021); and George Georgarakis and Robert Y. Shapiro, "Liberal Internationalism and Partisan Discontents Into the Post-Trump United States," H-Diplo/ISSF Policy Series: America and the World: The Effects of the Trump Presidency (Robert Jervis International Security Studies Forum, 2021).

18. See Keith T. Poole and Howard L. Rosenthal, *Ideology and Congress: A Political-Economic History of Roll Call Voting*, 2nd ed. (New York: Routledge, 2007); Nolan McCarty, Keith T. Poole, and Howard Rosenthal, *Polarized America: The Dance of Ideology and Unequal Riches* (Cambridge, MA: MIT Press, 2006).

19. On this assertion and debate, see Matt Grossman and David A. Hopkins, *Asymmetric Politics: Ideological Republicans and Group Interest Democrats* (New York: Oxford University Press, 2016); Thomas E. Mann and Norman J. Ornstein, *It's Even Worse Than It Looks: How the American Constitutional System Collided with the New Politics of Extremism* (New York: Basic Books, 2016); Norman Ornstein, "Yes, Polarization Is Asymmetric—and

Conservatives Are Worse," *The Atlantic,* June 19, 2014, https://www.theatlantic.com/politics
/archive/2014/06/yes-polarization-is-asymmetric-and-conservatives-are-worse/373044/;
Morgan Marietta and David C. Barker, *One Nation, Two Realities: Dueling Facts in American
Democracy* (New York: Oxford University Press, 2019); Pew Research Center.,2014. *Political
Polarization in the American Public,* and Robert Y. Shapiro, "The Evolution and Nature of
Partisan Conflict."

20. We cannot track this easily issue by issue for political leaders because in the case of congressional roll call votes, the same issues over time do not repeatedly come up for a vote.

21. Pew Research Center, *Partisan Polarization Surges in Bush, Obama Years; Political Polarization in the American Public;* ; and *The Partisan Divide on Political Values Grows Even
Wider.*

22. The Johnson administration passed an extraordinary range of social policy legislation. For
a compelling summary, see *Washington Post,* "Evaluating the success of the Great Society,"
https://www.washingtonpost.com/wp-srv/special/national/great-society-at-50/.

23. For the 2020–21 GSS survey, changes in responses observed in 2020–21 bearing on trends
may be due to actual changes in opinions or attitudes and/or may have resulted from
methodological changes made to the survey during the COVID-19 pandemic. This,
however, does not affect our observations about overall opinion trends for responses to
particular questions.

24. Lawrence R. Jacobs and Robert Y. Shapiro, *Politicians Don't Pander: Political Manipulation
and the Loss of Democratic Responsiveness* (Chicago: University of Chicago Press, 2000).

25. Michael Tesler, "Democrats and Republicans Are Increasingly Divided on the Value
of Teaching Black History," Monkey Cage (blog), *Washington Post,* February 28, 2018,
https://www.washingtonpost.com/news/monkey-cage/wp/2018/02/28/democrats
-and-republicans-are-increasingly-divided-on-the-value-of-teaching-black-history/;
Tesler, "Racial Attitudes and American Politics," in *New Directions in Public Opinion,* ed.
Adam J. Berinsky, 3rd ed. (New York: Routledge, 2019).

26. John R. Petrocik, "Issue Ownership in Presidential Elections, with a 1980 Case Study," *American
Journal of Political Science* 40, no. 3 (August 1996): 825–50, https://doi.org/10.2307/2111797.

27. The most recent tragedy when we drafted this chapter in 2022 was the murder of nineteen
children by an eighteen year-old gunman in a school in Uvalde, Texas.

28. Partisan differences increased on other issues, including prayer in school, sex education,
and birth control for teens. See the trend data by partisanship from the NORC General
Social Surveys, https://gssdataexplorer.norc.org/trends.

29. On the nationalization of politics, see Daniel J. Hopkins, *The Increasingly United States:
How and Why American Political Behavior Nationalized,* Chicago Studies in American
Politics (Chicago: University of Chicago Press, 2018).

30. An exception was the political fallout from Hurricane Katrina in August 2005. See Brigitte
L. Nacos, Yaeli Bloch-Elkon, and Robert Y. Shapiro, *Selling Fear: Counterterrorism, the
Media, and Public Opinion* (Chicago: University of Chicago Press, 2011).

31. For example, see the account in John M. Barry, *The Great Influenza: The Story of the
Deadliest Pandemic in History,* rev. ed. (New York: Penguin, 2005).

32. See "Are Liberals or Conservatives More Anti-Vaccine?," RealClearScience https://www
.realclearscience.com/journal_club/2014/10/20/are_liberals_or_conservatives_more_anti
-vaccine_108905.html.

33. This name refers to the speed of space travel in the *Star Trek* television series and movies.

34. Alan S. Blinder and R. Glenn Hubbard, "We Need to Fight COVID-19, Not Each Other.
Here Are the Keys to Compromise on a Relief Deal," *Washington Post*, Opinion, January 27,
2021, https://www.washingtonpost.com/opinions/we-need-to-fight-covid-19-not-each
-other-here-are-the-keys-to-compromise-on-a-relief-deal/2021/01/27/5c42ffd8-60cc
-11eb-afbe-9a11a127d146_story.html.

35. Shana Kushner Gadarian, Sara Wallace Goodman, and Thomas B. Pepinsky, "Partisanship,
Health Behavior, and Policy Attitudes in the Early Stages of the COVID-19 Pandemic"
(March 27, 2020), available at SSRN https://doi.org/10.2139/ssrn.3562796; Hunt Allcott
et al., "Polarization and Public Health: Partisan Differences in Social Distancing During
the Coronavirus Pandemic," *Journal of Public Economics* 191 (November 2020): 104254,
https://doi.org/10.1016/j.jpubeco.2020.104254; Matthew A. Baum et al., "The State of the
Nation: A 50-State Covid-19 Survey Report #14: Misinformation and Vaccine Acceptance,"
Covid-19 Consortium for Understanding the Public's Policy Preferences Across States,
September 23, 2020, vi. https://www.kateto.net/covid19/COVID19%20CONSORTIUM
%20REPORT%2014%20MISINFO%20SEP%202020.pdf; Paul Platzman and Robert
Shapiro, "Partisan Conflict and the Coronavirus: Public Perceptions of Presidential Per-
formance, Threat, Crisis, and the Health System" (working paper Columbia University,
2020); and Shana Kushner Gadarian, Sara Wallace Goodman, and Thomas B. Pepinsky,
Pandemic Politics: The Deadly Toll of Partisanship in the Age of COVID (Princeton, NJ:
Princeton University Press, 2022).

36. See Shapiro, "The Evolution and Nature of Partisan Conflict."

37. See Gary C. Jacobson, "The Presidential and Congressional Elections of 2020: A National
Referendum on the Trump Presidency," *Political Science Quarterly* 136, no. 1 (March 15,
2021): 11–45, https://doi.org/10.1002/polq.13133.

38. See Bill Hutchinson, "'Incomprehensible': Confrontations Over Masks Erupt Amid
COVID-19 Crisis," ABC News, May 7, 2020, https://abcnews.go.com/US/incomprehensible
-confrontations-masks-erupt-amid-covid-19-crisis/story?id=70494577; Deepa Shivaram,
"The Topic of Masks in Schools Is Polarizing Some Parents to the Point of Violence,"
NPR, August 20, 2021, https://www.npr.org/sections/back-to-school-live-updates/2021/08
/20/1028841279/mask-mandates-school-protests-teachers; *Limiting Workplace Violence Associated
with COVID-19 Prevention Policies in Retail and Services Businesses*, Centers for Disease
Control and Prevention, updated August 24, 2020.

39. Cf. Page and Shapiro, *The Rational Public.*

40. See John Zaller, *The Nature and Origins of Mass Opinion*, (Cambridge: Cambridge University Press, 1992); cf. Page and Shapiro, *The Rational Public.* On transformations of the
media, see Markus Prior, *Post-Broadcast Democracy: How Media Choice Increases Inequality
in Political Involvement and Polarizes Elections*, Cambridge Studies in Public Opinion and
Political Psychology (New York: Cambridge University Press, 2007).

41. See James Hamilton, *All the News That's Fit to Sell: How the Market Transforms Informa-tion Into News* (Princeton, NJ Princeton University Press, 2004); and Jacobs and Shapiro, *Politicians Don't Pander.*

42. Julian E. Zelizer, *Burning Down the House: Newt Gingrich and the Rise of the New Republi-can Party* (New York: Penguin, 2021).

43. Joseph A. Aistrup, *The Southern Strategy Revisited: Republican Top-Down Advancement in the South* (Lexington: University Press of Kentucky, 1996); Charles S. Bullock, Donna R. Hoffman, and Ronald Keith Gaddie, "The Consolidation of the White Southern Congressional Vote," *Political Research Quarterly* 58, no. 2 (June 2005): 231–43, https://doi.org/10.2307/3595625; Ira Katznelson, "Reversing Southern Republicanism," in *The New Majority: Toward a Popular Progressive Politics*, ed. Stanley B. Greenberg and Theda Skocpol (New Haven, CT: Yale University Press, 1997); Byron E. Shafer and Richard Johnston, *The End of Southern Exceptionalism: Class, Race, and Partisan Change in the Post-war South* (Cambridge, MA: Harvard University Press, 2006); Fred M. Shelley, Kimberly J. Zerr, and Adrienne M. Proffer, "The Civil Rights Movement and Recent Electoral Realignment in the South," *Southeastern Geographer* 47, no. 1 (2007): 13–26; and Harold W. Stanley, "Southern Partisan Changes: Dealignment, Realignment or Both?," *Journal of Politics* 50, no. 1 (February 1988): 64–88, https://doi.org/10.2307/2131041.

44. Morris P. Fiorina, *Unstable Majorities: Polarization, Party Sorting, and Political Stalemate* (Stanford, CA: Hoover Institution Press, 2017).

45. Ziva Kunda, "The Case for Motivated Reasoning," *Psychological Bulletin* 108 (1990): 480–98, https://doi.org/10.1037/0033-2909.108.3.480; Charles S. Taber and Milton Lodge, "Motivated Skepticism in the Evaluation of Political Beliefs," *American Journal of Politi-cal Science* 50, no. 3 (2006): 755–69; Charles S. Taber, Damon Cann, and Simona Kucsova, "The Motivated Processing of Political Arguments," *Political Behavior* 31, no. 2 (2009): 137–55; David P. Redlawsk, Andrew J. W. Civettini, and Karen M. Emmerson, "The Affec-tive Tipping Point: Do Motivated Reasoners Ever 'Get It'?," *Political Psychology* 31, no. 4 (2010): 563–93; R. Kelly Garrett, "Politically Motivated Reinforcement Seeking: Reframing the Selective Exposure Debate," *Journal of Communication* 59, no. 4 (2009): 676–99, https://doi.org/10.1111/j.1460-2466.2009.01452.x; Rune Slothuus and Claes H. de Vreese, "Political Parties, Motivated Reasoning, and Issue Framing Effects," *Journal of Politics* 72, no. 3 (2010): 630–45, https://doi.org/10.1017/s002238161000006x; and Todd K. Hartman and Adam J. Newmark, "Motivated Reasoning, Political Sophistication, and Associations Between Pres-ident Obama and Islam," *PS: Political Science and Politics* 45, no. 3 (2012): 449–55.

46. Morgan Marietta and David C. Barker, *One Nation, Two Realities: Dueling Facts in Ameri-can Democracy* (New York: Oxford University Press, 2019).

47. Angus Campbell et al., eds., *The American Voter* (Chicago: University of Chicago Press, 1976); Bernard Berelson, Paul F. Lazarsfeld, and William N. McPhee, *Voting: A Study of Opinion Formation in a Presidential Campaign* (Chicago: University of Chicago Press, 1954); and Donald P. Green, Bradley Palmquist, and Eric Schickler, *Partisan Hearts and Minds: Political Parties and the Social Identities of Voters*, Yale ISPS Series (New Haven, CT: Yale University Press, 2002).

48. Robert Jervis, *Why Intelligence Fails: Lessons from the Iranian Revolution and the Iraq War*, Cornell Studies in Security Affairs (Ithaca, NY: Cornell University Press, 2010).

49. Larry M. Bartels, "Beyond the Running Tally: Partisan Bias in Political Perceptions," *Political Behavior* 24, no. 2 (2002): 117–50; Peter K. Enns, Paul M. Kellstedt, and Gregory E. Mcavoy, "The Consequences of Partisanship in Economic Perceptions," *Public Opinion Quarterly* 76, no. 2 (2012): 287–310; and Shapiro, "The Evolution and Nature of Partisan Conflict."

50. There is little disagreement that the mass media and use of social media are part of the toxic politics chronicled in this book. Our narrative and evidence speak for themselves, and they echo what many other books and writings have analyzed and described especially with the rise of social media, though broadcast and other electronic media are part of the story as well. Finding and estimating specific causal effects of social and other media are complicated, and any effects are not automatic and may cumulate over time in ways that social scientific studies cannot immediately discern but may later become more apparent—as in the increase in the toxicity of the political environment. Based on reviews of existing research, it appears that in the United States, specific causal effects of social media on a variety of dependent variables, so to speak, have been found very roughly half the time they are studied. Everyone seems to think they are more pervasive than they are, probably due to the "third person effect," what people think about the attitudes and behavior of others. See Jonathan Haidt and Chris Bail, *Social Media and Political Dysfunction: A Collaborative Review*, accessed July 4, 2023, https://heystacks.com/doc/1185/social-media -and-political-dysfunction ; W. Phillips Davison, "The Third Person Effect in Communication," *Public Opinion Quarterly* 47, no. 1 (Spring 1983): 1–15; Andrew M. Guess, Pablo Barbera, Simon Munzert, and JungHwan Yang, "The Consequences of Online Partisan Media," *Proceedings of the National Academy of Sciences* 118, no. 14 (2021): e2013464118; Hunt Allcott, Luca Braghieri, Sarah Eichmeyer, and Matthew Gentzkow, "The Welfare Effects of Social Media," *American Economic Review* 110, no. 3 (20203): 629–76; Levi Boxell, Matthew Gentzkow, and Jesse M. Shapiro, "Greater Internet Use Is Not Associated with Faster Growth in Political Polarization Among US Demographic Groups," *Proceedings of the National Academy of Sciences* 114, no. 40 (2017): 10612–17; Moran Yarchi, Christian Baden, and Neta Kligler-Vilenchik, "Political Polarization on the Digital Sphere: A Cross-Platform, Over-Time Analysis of Interactional, Positional, and Affective Polarization on Social Media," *Political Communication* 38, nos. 1–2 (2021): 98–139; Yochai Benkler, Robert Farris, and Hal Roberts, *Network Propaganda: Manipulation, Disinformation, and Radicalization in American Politics* (New York: Oxford University Press, 2018); W. Lance Bennett and Steven Livingston, eds., *The Disinformation Age: Politics, Technology, and Disruptive Communication in the United States* (New York: Cambridge University Press, 2021); Matthew Levendusky, *How Partisan Media Polarize America* (Chicago: University of Chicago Press, 2013); Nathaniel Persily and Joshua A. Tucker, eds., *Social Media and Democracy: The State of the Field and Prospects for Reform* (New York: Cambridge University Press, 2020); Jaime E. Settle, *Frenemies: How Social Media Polarizes America* (New York: Cambridge University Press, 2018); Sinan Aral, *The Hype Machine: How Social Media Disrupts*

Our Elections, Our Economy, and Our Health—and How We Must Adapt (New York: Currency, 2020); Chris Bail, *Breaking the Social Media Prism: How to Make Our Platforms Less Polarizing* (Princeton, NJ: Princeton University Press, 2021); P. W. Singer and Emerson T. Brooking, *LikeWar: The Weaponization of Social Media* (New York: Mariner, 2018); and Max Fisher, *The Chaos Machine; The Inside Story of How Social Media Rewired Our Minds and Our World* (New York: Little, Brown, 2022).

51. On causality and relevant research, see the reviews provided by Druckman and Levy, "Affective Polarization in the American Public"; and Iyengar, "Affective Polarization or Hostility Across the Party Divide," 99–117. In addition to works cited earlier, see also, for example, Lori D. Bougher, "The Correlates of Discord: Identity, Issue Alignment, and Political Hostility in Polarized America," *Political Behavior* 39, no. 3 (2017): 731–62; Nicholas Dias and Yphtach Lelkes, "The Nature of Affective Polarization: Disentangling Policy Disagreement from Partisan Identity," *American Journal of Political Science* 66, no. 3 (2022): 775–90; Yphtach Lelkes, "Policy Over Party: Comparing the Effects of Candidate Ideology and Party on Affective Polarization," *Political Science Research and Methods* 9, no. 1 (2021: 189–96; and John C. Rogowski and Joseph L. Sutherland, "How Ideology Fuels Affective Polarization," *Political Behavior* 38, no. 2 (2016): 485–508.

6. WEAPONIZED WORDS AND DEEDS AGAINST DEMOCRACY

1. Jimmy Carter, "America's Democracy Is in Danger." *New York Times*, Sunday Review, January 9, 2022, 7.
2. Angelos Kissas, "Three Theses on the Mediatization of Politics: Evolutionist, Intended, or Imagined Transformation?," *Communication Review* 22, no.3 (2019): 223.
3. The transcript of the video's content is available at https://www.donaldjtrump.com /news9172bde9-a4e3-4024-846f-8f7fd7d06e9f, accessed July 7, 2023.
4. Ruth Ben-Ghiat, *Strongmen: Mussolini to the Present* (New York: W. W. Norton, 2021), 8.
5. The transcript is available at Rev, https://www.rev.com/blog/transcripts/donald-trump -tulsa-oklahoma-rally-speech-transcript, accessed July 7, 2023.
6. Matt A. Barreto et al., "The Tea Party in the Age of Obama: Mainstream Conservatism or Out-Group Anxiety?," *Political Power and Social Theory* 22 (2011): 6.
7. Bob Woodward, *RAGE* (New York: Simon & Schuster, 2020), Trump is cited on an unnumbered page preceding the prologue of the book.
8. Bob Garfield, "We've Lost," *Huffington Post* blog, updated June 17, 2017, https://www .huffpost.com/entry/donald-trump-2016_b_10523982.
9. Manuel Castells, *Communication Power* (New York: Oxford University Press, 2011), 154.
10. Anthony Pratkanis and Elliot Aronson, *Age of Propaganda: The Everyday Use and Abuse of Persuasion* (New York: W. H. Freeman, 1999), 165.
11. Ben-Ghiat, *Strongmen*, 93.
12. Robert O. Paxton, *The Anatomy of Fascism* (New York: Vintage, 2004), 16.

13. The transcript of Trump's speech is available at https://time.com/3923128/donald-trump
-announcement-speech/, accessed July 7, 2023.

14. Hitler's *Mein Kampf* is available in English at http://www.hitler.org/writings/Mein_Kampf
/mkv1ch06.html, accessed July 7, 2023.

15. Jan-Werner Mueller, *What Is Populism?* (Philadelphia: University of Pennsylvania Press,
2016), 35.

16. Mueller, *Populism*, 35.

17. Quoted in Greg Price, "Trump's Tweets Are Seen by Less Than One Percent of His
Followers, Social Media Expert Claims," *Newsweek*, January 3, 2018, https://www.newsweek
.com/trump-tweets-one-percent-mainstream-media-769207.

18. We looked daily at the first page in the print version of each newspaper (available online)
and thus captured the three most prominent stories without having to deal with the frequent breaking news on the publications' websites.

19. James W. Carey, "Political Ritual on Television: Episodes in the History of Shame, Degradation and Excommunication," In *Media, Ritual and Identity*, ed. T. Liebes and J. Curran
(London: Routledge, 1998), 67.

20. Timothy Snyder, *On Tyranny, Graphic Edition* (New York: Ten Speed, 2021), 45.

21. Martha Shanahan, "5 Memorable Moments When Town Hall Meetings Turned To Rage,"
NPR, August 7, 2013, https://www.npr.org/sections/itsallpolitics/2013/08/07/209919206/5
-memorable-moments-when-town-hall-meetings-turned-to-rage.

22. Shanahan, "5 Memorable Moments."

23. Matthew Bigg and Nick Carey, "Protesters Disrupt Town-Hall Healthcare Talks," *Reuters*,
August 7, 2009, https://www.reuters.com/article/us-usa-healthcare-townhalls/protesters
-disrupt-town-hall-healthcare-talks-idUSTRE5765QH20090808.

24. Ian Urbina, "Beyond Beltway, Health Debate Turns Hostile," *New York Times*, August 7,
2009, https://www.nytimes.com/2009/08/08/us/politics/08townhall.html.

25. Urbina, "Beyond Beltway."

26. Michael Finnegan and Janet Hook, "Republicans Stage 'Tea Party' Protests Against
Obama," *Los Angeles Times*, April 16, 2009, https://www.latimes.com/archives/la-xpm
-2009-apr-16-me-tea-party16-story.html.

27. Philip Weiss, "Who Is Barack Obama?," *New York* magazine, September 18, 2009,
https://nymag.com/news/politics/59265/.

28. Barack Obama, "A President Looks Back on His Toughest Fight," *New Yorker*, October 26,
2020, https://www.newyorker.com/magazine/2020/11/02/barack-obama-new-book-excerpt
-promised-land-obamacare.

29. The Aryan Nation's website no longer existed by 2020.

30. Stewart Rhodes, "Oath Keepers deploying to D.C," November 2021, https://oathkeepers
.org/2021/01/oath-keepers-deploying-to-dc-to-protect-events-speakers-attendees-on
-jan-5-6-time-to-stand/, accessed January 8, 2021.

31. Rhodes, "Oath Keepers."

32. The report is available at https://docs.house.gov/meetings/IJ/IJ00/20211019/114156/HRPT
-117-NA.pdf, accessed July 7, 2023.

33. The transcript of the September 29, 2020, debate is available at https://www.debates.org /voter-education/debate-transcripts/september-29-2020-debate-transcript/, accessed July 7, 2023.

34. Fabiola Cineas, "Trump Was Asked to Denounce White Supremacy. He wouldn't," *Vox*, September 29, 2020, https://www.vox.com/2020/9/29/21494841/trump-proud-boys-stand -white-supremacy.

35. Snyder, *On Tyranny*, 42.

36. Dominick Mastrangelo, "Trump Jr.: Trump Supporters in DC 'Should Send a Message' to GOP 'This Isn't' Their Party Anymore," *The Hill*, January 6, 2021, https://thehill.com /homenews/532886-donald-trump-jr-gathering-of-trump-supporters-in-dc-should-send -a-message-to-gop.

37. Cynthia Miller-Idriss, " America's Most Urgent Threat Now Comes From Within," *New York Times*, January 5, 2022, https://www.nytimes.com/2022/01/05/opinion/jan-6 -domestic-extremism.html.

38. Rachel Kleinfeld, "The Rise of Political Violence in the United States," *Journal of Democracy* 32, no. 4 (2021): 161.

39. The poll was conducted by the Quinnipiac University Polling Institute from January 7 to 10, 2021.

40. The Suffolk University/*USA Today* poll was conducted from February 15 to 20, 2021. Pollsters gave respondents a limited number of terms to choose from: a riot, a protest, an insurrection, a demonstration, or a gathering.

41. We listened to and transcribed the January 5 podcast of Bannon's "War Room" Episode 631, which was eventually removed from the site.

42. Walter Einenkel, "This Is the Video That Explains Why Rep. Mo Brooks Wants to Blame Coup D'etat on Antifa," Daily Kos, January 8, 2021, https://www.dailykos.com /stories/2021/1/8/2007179/--Start-taking-names-and-kicking-ass-Video-of-Alabama -congressman-hyping-the-insurrection-crowd.

43. Peter G. Berris, Michael A. Foster, and Jonathan M. Gaffney, *Domestic Terrorism: Overview of Federal Criminal Law and Constitutional Issues*, (report, Congressional Research Service, Washington, D.C., July 2, 2021), https://crsreports.congress.gov/product/pdf/R/R46829.

44. The document is available at https://www.justice.gov/usao-dc/press-release/file/1462346 /download, accessed July 7, 2023.

45. At the end of November 2022, Stewart Rhodes and Kelly Meggs, the leader of the Florida Oath Keepers chapter, were found guilty of seditious conspiracy by a federal jury, whereas other three Oath Keepers were convicted of other crimes.

46. James Fitzgerald, "Conspiracy, Anxiety, Ontology: Theorizing QAnon," *First Monday* 27, no. 4 (2022).

47. For incidents of QAnon violence, see the website of the Anti-Defamation League, https://www.adl.org/qanon, accessed July 7, 2023.

48. Elizabeth Crisp, "Trump Responds to QAnon Conspiracy," *Newsweek*, August 19, 2020, https://www.newsweek.com/trump-responds-qanon-conspiracy-i-understand-they-like -me-very-much-1526313.

49. Thomas B. Edsall, "Why Conspiracy Theories Flourish in Trump's America," *New York Times*, Opinion, June 22, 2022, https://www.nytimes.com/2022/06/22/opinion/trump-conspiracy-theories.html.

50. Andrew Sullivan, "Democracies End When They Are Too Democratic. And Right Now, America Is a Breeding Ground for Tyranny," *New York* magazine, May 1 2016, https://nymag.com/intelligencer/2016/04/america-tyranny-donald-trump.html.

51. Goebbels made this statement during a broadcast in April 1935, according to a selection of relevant citations published online under the header "Hitler as Messiah and God," http://www.net-abbey.org/hitler-as-god.htm, accessed July 8, 2023.

52. The text of the speech is available at https://research.calvin.edu/german-propaganda-archive/hess1.htm, accessed July 8, 2023.

53. Suzanne Mettler and Robert Lieberman, "Democracy Means Accepting Loss," *Bipartisan Policy Review* (Cornell University Institute of Politics and Global Affairs, January 2021), 14–15, https://cpb-us-e1.wpmucdn.com/blogs.cornell.edu/dist/1/8955/files/2019/09/bipartisanreview2021-final.pdf.

54. Ronan Farrow, "A Pennsylvania Mother's Path to Insurrection," *New Yorker*, February 1, 2021, https://www.newyorker.com/news/news-desk/a-pennsylvania-mothers-path-to-insurrection-capitol-riot.

55. Farrow, "A Pennsylvania Mother."

56. Dan Barry, Alan Feuer, and Matthew Rosenberg, "90 Seconds of Rage," *New York Times*, October 16, 2021, https://www.nytimes.com/interactive/2021/10/16/us/capitol-riot.html.

57. "Letters: Ordinary Citizens Turned Rioters on Jan. 6," *New York Times*, Opinion, October 21, https://www.nytimes.com/2021/10/21/opinion/letters/jan-6-capitol-riot.html.

58. "Letters: Ordinary Citizens."

59. Carey, "Political Ritual."

60. Craig Timberg and Drew Harwell, "The Donald's Owner Speaks Out on Why He Pulled the Plug on Hate-Filled Site," *Washington Post*, February 5, 2021, https://www.washingtonpost.com/technology/2021/02/05/why-thedonald-moderator-left/.

61. Timberg and Harwell, "The Donald."

62. Thedonald.win site was shut down by its owner in January 2021.

63. Elizabeth Dias and Jack Healy, "For Many Who Marched, Jan. 6 Was Only the Beginning," *New York Times*, January 23, 2022, https://www.nytimes.com/2022/01/23/us/jan-6-attendees.html.

64. Mettler and Lieberman, "Democracy Means Accepting Loss."

65. The Suffolk University/*USA Today* poll was conducted November 3–5, 2021.

66. Hannah Arendt, *On Violence* (New York: Harcourt Brace, 1970), 80.

67. For an important study of partisanship and violent hostility, see Nathan P. Kalmoe and Lilliana Mason, *Radical American Partisanship: Mapping Violent Hostility, Its Causes, and the Consequences for Democracy* (Chicago: University of Chicago Press, 2022).

68. While eventually more than one thousand persons were charged, some of them more than a year after January 6, we examined the cases of the first 659 people charged, according to the FBI documents that are available at https://www.justice.gov/usao-dc/capitol-breach-cases.

Most of our information was drawn from the FBI and related court documents; when crucial information was missing, we searched news transcripts and articles to fill in the gaps. In a number of cases, we were not able to find all the information we sought.

69. From the criminal complaint and arrest warrant, https://www.justice.gov/opa/page/file /1356116/download, accessed July 8, 2023.

70. The speech is available at https://www.presidency.ucsb.edu/documents/address-san -francisco-the-closing-session-the-united-nations-conference, accessed July 8, 2023.

71. The report "Freedom of the World Report: Democracy Under Siege" is available at https://freedomhouse.org/report/freedom-world/2021/democracy-under-siege, accessed July 8, 2023.

72. With support from the Political Instability Task Force, the Center for System Peace issues yearly reports on polity scores. See http://www.systemicpeace.org/, accessed July 8, 2023.

73. Barbara F. Walter, *How Civil Wars Start and How to Stop Them* (New York: Crown, 2022), 138.

74. KK Ottesen, "They Are Preparing for War: An Expert on Civil Wars Discusses Where Political Extremists Are Taking This Country," *Washington Post*, March 8, 2022, https:// www.washingtonpost.com/magazine/2022/03/08/they-are-preparing-war-an-expert -civil-wars-discusses-where-political-extremists-are-taking-this-country/.

75. Stephen Marche, *The Next Civil War: Dispatches from the American Future* (New York: Avid Reader, 2022), 177.

76. Paul D. Eaton, Antonio M. Taguba, and Stephen M. Anderson, "3 Retired Generals: The Military Must Prepare Now for a 2024 Insurrection," *Washington Post*, Opinion, December 17, 2021, https://www.washingtonpost.com/opinions/2021/12/17/eaton-taguba -anderson-generals-military/.

77. The text of the letter, signed by 124 retired admirals and generals, is available at https://img1.wsimg.com/blobby/go/fb7c7bd8-097d-4e2f-8f12-3442d151b57d/downloads /2021%20Open%20Letter%20from%20Retired%20Generals%20and%20Adm.pdf?ver =1620643005025, accessed July 8, 2023.

78. Anti-Defamation League, "Audit of Antisemitic Incidents in 2022," March 22, 2023, https://www.adl.org/resources/report/audit-antisemitic-incidents-2022.

79. Shana Goldmacher, Michael C. Bender, and Maggie Haberman, "Eyeing DeSantis, Trump Readies for a Long Primary Battle," *New York Times*, March 4, 2023, https://www .nytimes.com/2023/03/04/us/politics/trump-desantis-cpac-2024.html.

80. TruthSocial, @realDonaldTrump, March 24, 2023, https://truthsocial.com/@realDonald Trump/posts/110076529058362533, accessed July 8, 2023.

81. The content of the letter was widely reported in the news on March 24 and 25, 2023.

82. Mary Kay Linge, "Trump Slams Biden Admin's 'Weaponization of Justice System' as He Kicks Off 2024 Campaign with Waco Rally," *New York Post*, March 25, 2023, https://nypost .com/2023/03/25/trump-slams-bidens-weaponization-of-justice-system-at-waco-rally/.

83. Philip S. Gorski and Samuel L. Perry, *The Flag and the Cross: White Christian Nationalism and the Threat to American Democracy* (New York: Oxford University Press, 2022), 103.

POSTSCRIPT: TRUMPISM WITH AND WITHOUT TRUMP

1. See Robert Y. Shapiro, "Perspectives on Presidential Elections, 1992–2020: Introduction," In *Perspectives on Presidential Elections, 1992–2020*, ed. Robert Y. Shapiro (New York: Academy of Political Science), 1–52.

2. For June 2023 realclearpolitics.com reported polls that had Trump ahead of DeSantis by between twenty-one and forty-five percentage points, and Trump's support ranging from 43 percent to 61 percent.

3. Arizona Republican Congressman Andy Biggs (@RepAndyBiggsAZ), for example, tweeted on June 9, 2023, "We have now reached the war phase. Eye for an eye."

4. Claire Hansen, "Trump Calls Supporters to Action as He Prepares for Arraignment on Criminal Charges in Miami," *U.S. News & World Report*, June 12, 2023, https://www .usnews.com/news/national-news/articles/2023-06-12/trump-calls-supporters-to-action -as-he-prepares-for-arraignment-on-criminal-charges-in-miami.

   In another case, cooler heads prevailed: despite Trump's egging on his MAGA and Tea Party–inspired congressional supporters to shut the government down by not extending the debt limit, bipartisan agreement was reached to extend it.

5. Dana Milbank, "Opinion: As Trump Is Arraigned, Republicans Honor the Insurrectionists," *Washington Post*, June 16, 2023, https://www.washingtonpost.com/opinions/2023/06/16 /house-gop-trump-indictment-reaction-jan-6/.

6. Heather Cox Richardson from *Letters from an American*, June 22, 2023, received by email June 23, 2023.

7. Michael S. Schmidt, Alan Feuer, Maggie Haberman, and Adam Goldman, "Trump Supporters' Violent Rhetoric in His Defense Disturbs Experts," *New York Times*, updates June 14, 2023, https://www.nytimes.com/2023/06/10/us/politics/trump-supporter-violent -rhetoric.html.

8. Austin Sarat, "Opinion: Why Donald Trump Says His Enemies Are 'Communists,'" *Politico* Magazine, June 22, 2023, https://www.politico.com/news/magazine/2023/06/22 /donald-trump-red-scare-communism-00102990.

9. Aditi Bharade, "An Indicted Trump Once Again Posted a Bizarre Truth Social Holiday Greeting, This Time Wishing a Happy Easter to 'MARXISTS, & COMMUNISTS WHO ARE KILLING OUR NATION,'" *Insider*, April 9, 2023.

10. Brad Reed, "'Planted by Scoundrels!' Trump Demands GOP Allies Investigate Purported FBI Setup," *Raw Story*, June 22, 2023, https://www.msn.com/en-us/news/politics/planted -by-scoundrels-trump-demands-gop-allies-investigate-purported-fbi-setup/ar -AA1cT61N.

11. In one poll after the indictment in Miami, 76 percent of Republican voters responded that the indictment was politically motivated, and Trump held one of his greatest leads over DeSantis, 61 to 38 percent. See Anthony Salvanto, Khabir Khanna, Fred Backus, and Jeffiger De Pinto, "CBS News Poll: After Trump Indictment, Most See Security Risk but Republicans See Politics," June 11, 2023, https://www.cbsnews.com/news/cbs-news -poll-most-see-security-risk-after-trump-indictment/.

12. See Robert C. Lieberman, "Can Social Movements Save American Democracy? A Review Article," *Political Science Quarterly* 138, no. 1 (Spring 2023): 77–86.

13. Jonathan Swan, Maggie Haberman, and Nicholas Nehamas, "'This Is the Final Battle': Trump Casts His Campaign as an Existential Fight Against His Critics," *New York Times*, June 10, 2023, https://www.nytimes.com/2023/06/10/us/politics/trump-georgia-north-carolina.html.

14. Dessi Gomez, "DeSantis Tells 'Fox and Friends' He Will 'Destroy Leftism', 'Leave Woke Ideology' in the Dustbin of History.'" Yahoo.com., May 29, 2023, https://www.yahoo.com/entertainment/desantis-tells-fox-friends-destroy-222429178.html.

15. Jonathan Swan, Shane Goldmacher, and Maggie Haberman, "Five Takeaways from a Rocky 2004 Debut," *New York Times*, May 25, 2023, https://www.nytimes.com/2023/05/25/us/politics/takeaways-desantis-2024-twitter.html.

16. See Larry M. Bartels, *Democracy Erodes from the Top: Leaders, Citizens, and the Challenge of Populism in Europe* (Princeton, NJ: Princeton University Press, 2023).

17. See Chapter 5. See also, for example, Morgan Marietta and David C. Barker, *One Nation, Two Realities: Dueling Facts in American Democracy* (New York: Oxford University Press, 2019).

18. Thomas B, Edsall, "The Politics of Delusion Have Taken Hold," *New York Times*, Opinion, May 31, 2023, https://www.nytimes.com/2023/05/31/opinion/politics-partisanship-delusion.html.

INDEX

GPSR Authorized Representative: Easy Access System Europe, Mustamäe tee
50, 10621 Tallinn, Estonia, gpsr.requests@easproject.com

www.ingramcontent.com/pod-product-compliance
Lightning Source LLC
Chambersburg PA
CBHW022136020426
42334CB00015B/924